SAVING WASHINGTON'S ARMY

SAVING
WASHINGTON'S
ARMY

SAVING WASHINGTON'S ARMY

The Brilliant Last Stand of General John Glover at the Battle of Pell's Point, New York, October 18, 1776

PHILLIP THOMAS TUCKER

Skyhorse Publishing

Skyhorse Publishing books may be purchased in bulk at special discounts for sales promotion, corporate gifts, fund-raising, or educational purposes. Special editions can also be created to specifications. For details, contact the Special Sales Department, Skyhorse Publishing, 307 West 36th Street, 11th Floor, New York, NY 10018 or info@skyhorsepublishing.com.

Skyhorse® and Skyhorse Publishing® are registered trademarks of Skyhorse Publishing, Inc.®, a Delaware corporation.

Visit our website at www.skyhorsepublishing.com.

10 9 8 7 6 5 4 3 2 1

Library of Congress Cataloging-in-Publication Data is available on file.

Cover design by Kai Texel

Print ISBN: 978-1-5107-6937-3
Ebook ISBN: 978-1-5107-6938-0

Printed in the United States of America

Dedicated to Willard Thomas Tucker

Contents

Contents

Introduction

In one of the great ironies and most glaring omissions of the American Revolution, one of the most important battles of America's struggle for independence has remained virtually unknown to this day nearly two and a half centuries later. Compared to the famous New Jersey showdowns at Trenton and Princeton during the winter 1776–1777 campaign, and then at Saratoga, New York, in October 1777, very few Americans, including even Revolutionary War historians, have ever heard anything about the crucial Battle of Pell's Point, New York, which raged on Friday October 18, 1776. To ensure additional obscurity, this key battle fought just northeast of New York City has been long erroneously called the Battle of Pelham Bay and Pelham Heights, when this crucial engagement took place at neither location.

Exactly how important was this long-overlooked Battle of Pell's Point which was fought in a remote part of Westchester County, New York, just on the east side of Long Island Sound northeast of New York City? The longtime omission of the Pell's Point battle from the annals of Revolutionary War historiography has been extremely surprising, because no chapter of American history has been more romanticized and glorified than the American Revolution, especially the campaigns of General George Washington and American victories. Without adequate military experience or training at a military school or academy, Washington had relatively little realistic chance of achieving victory when facing the experienced professionals of the vastly superior British Army, which was fully demonstrated throughout the disastrous New York Campaign of 1776. In fact, Washington and his army only survived by the narrowest of margins on numerous occasions during this fiasco of a campaign in which he attempted in vain to defend New York City, which was an absolute impossibility.

Thanks to the demands of the political amateurs in the Continental Congress, General Washington's ill-fated defense of New York City during the disastrous summer of 1776 was a textbook example of ineptitude, because he made so many poor leadership judgments and decisions. Washington lost the Battle of Long Island on August 27 and then escaped with much of his army across the East River by the narrowest of margins to Manhattan Island on the night of August 29–30, thanks largely to the efforts of Colonel John Glover's mariners, mostly from Marblehead, Massachusetts, who rowed thousands of Washington's troops to safety during the night. It was only a matter of time before America's most prosperous port city fell. Forced to hastily evacuate New York City, Washington suffered one of the greatest disasters of the American Revolution in the early part of mid-September 1776, when he lost New York City to the superior forces of General William Howe.

Thereafter, the city served as the vital nerve center of the British military effort to subdue the wayward colonies for the war's remainder, thanks to its excellent deepwater port for British warships, which could strike anywhere along the Atlantic coast. But to be fair, Washington never had a realistic chance of successfully defending America's most important city, because it was surrounded by a maze of tidal rivers, narrow peninsulas, inlets, sounds, channels, and straits that had been carved out by the advance and retreat of glaciers millions of years before. During the New York Campaign, Washington faced nothing less than the most powerful navy in the world, when America had no navy in the area to counter the dominance.

The struggle for possession of New York City—America's second-largest city after the capital, Philadelphia, Pennsylvania—was of unparalleled strategic importance from the war's beginning. Washington lusted to capture the city for most of the war, including even at the beginning of the Yorktown Campaign during the spring of 1781. Washington was only reluctantly convinced by sound advice from French leaders to embark on the long march south with the French army to Yorktown, where American independence was won in October 1781. Washington's longtime obsession of capturing New York City had nearly wrecked the opportunity to capture Lord Cornwallis and his entire army on the Virginia Peninsula. Well into 1781, Washington had erroneously considered that the capture of New York City was the key to winning the war instead of operations in his home state of Virginia.

To be fair, Washington's strategic obsession was somewhat justified. New York City and the surrounding area were decisive ground from the American Revolution's beginning to the end. As noted, Washington lost New York City during the summer of 1776 to a mighty British invading force of 427 sailing ships with more than thirty thousand troops, the largest armada ever dispatched by England; Washington met the best-trained professional military in the world with only a ragtag army of around twenty thousand ill-equipped and poorly trained amateurs in rebellion and never had a chance.

Washington witnessed a whole series of fiascos largely of his own making around New York City, which were inevitable because of his lack of experience and his opponents' vast superiority on land and water. At Manhattan Island and then later in Westchester County just northeast of New York City, the fate of Washington's army and America's idealistic vision of a "New Israel" hung precariously in the balance during the early fall of 1776. Washington faced one crisis after another until a large portion of his army belatedly escaped from Long Island to Manhattan Island—which was a death-trap—and then withdrew north to the relative safety of Harlem Heights, New York.

Great Britain's most powerful expeditionary force in its lengthy history of invading foreign lands, especially nearby Ireland, missed still another golden opportunity to not only destroy Washington's fledgling army, but also to end the revolution in one stroke, because of what Colonel John Glover and his undersized Massachusetts brigade of four Continental regiments achieved against the odds of more than seven to one on October 18, 1776.

Howe's determined effort to encircle Washington's army and destroy Massachusetts Governor John Winthrop's idealistic dream of a "City on a Hill" not long after New York City's evacuation was frustrated by Colonel Glover, age forty-three, during the hard-fought Battle of Pell's Point. The persistent tendency to refer to the significant October 18 clash of arms as the "Battle of Pelham Bay" has caused some confusion about a land battle that was certainly not a naval action.

What these relatively few Massachusetts men of an undersized brigade under Colonel Glover achieved at Pell's Point, at a time when no other American troops were nearby to oppose the invasion, was extraordinary and quite unlike anything that was accomplished by comparable numbers of American fighting men during the course of the American Revolution.

Part of the reason of the longtime obscurity of the Battle of Pell's Point has been the excessive focus on General Washington, who was not present at the battle and had no bearing on its course or outcome, which was actually a positive development because, unlike Colonel Glover, the commander in chief was not tactically gifted or innovative, especially when it was necessary until his masterstroke at Trenton, New Jersey. This long-neglected battle in Westchester County was neither orchestrated nor planned by Washington, because it was solely left to Glover to do whatever he could to thwart the massive invasion of Howe's army. Glover created one of the war's great tactical masterpieces and bought precious time for the safe withdrawal of Washington's army north to White Plains, New York. However, the final result of the October 18 battle, in which the British retained the field and, therefore, claimed victory, was a foregone conclusion from the beginning, because Glover commanded fewer than eight hundred men against more than six thousand British and Hessian troops: the no-win situation of extreme importance made Glover's tactical contribution in delaying Howe's army for most of the day even more impressive.

Washington and the Continental Army were repeatedly saved by the contributions of the hard-fighting field grade officers of the

Continental Army, especially colonels of regiments and brigades. For instance, only days before the Battle of Pell's Point, Colonel Edward Hand and a handful of his Pennsylvania riflemen had initially saved the day by thwarting Howe's amphibious landing of his army on the narrow peninsula of Throgs Neck, buying time for the arrival of timely reinforcements, including Glover's Massachusetts brigade of four regiments. This surprising reversal forced Howe to then leapfrog only a few miles north to invade in Pell's Point to land at Washington's rear, which resulted in the October 18 battle and Glover's tactical masterpiece.

No American officer was more responsible than Glover for saving the day for Washington twice in less than a two-month period, beginning with the perilous evacuation from the trap on Long Island to the safety of Manhattan Island, after the miserable defeat of August 27 on Long Island and then the orchestration of his intricate defensive masterpiece at Pell's Point. More than any other Continental officer, Glover repeatedly compensated for the inexperienced commander in chief's lack of tactical ability and poor strategic insights in 1776, when the revolution might well have been lost. Quite simply, it took a good deal of skill and ability for Glover and his Massachusetts men to perform a series of miracles in 1776 to ensure the survival of Washington's army.

This was especially the case on October 18, when Glover waged a brilliant battle and delaying action to buy precious time on the New York mainland at Pell's Point to ensure that Washington's army lived to fight another day by escaping from its vulnerable defensive position at Harlem Heights and Manhattan Island to reach the New York mainland and then the safety of the high ground of White Plains. Quite simply, Glover played two key roles that saved the army and Washington in a short period of time by not only thwarting the British and Hessians at Pell's Point, but also by rescuing Washington from a lengthy list of his own tactical and strategic mistakes, especially in regard to the Long Island trap. But Colonel Glover's second vital role played for Washington in 1776 with his mostly mariners (the third one was when they ferried the main patriot strike force across the Delaware River on a stormy night so that they eventually would be in position to unleash a surprise attack that vanished an entire Hessian brigade of three regiments at Trenton on the snowy morning of December 26, 1776) was the most important one: the masterful delaying action of a brilliant defense in depth that thwarted Howe's invasion inland at an obscure place in Westchester County, New York, called Pell's Point.

While Glover's vital role in the Delaware River crossing to set the stage for Washington's first surprising victory at Trenton that turned the tide of the revolution has become world famous, Glover's brilliant performance at Pell's Point, which saved the day—like the escape from Long Island—during one of the struggle's darkest hours, has been long overlooked. However, Washington's masterful performance in reaping victory at Trenton, where fewer antagonists were engaged than at Pell's Point, cast a giant shadow over what Glover and his Massachusetts men had accomplished at Pell's Point barely two months before. Indeed, what has been most forgotten has been the fact that there would have been no miracle victory at Trenton to reverse the revolution's course without Glover's earlier success at Pell's Point.

On October 18, only a relatively few young men and boys—around 750 Continental soldiers—of a single undersized Massachusetts infantry brigade saved the day for Washington's army and the revolution. The defiant defensive stand ensured that General Howe's army would not march a short distance into Westchester County's interior on the New York mainland to strike Washington's withdrawing army, which was strewn out for miles and extremely vulnerable just to the west, and gain the Continental Army's rear to inflict a mortal blow to end the revolution in one stroke.

The undeveloped site of this key engagement just northwest of the Pell's Point Peninsula located in today's Pelham Bay Park in the Bronx has never been designated as a battlefield park. The long-overlooked battlefield where Americans, Hessians, and Redcoats fought and died when America's life was at stake—the same spot where religious contrarian Anne Hutchinson had fled the autocratic dictates of a Massachusetts theocracy in search of religious freedom and died at the hands of Native American warriors—is now covered mostly by modern development and a sprawling golf course. The ground where much blood was shed on October 18 even lacks solitude because of the roar of the nearby noise from a never-ending stream of traffic of cars and trucks pouring along busy Interstate 95.

From the beginning, the fascinating story of the American Revolution has been dominated by romantic myths and misconceptions, resulting in a gross distortion of the historical record. For nearly 250 years, far less important American Revolutionary engagements than Pell's Point have been glorified and embellished, while the Battle of Pell's Point has been consistently ignored by generations of American and English historians, almost as if it never happened. This has been an unfortunate development because the men and boys who fought and died in this forgotten engagement should be fully recognized and appreciated for what they accomplished against the odds to save Washington's army on a crucial mid-October day so long ago.

The supreme crisis unfolded when General William Howe's invasion force flooded into Westchester County in an effort to destroy General Washington's army, which was in a disorganized retreat only around half a dozen miles to the west. But fewer than eight hundred Americans, including beardless teenagers from across Massachusetts, stood firm against the onslaught from the morning to sundown on a beautiful autumn day in Westchester County. Against the odds and severely bleeding the enemy to buy precious time, they thwarted the strategic designs of a powerful opponent who was determined to destroy America.

The dramatic success of Colonel Glover and his relative handful of Massachusetts men in delaying the first British invasion on America's mainland has been long minimized by historians mainly because of the lack of primary documentation on both sides about this all-important battle. Despite the outpouring of publications during the

American Revolution's bicentennial and the longtime primary focus by historians on Washington's campaigns in the Middle Colonies and then at Yorktown, Virginia, the importance of Glover's success—not in winning the field but in buying precious time by thwarting the invasion—at Pell's Point has continued to be overlooked to this day to an extraordinary degree. Unfortunately, this rather remarkable development has occurred despite the fact that this key engagement when so much was at stake was not only the first battle on the American mainland during the 1776 campaign, but also the first stand-up fight between Washington's Continentals and mostly Hessian troops from Germany in a dramatic confrontation of extreme importance.

To his credit, the first modern professional historian to place the importance of the Battle of Pell's Point in a proper historical perspective was George Athan Billias in 1960. That year saw the release of Billias's work *General John Glover and His Marblehead Mariners*. Billias explained what has been fully supported by the facts and realities about this remarkable battle, when so much was at stake for not only Washington's army but also for America:

> Judged by the criteria normally employed by historians to evaluate the importance of a military engagement—be it strategic results, number of combatants involved, or casualties suffered—Pelham Bay deserves to be ranked among the more decisive battles of the Revolutionary War. . . . The true significance of the battle . . . lies in the fact that it saved the American army from encirclement and complete destruction.[1]

In his 2002 book *The Battle For New York*, Barnet Schecter described how "the tremendous strategic significance of the battle is beyond dispute. By obstructing the British advance for a day, Glover and his men helped Washington win the race to White Plains" and safety.[2]

However, Schecter's insightful analysis and appreciation of what happened at the Battle of Pell's Point is not typical or common among modern historians. For instance, historian Edward G. Lengel's fine

2005 biography, *General George Washington, A Military Life* relates that on "the 18th, thousands of British and German troops spilled ashore at Pell's Point, three miles north of Throgs Neck. If Washington had remained at Harlem Heights, the enemy would have cut him off. Yet when Howe noticed the Americans pulling back, he did not pursue. Instead his troops pushed slowly inland against a weak screen of Massachusetts Continentals."[3] Incredibly, in this example, no mention at all was made of how and why Howe's army had been slowed for the entire day of October 18, which was, of course, the magnificent tactical performance of Colonel Glover and his men.

Like so many other writers and historians, Lengel's otherwise excellent book has not only overlooked the Battle of Pell's Point, but also the strategic importance of Colonel Glover's last stand on the army's far eastern flank, while the men of Washington's army plodded north along the Albany Post Road during a lengthy withdrawal to White Plains. A small 1936 work by Troyer Steele Anderson revealed the truth of what really occurred on October 18 thanks to Glover's tactical masterpiece and why the battle was so strategically important for America: "the American resistance so impressed Howe that he waited for reinforcements before making a further advance."[4]

In addition, historian Lengel's point of view represented a classic example of one of the most persistent misconceptions and myths about the Revolutionary War: that only the inherent slowness, caution, and incompetence of General William Howe and his sympathy to the American cause were responsible for his failure to inflict a fatal blow on Washington's army. This widely accepted view, as if Colonel Glover and his men played no distinguished key role at Pell's Point on Friday October 18, was first developed by British leadership, who were in search of a convenient military scapegoat to explain the British Army's lack of success in America. Suspicion and criticism especially focused on the Howe brothers, General Howe and Rear Admiral Richard Howe, both during and after the conflict. Historians have only perpetuated the view that General Howe deliberately allowed decisive victory to slip out of his hands instead of any acknowledgment of the importance of Glover's skillful delaying tactics on October 18.[5]

Despite the supreme importance of the Battle of Pell's Point, even the fundamental facts about this key engagement have been misunderstood to this day by historians. Much of the battle's specific details, especially in tactical terms, have remained a mystery largely because of its absence from the history books to deny Colonel Glover and his Massachusetts men their just due. Even the battle's exact location has escaped legions of historians, buffs, and the experts to this day. As late as the spring of 2004 and as revealed in a *New York Times* article, historians conducted a professional investigative search in an attempt to determine the exact location where the battle, long shrouded in myth, was fought, and they were not successful.[6]

Strangely, even the name of this important battle that raged not far from the Long Island Sound has been confused in the history books. The dramatic clash of arms on October 18, 1776, has been called the Battle of Pelham and the Battle of Pelham Heights, even though the nearest town—the crucial bone of contention—was the village of Eastchester, New York, located just to the northwest. As mentioned, this early autumn 1776 engagement has most commonly been referred to as the Battle of Pelham Bay in the history books in a striking misnomer: the most popular designation seemed to have indicated a naval engagement, when Washington had no navy in the region. Such confusion has immeasurably contributed to the battle's obscurity in the annals of American Revolutionary historiography and in the minds of Americans. And Colonel Glover's name, which has been associated with the much better-known waterborne operations, especially the evacuation of Long Island in late August and dramatic Delaware River crossing before Washington's descent on Trenton in late December, has also bestowed a naval connotation to the battle fought on the New York mainland instead of on Pelham Bay.

Another fundamental reason to explain the battle's general obscurity for so long was because even the exact losses have been previously unknown and, therefore, unappreciated by historians, which would have demonstrated its scale. Hessian losses in the battle have been an enduring mystery and source of dispute among historians ever since the battle was fought. Because Hessian losses were reported by German officers back to the German princes who hired out their people as soldiers to King George III and not by General Howe to his superiors in London, the exact figure of Hessian losses has never been previously ascertained with any precision or exactness.

However, an abundance of evidence from rare primary source material has now revealed that Hessian casualties were exceptionally heavy at around one thousand men, making the Battle of Pell's Point one of the war's bloodiest engagements. In the past, of course, an accurate count of the Hessian losses would have partly emphasized the battle's scale and Howe's determination to break through Glover's three defensive lines situated on ever-higher ground. British troops played only a relatively minor role in the battle compared to other actions of the New York Campaign, and their losses were underreported by General William Howe for political reasons. As penned to his superiors in London, Howe's estimate of British losses was so low that it appeared to be hardly more a minor skirmish of little importance. For propaganda purposes and not to raise additional unrest in England on the political and domestic front, including opposition in the House of Parliament, British losses were officially kept at a minimum by Howe's gross underestimation. Therefore, both Hessian losses, which were not reported by Howe, and British losses have been misunderstood for nearly two and a half centuries. Of course, Colonel Glover and his men knew much better, and their words, including from letters, have revealed as much.

As usual, the truth about this forgotten battle in Westchester County can be more accurately ascertained from primary evidence, especially letters and diaries, rather than official documentation and general's reports dispatched back to London. Indeed, corresponding with other primary documentation and evidence, a most revealing November 6, 1776, letter came from an American soldier who told the truth of almost exclusive Hessian losses at the Battle of Pell's Point:

"The enemy were thought at the lowest computation to have lost five hundred men, some think not less than a thousand."[7]

Besides Colonel Glover's modesty, self-effacing manner, brief correspondence, and utter lack of self-promotion and as noted, the Battle of Pell's Point also has been forgotten because General Washington was not involved directly in the battle in any way, shape, or form. Had Washington been present on the field on October 18, then this engagement would have been acclaimed as one of his army's most impressive tactical successes of the war.

Instead, ironically, more focus has been placed by historians on the disastrous American rout at Kip's Bay on September 15, 1776 where Glover's men played still another key role in saving the day with other reinforcements by making a timely arrival. Unfortunately, in part because it was so shocking and the scene of Washington's most famous outbursts of temper, the fiasco at Kip's Bay, like the disastrous Battle of Long Island at the end of August, has completely overshadowed the sparkling tactical success achieved by Colonel Glover at Pell's Point only a short time later. Washington failed to rally thousands of routed American troops in the face of a British naval bombardment and amphibious landing of British and Hessian troops at Kip's Bay. A distraught Washington could only throw down his hat and cry out: "Are these the men with which I am to defend America?"[8]

What has been forgotten about this famous Washington quote was the fact that his key question was convincingly answered by the same troops who had helped to save the day at Kip's Bay and who were destined to make their tenacious last stand in Westchester County that saved the army shortly thereafter. The longtime widespread and almost total obscurity of Glover's amazing tactical defensive success at the Battle of Pell's Point has been especially ironic because 1776 was marked by an almost unbroken series of American defeats, fiascos, and retreats until Washington's unexpected victory at Trenton on December 26. Beginning with the debacle at the Battle of Long Island, New York, in late August 1776 and continuing until nearly the year's end, a lengthy string of American reversals and disasters (the revolution's darkest days) completely overshadowed Glover's most timely tactical success in buying precious time for General Washington's army to withdraw north from Manhattan Island to the safety of the high ground of White Plains, after delaying the powerful British and Hessian invasion force just northwest of the Pell's Point Peninsula. Ironically, even the success of Glover and his men in orchestrating the crossing of the Delaware for Washington's bold strike on Trenton has also cast a giant shadow to obscure what the Marblehead colonel achieved against the odds at Pell's Point.

Colonel Glover's remarkable tactical success in delaying General Howe's advance and buying precious time on October 18 to ensure the survival of Washington's army came at a time when the top American leadership proved especially tactically inept, especially the inexperienced commander in chief, who was literally learning about the art of war on the job: General Washington's lengthy list of mistakes in attempting to defend New York City included allowing himself to be entrapped on Long Island and then foolishly attempting to defend an indefensible Manhattan Island surrounded by waterways controlled by the British Navy with too few troops, while too belatedly realizing that Manhattan Island was a fatal trap like Long Island. Unfortunately for Washington and the American cause, even his top lieutenants proved equally tactically incompetent, especially General Nathanael Greene's ill-fated decision to defend a doomed Fort Washington situated on high ground at the northern end of Manhattan Island, after the army had already departed the island! In contrast to the litany of tactical errors committed by General Washington and his leading officers time and time again throughout the New York Campaign, Glover's tactical brilliance at the Battle of Pell's Point stood out not only in sharp contrast, but also as the most outstanding tactical success of the 1776 campaign around New York City.

Colonel Glover's success in buying time for the entire day and instilling greater caution in Howe to deter him for advancing deeper inland to the west to strike a fatal blow to the retreating rebel army ensured Washington's withdrawal north to the safety of White Plains.

This remarkable tactical success against the odds in Westchester County was one of the very few shining moments for American arms during the New York Campaign. In the words of historian Richard F. Snow:

> For ten weeks [Washington's forces] were whipped wherever they made a stand [but one of the few] bright spots [was] the terrific holding action found by Colonel John Glover and his indestructible Marbleheaders [of the 14th Continental Regiment and three other Massachusetts regiments] at Pell's Point.[9]

Glover's sparkling success on the army's far eastern flank in frustrating General Howe's thrust inland meant that Washington's army would not be entrapped in the narrow point of Manhattan Island that lay between the Hudson River, to the east, and Long Island Sound, to the west. The greatest mystery of the American Revolution was why the British commander, Sir William Howe, during the fall and early winter of 1776—a crucial two-month period—failed to deliver the lethal blow to destroy Washington's ill-trained army of amateur revolutionaries. Traditional explanations have routinely emphasized the failure as due to General Howe's caution that had been founded upon the traumatic experience that has been described by one historian as "Bunker Hillism." However, this explanation has become too generalized and simplistic, fostering stereotypical views that have been accepted as fact for too long, including by leading historians.

What has been most often overlooked was the fact that the punishment—nearly as severe as suffered by the attacking British troops at the Battle of Bunker Hill and more men than the British lost at the Battle of Monmouth, New Jersey—inflicted upon the sizeable British and Hessian invading force that poured into Westchester County on the morning of October 18, 1776, was actually the real key to Howe's lack of aggressiveness at a time when he could have won the war by aggressively pushing inland to destroy Washington's army. Colonel

Glover and his men inflicted losses from behind successive stone fences that made General Howe more tentative about the prospect of marching across a rural countryside covered with stone fences, after having lost hundreds of men. Hence, Howe thereafter advanced north up the coast to New Rochelle, New York, instead of pushing rapidly inland and directly toward Washington's army in the hope of delivering a lethal blow.

What Sir William Howe learned the hard way at the bloody Battle of Pell's Point was that American forces could prove to be most formidable by fighting guerrilla style, especially in setting up ambushes from the cover of woods, hilltops, boulders, and the lengthy stone fences. This unique brand of irregular warfare in which Colonel Glover added his own special touch to create tactical magic was very different from what Howe had previously learned, including at Bunker Hill, where the Massachusetts militiamen had fought in a conventional manner from fortified high ground. Glover's masterful delaying tactics demonstrated a degree of outstanding ingenuity and resourcefulness not previously seen in this war. Glover and his tough Continentals sapped the strength and momentum of any possibility of Howe's aggressive push west into the interior and toward Washington's vulnerable army in retreat, because the Massachusetts men so severely bled the attackers hour after hour. For Howe, this daunting prospect of facing the perils of guerrilla-style warfare—not from partisans but from well-trained Continentals like Colonel Glover's small command—was as menacing as facing regular (Continentals) American soldiers in a conventional manner on the battlefield, if not more so. Glover's tactical flexibility and ingenious delaying tactics of a defense in depth calculated to buy time and minimize casualties that he could not afford to lose resulted in a masterful and adroit blending of the most appropriate tactics—an unique mix of conventional tactics, such as volley firing, and asymmetrical tactics in using hidden positions behind stone fences to spring a series of successive ambushes on ever-higher ground of a defense in depth—that perfectly fit the exact battlefield situation based on the existing topography and the few available defensive positions.

After all, a heavily fortified position like a Bunker Hill (actually Breed's Hill) could always be outflanked, while guerrilla strikes, ambushes, and stealthy maneuvers could suddenly emerge without warning from almost any belt of woods, rock fence, or hilltop, before the Americans—fighting more like Native Americans than European troops—prudently retired to vanish seemingly into thin air. As demonstrated by Glover's unorthodox employment of his Continental brigade of a clever defense in depth and tactical success that relied upon a series of ambushes, such irregular tactics were ideally adopted to the mainland's terrain and against a more conventional opponent to sap the will and strength of an invading force in unfamiliar territory.

What Glover created on his own and on the fly was nothing less than the most brilliant tactics of the war up to this point in the conflict. In overall tactical terms, this little-known engagement in Westchester County on Friday October 18, 1776 was comparable to the Battle of Cowpens, South Carolina—nearly five years later on January 17, 1781—for the degree of its tactical brilliance and innovativeness of a masterful defense of depth: the tactical "father of Cowpens."

General Daniel Morgan's battle plan at Cowpens has been recently hailed as the most brilliant tactical plan of the war. Colonel Glover's battle plan that worked to perfection at Pell's Point can be compared most favorably to the tactics that reaped an amazing success at Cowpens. Glover's tactics at Pell's Point were fundamentally an innovative and masterful defense in depth of his regiments in echelon on ever-higher ground, but without any counterattack like at Cowpens that destroyed Lieutenant Colonel Banastre Tarleton's Loyalist command. The victory at Cowpens was basically a tactical repeat of what Glover had earlier orchestrated at Pell's Point with far fewer troops and against far greater odds in a much more important situation. General Morgan's tactics at Cowpens have gained widespread recognition, especially with the 1998 publication of Lawrence E. Babits's widely acclaimed *A Devil of a Whipping: The Battle of Cowpens*. Babits's excellent book made Cowpens famous as a tactical masterpiece of the American Revolution.[10]

But in fact, Colonel Glover's tactics at Pell's Point were equally, if not more, masterful, and actually more intricate and complex than General Morgan's tactics at Cowpens. The tactically gifted Marblehead colonel created an entire series of clever ambushes to exploit his opponent's overconfidence with a brilliant defense in depth. As noted, Glover commanded not raw militiamen, but seasoned Massachusetts Continentals, including many soldiers who once had been seamen in civilian life and militiamen who had harassed the British retreat from Lexington and Concord, Massachusetts, to Boston in April 1775.

When exposed on the army's far eastern flank and entirely on his own and far from support when Washington's main army was located to the west and then retreating north to White Plains, Colonel Glover faced greater odds, possessed fewer troops, and stood much less chance for success than General Morgan at Cowpens. Had General Morgan, a raw-boned Virginia frontiersman and former commander of Washington's finest marksmen, learned about the tactical details of the Battle of Pell's Point that had been fought more than four years before? The distinct possibility does exist because of the close similarity of their winning tactics and because Glover and Morgan served in the same army.

Glover's clever staggered defense in depth consisted of four separate defensive lines of each of his diminutive Bay State regiments, which were established behind consecutive stone fences located on ever-higher ground: in essence, a series of well-conceived ambushes— more in the case of the first three compared to the fourth which was his strategic reverse of his own regiment, the Fourteenth Massachusetts Continental Regiment. Most important, the Marblehead colonel's tactical ambush in depth was cleverly set up to bleed the enemy and buy precious time by exploiting overly aggressive British tactics and leaders, who had not known defeat on American soil, because General Howe was determined to gain a solid foothold by reaching the vital high ground, Pelham Heights, to ensure a successful invasion. Securing the high ground would give Howe a permanent toehold on the New York mainland, after a successful amphibious landing at Pelham Bay that was unopposed.

In a number of distinct ways, Colonel Glover's tactics were reminiscent of those of Hannibal, the great Carthaginian general from North Africa and the trading center of Carthage who crossed the Alps in his audacious march all the way to the gates of Rome. Hannibal relied on brilliant tactics, including those of Alexander the Great, to achieve one sparkling success after another over the much-touted Roman legions. Among Hannibal's winning tactics was his distinctive penchant of relying on a strategic reserve to surprise the enemy after having sent troops forward and who then prudently fell back as bait: the basic foundation of Glover's tactical plan at Pell's Point. Hannibal was especially adept at choosing the best terrain for setting clever ambushes to destroy large numbers of Roman legionnaires. And like the British and Hessians, the arrogant fighting men of ancient Rome could not have been more overconfident, which paid immediate dividends to Hannibal as they paid significant dividends to Glover at Pell's Point when facing an invading army that was considered invincible.

Colonel Glover performed at this best in leading an independent command while bestowed with a tactical freedom that allowed him the opportunity to create one of the most brilliant battle plans of the American Revolution on his own and in short order. On October 18, 1776 and on a scale not seen before, he demonstrated extraordinary tactical ability by blending colonial tactics of the French and Indian War and the tactics of Native American warriors stemming from the hard-learned lessons of frontier warfare with the best conventional tactics of eighteenth-century warfare in a masterful synthesis.

As mentioned, Glover's audacious defensive last stand in Westchester County bought precious time for Washington's army to withdraw north to White Plains to bypass Howe's forces, ensuring that the Continental Army would live to fight another day to keep the revolution's pulse alive. Against the odds and all chances for success, Colonel Glover's desperate defensive effort against the odds of facing the major invasion of Howe's army under his best top lieutenants, Sir Henry Clinton and Lord Charles Cornwallis, on his own protected the rear and extreme eastern flank of General Washington's army during its lengthy withdrawal north of around a dozen miles from Harlem Heights to White Plains and less than half a dozen west of Pell's Point. By comparison, the 1781 showdown at Cowpens was fought between relatively small task forces located a good distance away from the respective armies in the remote Piedmont hinterlands of northwest South Carolina.

Most important, and despite commanding only a diminutive Massachusetts brigade of four infantry regiments bolstered by three pieces of artillery that were left with a portion of his strategic reserve positioned on the high west bank of the Hutchinson River, Colonel Glover early took the initiative to boldly march forward on his own east of the river and without orders to oppose thousands of crack British and Hessian troops, who landed on the American mainland for the first time and in Washington's rear, when he could have chosen to retire or await reinforcements instead of fighting against the odds like other commanders would have ordered. To halt the overpowering numbers of invaders, Colonel Glover then pushed forward, or south, to gain favorable defensive ground to confront the invaders pushing north in overwhelming numbers.

However, the general obscurity of the remarkable story of Colonel Glover and his Massachusetts troops at Pell's Point has partly been the product of the sad lack of studies about the officer corps of the Continental Army because of the lack of records, documentation, and personal information, especially letters and diaries: not only in regard to Washington's top lieutenants, or generals, but also field-grade officers, or colonels like Glover. For this reason, Washington has almost seemed, especially from the pens of fawning historians who had endlessly glorified the "father" of the country, to have fought campaigns, including the New York Campaign, alone in a vacuum.

Indeed, since the American Revolution's conclusion, generations of traditional historians of the nationalist school have created the myth that Washington repeatedly saved and won the revolution, as if he possessed neither top lieutenants or talented field-grade officers, especially colonels. Indeed, in truth, it was the forgotten hard-fighting and tactically skilled officers like Colonel Edward Hand and Colonel Glover who actually deserved the lion's share of the credit for playing key roles in saving the day during the New York Campaign. Because he ultimately prevailed in his war at Yorktown, Washington has naturally long reaped the lion's share of the credit. But in fact, it was these forgotten lower-level commanders like Glover who early often did the hard fighting and tactical thinking on their own without Washington nearby to save the day.

The general obscurity of Revolutionary War leadership in the Continental Army below the commander in chief has been the anthesis of the situation of Civil War historiography in which biographies have regularly appeared year after year about everyone of a high officer's rank, especially general officers, on both sides. For instance, in regard to Revolutionary War historiography, there is nothing comparable to the detailed analysis found in Douglas Southall Freeman's classic work *Lee's Lieutenants: A Study in Command.*

Especially when compared to Civil War historiography, the entire Revolutionary War period has suffered from general obscurity, thanks partly to the different degrees of literacy among patriots that ensured the lack of primary source material. Therefore, many of Washington's field-grade officers in the New York Campaign have remained shadowy and remote figures to this day. Quite simply, Washington and his army would not have persevered without the talented officer corps that served under him, especially because the Virginian had not yet wised up to avoid matching conventional tactics with his superior opponent during the New York Campaign.

While General Washington primarily thought in terms of waging a conventional war like his British opponent, it was the most unorthodox, free-thinking, and tactically flexible colonels in the Continental Army who repeatedly saved Washington and his army of amateurs from self-destructing themselves and the revolution itself, because of the commander in chief's faith in strict orthodoxy and conventional tactics, almost as if he was wearing the scarlet uniform of a British officer. Washington embraced the conventional strategies and tactics that were nothing less than folly because such a strict adherence to traditional ways of waging war guaranteed defeat at the hands of experienced professionals, who had been schooled at some of Europe's finest military academies. Thankfully, Glover did not think or fight conventionally—the secret of his amazing success in thwarting the ambitions of Howe and his powerful British-Hessian Army with only a relative handful of fighting men on October 18.

Washington repeatedly came perilously close to having lost the war during the New York Campaign because of his blundering, miscalculations, and lack of strategic insight and tactical abilities. Indeed, barely a year after the signing of the Declaration of Independence in Philadelphia, the people's rebellion very nearly came to an abrupt end repeatedly during the ill-fated New York Campaign—an absolute disaster that would have dramatically changed the course of world history. Of course, the reality that the American Revolution repeatedly almost ended during the New York Campaign has not been generally acknowledged or appreciated by historians in large part because Washington eventually won his war, thanks to extensive French land and sea power, which made decisive victory at Yorktown possible.

Contrary to the seemingly endless romantic myths and nationalist narratives that have always bestowed the lion's share of the credit to Washington, the real truth of the matter was that the commander in chief would probably have been hanged for treason and the Continental Army destroyed during the New York Campaign, if not for the hard-fighting abilities and tactical skills of his unknown brigade commanders, especially John Glover.

This current book is the most detailed study and first modern work in nearly a century and a quarter devoted to the dramatic clash of arms between 750 Massachusetts soldiers of the Third, Thirteenth, Fourteenth and Twenty-sixth Massachusetts Continental Regiments and a mighty invading force of thousands of well-trained British and Hessian soldiers. Clearly, on the eve of the 250th anniversary of the

Battle of Pell's Point, it is now time to explore a forgotten tactical masterpiece of the American Revolution in greater detail than ever before.

Even though the October 18 engagement in picturesque Westchester County was fought within sight of New York City, the Battle of Pell's Point has been unremembered even by generations of New Yorkers, who have allowed their distinguished revolutionary past to fade away. Ironically, tens of thousands of New Yorkers continue today to visit the pleasant confines of Pelham Bay Park—the largest park in the Bronx—on family gathering and picnics without ever realizing that the American nation had been saved by the hard fighting and tactics of a relative handful of Massachusetts Continentals exactly where they have long walked and played with family members for years. Nor, of course, have they realized that the decisive day in early autumn had been saved by Colonel John Glover by employing some of the most masterful tactics seen during the course of the American Revolution. However, this unfortunate situation has been understandable, because no historic monuments or statues stand in honor of Glover and his men at Pelham Bay Park to this day. From all appearances, it is as if no battle was ever fought there on October 18, 1776, especially one of extreme importance in regard to America's destiny and future.

Consequently, this current book has been written partly in the hope that the forgotten heroics of a small band of Continentals who battled against the odds will never before forgotten. After all, these young Massachusetts men and boys fought a tactically brilliant delaying action in Westchester County for the dream of an independent nation that would have died an early and ugly death if they had failed to hold firm against thousands of invading British and Hessian troops in nothing less than perhaps the most important defensive stand of the American Revolution. During one of the darkest periods in American history, when the future of the infant republic looked especially bleak and without hope of any kind, Colonel Glover's Massachusetts men repeatedly proved their worth when the life of their floundering nation was at stake.[11]

The remarkable story of what a relative handful of American fighting men accomplished against the odds will be told in full in this current book, thanks to the discovery of new primary research and documentation that has revealed the truth of what really happened in this remote part of Westchester County on October 18, 1776. What will be revealed for the first time was that the Battle of Pell's Point was in fact one of the bloodiest and most important battles of the American Revolution. It was also one of the most one-sided American successes of the war in terms of inflicting disproportionate losses and thwarting General Howe's mighty invasion force from striking inland to hit Washington's army, when it was most vulnerable and in extremely bad shape during a miserable retreat north from Manhattan Island. Hopefully, the memory of these hard-fighting Bay State men, the irrepressible Colonel John Glover, and the crucial engagement in which they battled with distinction will finally be appreciated by Americans in the present day and far into the future.

In 1906 and 130 years after the Battle of Pell's Point, American artist Howard Pyle completed a truly masterful painting entitled *The Nation Makers*. Unlike previous American historical painters whose subjects were highly romanticized versions of great leaders and battles of the American Revolution, Pile devoted his fine artistic work to the common soldiers who were the ones who truly made America with their personal sacrifices and their blood spilled on the battlefield. These ill-clothed, poorly equipped, and seldom paid young men and boys, including mostly lower-class immigrants, African Americans, substitutes, and even indentured servants, were the ones who fought year after year and all the way to the final victory at Yorktown in October 1781, especially in the Continental's ranks.

To magnificently capture the irrepressible fighting spirit and die-hard commitment of mostly lower-class and middle-class fighting men, who were primarily common yeoman farmers and men of the soil, in his excellent 1906 painting, Pyle depicted a motley and battle-worn group of Revolutionary War soldiers who gave the distinct appearance of having been the very antithesis of crack members of a professional fighting force. However, it was such common and ordinary men without sufficient weapons, uniforms, and supplies who never gave up and continued to fight against fate and the odds year after year, despite the seemingly endless failures of their upper class leaders and bungling government in Philadelphia to eventually win their war for liberty.

Artist Pyle's excellent painting has presented an extremely realistic look at the common soldiers of Washington's Army that has contrasted sharply with the popular and stereotypical images of the most romanticized war in the annals of American history. These ragged, unsoldierly looking fighting men sacrificed their all to an inordinate degree with blood, sweat, and tears from 1775 to 1783. Most of all and quite unlike any other painting depicting a battle scene from the American Revolution, Howard Pyle brilliantly captured the feisty, never-say-die spirit of Colonel John Glover and his Massachusetts soldiers during the Battle of Pell's Point, where they faced impossible odds when thwarting the British-Hessian Army from rapidly pushing inland to strike the exposed right flank of Washington's unprepared army during its chaotic withdrawal north, which would have extinguished the life of the reeling Continental Army and America in short order.

In consequence, the excellent design team at Skyhorse Publishing has thoughtfully graced the cover of this current book with not only this masterful Howard Pyle painting, but also with a fine sketch of Colonel John Glover in this prime: a perfect combination for a book devoted to the forgotten Battle of Pell's Point and Glover's tactical masterpiece. Indeed, in many ways, the Pyle painting seemed to have been painted for the express purpose of representing the heroism of the saviors of Washington's army twice in the New York Campaign, especially during the dramatic showdown at Pell's Point on October 18, 1776, while demonstrating that Glover was Washington's most indispensable colonel and his Massachusetts soldiers were America's most versatile fighting men throughout the turning point year of 1776. In fact, the title of Pyle's painting might well have been *The Fighting Spirit of John Glover and his Men at the Battle of Pell's Point.*

By the end of the American Revolution and while still basking in his great victory reaped at Yorktown that ensured the independence of a new nation, General Washington's improbable success seemed inexplicable and impossible. In fact, a central mystery about America's struggle for liberty has continued to exist to this day: how was it even possible that an inexperienced and unschooled former militia officer and Virginia Tidewater planter from his beloved insular world of Mount Vernon ultimately could have possibly prevailed over the finest military establishment in the world? How had the mighty British empire and its superior military leadership lost America? Such intriguing questions have continued to be debated by historians to this day.

After all, it seemed as if nothing less than a miracle had allowed Washington, who was saddled with a long list of strategic and tactical limitations as an inexperienced commander that led to a host of strategic and tactical mistakes on a scale which astounded friend and foe alike throughout the New York Campaign, to prevail in the end. The Tidewater Virginian literally had to learn about the art of war on the job and it was an extremely painful process that led to disastrous results. In consequence, many Americans, both soldiers and civilians, including Washington himself, ultimately concluded how only a kind and smiling Providence had been most, if not solely, responsible for bestowing decisive victory upon the infant republic and its amateur armies, which continued to blunder almost to the war's conclusion. However, in truth, the best explanation for how and why Washington's army was repeatedly saved during the disastrous New York Campaign may be found in the timely contributions and performances of Colonel Glover and his Massachusetts men, especially at the Battle of Pell's Point.

Fortunately, General Washington possessed not only an ace in the hole but also a secret weapon that he repeatedly employed with outstanding success during the darkest days of 1776: Colonel John Glover and his Massachusetts men mostly from the port of Marblehead. Indeed, what saved Washington and the Continental Army three times in barely less than four months in 1776 and twice during the New York Campaign in less than two months was one of Washington's best lieutenants and his elite regiment of Massachusetts mariners, who were as capable on land as on water: the timely rescue of thousands of Washington's men during a risky evacuation off the death trap of Long Island before they were destroyed or forced to surrender; the Battle of Pell's Point, in which they kept Howe's army at bay and away from Washington's flank and rear to allow the Continental Army to safely retreat from the death trap of Manhattan Island to the safety of White Plains unmolested; and then ferrying the army, including a large amount of artillery, across the swirling waters of the Delaware River in Durham boats on a stormy night in late December that bestowed Washington with the opportunity to strike his masterful blow at Trenton that saved the revolution. Indeed, no Continental troops in Washington's army played larger and more important roles in having repeatedly saved the day for Washington's army than the Marblehead colonel and his unorthodox, versatile Massachusetts men, who proved themselves to be Washington's most invaluable soldiers.

Without the timely contributions of Colonel Glover and his crack command, the American Revolution would have ended in defeat and the United States would never have won its independence. This book has presented the dramatic story of Washington's most elite and dependable soldiers from a distinctive seafaring community in Massachusetts and their incomparable role in saving the day at Pell's Point. Throughout 1776, they repeatedly bailed out their fumbling commander in chief to compensate for his tactical mistakes to the point that they evolved into Washington's saviors, who repeatedly rose to the challenge.

This book has continued the author's longtime focus on the remarkable stories of America's elite combat units from the French and Indian War (*Ranger Raid, The Legendary Robert Rogers and His Most Famous Battle*, 2021) to the Civil War (multiple volumes) to reveal how the crack troops of America have often reversed the course of human conflict to decide the fate of nations by rising to the stern challenge of the most dire battlefield situations. Colonel Glover and his Massachusetts men fit neatly into the rare and distinguished group of elite soldiers who helped to determine America's destiny and future, emerging as Washington's most reliable troops during the crucial New York Campaign and for the remainder of 1776.

Most of all, this groundbreaking book is unique because it is the first detailed and in-depth study of the crucial role played by a single Continental brigade in one of the most important battles of the American Revolution: an unprecedented close look and analysis of a brilliant commander, John Glover, and his tactical masterpiece that he orchestrated with consummate skill on Friday October 18, 1776 to save Washington's Army.

Phillip Thomas Tucker, PhD
Central Florida
August 20, 2021

Chapter I

Unprecedented Disasters at Long Island, New York City, and Kip's Bay

A former commander of ragtag Virginia militia during the French and Indian War, General George Washington was the commander in chief of the Continental Army and a man who had to learn the business of war on the job. The greatest love of the forty-four-year-old commander in chief of America's army of hopeful revolutionaries and rustics in rebellion was his sprawling Mount Vernon plantation in the Virginia Tidewater and not the art of war. Washington's mansion sat majestically on the bluffs overlooking the wide Potomac River and the gently rolling hills of southern Maryland across the river just to the east.

Inexperienced at commanding his poorly prepared army in his first major campaign to defend New York City, Washington was fated to lose the second-largest city in North America in September 1776 largely because of the ill-advised decisions of the politicians of the Continental Congress, which had insisted that he defend the city at all costs. In keeping with the dictates of a truly republican government of the people by obeying Congress, Washington deferred to the amateur judgments of the politicians, who themselves possessed even less military experience than the Virginia planter from Mount Vernon: a shaky and unproven civil-military arrangement in the republican tradition that guaranteed disastrous results. Like the naive civilian political leaders in Philadelphia, Pennsylvania, where the Declaration of Independence had been drafted barely a year before, these civilian amateurs in the military arts insisted that Washington attempt to hold the entirely indefensible New York City.

Still heady from having boldly issued their earthshaking Declaration of Independence during the summer of 1776 against the time-honored concept of monarchy and the divine right of kings, America's top politicians were convinced that the strategic city's loss would so severely damage public spirits and morale of the rustics in rebellion that the revolution would die an ugly death. However, the amateur politicians of Philadelphia, who had already become excessively meddling in military affairs, seemed to have ignored the simple fact that the revolution would succumb even more quickly if Washington's army attempted to fulfill the impractical demands of Congressional novices at war. Ironically, the infant republic and army now risked dying of an overabundance of the spirit of republicanism during the defense of New York City.[1]

During a scorching-hot August 1776 that gave no hint of autumn's approach to diminish the intense heat and humidity and despite commanding too few troops when attempting to hold impossibly hopeless defensive positions around New York City as ordered by Congress, Washington busily prepared the infant American Army in its first major confrontation against the powerful concentration of the British Empire's military might. Like America's politicians in the bustling city of Philadelphia, the former French and Indian War veteran felt that the upcoming struggle was one that very well might decide the fate of America. However, Washington possessed no navy at his disposal to defend a city surrounded by waterways and controlled by the Royal Navy, under Vice Admiral Richard Howe, which was a liability that could not be overcome.

Equally discouraging, Congress and Washington had already seriously overextended themselves by having dangerously embraced the heady strategic vision that Canada could be easily conquered to become the fourteenth colony of the young United States. The ill-founded American belief was prevalent that Canadians would love nothing more than to join a new confederation of republican states and that they would not see United States soldiers as barbarian invaders of their beloved homeland: an entirely misplaced concept that defied logic and rational thought given the history of nationalism around the world. Therefore, an entire republican army had been early dispatched by Washington, with the blessings of Congress, north to conquer Canada. However, on the last day of 1775, Ireland-born Richard Montgomery's desperate assault on the mighty fortress of Quebec in a snowstorm ended in bloody fashion with his death and the first great defeat for American arms on British soil.

However, what little was left of the depleted American Army, which had failed to capture Quebec, stubbornly hung with an icy grip onto Canadian soil despite the arrival of sizeable British reinforcements. Then Washington lost additional good fighting men whom he could ill afford to lose when Congress dispatched additional troops north in April 1776 to bolster the ragged band of fighting men in Canada. Washington was shortly to pay a high price for his own strategic miscalculation and the Philadelphia politicians' desire to gain Canada rather than focusing more on defending New York City, when everything was at stake for the infant nation.

If and when the British and their Hessian allies arrived in force by water in a mighty armada as long feared, then the struggle for New York City might well decide America's future destiny. In Washington's words from a letter to the governor of Connecticut, Jonathan Trumbull, in a desperate plea for reinforcements at a time when the stakes could not have been higher: "You are sensible, Sir, of the great importance of a strenuous exertion at this critical period, a period which may in its consequences determine the fate of America."[2] In the end, General Washington's appeals paid dividends, because two-thirds of his army consisted of New Englanders, of whom more than one-third hailed from Connecticut by the time of the New York Campaign.[3]

Most important, New York City was well worth fighting and dying to hold. In early 1776, John Adams described the prosperous port city as the "key to the whole continent."[4] Therefore, it was only a matter of time before the British struck with a vengeance, but exactly where around New York City? After General William Howe had evacuated Boston in mid-March 1776 after Washington's successful siege and then sailed away to Halifax, Canada, because the New England army had secured Dorchester Heights, which overlooked the port city on the south, the British had reorganized and made thorough preparations for a massive offense that targeted New York City in the summer of 1776.

Consisting of contingents of experienced troops from England, Nova Scotia, the West Indies, Scotland, Ireland, Gibraltar, and the Carolinas, England sent forth the largest armada of British warships in English history, under Rear Admiral Richard "Black Dick" Howe who was William Howe's brother. This mighty force represented Great Britain's attempt to end the rebellion in one blow by capturing New York City and destroying Washington's army. British warships carrying large numbers of well-trained regulars steadily began to descend upon the New York City area under General Howe, who benefited from excellent top lieutenants in Sir Henry Clinton and Lord Charles Cornwallis. He found a perfect staging area on Staten Island, located only seven miles south of New York City, from which to launch a strike.[5] All in all, this immense force of eventually more than thirty-thousand men was "the best officered, disciplined, and equipped that Great Britain could then have mustered for any service."[6]

However, the aristocratic General Howe took his time before unleashing an attack to Washington's great relief, while building up his massive strength and making thorough preparations to end the rebellion. In the words from an August 13 letter from a young Maryland officer, Tench Tilghman, who served with distinction on Washington's staff:

> 96 Sail of Vessels have arrived at the watering place [and] We suppose they are the Transport with Foreign [Hessian troops from Germany] Troops—To our great amazement they still continue inactive, which is much in our fav[o]r for we are receiving Reinforcements every day.[7]

On August 22, a letter published in the *Pennsylvania Journal*, Philadelphia, revealed how: "we have reason to expect the grand attack from our barbarian enemies."[8] One of Washington's anxious men penned in an August letter:

> The enemy have a very formidable Army . . . and from the best intelligence it is expected they will give us Battle soon, at which time I hope God in his infinite mercy will be on our side, and we shall have no occasion to dread their numbers or experience. Our cause being so just, I cannot but hope for success.[9]

Religious-minded and gentlemanly Captain Nathan Hale, a dedicated Connecticut soldier who had destined for a British hangman's noose on September 22, 1776, wrote in an August 20 letter:

> For about 6 or 8 days the enemy have been expected hourly, whenever the wind and tide in the least favored [and therefore] We keep a particular look out for them this morning. The place and manner of attack time must determine. The event we leave to Heaven. Thanks to God! we have had time for compleating [sic] our works and receiving reinforcements [and] We hope, under God, to give a good account of the Enemy whenever they choose to make the last appeal.[10]

And one of Washington's colonels penned a confident letter to another colonel on August 15 from his encampment on Long Island:

> I am yet fully in the Belief they will Land on Long Island for One of their Places & where else I don't know, but I'm fully persuaded, in more Places than One, I wish you & your Regiment all Happiness. I know you will all play the man—the critical Hour of America has come; beat 'em once, they are gone.[11]

Having little intimate knowledge about the nuances of sea power and how decisive it could be in wartime, Washington had focused on creating a vast network of defenses to protect New York City, including Brooklyn Heights on Long Island that guarded the water side of New York City, in the hope that the British would foolishly launch an amphibious assault as at Bunker Hill, where more than one thousand British soldiers had become casualties on June 17, 1775, a year before the issuing of the Declaration of Independence.

But General Howe had learned his lesson the hard way at Bunker Hill, where his men had been slaughtered in attacking a high ground fortified position. He would not make the same grievous mistake twice. Therefore, he would wisely rely on outflanking maneuvers to easily negate Washington's complex of defenses, wherever he found them during the course of the New York Campaign. With relatively little military knowledge in the art of conventional warfare as taught at military academies across Europe, Washington never imagined how easily even the strongest fortifications on seemingly impregnable high ground could be easily outflanked by the combined operations of the Royal Navy and the army's crack regulars led by experienced commanders, thanks to the intricate system of waterways that surrounded the city and the fleet of British warships that could deposit large numbers of troops at any point at will with complete impunity.

As could be expected when Washington and other officers had only decided to defend the water side of Long Island at Brooklyn Heights facing west, the end result was all but inevitable when Howe struck the land side, or the defender's rear on the east, with a mighty army: America's most disastrous defeat of the war to date at the Battle of Long Island. With relative ease after the British Navy had landed an invasion force on Long Island and marched inland behind the American defenders, who still faced the wrong way or toward the water, and after the British easily turned their unguarded left flank and gained their rear with almost effortless ease, Washington's rookie army was soundly defeated on August 27, 1776, during the largest battle of the American Revolution to date: ironically, an engagement that should not have been fought because a defense of Brooklyn Heights on Long Island was doomed from the start because the British controlled the waterways. The disaster was greater because a tactically clueless Washington had steadily poured reinforcements into Long Island to bolster the defenses on an island that had become a trap.

What was left of the battered Continental Army now stranded on Long Island and seemingly about to be destroyed by Howe's victorious troops was only saved by their timely escape west across the East River and through its strong currents, thanks largely to Colonel John Glover and his mariners of the Marblehead regiment, or the Fourteenth Massachusetts Continental Regiment. Glover's command was known as the "Marine" regiment, which was one of the most exceptional units of the American Revolution. During the stealthy evacuation of Long Island, Glover's men used oars muffled with woolen blankets while rowing to New York City and back nearly a dozen times to Long Island during a quiet movement across the East River that caught Howe by surprise. The mostly Marblehead men were assisted by another Massachusetts regiment of seafarers under Israel Hutchinson from the nearby port of Salem. Against all expectations, these Massachusetts seafarers from two neighboring fishing communities on the Atlantic just north of Boston labored all the night of August 29–30 at the oars, ferrying nearly ten thousand of Washington's troops across the wide waterway that separated Long Island from the lower end of Manhattan Island. During nothing less than what was the remarkable Dunkirk of the American Revolution, Washington's men were then disembarked safely in New York City throughout the foggy darkness in what was nothing less than a minor miracle.

Thanks to the irrepressible Colonel Glover, the amazing escape of thousands of Washington's men from Long Island was extremely narrow and the closest of calls. Washington was—much to his credit—in the last boat oared to safety by Glover's mariners, and he and his men thanked God for a miraculous deliverance. The escape from Long Island convinced the rustic revolutionaries even more that a kind Providence had saved the day and had blessed this people's struggle against an autocratic king, who believed that he had been divinely appointed to rule the American people in any manner he deemed appropriate. But Washington and other Americans already had a king—God—and certainly did not need another one who issued harsh edicts from faraway London.

On September 7, 1776, and with the powerful British Army occupying Long Island, which it had won by use of Howe's clever tactics, a troubled Washington, who was learning about the importance of naval superiority, held a much-needed council of war. After much discussion, Washington and his top lieutenants reached a tactical compromise that boded ill for the future. Not having learned their lesson in attempting to defend both Long and Manhattan Islands (two traps) with defenses only on the water side and along a too-widely extended front surrounded by water when the British possessed complete naval superiority, Washington and his army of amateurs now planned to attempt to preserve both New York City and most of sprawling Manhattan Island in still other example of folly stemming from badly misplaced overconfidence and the lack of strategic and tactical insights. Because of the disadvantageous geography of an extensive archipelago with strong-points widely scattered to cover too many key strategic points, this ill-advised decision called for a wider dispersal of the ever-decreasing number of American troops under arms across Manhattan Island: the recipe for yet another disaster in the making. But most of all, the ill-fated strategic decision of attempting to simultaneously defend both Manhattan Island and New York City ensured that additional fiascos already loomed ahead for Washington's ragtag army of innocents at war.

Indeed, Washington and his top lieutenants, under the convoluted guidance of the bungling civilian amateurs of Congress, had committed absolute folly, because like

> most compromises, this one served neither purpose; it was
> not effective to save the city, nor yet the army [because] it was
> a thoroughly bad decision; it strung the army out [over] 15

miles, with its weakest point midway between its extremities, and so invited the British to cut it in two in the middle and defeat the ends separately.[12]

But to his credit and now knowing that even greater challenges for his ill-trained and under-equipped army lay in store in the days ahead, Washington at least made one brilliant decision in a disastrous campaign in which American errors, mistakes, and miscalculations seemed to have no end. On September 4, 1776, he demonstrated wisdom by officially appointing a new brigade commander to lead four veteran Continental regiments, Fourteenth, Third, Thirteenth, and Twenty-sixth Massachusetts, Colonel John Glover. The modest, unassuming colonel from Marblehead, Massachusetts, now took command of Major General James Clinton's brigade.[13]

Continuing to greatly benefit from the stealthy and swift mobility of the powerful Royal Navy's warships under Vice Admiral Howe that faced no opposition, British and Hessian forces soon exploited an obvious opportunity by landing on the east side of the East River about four miles north of New York City to gain a grip on the eastern edge of lower Manhattan Island. From five British warships anchored on either side of Kip's Bay in lower Manhattan and facing west toward a thin line of American defensive works, a large number of flatboats prepared to carry thousands of well-trained Hessian and British troops toward the Manhattan shore. About an hour before noon on September 13 and after having moved without opposition across the East River, eighty cannon from the five British warships lying in the limpid waters pounded the thin line of light earthworks and its New England defenders with a fury. This intense bombardment by expert British naval gunners was kept up for nearly two hours, sweeping the targeted area with a hail of cannonballs to set the stage for an audacious amphibious landing with the same ease as at Long Island, which had resulted in an one-sided British-Hessian victory from which the reeling Continental Army had yet to recover.

Then at last and as feared by the nervous New England militia-men, the "terrible and . . . incessant roar" from the British cannon on the warships suddenly ceased around 1:00 p.m., and a strange calm descended over the west side of the wide East River—a most omi-nous portent. And, right on cue, a vast armada of flat-bottomed troop transports, manned by British sailors at the oars working vigorously through the waters of Kip's Bay, carried large numbers of General Howe's men toward the Manhattan shore. As General Howe and other British leaders had hoped, what awaited thousands of British and Hessian troops, after a softening up of the defensive works with the naval bombardment, was not a tenacious Bunker Hill–like defensive stand of New England's famous fighting farmers, as fondly envisioned by Washington. While the Britons and Germans in bright uniforms drew ever-closer to the landing site of the sandy beach, the lengthy line of American earthworks remained strangely quiet. With no vol-leys pouring forth from the defenses or cannon erupting like thunder as expected, Howe's puzzled men splashed ashore unopposed. They were shortly basking in one of the easiest victories of the American Revolution without the loss of a single soldier. After all, what Howe's men now saw before them was almost unbelievable: thousands of American soldiers fleeing for their lives across the open fields instead of fighting in defense of their own home soil as ordered.[14]

The humble son of a Massachusetts preacher and concerned about maintaining religious observance on this day of rest on the holy Sabbath like a good son and obedient Christian, young Private Joseph Plum Martin described one of the great fiascos of the American Revolution that once again proved an amateur army's ineptness that seemingly could do nothing right. He wrote about the absolute disas-ter for American arms:

> It was on a Sabbath morning, the day in which the British were always employed about their deviltry, if possible. . . . We kept the lines till they were almost levelled upon us, when our officers, seeing we could make no resistance, and no orders

coming from any superior officer, and that we must soon be entirely exposed to the rake of their guns, gave the order to leave the lines.[15]

Among the British-Hessian landing force, Thomas Sullivan, who had been born on the Emerald Isle in 1755 and served in the 49th Regiment of Foot, could hardly believe how easy this one-sided British victory had been achieved over the fumbling revolutionaries. As he penned in his journal:

The firing of the shipping being so well managed and so incessant, that the Enemy could not remain in their works, and the descent was made without the least opposition [and] the conduct of the Officers of the Navy, did them much honor; and the behaviour of the Seamen belonging to the ships of War and Transports, employed to row the boats, was highly meritorious.[16]

From the safe confines of Fort Constitution, soon to be renamed in honor of his division commander, General Charles Lee, situated on the west side of the North, or Hudson, River on New Jersey soil, Colonel John Glover wrote in an October 7 letter to his mother Tabitha in Marblehead, Massachusetts, how: "the enemy had landed 18,000 men [at Kip's Bay] on the East side [of Manhattan Island] about 4 miles from the City, covered by 10 sail of men of war, and opposite to them on the North [Hudson] River came up three large ships [and] The whole kept up a constant cannonading with grape shot and langrage [sic] quite across the Island" of Manhattan.[17]

Incredibly, General Washington's soldiers had proved unable to not only adequately defend their own homeland against Howe's amphibious landing to outflank Washington's army on the east, but also could not even put up a mere token defense when holding light earthworks—an unprecedented tactical development that mocked the illusionary image of additional Bunker Hill-like victories that

American leadership fondly expected to come like the rising of the sun. While the success at Bunker Hill had resulted from the strong defenses having been located on the high ground of Breed's Hill, the light defenses on lower Manhattan Island at Kip's Bay were situated on low-lying terrain. As during the disastrous Battle of Long Island, this almost effortless rout of so many of Washington's troops revealed the supreme confidence of British leaders, who doubted that the Americans could stand up to the British on the battlefield when even holding defenses, which had proven well-founded and prophetic.

Ironically, the mostly upper-class members of Parliament on the Thames River in London, the center of a vast empire based on an aggressive colonialism, imperialism, and mercantilism that had created a prosperous global empire, had never seen America or its people. Nevertheless, they held tight to the pervasive stereotypes that these American colonials simply lacked the character and moral courage to stand up to British bayonets. At this time, most Britons were convinced that these homespun Americans would surely run at the first sight of onrushing regulars with eighteen-inch bayonets fixed at the end of their "Brown Bess" flintlocks, in bright scarlet uniforms. The common stereotype among British military and civilian leadership was that the American fighting man was nothing more than an abject coward, and what happened at Long Island and Kip's Bay in only a few weeks seemed to have provided ample evidence of such harsh opinions about the lack of American character and courage, when the fate of America was at stake. If these American fighting men had failed to fight and die for their country, then was there even a republican nation anymore? Why were they no longer fighting for freedom with the enthusiasm of 1775?

The Earl of Sandwich, the First Lord of the Admiralty, bragged with complete certitude how the Americans would "never meet our people in fair conflict [and] will throw down their arms and run away" from the advance of highly disciplined British soldiers. Partly based on familiar stereotypes that had grown to new highs from experiences stemming from the French and Indian War, he even boasted about the common sentiment so pervasive across England and Europe how "only a few of our troops will rout the greatest number of them."[18]

As if that was not enough, the haughty First Lord of the Admiralty even declared that during the confrontation for possession of Boston at the war's beginning that if he learned that "20,000 New England men were coming against me, I should wish that they were rather thirty or forty thousand." Incredibly, he believed that the larger number of American soldiers, then "the greater the stampede"—a common view that was ever-popular in London, which had partly resulted in the sending of a mighty armada to New York City partly in the belief that such a strong show of force would be enough to cow the revolutionaries and make them immediately come to their senses without offering the slightest resistance. Ironically, an entirely believable scenario to Britons had been played out in full at Kip's Bay on a Sunday morning north of New York City.[19]

Indeed, now in the following year after he presented his popular view that dominated England, it seemed as if Lord Sandwich's prophesy had been fulfilled by the shameful Kip's Bay rout, which represented a new low for the young American army that was learning on the job like its equally inexperienced commander. The dismal performance of Washington's troops at Kip's Bay was shaping up to be the worst disaster of the war to date, outdistancing even the rout stemming from the recent Long Island defeat.

But almost at the last moment in the disaster at Kip's Bay, all was not lost for the hapless Americans because of the arrival of veterans who had already proved to have been saviors of the retreat off Long Island during the rescue of thousands of Washington's soldiers before it was too late. There was one last hope to salvage something positive from the unprecedented fiasco at Kip's Bay to gain lost respect for America's revolutionary defenders, who proved no match for Howe's veterans even before having fired a shot in anger. In timely fashion, one of Washington's reinforcing units that rushed forward to stem the tide of the shameful rout at Kip's Bay was Colonel John Glover's Fourteenth Massachusetts Continental Regiment and its three sister regiments from the Bay State. In a smart decision, Glover's regiment had been pulled from Harlem Heights on September 14 and ordered east at a brisk pace to reach the scene of disaster just in time. If any command could reap a measure of American honor from the most embarrassing humiliation of the war, it was this remarkable Massachusetts unit of mariners. After all, the Fourteenth Massachusetts was a crack regiment that was the most versatile and disciplined command in the Continental Army. Under Colonel Glover's able leadership, this dependable amphibious regiment was one of the finest in Washington's army, as recently demonstrated during the risky Long Island evacuation. By this time and either on land or water where it excelled when the challenge was greatest, the Fourteenth Massachusetts Continental Regiment was "the best equipped, best disciplined and most reliable Corps in the Army."[20]

In shocking fashion, the debacle at Kip's Bay revealed how Washington and his men were no match for hardened professionals from across the sea. By this time and throughout the ill-fated New York Campaign, what was being played out in overall strategic terms by way of Howe's tactical expertise was "a cat-and-mouse game [in which] Washington was a rather bewildered mouse," who was always caught by surprise whenever Howe decided to make a clever move.[21]

Consequently, "to my great surprise and Mortification" in riding down the Boston Post Road, General Washington had been stunned by what he saw at Kip's Bay. However, he was unable to stop the rout when so many troops "were flying in every direction and in the greatest confusion" despite his best efforts. The commander in chief now saw that he no longer commanded these panic-stricken men because he no longer exercised any control of them. A thoroughly disgusted and frustrated General Washington asked during the height of the Kip's Bay stampede, when hundreds of panicked troops streamed around and past him, "Are these the men with which I am to defend America?" His question was about to be convincingly answered by Glover's soldiers, who shortly played a key role in halting the rout that

Washington had been unable to accomplish to his ever-lasting disgust, at an obscure place north of Kip's Bay called Pell's Point.[22]

The Most Unique and Distinctive Soldiers of Washington's Army

Hailing mostly from the longtime fishing port of Marblehead situated on a rocky peninsula located just north of Boston and founded by hardy settlers who had been mostly seafarers from small fishing villages located primarily in east, west, and southwest England, including Cornwall, and the Channel Islands, the soldiers of the Fourteenth Massachusetts Continental Regiment were special by any measure.

The young men and boys of Glover's "Marine" regiment were the most unique and unorthodox soldiers in Washington's army. Having grown up in the picturesque port city, individuals of this distinctive seafaring community on the Bay State's rocky coast were known for their rugged individualism, free thinking, natural skepticism that bred a measure of ingenuity, and a distinctive unorthodoxy to an excessive degree: the making of an ideal republican soldiery to meet even the stiffest challenges in 1776. Most of all, these self-reliant and naturally nonconformist seafaring men from mostly Marblehead believed in God, freedom of the seas, the virtues of self-government, defiant independence, and the rights of the individual, which all helped to translate into a tactical flexibility and a can-do attitude despite the odds on the battlefield.

All in all, this excellent regiment was a godsend to General Washington, especially during the New York Campaign, because Glover's men were members of America's first amphibious and marine command with both land and water fighting capabilities, which were well beyond the ordinary. Most of these men had been fishermen, sailors, and seafarers before the war, having made a living sailing and working the waters of the cold Atlantic, especially in fishing expeditions to the world's finest fighting grounds—the Grand Banks of the northwest Atlantic. Here, most of these young men and boys in the ranks had long fished the underwater plateaus of the continental shelf to reap a rich harvest of cod that had long made Marblehead prosperous. For such reasons, Glover and his men had become the undisputed master of amphibious operations second to none.

Ironically, evolving into Washington's trusty saviors was more of a natural development rather than an evolution created in wartime partly because they hailed from a unique cultural environment of the largest commercial fishing port in all North America, Marblehead. Also from the ports of Salem, Lynn, and Beverly, Massachusetts, but fewer in numbers than Marblehead in Essex County, Massachusetts, these men were the most disciplined soldiers in Washington's army partly because of their difficult and demanding lives stemming from their seafaring experiences. From Marblehead situated on the long, rocky peninsula known to the locals as the Great Neck and covered in hollyhocks (Marblehead had been long called "Hollyhock Town") that added greenery and located around sixteen miles northeast of Boston, Marblehead presented a highly unusual appearance. The town consisted of clutters of small houses and fisherman cottages of every shape, form, and size in a jumbled mass on the high ground overlooking the harbor of blue: a distinctive individualism, self-reliance, and independence personified. This lucrative fishing community rested on the foundations of typical New England practicality, hard work, and frugality. When not at sea, the people of Marblehead stoically endured the harsh winter winds and icy storms sweeping in from the northeast, but spring and summer were delightful at one of the most picturesque harbors in New England.

In the shape of a giant lobster claw, the north–south harbor of Marblehead lay nestled between the Great Neck on the left, or west, and the smaller pincer claw on the right, or east. Before the war, these men had been part of a vast fishing fleet of more than 150 vessels that annually journeyed more than five hundred miles to the great fishing grounds of the Grand Banks off the coast of Nova Scotia to reap rich harvests of cod for the European market, especially in Spain, and the sugar islands of the West Indies to feed the great multitudes of enslaved Africans who far outnumbered the white population.

Fully able to perform specialized missions on either land or water on a moment's notice when such orders were handed down from Washington's headquarters, Glover's men still wore their distinctive seafaring garb—short blue jackets with leather (waterproof) buttons and baggy, light trousers—with pride instead of the standard Continental uniforms of blue. Indicating the depth of their distinctive cultural and occupational backgrounds connected so closely to the sea and unique composition in a people's army made up mostly of farmers, the revealing appearance of the Marbleheaders, who looked almost as if they had just stepped off a fishing vessel from the Grand Banks, set them apart from Washington's other troops. Most important, Colonel Glover's men knew the supreme value of teamwork and the spirit of a perfect sense of equality between divergent individuals, including in regard to race, because of their years in working closely together at sea to create a hardened brand of discipline. Even more, they spoke with a peculiar Marblehead patois and a seafaring slang that revealed the isolation of their insular fishing community with its picturesque harbor and their distinctive way of life. These men intimately knew the ways of a sailing ship and the sea better than what they knew about farming the land and the mysterious society of landlubbers farther inland. They hailed from the largest and most successful commercial fishing community in America, thanks to Marblehead's magnificent harbor and the most lucrative cash crop that could be found in the dangerous waters of the North Atlantic, cod.

Most of all, these soldiers of Colonel Glover's regiment were a breed apart not only in the civilian world, but also in the ranks of the Continental Army—a unique double distinction of the most unorthodox and unconventional fighting men known for their can-do attitudes and seafaring ways. By any measure, Glover's mariners were tough, hardy men, who hailed from a rugged, harsh place on their rocky peninsula. In a paradox, Marblehead smacked of indiscipline at first glance. It was a haphazard-looking fishing community of small, wooden clapboard houses situated amid a maze of dirt streets, alleys, and lanes, including the appropriately named "Mariners Lane," without any conceivable order or reason. For generations, men had departed from this chaotic-looking community—looks were most deceiving in this regard—on sailings ships to engage in one of the roughest of all occupations in America. All of these distinctive environmental factors had transformed these unorthodox men into an exceptionally durable soldiery, more resourceful and versatile than any other soldiers in Washington's army.

Far more distinctive than their traditional and colorful seafarers' garb, including baggy and light trousers that were ideal for climbing riggings, raising sails, and other mariner duties aboard ship, these seafaring men possessed something that was badly needed in Washington's often-defeated army: the hard-fighting, discipline, and resilient qualities of this elite infantry regiment. From beginning to end, these hardy New Englanders of the Fourteenth Massachusetts Continental Regiment demonstrated at every possible opportunity that they were among the army's finest soldiers. Consequently, Glover's soldiers, who served either as infantrymen or mariners depending on the specific situation, basked in the entire army's and Washington's high esteem for having successfully transferred around ten thousand trapped and doomed soldiers across the East River from Long Island to the safety of Manhattan Island on the night of August 29–30 to keep the fires of revolution alive in what was "an escape pivotal to the outcome" of the American Revolution. Because of these reasons, just the mere sight of the highly disciplined New Englanders, who still carried the aura of the sea with them, inspired confidence in other Continental troops, especially during crisis situations.

Indeed, other soldiers knew that the army's elite troops had arrived when they saw Glover's men, although they certainly did not look the coveted part because of their coarse, homespun appearance that served as a walking advertisement of a life at sea. Watching the mysterious, magical effect of Glover's can-do men inspiring other Continental troops at Long Island to stand firm while contemplating the striking paradox, one young Pennsylvania officer from the upper crust of the nation's capital in Philadelphia, Alexander Graydon had anything but complimentary words for Washington's "motley army" that consisted of an "multitudinous assemblage" of citizen-soldiers.[23]

But most significant, he also carefully noted how of all Washington's troops, the

> only exception [to the disorder and ill-discipline of] these miserably constituted bands from New England, was the regiment of Glover from Marblehead. There was an appearance of discipline in this corps; the officers seemed to have mixed with the world, and understood what belonged to their stations. Though deficient, perhaps, in polish, it possessed an apparent aptitude for the purpose of its institution, and gave a confidence that myriads of its meek and lowly brethren were incompetent to inspire.[24]

Of course, these exceptional qualities inherent in the crack mariners of Glover's disciplined regiment became most obvious when thousands of hapless Americans had been trapped on Long Island, when they rose splendidly to the challenge. Alexander Graydon, who served in the ranks of a Pennsylvania command, emphasized how the mostly Marbleheaders of Glover's regiment

> inspired no inconsiderable degree of confidence. The faces that had been saddened by the disasters of yesterday, assumed a gleam of animation, on our approach; accompanied with a murmur of approbation in the spectators occasionally greeting each other with the remark, that "these were the lads that might do something."[25]

The mysterious inspirational influence of the army's elite troops over other soldiers, both Continentals and especially militiamen, most recently became apparent when American fortunes reached a new all-time low at the Kip's Bay disaster. During the fiasco of Kip's Bay and with other arriving colonial troops who had been dispatched down the Boston Post Road, the timely arrival of Glover's men brought a much-needed stability to the chaos that the presence of General Washington was not able to achieve, providing inspiration and hope to throngs of defeated soldiers, who could not be rallied only a short time before. Indeed, the thousands of "Americans that had fled upon the approach of the enemy, stopped not till they were met by Col. Glover's and the five other brigades."[26]

However, it was mostly the sight of Glover's troops that gave the most confidence to the routed militiamen from Connecticut and finally instilled them with the resolve to stand firm. Indeed, the

> officers of Colonel Glover's regiment, one of the best corps in the service . . . immediately obliged the fugitive officers and soldiers, equally, to turn into the ranks with the soldiers of Glover's regiment, and obliged the trembling wretches to march back to the ground they had quitted.[27]

The Loss of America's Second-Largest City

In overall strategic terms, the humiliating debacle at Kip's Bay possessed far-reaching ramifications because Washington's army had been outflanked on the east or on the right. Indeed, the Kip's Bay fiasco "fixed the fate of New York [and this] defeat was as grievous in loss of property as it was shameful cowardice it uncovered [and] There never had been a more outrageous affair and seldom so complete a British victory for so small an expenditure of blood and bullets."[28]

In consequence, New York City was doomed to fall because of the defeat at Kip's Bay, because Washington was forced to withdraw north from lower Manhattan to avoid getting cut off. Author Russell Shorto perhaps best explained the importance of New York City and Manhattan in his 2004 book *The Island at the Center of the World*. Indeed, by the time of the American Revolution, New York City was the center of the North American colonists' world and the "greatest natural harbor" on the eastern seaboard, which made it the center of trade for all thirteen colonies, while having long served as the most direct commercial link between the Mother Country and British possessions in the Caribbean Islands and North America.

In the words of Barnet Schecter in his 2002 work *The Battle For New York*: "Because of its geography, its culture, its people, and its hold on the imagination of eighteenth-century military strategists, New York was, without exaggeration, the pivot on which the entire Revolutionary War turned."[29] And now Washington had lost America's great city during the most humiliating and disastrous of military campaigns. In the words of Maryland-born Tench Tilghman, who served on Washington's staff, from a September 16 letter in which he described the abandonment of New York City:

> Our Army totally evacuated New York City yesterday, the Enemy landed a party of about 3000 from Appearance four miles above the City [at Kip's Bay and] while their Men were landing [and] no Body opposed them. . . . We removed everything that was valuable, some heavy Cannon excepted, before we left the Town two [New England] Brigades ran away from a small advanced party of the Regulars [at Kip's Bay], tho' the General [Washington] did all in his power to convince them they were in no danger. He laid his Cane over many of the Officers who shewed their men the Example of running. These were militia, the New England continental Troops are much better.[30]

One of the greatest ironies of the American Revolution was that New York City's loss at the time seemed an unprecedented disaster for American arms and one from which there would be no recovery. However, as the British eventually learned, this war for America could not be won by capturing even the largest cities, including its capital, like in Europe, because this was a people's rebellion. Even more, the myopic focus on retaining control of New York City saddled British leadership with the illusion that they were still winning the war as late as 1781: a fantasy that might well have cost them America in the end.[31]

Perhaps more than anyone else because he was a seafaring man and the fact that New York City was encircled by a complex maze of waterways, Glover fully realized how close Washington's army had come to having been trapped by committing the folly of attempting to retain possession of New York City, when it was impossible under the circumstances. In an October 7, 1776, letter to his mother from Fort Constitution, Glover wrote of when "we evacuated New York [City], and happy for us we began the retreat so timely as we did, otherwise the whole that were in the City must have been cut off."[32]

In a replay of the narrow escape and evacuation from Long Island, Glover played a key role in the city's evacuation before Howe's army circled north in another amphibious landing to cut off Washington's line of retreat as feared. As Washington penned to Congress: "We are now taking every method in our power to remove the stores [from the city], in which we find almost insuperable difficulties [which are] great [and] Our sick are extremely numerous [about one-fourth of the army], and we find their removal attended with the greatest difficulty."[33]

Once again, General Washington had relied heavily upon Colonel Glover even before the disaster at Kip's Bay after having made the decision to disperse his troops over a wide area of sixteen miles to guard numerous strategic points, including Kingsbridge, which linked Manhattan Island to the American mainland—and leaving Major General Israel Putnam's Division in New York City. Glover had fulfilled the difficult assignment of transporting military supplies and around five hundred sick soldiers around twenty miles north up the Hudson to Orangetown, New York. On the night of September 12–13, these ill soldiers were transported to the safety of New Jersey by Glover's men, before they had then received urgent orders to march to Kingsbridge and then farther south to ensure that Glover and his troops helped to save the day at Kip's Bay.[34]

Colonel Glover described the evacuation of New York City, feeling thankful because on "the 15th . . . we evacuated New York and happily for us [since] we began the retreat so timely as we did otherwise the while that were in the City must have been cut off the enemy having landed 18,000 men on that day on the East Side about four miles [north of] the City" at Kip's Bay.[35]

Glover and his mariners were destined to twice rise to the fore when the army seemed well on its way along the road to extinction, after one fiasco after another in rapid succession: Pell's Point during the New York Campaign and then barely two months later during the Trenton Campaign.

Whenever a crisis or no-win situation called when the life of the army and the new nation were on the line, consequently, Washington always kept in mind how the little Marblehead colonel, who still talked like a sea captain who had just returned from a fishing expedition to the Grand Banks, and his disciplined seafaring men—basically the army's marines—were the ones he could always rely upon to rise to the challenge. Now an acting brigadier general (he would win this rank in 1777) in command of a fine Massachusetts Brigade after the disaster at Kip's Bay and since early September, Colonel Glover stood out as a shining star amid a galaxy of mediocre, incompetent American officers, including Washington to a shocking degree. Glover was special, and Washington, to his credit that revealed he was an excellent judge of character, had early realized as much. In private moments of doubt, a frustrated Washington lamented how his Continental troops, who were better trained and disciplined than the militiamen who in theory were to rally around the regulars, "never had officers, except in a few instances, worth the bread they eat."[36]

And, as usual another crisis was shortly looming for the Continental Army during this seemingly doomed campaign in which New York City already had been lost, when it had been Washington's primary responsibility to save the city. Therefore, it was feared by Americans that the Kip's Bay disaster had been only the beginning of what lay in store for the error-prone Washington and his bungling army, because of Howe's tactical skills and the British navy's control of the intricate system of waterways around New York City and Manhattan Island. Therefore, while positioned on Manhattan Island, the strategic situation could not have been more dire for the Continental Army, which was already losing this war in embarrassing fashion: "Washington's position was precarious [especially] With the enemy on three sides, his army was in danger of being cut off from further retreat and destroyed."[37]

As Washington wrote in a letter to the Continental Congress about the crisis now faced by the infant nation conceived in liberty:

> It is evident the enemy mean to inclose us on the island of New York [Manhattan] by taking post in our rear while the shipping secures the front, and thus, by cutting off our communication with the country, oblige us to fight them on their own terms or surrender at discretion, or by a brilliant stroke endeavor to cut this army in pieces.[38]

Despite New York City's loss and again committing the folly of attempting to defend too many points over too wide of an area of Manhattan Island, Washington's forces remained extremely vulnerable. The unique geography of the New York area had already handed General Howe much of what he needed to win a decisive victory to win the revolution, while commanding a seemingly invincible army and enjoying complete naval superiority in the waters around New York City.

Nevertheless, General Washington and his top commanders were yet undecided about the specifics of Howe's next tactical move despite that fact that it was obvious that he would never again foolishly launch frontal assaults like he did at Bunker Hill and that he would rely on outflanking maneuvers. In consequence, the greatest fear among American leadership was that Howe would conduct an amphibious landing at some point to the north from Long Island Sound in an attempt to not only outflank and cut off Washington's strong position at Harlem Heights, but also to gain the Continental Army's rear to trap it on Manhattan Island. These menacing tactical possibilities were taken into consideration, but they could not be stopped because America possessed too few troops and no navy to thwart the British Navy from easily landing thousands of troops at any point of their choosing at any moment. Washington, therefore, attempted to guard against all tactical possibilities over a wide area with too few troops: an impossible task. Consequently, some ten thousand American troops remained at and around Fort Washington on the northern tip of Manhattan Island and on the Hudson's east side. General Nathanael Greene, who was Washington's top lieutenant, commanded another five thousand troops in and around Fort Lee, the former Fort Constitution, on the Hudson's other side.

Most important, Major General William Heath, born in Roxbury, Massachusetts, in 1737 and one of Washington's top lieutenants, and another ten thousand men held the Kingsbridge area on the mainland to the north to resist a British amphibious landing. For ample good reason, it was feared at headquarters that Howe would conduct a strike inland north of Kip's Bay in an attempt to ease north of Washington's army and trap it. The crucial link from Manhattan Island to the mainland was Kingsbridge—a small wooden bridge, which crossed the Harlem River at a narrow point that had been uniquely named Spuyten Duyvil Creek, which Glover wrote as "Spitting Devil Creek" in a letter, of vast strategic importance: the vital avenue of escape from the trap of Manhattan Island for Washington's army, which was yet reeling from a series of miserable defeats and gloomy withdrawals in rapid succession.[39]

The next crisis of the amateurs in rebellion against seasoned professionals was only a matter of time. However, Glover remained confident, despite the reduced size of his Bay State regiment and brigade from the usual attrition, especially from disease, which always took more lives than British bullets and cannonballs. On September 20, for instance, the Fourteenth Massachusetts Continental Regiment consisted of only 279 men, because another 126 soldiers were serving at Beverly, Massachusetts, in Washington's infant navy.[40]

New Outflanking Threat, British Landing at Throgs Point

As throughout this disastrous summer-fall campaign around New York City when America's life was at stake during the most desperate of times, Washington repeatedly committed tactical folly. He continued to demonstrate his lack of experience in the art of war, while repeatedly bringing the revolution precariously close to abruptly ending hardly before it had begun. Embracing a course of folly, he still wanted to retain possession of the northern part of Manhattan Island despite New York City's recent loss, which was a strategic incompatibility under the circumstances and geography, especially in regard to the intricate system of waterways that seemed to run in every direction: a virtual impossibility and a far-fetched fantasy that revealed the extent of the surprising overconfidence and self-delusion of the army's inexperienced leader.

General Washington, however, still believed that he could accomplish his outdated plan to bait the British into launching foolish frontal assaults by occupying the strong defensive position at Harlem Heights, a rocky plateau on Manhattan Island located between the Hudson River to the Harlem River. Once again risking his army's life unnecessarily as throughout this campaign, Washington made the mistake of not abandoning Manhattan Island as soon as possible. This wise maneuver would have early allowed him to transfer his army north in a timely manner across the Harlem River to the relative safety of Westchester County on the New York mainland.[41]

Because the British Navy controlled the waterways around New York City and thanks to the disaster at Kip's Bay that outflanked his stationary position on the right or east, this best avenue—the Harlem River by way of strategic Kingsbridge just east of the Hudson River—for Washington to abandon Manhattan Island and escape north could be easily cut off by British warships, however. But despite the risks, Washington was convinced that he had adequate defensive arrangements in place to thwart the possibility of his army's entrapment. Besides Harlem Heights, Washington's forces held Fort Washington on the northwest side of Manhattan Island and Fort Constitution, which guarded a strategic bend of the Hudson just north of West Point on the river's west side unlike Fort Constitution, causing him to incorrectly believe that the passage of British warships could be stopped by rows of cannon, although manned by inexperienced gunners, poised on the high ground.

And he had positioned a force east of the Harlem River to guard his flank just in case an emerging threat suddenly appeared from the east. Washington believed that he could yet easily escape Manhattan Island like from New York City, as if the factor of time was unimportant: a delusion of monumental proportions, because far too much was now at stake—the army's life and that of the revolution—to roll the dice on a risky gamble. Washington should have felt no confidence whatsoever in being able to maneuver his army out of harm's way in an efficient manner at the first sign of trouble when he again met the tactically astute General Howe in the all-important chess game not only for possession of Manhattan Island, but also the life of the revolution.[42]

Giving him some comfort and also fueling a false sense of confidence, Washington's defensive position along the commanding high ground of Harlem Heights was a good one, while thoughts of Bunker Hill glory continued to flash through his head. However, Washington remained vigilant, wary of mysterious and stealthy British movements that he could not yet fully decipher or understand. By September's end and with the advent of the arrival of cooler weather, he had his troops ready for another surprise British-Hessian assault, including at night. As noted, Howe had learned a lesson from having seen hundreds of redcoats slaughtered on the bloody slopes of Bunker Hill, or actually Breed's Hill. In the words of historian Thomas Fleming, who was not guilty of exaggeration: "Even a mere [British] captain could see the folly of a frontal assault on Harlem Heights."[43]

Captain Frederick MacKenzie, of the Twenty-third Welsh Fusiliers, reasoned correctly upon viewing the strength of the defensive position and the busy preparations of Washington's troops for receiving an assault at Harlem Heights: "I am of opinion Genl Howe will never attack them in front in their present position [therefore] He certainly intends something very different."[44]

Clearly, this was the correct tactical evaluation, because the British commander in chief wisely had the art of outflanking Washington's army on his mind, after that tactic had recently worked like a charm on Long Island. Howe had already learned his hard-earned Bunker Hill lesson, which was a searing experience that he never forgot as long as he lived. In this New York campaign, therefore, Howe would continue to rely on flanking and encircling movements, while Washington was still thinking in terms of Bunker Hill: a dangerous discrepancy that was the recipe for disaster. Consequently, the freshly dug lengthy line of defenses spread across Harlem Heights were too formidable for Howe to be tempted to commit the ultimate folly. Indeed, the "American works on Harlem Heights were too well planned and too strongly defended, by nearly 15,000 men, to invite a frontal attack" for a commander of Howe's talents, which only revealed Washington's naivety and wishful thinking.[45]

Anticipating another trick from the wily Howe, the experienced General William Heath, a New Englander and former volunteer of a Boston artillery command that he had joined in 1765 to gain experience and who now commanded American troops in Westchester County on the New York mainland, had prudently ordered a line of pickets to watch the sprawling coastline at Throgs Neck. The neck, located about a dozen miles north of Kip's Bay and just southeast of the town of Westchester, Westchester County, offered an ideal landing site for British amphibious operations on the west side of the East River and northeast of Harlem Heights: a most advantageous position to the north from which to advance west and stealthily ease behind Washington's army. Here, in south Westchester County, Throgs Neck was situated on a narrow peninsula that gradually widened between the Hudson River on the west and Long Island Sound on the east. To his credit, therefore, Washington ordered Ireland-born Colonel Edward Hand and his Pennsylvania men armed with long rifles, to guard Throgs Neck, which was located at the end of a small, narrow peninsula protruding into the deep tidal waters of the East River.[46]

Fortunately for America, Hand was an exceptional leader and skill-ful fighting man of outstanding ability. Ironically, Hand had arrived in America in 1767, while wearing a scarlet uniform of a surgeon's mate in the British Army. He resigned from serving the king to make a life for himself in America, which presented boundless opportunity com-pared to the impoverished Emerald Isle so far away. Instead of return-ing to the bleakness of Ireland, he had acquired more than 1,400 acres of prime Pennsylvania land. With considerable skill, Colonel Hand now led the reliable Continentals of the First Continental Infantry Regiment (first known as the First Pennsylvania when formed in 1775) of the Pennsylvania Line. Hand and his Pennsylvania boys had earlier played a key role in harassing and delaying the enemy's advance after first landing unopposed on Long Island by the sharpshooting skills of the unit's frontier marksmen, winning Washington's trust and respect for their harassing irregular tactics.[47]

For all the right reasons, General Howe wisely wanted at all costs to avoid the prospect of hurling long lines of redcoats against Washington's earthen defenses aligned across the excellent high-ground perch atop Harlem Heights. Therefore, the most logical and appropriate strategy that ideally fit the overall tactical situation evolved from an all-day council of war held by General Howe with his top commanders on October 8. Rear Admiral Richard Howe pro-posed another amphibious landing to the north to catch Washington by surprise and gain his left flank.[48]

Enjoying complete control of the network of waterways around New York City, the British now relied on a bold strategic plan at the beginning of October's second week that called for outflanking the Harlem Heights defensive position by way of easing Vice Admiral Howe's vast armada of warships and transports north from Kip's Bay and up the East River and launching an invasion of Westchester County, after landing north of and far beyond Washington's left flank on the east and toward the East River to entrap the Continental Army on Manhattan Island. To disguise the flanking movement and to occupy Washington's attention, Lord Percy and several brigades were left to demonstrate and feign an offensive thrust before Washington's main body of troops, who were still holding firm along Harlem Heights, anticipating assaults at any moment.

But in fact, Howe missed a golden opportunity. At the October 8 council meeting, the astute General Henry Clinton had advocated a landing of troops in east Westchester County at or near New Rochelle, New York, which was located north of Pell's Point, on Long Island Sound. Howe overruled the proposed on-target strategy of landing farther north at New Rochelle—a guarantee to entrap Washington's army—because Vice Admiral Howe was concerned about the safety of its vulnerable fleet at such an unsheltered location in the more open waters of the Long Island Sound compared to the narrower East River, because of the ravages of a possible hurricane near the height of the hurricane season. Howe finally settled on the seemingly more suitable landing site in his mind, which was actually not the case, for slipping north to outflank Washington's Harlem Heights position chosen by members of the war council for this amphibious envelopment at Throgs Neck or Point, in Westchester County. The landing site was located at the southern end of Long Island Sound where the East River met the Long Island Sound, northeast of New York City, and at the eastern corner of Westchester County.[49]

Clearly, the capture of Kip's Bay around a dozen miles south of Throgs Neck and the successful amphibious landing at that vital point now paid additional dividends besides having doomed New York City. Now, the British Navy could push off from the calm waters of Kip's Bay, proceed north unopposed at any moment, and then land farther north to not only outflank Washington's heavily fortified position on the east, but also isolate Fort Washington and its large garrison of Continental troops situated at the north end of Manhattan Island.[50]

Howe's amphibious landing at Throgs Neck targeted a small spit of land that thrust southward into the southern end of Long Island Sound and near the junction of the East River and the sound about three miles southeast of the town of Westchester, which located farther north and higher up on the peninsula, and around eight miles from Kingsbridge to the northwest and not far from the Hudson's east bank. A successful British-Hessian thrust inland from Throgs Neck promised much in strategic possibilities. Located in southern Westchester County and separating Long Island Sound from the East River, Throgs Neck, originally Throckmorton's Point but now known among the locals as Thock's Neck, Frog's Neck, and then Frog's Point after the name had been repeatedly shortened over the years, was situated at the lower, or southernmost, tip, a small north–south peninsula about two miles in length that paralleled the south end of Long Island Sound.

By this time, General Howe had also made a key mistake by having spent too much time at Kip's Bay to make the patriots more wary about his next move. Because the Throgs Neck Peninsula was located almost directly east of Washington's defensive position on Harlem Heights, it could be easily outflanked by an amphibious landing to the east from Long Island Sound, which Washington immediately recognized. However, as an effective diversion to disguise such a landing, several British brigades positioned before Washington's defensive line along Harlem Heights focused Washington's primary attention on the immediate threat that loomed before him rather than his vulnerable left flank near Long Island Sound. This same strategy had already proved successful to verify that Howe was a master flanker in orchestrating amphibious landings at Long Island, where the Americans and especially Washington least expected a landing, and then at Kip's Bay.[51]

Politician William Duer, who had been born in England, wrote to Tench Tilghman in a September 20 letter that prophetically told of Howe's next tactical move because it was so logical:

> I can easily imagine that Genl. Howe must be both chagrined
> and disappointed at the Retreat of our Army from New York.
> I have no doubt but what he expected fully to have taken
> them in a net, and he certainly would have succeeded had
> we pertinaciously persisted in the plan of defending the city

[and now the Hudson] River is sufficiently obstructed that our lines will keep the enemy from making any progress in front . . . but you must recollect that the [Long Island] Sound is, and must ever be, open; and if they should succeed in landing a Body of Men in Westchester County, they might, by drawing lines to the North [Hudson] River, as effectually hem us in, as if we were [still] in New York [City].[52]

After having waited throughout the late summer and early fall in New York City, Howe was emboldened by the arrival of five thousand Hessian reinforcements of the Second Division (the First Division of German troops had already joined the army at Staten Island on August 12), whose services had been bought at a high price by King George III from German princes of individual states, especially Hesse-Kassel. These well-trained German troops, who were uniformed in blue coats, landed on New York soil to mark a historic moment, which infuriated Washington's men: Britons were considered "cousins," but the Hessians were mercenary foreigners who had been hired to kill Americans and rob them of their liberty. All the way from the mountains and rolling farmlands of Germany, the proud Hessians fought for the honor of their Teutonic people and their principalities. In the darkness of 3:00 a.m. on Saturday October 12, therefore, a more confident Howe finally decided to renew the offensive with a reinforced army of around 35,000 men, both Britons and Hessians, in a final bid to entrap Washington's army.

General Howe reasoned that he could now keep a tight grip on New York City and also embark on the offensive to the north against Washington's army to turn its weak left flank. In consequence, General Henry Clinton began to embark five thousand troops aboard flatboats at Kip's Bay for a push north up the East River and toward the southern end of Long Island Sound, before launching an amphibious landing for the push inland west in an attempt to outflank and then pin Washington's army against the Hudson River to the west, where it could be easily crushed at will, after outflanking the strong defensive ground of Harlem Heights so that there would be no bloody Bunker Hill repeat.[53]

British warships under Rear Admiral Richard Howe planned to escort the vast fleet of flatboats filled with seasoned fighting men across East River's wide waters, which were almost lake-like in appearance except for the swirl of the strong currents, to gain the new landing site at Throgs Neck in southern Westchester County. Most of all, General Howe had set his sights on the all-important strategic roads that led northwest to Kingsbridge, only about four miles distant, and straight to the vulnerable rear of the majority of Washington's army poised on Harlem Heights and looking south in the wrong direction for trouble: the ideal scenario for entrapment of Washington's army on Manhattan Island.[54]

In his report to leadership in London, General Howe described the grand movement north by water to gain Washington's vulnerable left flank, while revealing the Briton's tactical astuteness: "All previous arrangements being made, the army embarked [from Kip's Bay], on the 12th of October, in flat boats, and other craft, and pressing through the dangerous navigation of Hell-gate, in a very thick fog," while pushing farther north up the East River toward the ultimate target of Throg's Point.[55]

One of Washington's soldiers presented the American perspective in regard to Howe's tactics around this time in a letter: "About the 15th [12th] of October, the great movement, the enemy up the [Long Island] sound," began with "lord and general Howe there in person [because] Howe's plan was to make a bold stroke, and hem in and cut off our army at once."[56]

Indeed, after the armada of British warships and flatboats passed through the turbulent waters of Hell's Gates and a late-summer fog, known to hug the Atlantic coastline at this time of year, that was as thick as soup, the British landed at Throgs Point on the morning of October 12 without meeting opposition—to Howe's delight and as he planned because he possessed the Royal Navy under his capable brother and complete naval superiority to guarantee a surprise landing, because no American defenses had been erected along the sandy shore or beach at low-lying Throgs Neck. In fact, no American soldiers were near enough to even attempt opposing the landing at Kip's Bay. Howe's landing at Throgs Neck gained the strategic advantage of catching Washington by surprise like on Long Island that had led to disaster.

An oddly yet confident, if not somewhat delusional, Washington now faced a greater peril than imagined. Washington's army on Harlem Heights risked more than being simply outflanked on the left, or to the east. Washington's army now risked a clever double envelopment. Since British warships could also sail north up the Hudson and past Fort Washington, another landing of British troops could come north to strike the American's right flank or in the rear of Washington's position at Harlem Heights, while a vigorous British drive across the peninsula west from Throgs Point could smash into the Continental Army's left flank and gain Washington's rear: the tactical formula for ending the life of Washington's upstart army.[57]

While feeling secure on the high ground and behind the formidable defenses of Harlem Heights, it was only a matter of time before Washington's excellent defensive position was entirely compromised. Indeed, the "danger was that the jaws of the trap would be closed suddenly [and] American forces might be compelled to fight when and where the enemy pleased or might be cut and starved into surrender."[58]

But to his credit and taking no chances, Washington had wisely already personally reconnoitered Throgs Neck on October 3 with Colonel Edward Hand, who led the "rifle corps" of Pennsylvanians armed with deadly long rifles. Attempting to ensure that he would not be again surprised like on Long Island, Washington had ordered Hand to pick about thirty of his best Pennsylvania riflemen to defend the key ford at a tidal creek and the west end of the narrow causeway spanning a brackish creek and millpond situated just beyond the neck's shoreline. This was a natural choke-point, or "pass," ideal for a defensive stand to be made by only a relatively few soldiers when armed with long rifles. Colonel Hand directed nearby piles of cordwood to be used to enhance the defensive position and ordered the bridge's wooden planks to be taken up to impede a British crossing of the causeway. Hand's timely actions partly reflected his experience during a past career in the British Army before retirement to become an American citizen.[59]

Additionally, General Howe had already made a serious tactical mistake because of his lack of detailed intelligence about the area around Throgs Neck, assuming that it would be perfect for a surprise landing. But in the end, it would be Howe who was most surprised by what he found at Throgs Neck. While Howe's bold plan to launch an amphibious landing north to catch Washington from the flank was well thought out, the landing site was not. The small peninsula of Throgs Neck was more of a low-lying island, surrounded by saltwater marshes and subject to flooding with the arrival of the daily high tide and heavy rains, than a firm peninsula of solid ground where the British Army could gain a permanent toehold and erect defenses, if necessary. Most of all, Howe needed to gain a high-ground landing site for a permanent toehold. At high tide, only a narrow, wooden causeway and rickety old bridge over the tidal creek at the peninsula's lower end connected it most tenuously to the New York mainland of southern end of Westchester County east of the village of Morrisania in the Bronx.[60]

By this time, Washington possessed the good fortune to have one of the finest field grade officers in his army guarding this key position on his army's far left flank, Colonel Edward Hand. As noted, Hand was a talented Irish immigrant who had resigned from the British Army, in which he had formerly served as surgeon's mate, in 1774. After having fallen in love with America and a pretty American woman, he had settled in Pennsylvania with his wife. In terms of skills and abilities, Hand was second only to Colonel Glover as Washington's top mid-level commander. To stop the invader from pouring inland like a flood, the Irishman knew that the enemy had to be stopped at the causeway over the creek that connected Throgs Neck to the mainland of Westchester County, which called for decimating any advancing troops attempting to push inland with an accurate fire from his men armed with the Pennsylvania long rifle.

Knowing the position's supreme importance, not only General William Heath early in October, but also General Washington inspected the position on October 11, as if expecting the worst and anticipating Howe's next tactical move in a classic chess game. Most of all, with Hand commanding only around thirty crack riflemen of the Pennsylvania Continentals, Washington knew he would have to rush reinforcements to this distant point east of Harlem Heights and all the way to the peninsula's other side, if the British landed in force.[61]

Meanwhile, after the bombardment from British warships, some four thousand British troops landed on Throgs Neck near the Ferris family estate and easily gained south Westchester County soil without facing opposition. British soldier Thomas Sullivan was amazed by another easy success, writing in his journal: "When the Rebels perceived us in the Boats, they abandoned the Neck," withdrawing on the double in what seemed like a replay of Kip's Bay.[62]

Sensing a dramatic victory in the making, General Howe's advance elements marched swiftly up the peninsula to reach the little wooden bridge across the murky saltwater creek that separated the peninsula from the low-lying mainland. For a successful British thrust inland, this small, bridge—or causeway—had to be secured by Howe's foremost troops at all costs to ensure the army could pass over the brackish salt marsh and then pour inland to gain solid ground. However, the first British soldiers were frustrated to discover the bridge had been disabled by large wooden planks having been removed by the Pennsylvanians. Thanks to General Heath's orders, Colonel Hand and his Pennsylvania riflemen had beaten the British to the punch. On the night of September 12 and as mentioned, the competent colonel from the Green Isle had ordered his Pennsylvania boys to pull up the bridge's wooden planking to ensure no passage of enemy troops across the narrow span across the creek.[63]

As revealed in a October 19, 1776, letter from one of Washington's soldiers, who was caught by surprise by Howe's stealthy maneuver to the north:

> Last Saturday a number of the King's troops landed at a place called Throgs-Point [but] Soon after they landed, they attempted to pass at the mills opposite West-Chester Town,

but the bridge being taken up, and the pass well defended by a part of our army, the enemy thought proper to retreat, and immediately encamped, since which, little more has been done on either side, in that quarter, than a small cannonade.[64]

British soldier Thomas Sullivan described in his journal how the hated "Rebels" had gone to work and "cut down the wooden Bridge that was on the gut or Rivulet to hinder our following them to ye main Continent. They were within Gunshot of us on the other side of the Gut; where they began to intrench themselves in our front, and kept continually firing" on us.[65]

Deployed in expert fashion by Colonel Hand, the sharpshooting Pennsylvania boys and their blazing long rifles from the western frontier now showed their value, keeping the redcoats at a respectful distance. Washington had responded in time to the serious threat, as he had promised the hard-fighting Irish colonel, who had hurriedly dispatched a messenger to army headquarters to secure assistance. Therefore, Washington had ordered reinforcements, including an artillery piece, to bolster the sharpshooting Pennsylvanians, including Colonel Hand, who blazed away with a rifle to inspire his men to stand firm and cut down additional redcoats. Increased rifle fire and booming artillery with the arrival of reinforcements convinced Howe that he faced far more of Washington's men at Throgs Neck than actually was the case. General Howe now realized he had committed a tactical error in attempting to force an advantage at Throgs Neck, which was a no-win situation for his army as deemed by the dictates of geography, Colonel Hand, and the blazing fire of the Pennsylvania long rifles.[66]

Colonel Glover and his mostly Marblehead men had played a forgotten role in helping to save the day at Throgs Neck. In the nick of time, around 1,800 Massachusetts men, including Glover and his Fourteenth Massachusetts, and the New York Continentals bolstered Hand's band of fast-working Pennsylvania sharpshooters with two cannon. Thanks to what happened at Throgs Neck, General Washington

gained even greater confidence in his Massachusetts troops, especially the men of Glover's versatile command, who once again proved
that they were as formidable on land as on water. These timely reinforcements had managed to stop the invasion and thwarted Howe's
best-designed tactical plan, while saving Hand's small Pennsylvania
command from destruction. More important, Washington gained
greater insight into the tactical thinking of his opponent, knowing
beyond all doubt that Howe's strategy consisted "of getting in our rear
& cutting off our communication with the Country."[67]

Chapter 2

Dark Days and Another Dismal Washington Withdrawal

The startling news that large numbers of British troops had landed at Throgs Neck sent shock waves rippling through Washington's headquarters and army at Harlem Heights. By now, the truth of Howe's sinister intentions had been revealed in full: to cut off Washington's army and to deliver a death stroke to it.

One of Washington's officers who realized as much was talented General Charles Lee. Born in England, he now demonstrated his expertise from his many years of military experience, including the recent successful defense of the vital port of Charles Town or Charlestown (later Charleston), South Carolina. As revealed in an officer's letter about the October 16 commander's conference where Washington presided, General Lee knew exactly what was on Howe's mind, anticipating his tactical moves with clarity. He

> thought that the [strategic] situation of the army at the gates of America was much too confined and cramped, and that it could not be a good policy to lie still in such a situation, or to hazard the great cause in which were embarked, in one general action, in which if we should not succeed, the army might be lost, or a retreat would be extremely difficult, if not impossible. It was determined by the generals [Washington included] therefore to counteract the enemy by a general movement.[1]

As decided at this commander's conference on October 16, to counter Howe's landing at Throgs Neck Washington planned to order reinforcements to such strategic locations as Fort Washington at the north end of Manhattan Island, spreading out his forces to ensure that they could not be captured in one large concentration if Howe's plan to cut off and surround the army succeeded. Therefore, as written by an American officer in a letter, alerted Continental units, including Glover's brigade (recently Major General James Clinton's brigade) of Charles Lee's Division, soon would be "ordered over Kingsbridge, and marched on towards the enemy, to counteract them in their operations."[2]

New Englander Joseph Plumb Martin wrote of the dangerous strategic situation for Washington's army at this time: "the British landed at Frogg's neck, or point, and by their motions seemed to threaten to cut off our retreat on York-Island," or Manhattan Island.[3]

Indeed, Manhattan Island continued to loom as a deadly trap for Washington, who had almost seemed oblivious to the disturbing grim reality until it was almost too late. At an early date, the ever-analytical Colonel Joseph Reed, a gifted staff officer at headquarters and who was becoming increasingly critical of Washington's generalship because of what he had often seen firsthand, instinctively knew as much. Ascertaining that lower Manhattan Island was a fatal trap, Reed had penned in a September 2 letter how the American army was "cooped up or in danger of so being on this tongue of land where we ought never to have been."[4]

Therefore, Washington's soldiers were about to engage in still another long and gloomy withdrawal north—a dozen miles from Harlem Heights to White Plains, New York—and, in one soldier's words, "the stores, baggage, &c, were [ordered shortly to be] moved to places of safety with the greatest expedition," because a new crisis was at hand.[5]

The Eccentric Major General Charles Lee

After the successful defense of Charlestown in which he emerged as the city's savior in the popular imagination after having been dispatched south by Washington, Major General Charles Lee had returned to Washington's army in mid-October to take command of General William Heath's Division, which included Glover's Massachusetts brigade. Almost everything about General Charles Lee, who was second-in-command of the Continental Army, was either repulsive or offensive to the more refined gentleman of the upper class around him. Partly because he had been born in England and possessed so much experience, Lee was arrogant and conceited to a degree seldom seen in polite circles. Most of all, the cantankerous Lee was obsessively antisocial, preferring his beloved dogs to his fellow humans. His own towering arrogance, hot temper, and inflated sense of self-worth ensured the controversial general's emotional isolation from others of all ranks. As eccentric as he was odd in a day when gentlemanly qualities were most admired, General Lee was convinced that he was a military genius, superior in intellect to everyone else in General Washington's army, especially the commander in chief. However, he was bright, persuasive, and articulate in a way that allowed him to sound militarily brilliant, convincing those around him at Washington's headquarters of his views. Not only was he considered a military genius in Washington's army, but even the British believed that Lee was the most capable military man on the American side, because of his high level of military experience.

Indeed, General Lee possessed one invaluable trait lacking among Washington and his top officers at this time: decades of solid military experience in both the British and Polish Armies. Therefore, General Lee's military advice was invaluable to an army of amateurs in which generals knew almost as little about military affairs as the privates in the ranks. Consequently, General Lee had provided General Washington with the best advice possible at the time: evacuate Manhattan Island because it was indefensible and untenable, when the British Navy controlled the waterways around the island and Howe's invasion force had landed farther north, making it a deadly trap from which there was no escape.

Clearly, Wednesday October 16 was an important date in the infant Continental Army's life, because the extent of the crisis had been faced head-on by army leadership. Thanks to General Lee's growing concerns about impending disaster because the army could be so easily trapped on Manhattan Island, General Washington's timely commanders' conference at his headquarters on this early fall day was forced to deal with an escalating crisis situation, although Howe's frustrated troops had been unable to push inland thanks to Colonel Hand's actions and arriving reinforcements. Here, among the low-lying salt marches, the British were destined to remain at Throgs Neck for nearly a week, swatting mosquitoes and cursing their fate.

General Washington had just returned from his second timely reconnaissance of the Pell's Point Peninsula that was located around five miles north of Throgs Neck, revealing that he was increasingly concerned about future amphibious landings farther north. Clearly, this timely high-level meeting at Washington's headquarters was all-important because of the acceptance of the reality that Howe could land at any point and at any time from Long Island Sound to outflank Washington's army and entrap it to end its life.

Thanks largely to General Lee's persuasive arguments and considerable influence that dominated this all-important October 16 conference at Washington's headquarters and after having been outflanked to the east at Throgs Neck, Washington and his top lieutenants came into common agreement: it was now time to abandon the defensive position at Harlem Heights and the Kingsbridge defensive line located at the head of Manhattan Island before it was too late. It was clear to one and all that the tactical situation now called for a hasty withdrawal north to escape Manhattan Island and gain the New York mainland.

But even though Howe had been stopped at Throgs Neck, the vulnerability of Washington's army only increased because it could continue to be outflanked on the east by the British moving ever-farther north by water in the future. Therefore, lingering any longer on Manhattan Island would spell certain disaster, because the highly mobile and efficient British Army could land farther north of Throgs Peninsula and anywhere along the Long Island Sound on a moment's notice. Without a choice, General Washington decided on

October 16 that his army would now have to conduct a withdrawal of around a dozen miles north to the high ground—an excellent defensive position—of White Plains to escape the noose that Howe had tightened.[6] What now developed was nothing less than a desperate "race for the hills above White Plains" to escape, because so much was at stake and little time remained.[7] Colonel Joseph Reed, who had been born in Trenton, New Jersey, was convinced that it had been General Lee who had been the guiding light in ensuring that the Continental Army would not be destroyed on Manhattan Island and not Washington.[8]

North of New Rochelle, which was located about halfway between Throgs Neck and White Plains and situated about in the narrow peninsula's center between the Hudson to the west and Long Island Sound to the east, the army's safety was now offered by the high ground of White Plains, which had suddenly become strategically important. The longtime county seat of Westchester County, the town stood at the junction of the main land route—the Boston Post Road—linking New York to New England and the road leading north to Albany up the Hudson River.[9]

Therefore, the long retreat north along the Albany Post Road, which paralleled the Hudson, by the vast majority of Washington's army from Harlem Heights to White Plains was destined to begin the following day after the conference with the first contingent of troops heading north on October 17, while leaving behind more than one thousand soldiers to defend Fort Washington—a great mistake—on the Hudson in the northwest corner of Manhattan Island. Washington's decision called for a lengthy withdrawal north across the Harlem River at Kingsbridge and then north up the west bank of the Bronx River along the Albany Post Road to present a most formidable challenge. Indeed, the life of General Washington's army now hinged upon a simple strategic reality that could not be denied if Howe's army landed farther north: the all-important race north because the infant republic's and revolution's existence now depended upon which side won the high-stakes race to White Plains.

If General Howe's troops reached White Plains first after land-ing at some point north of Throgs Neck or if they struck the with-drawing revolutionaries on the right flank, then General Washington and the Continental Army could be easily destroyed by thousands of well-trained British and Hessian professional fighting men. Therefore, without a tactical option remaining if such a disadvantageous sce-nario developed as feared, then Washington would be forced to hurl his men head-on into Howe's legions in an attempt to break through or would have to surrender or face annihilation, if the enemy landed farther north and then pushed inland, or west, to strike Washington's withdrawing army on the right flank. Therefore, a lengthy "race for the hills above White Plains," with everything depending on who won this next phase of the chess game.[10] In one soldier's words about the beginning of the retreat north from a letter: "On the 17th, [the army] had orders to march to Mile Sqr [Miles Square, Yonkers], which we reached the next day [north] towards the White plains."[11]

Washington's Severe Crisis in Command

The successive defeats and withdrawals had badly dispirited large num-bers of Americans, both soldiers and civilians, who had lost faith in the revolution and its lofty promises of easy victories over evil invad-ers. To Congress, Washington lamented the rise of desertions that had been fueled by the seemingly endless setbacks, especially among the militia, writing how these disheartened men, who were fair-weather patriots, departed the army "almost by whole Regiments, by half ones and by Companies at a time."[12]

At this time, however, Washington's army of around thirteen thou-sand men was ready for anything but a long-distance race north across the New York mainland to escape to White Plains. Thousands of sol-diers were diseased, foot-sore, and weary of the war that appeared to be a losing one. Large numbers of wounded men had to be loaded up and transported in slow-moving wagons and carts, including rickety vehicles pulled by lumbering oxen, during the push along the dusty

Albany Post Road to White Plains, ensuring that columns were strewn out for miles. And even Washington's healthy soldiers, dispirited by so many losses and fiascos, also straggled. All in all, this deplorable situation presented a golden opportunity for Howe to strike a killing blow upon Washington's army, if he gained a permanent toehold on the New York mainland after making a successful amphibious landing farther north. To make things even worse if that was at all possible, rations were nonexistent with the breakdown of logistics, morale, and lines of communications. Clearly, Washington's common soldiers were in especially bad shape, including men who were starving while the finely-uniformed officers of a higher class ate relatively well to erode the revolutionary sense of brotherhood. Therefore, the discouraged common soldiers in the ranks became both "tired and faint" from the twin curses of hunger and exhaustion, while "keeping up the old system of starving," wrote young Private Joseph Plumb Martin, during the gloomy withdrawal north toward White Plains.

Complicating matters was the fact that discipline was virtually nonexistent in Washington's army by this time, which had steadily plummeted with each new defeat and urgent retreat. Regardless of age or rank and as if back on the farm or at a rowdy New England town meeting, many soldiers now did exactly as they pleased, including not listening to their commanding officers and abandoning assigned camp baggage and gear during the dreary retreat along the road leading to the safety of White Plains. Veteran officers realized that such a lengthy withdrawal of around a dozen miles was a certain guarantee that even more of the shrinking army's precious manpower would continue to dissolve into thin air like the dimming spirit of patriotism. Soldiers with enlistments up at war's end simply walked off from the stretched-out columns of ill-clad men choking in clouds of swirling dust, heading through the brownish fields of early autumn and making for home. After all, early fall was the traditional harvest time and much work had to be completed on the farm in preparation for winter, especially after wasting the summer away in a futile campaign to keep the British out of New York City. Left on their own for far too long, soldiers' families far away from Manhattan Island had to be prepared to survive the upcoming winter, which was especially harsh in New England.

Even worse, the progress of Washington's army, encumbered with too much surplus baggage and equipment and lacking adequate transportation to haul everything to White Plains, slowed dramatically during a disastrous withdrawal. Wagons and carts were in short supply, ensuring additional problems and delays that seemed to have no end. Cursing all the way, angry teamsters unloaded wagons on the side of the road to lighten their heavy loads to hasten their flight rearward to the relative safety of White Plains. Not enough horses and oxen were available to move supplies and artillery pieces greatly slowed down progress. Some determined artillerymen were forced to move heavy guns up the road leading north by hand, with cannoneers sweating and pulling under a scorching sun and in heat that seemed more like July than mid-October.

Therefore, Washington's badly conducted and lengthy withdrawal north more resembled a retreat after a battlefield defeat rather than a traditional retrograde movement. By any measure, this "new retreat was a nightmare [and] The American Army was a long, exposed line of 13,000 weary, dispirited men [and therefore] Washington's army crawled painfully" north toward the salvation offered by the high ground of White Plains.[13]

The combination of the terrible shape of Washington's army and the withdrawal's length of around a dozen miles seemed to herald future disaster, especially if struck by the British Army in the midst of withdrawal if Howe landed north of Throgs Neck and then gained Washington's rear, which might well mean the ending of Washington's army and America's sagging resistance effort, which had now become less popular than in the hopeful springtime when a great victory had seemed inevitably on the horizon.

If the American Army could not stand up to the British Army in an open-field fight, as had been repeatedly demonstrated throughout this ill-fated campaign for New York, then certainly it would have no chance of survival if struck by Howe in the midst of such a chaotic withdrawal. Quite simply, Washington's army would be easily cut to pieces like the overall hopes for America in winning this war. Therefore, in many ways, the long withdrawal to White Plains was potentially more dangerous for Washington's army than even a traditional showdown on a conventional battlefield, because it was now more vulnerable than ever before during the struggle of pushing north.

While General Washington's troops slogged through the swirling clouds of dust toward White Plains, General Howe concluded that the decision to attempt to land at Throgs Point and to launch an invasion inland from that point had been a strategic error of the first magnitude. In regard to the Throgs Point strategy, the first mistake had been to believe that Throgs Neck was part of a solid peninsula. Instead of gaining the solid ground of a peninsula leading inland to reach higher and solid ground, it was only an island at high tide, separated from the mainland by tidal waters of Westchester Creek and a broad expanse of wetlands covered in tall grass of expansive salt marshes. Therefore, even without Colonel Hand's band of hardy Pennsylvania defenders, the Throgs Neck Peninsula was simply not the proper avenue by which a British Army could march inland to outflank General Washington's army, cut off his links to New England, and gain the army's rear to inflict a decisive blow.[14]

General Howe, therefore, now hoped to compensate for his grievous mistake. Therefore, he looked longingly north for a better site for an amphibious landing with the same wise tactical plan of securing a position above, or north, Washington to gain his rear and cut off the Continental Army. This more suitable landing site was located only around five miles north of Throgs Point at Pelham Point, which was just east of the Hutchinson River and at the southern tip of a peninsula in the lower, or southern, part of Long Island Sound. Unlike low-lying Throgs Neck Peninsula, dominated by marshy ground, wetlands, and high tides, the approximately three-mile-long peninsula, stretching in a north-south direction parallel to Long Island Sound to the east, of Pell's Point was "a true peninsula" that consisted of solid ground that rose ever higher. But best of all for British fortunes, there were no large number of American defenders, only a handful of New York militiamen, situated along the shore of the northern end of Pelham Bay.[15]

Most important, a good, well-worn road, the Boston Post Road—the old mail route from New York City to New England—was located on the mainland above, or north, of the Pell's Point Peninsula. The Boston Post Road led through northwest to the town of Eastchester, located just southwest of New Rochelle on Long Island Sound and farther inland than New Rochelle. Meanwhile, the withdrawal route of General Washington's army was along the Albany Post Road that ran close to and parallel to the Hudson and "within easy striking distance" of the vital Boston Post Road that led from Kingsbridge north to Connecticut and the rest of New England. The Eastchester Road led west from Eastchester to the Albany Post Road and Washington's retreating army, which continued to head north for the safety of the high ground of White Plains. By targeting the Albany Post Road along the Hudson's east bank by way of the Eastchester Road that ran west to Washington's route of retreat, the wily General Howe was "aiming to get in the rear of the Americans."[16]

Compared to the far more plentiful advantages of the Pell's Point landing site, the Throgs Neck Peninsula had been located too far south of this strategic road (the Boston Post Road) upon which the fate of Washington's army was now based. The Boston Post Road ran west to east where it crossed the Hutchinson River (originally known as Eastchester or Hutchinson Creek) at the little Eastchester bridge situated just north of Pelham Bay. Even more, the Pell's Point Peninsula was situated far closer to the Boston Post Road than the more remote Throgs Neck Peninsula.

Fortunately for the patriot cause, some British deserters on October 15 informed the Americans of Howe's ambitious plan to land at Pell's Point in his next attempt to reap the success that he had fondly envisioned in landing at Throgs Point by a stealthy ambitious landing to the north. These talkative men were five British sailors from Rear Admiral Howe's fleet who had deserted from the harsh discipline aboard the HMS *Brune*. As Major General William Heath recorded this intelligence coup of the first magnitude: "They informed, that there was a large body of British on Frog's Point, and that an attack might soon be expected" farther north.[17]

On October 16 and before the decision to withdraw to White Plains had been made during the general officer's conference on the same day, General Washington, some of his top lieutenants, and the finely uniformed members of his trusty staff had made a hasty, but most timely, reconnaissance of the Pell's Point Peninsula. Here, they had surveyed the ground from a high point, including the eastern edge of Pelham Heights on the north end of the Pell's Point Peninsula, that overlooked a wide area to the east, including the Long Island Sound. As Major General Heath, a thirty-nine-year-old farmer from Roxbury, Massachusetts, who had rushed to the assistance of his fellow Bay State Minutemen at Lexington on April 19, 1775, wrote how on October 16:

> The General Officers of the army rode to reconnoitre [sic] the ground at Pell's Neck &c. and it was determined that the position of the American army should be immediately changed; the left flank [or the right flank during the northward withdrawal as opposed to a defensive stance facing south] to be extended more northerly, to prevent its being turned by the British.[18]

Indeed, General Washington and others, including General Charles Lee, second-in-command of the army, "who had been watching their motions," was highly impressed by the fact that some possibilities for a defensive fight existed in the area just north of Throgs Neck because this pristine section of Westchester County and the surrounding area consisted of an agricultural and rural "district of stone fences that would confine [British] artillery and large bodies of infantry to the main roads."[19]

With the unforgettable lessons of Bunker Hill in mind, Washington had been impressed by the defensive possibilities that he saw in this picturesque rural countryside crisscrossed with seemingly countless stone fences that covered the early autumn landscape. Along with cutting down trees and uprooting stumps, generations of Dutch farmers of Westchester County had cleared the fertile countryside of rocks, which had been left behind from the retreat of the glaciers millions of years ago, to grow more crops. Carefully constructed from the immense supply of glacial rocks which had been placed by farmers on the roadsides, these high stone fences covered the landscape and seemed to have no end, while also designating not only landownership but also to divide different crops, grazing sheep and cattle, and grassy pastures. Almost certainly, Irish immigrants, including stonemasons, had also worked in this construction because such stone fences are pervasive in Ireland to this day like in past centuries.

Most of all and to his credit, General Washington knew that this unique feature of this land—interlaced networks of stone fences—might well spell the difference between victory and defeat, if properly used by even a relatively small band of defenders of Westchester County soil. After all, these stone fences were ready-made defenses that did not call for eroding the morale of the American fighting men by ordering them in the laborious construction of earthworks. Largely untrained and inexperienced militiamen most often needed an extra measure of confidence in facing the world's finest troops from both Britain and Germany. Washington said, "Place them behind a parapet, a breast-work, stone wall, or any thing that will afford them shelter, and . . . they will give a good account of their enemy."[20]

And before the bloody Battle of Bunker Hill where he became a hero known for having ordered his Bay State men not to fire until you see "the whites of their eyes," crusty General Israel "Old Put" Putnam, a former Connecticut Ranger during the French and Indian War who was now one of Washington's top lieutenants, had humorously emphasized in regard to his inexperienced Massachusetts troops:

"Americans are much afraid of their legs [but] Cover them and they will fight forever."[21]

As noted, Wednesday, October 16, had been one of the most important days in the history of the infant Continental Army, because of the key decision made by leadership during Washington's council of war that Harlem Heights should be immediately evacuated "with the greatest Expedition," despite its considerable natural strength. As revealed in an officer's letter about the new strategic plan, Washington's troops had been ordered to "march [north toward White Plains] into the country, to prevent the enemy [under General Howe] from ravaging the coast and surrounding us, and, by our movements, to lead them into the country."[22]

Knowing that Pell's Point had to be defended to protect his vulnerable rear because it was too tempting of a landing site to Howe because of the wide, placid waters of Pelham Bay that allowed easy access for scores of warships and troop transports, General Washington had sent General Charles Lee, who had been "watching their motions" and now commanded the division (Lee had taken over Major General William Heath's Division upon his arrival from Charles Town in mid-October) of which Colonel John Glover's Massachusetts brigade was a part, new orders. At this time, Lee's Division was positioned north of the Harlem River and Kingsbridge at Valentine's Hill almost directly west of Eastchester and just northeast of Kingsbridge and near the Bronx River. Lee was directed by Washington to dispatch a full brigade to the Pell's Point Peninsula located about three miles north of Throgs Neck Peninsula. At this time, Lee commanded the army's right wing during the long withdrawal to White Plains. To his credit and knowing the extent of the threat and remembering their vital role during the Long Island evacuation, Washington naturally chose his best men for the mission, Colonel Glover and his Massachusetts Brigade—one of Washington's finest leadership decisions of the New York Campaign. In addition, General Lee also deserved credit because he had also early seen the need to position Glover's brigade just southeast of Eastchester—northwest of the Pell's Point Peninsula—to guard against a British landing from the nearby Long Island Sound. Therefore, Glover and his seasoned mariners, who had been ordered to join the main army at Kingsbridge when Howe had landed at Throgs Neck and then to reinforce Colonel Hand's position, were dispatched eastward on October 16 across the peninsula to guard the road leading from Pelham Bay and take a position just southeast of Eastchester before Pelham Bay, while unwittingly setting the stage for the Battle of Pell's Point.

Most significant for this crucial assignment, General Washington specified exactly what troops he thought could handle a most formidable challenge of holding the army's easternmost flank, under General Lee's command, as trusty guardians on the east and around three miles farther north of Throgs Neck, which included guarding the Boston Post Road at Pell's Point.

He also chose the promising New England officer because he was exactly the kind of resourceful and imaginative can-do officer who could handle such an important assignment, Colonel John Glover. This seasoned infantry brigade of Bay State soldiers included the premier unit, Glover's old Fourteenth Massachusetts Continental Regiment of mostly Marbleheaders. By this time, not only General Washington but also the rest of the Continental Army retained complete confidence in Colonel Glover and the Fourteenth Massachusetts Continental Regiment for what they had already accomplished throughout the New York Campaign. All in all, General Washington could not have made a better decision in regard to handing the crucial mission of defending the Pell's Point Peninsula to Glover.[23]

However, ironically, this timely decision to rely on the Massachusetts men might not have been embraced by this aloof gentleman farmer from Mount Vernon only a short time before, after he had first taken command of the New England at Cambridge, situated just outside Boston, in June 1775. General Washington had gradually overcome his own considerable prejudices of the Virginia Tidewater planter class elite, which was dominated by Southern values and cultural proclivities, against New Englanders by the steadfast performance of Glover and his men, especially during the August 29–30 withdrawal across the East River to Manhattan Island from Long Island and elsewhere. At this time when the revolutionary resistance effort had reached a new low point, one of Washington's greatest concerns was the lack of quality officers, who were dependable and trustworthy in crisis situations. As if in recognizing his own limited tactical abilities, General Washington most of all needed talented and tactically astute commanders who he could rely upon with the most important assignments like Colonel Hand had recently demonstrated at Throgs Neck.

In regard to General Lee, who was second-in-command of the reeling Continental Army, General Washington doubted "the stability [and] perhaps the dependability" of his England-born top lieutenant, because of his erratic personality. For instance, in a letter to his brother, Washington wrote how the eccentric, but talented, Englishman of an especially prickly nature was "rather fickle and violent I fear in his temper."[24] However, the general's eccentricities and the fact that he was known as "Mad Lee" did not matter to an admiring Washington because Lee's military expertise had repeatedly shined. In regard to the retreat from Harlem Heights to White Plains and as mentioned, Lee had been early adamant in the council room with Washington and the other generals. In the words from a letter that explained the crucial decision to withdraw north to White Plains to escape entrapment at nearly the last moment:

> The great Movements of the Enemy up the South, their Land[ing] in large bodies at Frogs [Neck,] & the Intelligence which the Generals obtained that the Enemy with their whole force were off against E[ast]. Chester & N[ew] Rochel[le], & that both L & Gen. Lowe were there in person, gave the Generals full satisfaction, that gen. Hows [sic] plan was to make a bold stroke & hem in & cut off our Army at once. Gen. Lee I have understood tho't that the Situation of the army of the States of America was much too confined & crampt, & that

it could not be good Policy to lie still in such a Situation, or to hazard the great Cause in which we were embarked in one General Action, in which if we should not succede [sic], the Army might be lost, as a Retreat would be extremely difficult if not impossible. It was determined by the Generals therefore to counteract the Enemy by a general Movement.[25]

But in the end, Washington could not trust the intriguing and conniving Lee, who sincerely believed that he should replace Washington as the army's commander in the future and acted accordingly, including in a devious manner. Even the trusty officers among Washington's personal staff, or "family," proved untrustworthy as Washington learned to his shock, such as his own staff officer Colonel Joseph Reed, or disappointingly incompetent, such as Ireland-born Quartermaster General Stephen Moylan.[26] Worse of all and like General Lee, Colonel Reed evolved into one of the influential officers who became "extremely dangerous enemies" to General Washington. Like an ever-increasing number of other Continental officers, Reed considered the Virginia Tidewater planter and former militia officer too incompetent to command the Continental Army and in time sought his removal from command.[27]

In fact, as demonstrated during the twin disasters at Long Island and Kip's Bay, Washington could not even trust his own men. In a letter to Congress, he admitted his "want of confidence, in the generality of the Troops," who were the only ones who now could possibly save America when they could not even save themselves.[28] In a letter to his mother, Tabitha, in Marblehead, a disgusted Colonel Glover had even harsher words for the men who had failed miserably to rise to the challenge during this all-important campaign when everything was at stake for America:

In Short if Some example is not made of such Raskely Conduct, there will be no incouragement for men of Spirit to Exert themselves. As in Case now is they will all ways fall a

Sacrifice wile Such Low Lives Scoundrils that have Neither Honour nor the Good of their Country at heart, will Sculk behind and Get off Clear.[29]

The lack of faith in Washington was well-founded, as the New York Campaign fully demonstrated. After all,

Washington's [prior military] service had been confined to frontier warfare [and Virginia militia service], in a relatively junior capacity. He had no firsthand acquaintance with cavalry tactics or the use of massed artillery, not to mention the handling of a large composite force [so therefore] He could not afford to trust his own judgment while so much remained a closed book to him.[30]

As Washington had penned in a letter during the French and Indian War and which was no exaggeration and applied to the New York Campaign that revealed why he was so shocked by personal betrayals, because he was not a conniving political player who maneuvered behind the scenes like so many other leaders who would do almost anything to get ahead at the expense of others, Washington had confessed with honesty with a genuine frankness: "My nature is open and honest and free from guile!"[31]

A growing number of politicians were already aware of Washington's severe limitations from inexperience, especially in tactical terms. Ever-mindful of Washington's limitations, Marylander William Duer, a member of the Convention's Committee of Correspondence, had recently penned with diplomatic delicacy and considerable understatement to Tench Tilghman, who served on Washington's staff, on October 2 before Howe's next move north that he fully expected:

I wish they would delay this [inevitable northward offensive by Howe] attempt till Genl. Lee arrives [from Charlestown], or till [Philadelphia-born General Thomas] Mifflin comes from

Philad. I am sensible that however great General Washington's abilities and vigilance are, he must stand in need of the assistance of such excellent officers [and] If [General Nathanael Greene] could be spared [then] his presence, I think, would be of great consequence . . . what, with the situation of our enemies in your quarter and the cursed machinations of our Internal Foes, the fate of this State hangs on a single battle of importance.[32]

With great relief, Washington knew that he could always trust Colonel Glover, which had been proven in full during the risky evacuation from Long Island and throughout the New York Campaign and elsewhere. Therefore, and unlike others in General Washington's army who failed the commander in chief, Glover was not only dependable and competent, but also blessed with the tactical ability and natural aggressiveness that made him an ideal choice for an independent command on an all-important mission of holding and guarding the army's far eastern flank near the Long Island Sound, when Howe had outflanking and trapping Washington's army on his tactically agile mind. In the words of historian Barnet Schecter, by the fall of 1776, the Marblehead colonel "had won him Washington's gratitude and confidence, and [consequently] Glover was charged with protecting the retreating army by delaying the British should they land at Pelham" Bay.[33]

Thanks to his distinguished efforts earlier this summer during the struggle for New York, especially the narrow escape from Long Island during a foggy late August night, the ever-versatile Colonel Glover had won General Washington's complete confidence, which had been well-placed by the Virginian who had learned to admire and respect New Englanders by this time. Hiding a burning ambition, Colonel Glover's subdued manner, short and stocky stature, and the almost dandified appearance of a proper New England gentleman hid a host of rare qualities—tenacity, fierce determination, and never-say-die—that were most admired by Washington at a time, when his amateur army needed capable leadership more than ever before. Glover was a rather plain-looking redhead of a mature age. He was distinguished by a high forehead and a jutting jaw that befitted his sense of determination to excel against the odds. Before the war, he had possessed a distinctive penchant for dressing in elegant fashion because he was a respected member of the "codfish aristocracy" of Marblehead, while Washington represented the Virginia Tidewater aristocracy: factors that served as a common bond among these two proper upper-class gentlemen from two vastly different worlds, whose homes were separated by around 475 miles.

One of Glover's few weaknesses was his fastidiousness and obsession with maintaining a resplendent military appearance at all times, which included wearing fine Dutch shirts and a fancy blue uniform that displayed his colonel's rank for all to see. But despite his gentlemanly appearance as a member of Marblehead's elite, he was a hardnosed fighter and scrapper, who had never lost the common touch because of his humble background. Feisty and tough, Glover possessed a rugged nature and disposition that was closer to a common seaman than a refined gentlemen of Marblehead's upper-class elite. He had been born on November 5, 1732, in Salem, Massachusetts, where he was baptized on November 26, as the son of Jonathan Glover and Tabita Bacon-Glover. The men of the Fourteenth Massachusetts never saw Glover as a member of the aristocracy, but more like a common soldier in the ranks who always shared the same hardships and dangers with them.

Belying his proper demeanor, Glover was a self-made man, even more so than Washington who had inherited great wealth, including large numbers of enslaved persons, from his family and his extremely fortunate marriage to a rich widow, Martha Curtis. The taciturn colonel from Marblehead began life as a humble cobbler, before his rise to upper-class status. Glover's wealth, as verified by his large house on the stony ridge overlooking Marblehead Harbor, was not inherited, but earned by years of hard work, determination, and business savvy. For such reasons, the talented colonel never lost his commonness, which was a quality that endeared him to his Massachusetts men. He was just the type of commander who Washington knew was ideal for any desperate undertaking, when hard fighting and tactical flexibility would be required, especially if Howe landed his army at Pell's Point. Blessed with a rare blend of intelligence, resourcefulness, and good common sense that was most needed for a highly effective officer or a captain on his own ship on the open seas, Glover could be depended upon completely in a crisis situation, including when the life of the Continental Army and America were at stake, which would be the case on October 18, 1776. A quiet Congregationalist and devoted family man without known vices, Glover seemed to be the antithesis of a diehard fighting man imbued with revolutionary zeal at first glance, but he came alive on the battlefield to become a dynamic commander when the challenge was greatest.

For all of these reasons, Washington could not have made a better choice than Glover for such a crucial assignment of holding the far eastern flank during the army's confused withdrawal, if General Howe's army attempted an amphibious landing in Westchester County north of Throgs Neck, which was only a matter of time because of his penchant for maneuvering north in attempting to trap the Continental Army like a rabbit in a snare. Glover's small size and placid appearance belied his fighting spirit and feistiness, but looks were most deceiving in this regard. During active campaigning, he had proved to be especially innovative, resourceful, and energetic, with the uncanny ability to rise to any challenge of a seemingly impossible nature in a no-win situation. Perhaps no colonel in all the Continental Army was more pugnacious and tough-minded than John Glover, and Washington realized as much after having witnessed the miracle of the escape from Long Island and other good service.

Since Washington had taken command of the Continental Army around New York in April, he had been saddled with a good many subordinates who were either incompetent, inexperienced, or both. He wrote to Glover in an April 1777 glowing letter of praise that was rarely forthcoming to anyone from the austere commander in chief, especially after what the colonel had accomplished at Pell's Point: "I think I may tell you without flattery, that I know of no man better qualified than you to conduct a Brigade."[34] This astute conclusion by General Washington, much to his credit, was no exaggeration and right on target, when it came to one of his top lieutenants.

What was most infuriating about the Kip's Bay rout of the Connecticut militia to Washington was the fact that it had been led by officers. The enraged commander in chief had targeted these panicked officers with blows from his wooden cane, but to no avail as they simply ran past him as if in a wild footrace to the rear. Teenage Private Joseph Plump Martin, who was one of the Connecticut boys in the panicked ranks, summarized the deplorable situation that revealed the widespread lack of capable officers in the New England militia:

> Every man that I saw was endeavoring by all sober means to escape from death or captivity, which at that period of the war was almost certain death. The men were confused, being without officers to command them. I do not recollect of seeing a commissioned officer from the time I left the lines on the [west] banks of the East River in the morning until I met with the *gentlemanly one* in the evening. How could the men fight without officers.[35]

From the beginning, Colonel Glover was the antithesis of these kind of fainthearted officers, who talked bravely but achieved little on the battlefield. Of English descent and with seafaring in his blood, Glover was one of a kind. After he was born in the fishing port of Salem, Massachusetts, the family had shortly moved around four miles to the southeast, settling down in the magnificent port of Marblehead. With the town nestled along the high ground on the west side of Marblehead Harbor, Glover's plain two-story Georgian gambrel house, built in 1762, overlooked the sizeable harbor—a natural refuge for New England's largest fishing fleet from the Atlantic's storms when the fishing season was over—and the seemingly endless expanse of the Atlantic that dominated the eastern horizon as far as the eye could see. Rather than from a desire to display his wealth, Glover's family needed a large house because he and his first wife, Hannah, had a good many children who they dearly loved.

Most important, Glover had gained considerable military experience before the start of the American Revolution, providing him with an invaluable edge in regard to the overall low quality in Washington's officer corps that was found seriously lacking during the disastrous New York Campaign. He had been appointed an ensign of the Third Military Foot Company—the Marblehead militia unit—in 1759, when the French and Indian War ended. In 1762, Glover had been then appointed to the rank of captain lieutenant of the Marblehead militia by the Massachusetts governor in Boston. In appreciation for his fast-growing reputation, a captain's rank was forthcoming to Glover from Governor Thomas Hutchinson in 1773 on the American Revolution's eve. During these years before war with England, Glover learned how to handle men under arms and the intricacies of military ways, which he put to good use in 1776, especially during the dramatic showdown at Pell's Point. Without hesitation, the good citizens of Marblehead had elected him to command the "Marine Regiment" of mostly Marblehead soldiers by the time they marched off to war to join General Washington's army at Cambridge, Massachusetts, during the summer of 1775.[36]

Using leadership skills learned at sea when he had been the enterprising captain of his own sailing ship, Glover was a hard-nosed disciplinarian who had first trained his men on the meadow-like grass of the Marblehead Commons on Windmill Hill overlooking the picturesque harbor. Here, he had begun the process of molding the Fourteenth Massachusetts Continental Regiment into an elite command by way of his own abundant abilities and distinctive leadership style, which had been forged for years at sea and on land during the prewar years. Glover's deep-seated discipline and duty-mindedness stemmed from years of having faced the many difficult challenges on both land and sea. His mostly Marblehead men had early understood the supreme importance of discipline on sailing ships when journeying to the Grand Banks and this distinctive quality paid immense dividends to Washington and his army, especially during 1776, including at the Battle of Pell's Point. To the colonel and his Massachusetts men who still carried the essence of the sea with them during the New York Campaign, this struggle against the Mother Country and its German allies was a righteous cause and a moral crusade with powerful religious overtones.

Deeply motivated by what he had long read in the pages of the Old Testament, Glover was very much a religious warrior engaged in a holy war in 1776. When no regimental or brigade chaplain was available for his command, Glover then presided over the religious affairs of his unit that was more like a close-knit community—a mini-Marblehead—in the seafaring tradition and more so than in other Continental regiments. As the fatherly Moses who was revered by the men of his Massachusetts regiment, he presented rousing sermons to his troops to fortify their resolve and faith during the struggle to protect their people and distinctive way of life, which had been known for seemingly countless generations in their home port on the rugged coastline just north of Boston.[37]

Colonel Glover's moods occasionally swung from a belief in inevitable victory to doubts about chances for American success in this war, depending on the time and situation, especially during the disastrous New York Campaign. However, he never once wavered from his faith in the righteousness of the struggle, despite doubting that he would survive the war in the fatalistic Congregationalist tradition. On October 18, therefore, he would battle against the British and Hessians with a righteous zeal and like the ancient Hebrew warrior Joshua against the barbarian tribes, whose "unclean" people worshipped many Gods in the ancient land of Canaan.

Indeed, Glover's most dominant characteristic was the burning desire to accomplish all that he could possibly do to win a new nation's independence at any cost or sacrifice. For Colonel Glover, this patriotic determination, which was almost spiritual and bordered on the fanatical, was based on a zealous faith that burned deep within his heart and mind because of his belief in the sacredness of the cause of liberty. Glover's total commitment to the struggle was revealed in one of his letters: "We must and shall all share the same fate, either free-men or slaves [and a total effort] was absolutely necessary to defend and secure the liberties of America [and] Every man who has the good of his country and posterity at heart ought to put his shoulders to the burthen, and bear part of the weight."[38]

Ironically, the aristocratic General Howe, who was bestowed with the title of Sir, which had been long used to designate a knight since the 1200s in England, for his one-sided victory at Long Island, thought much like Colonel Glover in this regard. Like one of his top lieutenants, Lord Charles Cornwallis, he was proud to now have been given the opportunity to fight for King George III and to be in "ser-vice my country in distress [and] Every man's private feelings ought to give way to the service of the public at all times, but particularly when of that delicate nature in which our affairs stand at present."[39]

As was about to be demonstrated on the forgotten field of Pell's Point, Colonel Glover was possessed with a deep-seated sense of republicanism that would never die, while battling for a people's republic against the strongest monarchy in the world. As he penned in a heartfelt letter about what was needed for America to prevail in this war: "Every man who has the good of his Country and posterity at heart ought to put his shoulders to the Burthen, and bear part of the weight; he that does not ought to be discarded and not suffered to breathe American Air."[40]

Glover was anything but the stereotypical aristocratic New Englander who has been long viewed as narrow-minded, opinionated, and full of regional prejudices—unfortunately, a popular myth about perhaps the most naturally gifted and talented New Englander in the Continental Army. Colonel Glover's popular image has been unfairly portrayed in books and films, resulting in negative perceptions about him that have persisted to this day. For instance, in the popular Arts and Entertainment 2000 production of *The Crossing*, which was based on the novel by Howard Fast, the author was guilty of presenting the old negative personal stereotypes about Glover. These long-accepted views were extremely misleading, while he, like almost all authors, presented General Washington as a flawless leader and almost saintly figure in the nationalistic tradition, which was certainly not the case: actually, the opposite was closer to the truth.

Contrary to the pervasive myths and stereotypes, Glover was a man of passion and warmth, possessing a sense of humor and distinctive dialect that was more sea-based than that of other colonels in Washington's army. He liked to have a good time with friends when the occasion allowed and loved his family back in Marblehead. Like other members of his elevated class in Marblehead, Glover enjoyed fine wine such as Madeira, bountiful foods caught fresh from the sea, and fellowship with his men of all ranks, while leading from the front to provide an inspirational example. He shared hardships with his men like a common soldier and as if still the captain of his own sailing ship on the Atlantic. As early as 1769, Glover and leading members of Marblehead's elite had met every Tuesday evening to discuss world events, especially in regard to the colonies' increasingly fractured relationship with Great Britain. These were the gatherings of the Tuesday Evening Club whose meetings were held on the second floor of the fine home, built in 1724, of Joshua Prentiss. Here, fine wines, "good punch," and high-quality tobacco were enjoyed by the social club's enthusiastic members. Even more, Glover had evolved into a savvy businessman who gained considerable wealth and comfort for his family. After first having first worked as a lowly shoemaker in his teenage years to learn about existence at the bottom of society, Glover had then advanced in life by opening up his own tavern in Marblehead and then captained his own ships. He had gained his own commercial fleet by the time of the American Revolution.

A true Renaissance man with a zest for life, Colonel Glover's aggressive leadership style and penchant for discipline hid the sunny side of his personality, including the deepest of personal affections for those who he loved at home. As he confessed in a letter to General Washington at a time when few men admitted his personal and private proclivities in written words, Glover described himself as "one who is very particularly attached to his children; this may be called a weakness in me; however it's such a weakness as I at all times take pride in showing."[41]

The Marblehead colonel described his army life as that of a "Military Monk" on one occasion, because he was naturally a stoic and self-sacrificing man without the kind of ego that led to unnecessary personal clashes with fellow officers or made rash decisions in an attempt to win glory on the battlefield with the lives of his men: all qualities that helped to make to make him an ideal republican officer. He had risen through the ranks on his own abilities and talents rather than backdoor political maneuvering like so many of his fellow officers. Revealing his lighter side when serving his country, Glover was not out of character when he lamented the lack of fine liquors, especially fine dark wines from Portugal and Madeira, in a letter: "It's an exceeding dry time with us, not a single Glass of Wine to be had here [and] Judge you how long one poor Cask [of wine] will Last, among so many [high-ranking general and senior officers who] can drink a Glass when it comes in their Way."[42]

By the morning of October 18, which was a Friday in a beautiful fall that was refreshing after the intense heat of a scorching summer, the seasoned Massachusetts soldiers of Colonel Glover's Brigade, which naturally included his mostly Marblehead regiment, had much to prove, while serving as guardians on Washington's eastern flank during the army's miserable withdrawal to White Plains just to the west, because a dark stain had been placed on New England soldiers. The recent dismal performance of New England troops at Kip's Bay, where the Connecticut militiamen had run for their lives, had cruelly mocked the leading role played by the New Englanders in having sparked the revolution in 1775. Delaware's Caesar Rodney, a signer of the Declaration of Independence, admitted in a letter to his brother Thomas: "That the New England men placed to defend the land-place [at Kip's Bay], behaved in the most dastardly, cowardly, scandalous, manner is most certain."[43]

In consequence, the Maryland, Delaware, and Pennsylvania troops held the New Englanders, who were generally less disciplined than the better-uniformed men from Maryland and Delaware who were considered crack "southern" troops, in absolute contempt. Ireland-born Colonel John Haslet, who commanded the Delaware regiment which was one of Washington's best combat units, wrote, "Some officers have poured much contempt upon the Eastern Troops & great Animosity subsists just now among them."[44]

Of course, one fundamental reason for this drop-off in reliability and fighting prowess of the northeastern troops in general by this time was due to the fact that the New England men were no longer defending their home region: ironically in a contradiction of sorts in this regard, a situation that certainly failed to apply to Glover's men, who seldom deserted, largely because of the Marblehead colonel's inspirational brand of leadership and the fact that they mostly hailed from a single seafaring community. For most New Englanders in the Continental Army, because of their provincial natures before the rise of a greater sense of American nationalism, battling the British and Hessians to save Long Island, New York City, and Manhattan Island was simply not the same as defending Boston or hometowns in New England. In contrast and because they fought closer to home, the Continental troops from the Middle Colonies, such as Pennsylvania, Delaware, and Maryland, had become the best and most dependable combat troops in General Washington's army by this time and as repeatedly demonstrated throughout the New York Campaign.

This overall situation caused considerable distrust between Washington's troops from New England and those soldiers from the Middle Colonies, which reached new highs at this time with old regional rivalries rising to the fore. The existing regional prejudices of soldiers from the Middle Colonies only grew into a deeper contempt for the New Englanders after the Kip's Bay fiasco. Under the circumstances, this fractionalizing based on different regions was a natural development in a fledgling national army in which allegiance to home regions was often stronger than those to the young nation, which was nothing more than a new creation of barely a year's duration by this time. Fueled as much by old regional animosities, jealousies, and prejudices as recent battlefield performances, such open disdain and even hostility among Washington's troops toward soldiers from different regions—not only north and south but also east and west—grew to such an extent that a mutual hatred developed to the point where "the northern and southern troops would as soon fight each other as the British."[45]

Colonel Glover's Forgotten Black Fighting Men of the Bay State

One of the major forgotten differences, besides cultural, regional, and demographic factors of different regions that created a fragile national army and even more delicate sense of American nationalism, that existed between Washington's New Englanders and the troops from the Middle Colonies and the South was the factor of race. This fact has been long overlooked by traditional historians, especially of the nationalist school, as if there was not a Black presence in the Continental Army and as if they had made no contributions in the struggle for liberty. For more than two hundred years, historians and scholars, especially nationalists, have too often mistakenly viewed Washington's army as a homogenous entity, ignoring considerable cultural and ethnic diversity that was the antithesis of the stereotypical white, Anglo-Saxon, Protestant soldiery according to the popular nationalist myth. Indeed, Washington's army, a heterogenous mixture, mirrored the demographics of colonial America.

For instance, in the elite ranks of Glover's command were a number of Black soldiers. From the beginning, Marblehead, Essex County, Massachusetts, was a fishing community with a diverse mixture of people, including Black residents and Native Americans. Compared to life on land, the greater equality found in the seafaring experience had early served as a magnet for free Black men to serve at sea, although slavery still existed in Marblehead and across Massachusetts in 1776. However, slavery in Marblehead consisted almost exclusively of domestic or house servants, both men and women, because the port was not an agrarian community like the vast majority of Massachusetts towns. By 1776, the highest number of Black residents lived in the seafaring communities of Essex County, including Marblehead, in a mostly agrarian Massachusetts with a total Black population of 4,800.

In the ranks of Glover's regiment, these young men of African descent were not servants, cooks, or camp followers as commonly assumed by many Americans, but legitimate fighting men like Emmanuel "Manuel" Soto and Romeo, who was a former seafarer like most regimental members of the Fourteenth Massachusetts. Indeed, they were proud African American soldiers who compiled distinguished records. These Black patriots served with distinction side by side with the white troops of Glover's regiment to share in the unit's most stirring contributions from the evacuation of Long Island to the Battle of Pell's Point and then to the crossing of the Delaware and the Battle of Trenton and well into future years.

Consequently, Glover's Fourteenth Massachusetts Continental Infantry Regiment was an integrated unit ahead of its time, which made this a most distinctive combat command in Washington's army. This stunning reality of an integrated Continental regiment shocked troops from the Middle Colonies and men, especially slaveholders, from the South, where slavery thrived in an agricultural economy to a degree not seen in New England. One aristocratic Pennsylvania officer from the streets of Philadelphia wrote with disgust during the summer of 1776 upon observing the diversity of Glover's regiment, because of the appearance of Black troops in the ranks. In Alexander Graydon's words, which indicated the day's typical aristocratic sensibilities and racial prejudices even when a new sense of equality had risen to the fore during the new republican experiment in nationhood: "But even in this regiment there was a number of negroes, which, to persons unaccustomed to such associations, had a disagreeable, degrading effect."[46]

The fact that African Americans served in Glover's ranks with pride and distinction as equal fighting men was understandable because both free and enslaved Black residents had been long part of the Marblehead community. What has been most generally forgotten today was the fact that New England possessed a history and legacy of slavery almost as old as that of the South.

Quite likely carrying the first enslaved Africans, almost certainly West Africans and perhaps even some Muslims, brought to New England in an American-built vessel, Marblehead captain William Pierce's ship, which had been constructed in Marblehead, was landed in Boston in 1638. At this early date, these "Moors"—as white Europeans commonly called Africans (a legacy stemming from the eight hundred years of warfare that raged between the white Christian Spaniards against the Moors of North Africa for control of the Iberian Peninsula)—were considered necessary, as in the South, to fulfill the manpower requirements of labor-short New England. At Marblehead from the beginning, good men were needed in the fishing industry, and color made no difference on the open seas.[47]

In Marblehead, most African Americans in Glover's ranks had been seafarers, while others had worked as domestic "servants" in the homes of leading Marblehead merchants and shippers, as opposed to enslaved persons in the South. Whereas in the South, these transplanted Africans mostly labored in raising cash staples, as in the sweltering rice fields of coastal South Carolina, as part of a larger plantation system, Black residents of Marblehead early became integrated with the white community because they were in the mainstream of economic activity, becoming fishermen and sailors: a relatively easy and natural assimilation into the fishing community that was mirrored in other New England ports, including nearby Salem, which was the sister fishing community of Marblehead.

Rather than sailing to the Grand Banks to reap a lucrative crop of cod, other Black residents stayed behind in the port town to work at the fish flakes, where cod was dried in the sun before the final product was transported around the world. Ironically, the fishing industry of Massachusetts port towns "relied" in part upon Black labor to feed the tens of thousands of enslaved Africans in the Caribbean. Free Black residents lived in a separate section of Marblehead in the town's rear near the Black burial ground, where the races were separated in death. However, favorite Black servants were often buried with white families in the white cemetery on Burial Hill, which overlooked picturesque Marblehead Harbor. Black sailors had experienced more equality at sea and in the crews aboard ship than on land, where color made more of a difference than when sailing to the rich fishing grounds to the northeast off the coast of Nova Scotia.[48]

This greater equality found by Marblehead's African Americans on the high seas than on land and years of serving on fishing vessels had helped to instill a high degree of discipline—for Black as well as white sailors—that helped to make them disciplined soldiers and excellent fighting men in the ranks of Glover's regiment. Not surprisingly, consequently, a life on the ocean had long beckoned to generations of African Americans across New England, especially in Massachusetts. Therefore, small and culturally vibrant Black communities developed in the major seaports of New England, including in Marblehead.

Far from society's artificial social customs and constraints on land, Black and white seafaring men worked side by side and lived closely together aboard ship, while forging a common bond and camaraderie that was based on life at sea. Members of different races, including Native Americans, who also worked in the fishing industry at Marblehead, came closer together as one and far more than was possible on land. And most important, Black and white fishermen relied upon each other at sea not only for successful catches of cod but also for the ship's survival, erasing artificial color lines out of necessity in facing the dangers posed by one of the most hazardous environments and occupations in America.

Life at sea neatly erased the ugliness of racial prejudice like no other experience because Black and white seamen needed to be united as one and closely depended upon each other: a common experience that revealed a common humanity born of mutual dependence on every other member of the ship's crew. Ironically, however, both Black and white sailors and fishermen developed a strong contempt for their fellow man not based on skin color, but toward the despised "Landsmen," who had never gone to sea to put their manhood and courage to the test.

Significantly reducing toxic racism and prejudice based upon nothing more than skin color because a seaman's abilities and skills were far more important, close interracial working relationships and trust forged on the high seas created an open and honest egalitarian environment far from civilization's artificial restrictions, which translated into a natural development in the minds of Marbleheaders by the time of the American Revolution. Consequently, both Black and white soldiers served side by side in the ranks of Glover's regiment, just like when they had served as crew members on vessels that had long sailed out of Marblehead's harbor and spent long periods of time at sea.

Clearly, the greater equality that existed between Black and white seamen and then soldiers of Glover's command was an amazingly smooth transition. Naturally because the maritime and fishing industries were so thoroughly integrated, so were New England's seacoast communities to a degree not seen farther inland: the central foundation to ensure that Blacks and whites served together in community-like companies just like on fishing vessels. Like his fighting men, Glover was open-minded in regard to race because he hailed from an integrated environment at sea and also Marblehead community and understood racial equality on an intimate level.

For example, Glover had long worshipped in the same church where African Americans prayed during the same religious service on Sundays. Here, Blacks and whites worshipped and prayed together, while giving thanks to God for their blessings. Because of this heightened degree of integration in both Marblehead and on the high seas, Black and white soldiers had rowed the boats together during the rescue of a large portion of Washington's army from Long Island and then fought together at Pell's Point because men of African descent were not only part of the community but also part of the seafaring and maritime experience and equal members of the Fourteenth Massachusetts. Blessed with healthy self-identities nurtured from the seafaring experience and the sharing of common dangers both at sea and then on the battlefield, African Americans of Marblehead served as equal members of Glover's regiment, fighting and dying just like white soldiers in battling for their country's liberty. They had been free Black seamen before they served as free Black soldiers who were fueled by "a radical African American patriotism," which advocated greater inclusion and equality for Black people in everyday life across America.[49]

This close bond long forged between the Black and white soldiers of Colonel Glover's regiment early shocked disbelieving Southern troops, who hailed from the largest slave-owning state in the Union, Virginia. The deeply entrenched racial animosity of white Virginians resulted in a wild brawl at the army's Cambridge, Massachusetts, encampment, which had to be broken up by an irate Washington. The western Virginia frontiersmen of Daniel Morgan's rifle command, who had virtually no association with Black people out of bondage while living in the hills of prewar Virginia, including today's West Virginia, clashed violently with the Marbleheaders because of "the presence of negroes in Glover's regiment."[50]

As seen from this ugly incident, the open hostility demonstrated by white Southern troops toward Black soldiers from Marblehead was most ironic. After all, these men of African descent more deeply felt a love for liberty that exceeded that of most whites in general because they had either experienced slavery themselves or, if free, had relatives in bondage and knew all about the horrors of enslavement. If anything, these angry Virginians would have been wise to have embraced African Americans to serve in their own ranks to fight this war against the greatest power on earth, because they were all true republican brothers in arms that should, in theory, have superseded color and cultural differences.

Not only serving in Colonel Glover's Fourteenth Massachusetts in which soldiers like Private Manuel Soto carried muskets with pride, Black fighting men were also found in the ranks of the other

Massachusetts regiments of the Bay State brigade. For instance, Pomp Magus had first enlisted in Colonel Loammi Baldwin's Twenty-sixth Massachusetts Continental Regiment, which was part of Glover's brigade, in 1775 and served in 1776, evidently including at the Battle of Pell's Point.[51] Most appropriate and symbolic, Private Caesar Glover, a former seafarer who possessed connections to the Glover family as a domestic servant, also served with distinction in fighting America's battles in the ranks of the mostly Marblehead regiment.[52]

Chapter 3

Brilliant Delaying Tactics in Westchester County that Saved Washington's Army

By the time the first leaves of autumn had turned yellow and brown on the hardwood forests around Manhattan Island and a pristine agrarian land of large and small farmers, General William Howe had missed his golden opportunity to exploit his successful landings at Kip's Bay and then at Throgs Neck in bold attempts to gain the rear of General Washington's army, entrap it on Manhattan Island, and end the revolution in one stroke. However, Howe had hit upon the winning formula and exactly the right tactics and the right place farther north after these two previous failures that had been launched too far south. Indeed, in overall strategic terms, "Howe had chosen the wrong spot to begin his encircling movement [and] Had he landed his men further" north, then "he might indeed have cut off at least a part of the American army."[1]

However, to his credit, Howe was an irrepressible type, which was always a top quality of a good commander in the field. In consequence, he was now determined to try again. This time, he was determined to land farther north to fulfill his ambition of cutting off Washington's army and trapping it, which might well result in the ending of the war. Most of all, he knew that he must not commit the folly of unleashing frontal assaults on the lengthy line of defenses atop Harlem Heights to avoid Bunker Hill–like losses. He, therefore, would once again rely upon another flank movement to the north in a bid to deliver a deadly blow to the amateur army of rustic revolutionaries.

In a September 25 report to George Sackville, or Lord Germain who was the Secretary of State of the American Colonies and directed the war effort, Howe requested additional troops to build up his strength to around seventy thousand troops for his next bid to finally end the career of the bungling upstart named Washington and secure decisive victory for King George III. Prospects were extremely good for decisive success, because defeating Washington had already proved surprisingly easy in this campaign, because of the employment of flanking maneuvers and the depth of Washington's ineptitude and the inexperience of his troops.[2]

Among these reinforcing troops that had caused Howe to remain in position for five days at Throgs Neck under the balmy early autumn sunshine were three full battalions of Hessians, or nearly three regiments. An Irish soldier who had had enlisted in Dublin, Ireland, in the Forty-ninth Regiment of Foot, Thomas Sullivan penned in his journal about what he believed to have been the predominant strategic thinking of General Howe and his top leaders on October 12:

> The very strong Positions the Enemy had taken on New York Island, and they having fortified it with incredible labour, occasioned the Generals determining to get upon their Principal Communication with Connecticut, with a view of forcing them to quit their strong holds in the neighborhood of King's Bridge, and, if possible, to bring them to action.[3]

Perfect Landing Site for Slipping Behind Washington's Army

But in fact, Howe's strategic plan was far more optimistic. To not only outflank General Washington's army now aligned in a strong defensive position on Harlem Heights and to compensate for the missed opportunity at Throgs Point and after having wasted six days of inactivity at this obscure location amid low-lying swamps so disfavored by geography for a massive drive inland to the west, General Howe once again prepared to launch yet another ambitious flanking maneuver to the north with an amphibious invasion higher up and about five miles north of Throgs Neck. Thanks partly to the influence of his rear admiral brother Richard, William Howe used his masterful understanding of amphibious warfare with his decision to land his invasion force on the Pell's Point Peninsula, thanks to the calm waters that sheltered Pelham Bay that could be filled with countless warships and troop transports, because no rebel defenses filled with amateur revolutionaries or American cannon lined the shore. Most important, this targeted point of the thin peninsula nestled between the Hudson River and Long Island Sound was a shorter distance west from Pell's Point to the Hudson than had been the case of Throgs Neck for the overall goal of striking Washington's army and trapping it on Manhattan Island.

Best of all, the new target site for landing his army selected by General Howe offered an ideal series of bays (first Eastchester Bay to the south and then Pelham Bay just to the north) that looked much like broad lakes to offer easy access to the Pell's Point Peninsula and high ground a short distance north and northwest: a much better place to launch an amphibious invasion than the low-lying, swampy terrain around Throgs Point, where a vigorous push inland had proven impossible. Pelham Bay was a wide, lengthy, north-south-running body of water located only a relatively short distance north—around three miles—of Throgs Point and paralleling Long Island Sound just to the east. This wide bay of tranquil water lay just below, or south, of the peninsula. The Pell's Point Peninsula offered an ideal place for an amphibious landing of thousands of troops to pour inland to more quickly gain solid and higher ground than in the case of Throgs Neck, fulfilling Howe's lofty ambitions.

While Throgs Neck might have been one of the worst places north of New York City to attempt an amphibious landing, Pelham Bay was the best place of all to ease behind Washington's army and cut it off, after striking it on the western flank during the army's lengthy withdrawal. Most important and the anthesis of the deplorable situation at Throgs Neck, Howe's targeted area was located only "three miles to the eastward, at Pell's Point [and the entire Pell's Point Peninsula was] a part of the mainland [that now] offered no serious natural obstacles."[4]

In regard to a landing site for the British-Hessian Army, the differences between Throgs Neck and Pell's Point revealed one of the war's great ironies: General Howe might well have won the war had he earlier chosen to invade and pour inland only a short distance north at Pell's Point instead of wasting nearly a week at Throgs Neck. This simple difference of only around three miles farther north was the narrow margin that meant the difference between the life or death of the Continental Army and the United States of America.

As General Howe explained his well-thought-out tactical and strategic reasoning for his most recent decision—the same as that which led to his earlier targeting of Throgs Point—to land his mighty force of invaders at Pell's Point: "The very strong positions the enemy had taken on this island [Manhattan], and fortified with incredible labour, determined me to get upon their principal communication with Connecticut, with a view of forcing them to quite the strong holds in the neighborhood of Kingsbridge, and, if possible, to bring to action," where they could be decisively defeated.[5]

After landing at Pell's Point and according to plan, Howe's invasion force could then easily march inland, or west, only a short distance along good roads, especially the Eastchester Road that led southwest from the village of Eastchester, on the New York mainland nestled between the Hudson and Long Island Sound to gain Washington's rear and strike the Continental Army in retreat. The Boston Post Road, which ran through Eastchester, led northeast to Boston and New England. The British and Hessian invaders could push west a relatively short distance along the Eastchester Road to intercept the army's long escape attempt north to White Plains.

Best of all for the prospects of a successful landing at Pell's Point on the New York mainland, neither earthen defenses, artillery emplacements, or forts guarded Pelham Bay on the army's far eastern flank and for the around half a dozen miles inland all the way west to the Hudson, where Washington's army was now in retreat along the Albany Post Road. Reeling from the series of defeats and dreary withdrawals, the dispirited units of General Washington's army were situated far too far to the west to oppose the landing or even respond to it in time. Even more, the Westchester County, New York, militia was not called out to defend their own homeland by this time in part because this was a largely Loyalist country. Instead, the many Loyalists of Westchester County prepared to welcome the invaders with open arms. Despite a number of fiery rebels in the area, most people of Westchester County were Loyalists who either strongly supported the Crown or wanted to live their lives unmolested.

Indeed, despite an obvious landing site for Howe's next offensive effort, the entire Pell's Point peninsula, which was about three miles in length, was undefended without any defensive structures, while free of natural obstacles that would slow a British push inland across a fertile agricultural region more dominated by open farmlands than heavy forests. Seemingly nothing could deny General Howe his strategic objective of conducting a successful invasion of the New York mainland to gain Washington's rear and destroy the Continental Army—America's best last hope for a successful revolution. Not only blessed with disciplined, experienced, and expertly trained troops who were highly skilled in the art of war, Howe also possessed the luxury of landing at any point off Long Island Sound to gain the eastern shore of Westchester County and then move inland between the Hudson and the Sound without encountering any American naval forces on water or defensive lines on shore.

After moving inland from Pell's Point, the invading British and Hessian troops then

> could quickly cut the main road [Boston Post Road] to New England and be only a short march [north] from White Plains, the key position in Westchester County, astride a network of roads [and] With ships in the Hudson [to the west] already cutting off all Washington's waterborne supplies, [Washington's] army would have no choice but to starve, disperse, or fight under very disadvantageous circumstances.[6]

Quite simply, a successful landing of his powerful army on the undefended Pell's Point Peninsula and its easy access to key roads, especially the
Eastchester Road that led west from the Boston Post Road and Eastchester
to retreating Washington's army, would provide General Howe with the
golden opportunity to end this pesky American rebellion once and for all.
After all because of his superior tactical skill as opposed to his fumbling
former-Virginia militia colonel opponent, he had "repeatedly declared [to
London throughout the late winter and spring of 1776] that he wished
to bring the Continental Army to a decisive action, for only a resounding
British victory would, he thought, end the rebellion."[7]

As Colonel Glover, whose knowledge of seamanship was extensive
like his on-target strategic insights, lamented in a letter:

> We cannot tell this day where we shall be the next, and this
> ever will be the case while the enemy commands the River[s]
> [and other waterways around New York City, including Long
> Island Sound], by which they can bring their whole force to
> one single point, with great ease and in a very little time.[8]

The chances of General Howe finally achieving decisive success
and ending this war with one blow seemed inevitable with any successful British invasion of Westchester County just north of Throgs
Point, located about three miles north on the Pell's Point Peninsula,
after sailing north on the night of October 17 to Pelham Bay just
off the point. Indeed and as noted, the Pell's Point Peninsula offered
this ideal opportunity for an amphibious landing and then a painless
march up the north-south peninsula and then deeper, or west, into
Westchester County to gain the strategic Eastchester Road and then
cut off Washington's retreat north to White Plains and trap his weak,
vulnerable army, which could then be destroyed or forced to surrender to end the revolution. In truth and in an understatement, one
historian has maintained that had General Howe "gone immediately
to Pell's Point rather than to Throgs Neck, he would have had a much
better chance to injure the Patriot army."[9]

Worst of all, for British fortunes, Howe had tipped his hand about what would be his next strategic move and one not only in the same direction—north—but also up the same north-south body of water. For the befuddled General Howe, Throgs Neck had possessed "no strategic advantages, beyond signaling Washington [and especially General Charles Lee] that the British were outflanking him again and he had better abandon New York" as soon as possible.[10]

Unlike the disastrous choice of Throgs Point as a landing site and to his credit, Howe had finally smartly targeted an area that was finally the right place—"a true peninsula where there had been no American defenders"—and the best opportunity of the war to trap and destroy Washington's army, when it was the most vulnerable while in a long, disorganized retreat, in short order. In consequence, if Howe's ambitious plans worked as planned, then the war would almost certainly come to an end—a sort of Yorktown in reverse half a decade before the final major decisive battle of the American Revolution in the faraway Virginia Tidewater.[11]

And most important compared to the Throgs Peninsula, this new threat that was about to suddenly emerge at Pell's Point was "only three miles above [Throgs Neck, and it] would be vastly harder for the Americans to defend," especially if Howe gained a toehold on the high ground just north of the landing site.[12] With his brother's powerful navy having complete control of the maze of waterways around New York and with the clock ticking on the Continental Army's life, Howe realized that it was only a matter of time before he managed to strike Washington's withdrawing army on its eastern flank to end the revolution in one stroke.[13] By this time, General Washington knew all about the greatest danger facing his army from intelligence reports: "they mean to Hem us in by getting above us and cutting off all communications with the [rest of the] Country."[14]

Therefore, the construction of an elaborate network of fortifications at any point, especially at Harlem Heights, to defend Washington's army from a frontal assault from the south was now nothing more than a waste of time, because the real threat lay not to the south, but to the north. Acting Engineer Rufus Putnam, a former millwright, farmer, surveyor, and Massachusetts militia officer who had been a chief architect of the fortification of Dorchester Heights by the way of prefabricated defenses that had forced Howe to evacuate Boston in March 1776, had early realized as much. Like General Lee, he had informed General Washington about the sheer folly of attempting to defend Manhattan Island because the British could land thousands of troops at any time and at almost any point to the north that they chose to negate the defensive network on Harlem Heights or any other defensive point on Manhattan Island.[15]

Right Place, Right Time, Right Soldiers

Around three and a half miles northwest of Pelham Bay and just west of Long Island Sound, only a small band of Massachusetts soldiers— an undersized and depleted Continental brigade that badly needed new recruits to bolster its thinned ranks—of General Charles Lee's Division was the only force that stood between the upcoming mighty British-Hessian invasion and General Washington's army. By the night of October 16, Glover's placement just southeast of the Eastchester was most fortuitous and by deliberate design.

Protecting the far eastern flank of Washington's withdrawing army now struggling north along the dusty Albany Post Road, Colonel Glover's diminutive force had been dispatched by Major General William Heath on October 14 to watch the Eastchester Road that led southwest to Valentine's Hill and west to the vulnerable American army in the midst of withdrawing to White Plains and to guard the area around Pelham Bay, where General Howe's invasion force was almost certainly to land on the soil of Westchester County—the New York mainland—at any moment.[16]

With still no intelligence or indications that the British were moving north by water and landing anywhere above Throgs Neck in Westchester County, Glover's Massachusetts soldiers had spent October 17, Thursday, quietly in camp on the Boston Post Road just southeast of Eastchester. Here, they cleaned weapons, drilled smartly, and engaged in routine camp chores. No doubt the more pious Bay State men, many of whom wore their hair long and tied in queues in the back in the popular style of the day, contemplated attending church services at the unfinished St. Paul's Episcopal Church, a stately structure made of finely chiseled gray stone in a long-lasting tribute to God, in Eastchester for the upcoming Sunday, October 20. The quiet agricultural community of Eastchester was situated atop a commanding knoll, surrounded by low hills, which overlooked a picturesque surroundings of salt marshes, stands of tall hardwood timber, grassy meadows, and fields of crops. Located on the Boston Post Road that led north and the Eastchester Road that led west, the small town was situated about one-third of the way to the Hudson to the west, while the Long Island Sound lay just to the east. All in all, this was an excellent place from which the Massachusetts brigade, now acting as a strategic reserve in case of enemy landings, could be hurriedly dispatched southeast if Howe landed at Pelham Bay.

This Thursday October 17 was another magnificent day of an Indian summer that was one of the finest in recent memory and pleasant enough to make a young soldier from Marblehead momentarily forget about the war's horrors. Here, just west of the Hutchinson River southeast of Eastchester, the Bay Staters rejoiced in the fact that it was warmer in this area at this time of year than back home in New England. Like in the eventful summer that had just passed during the struggle for possession of New York City, the autumn sun shone and the skies were cloudless. Only the slightly cooler nights and shorter hours of daylight indicated that yet another winter was on the way. Summer was still in the process of slowly dying, but this was a classic Indian summer—a name derived from when Native Americans had so often launched slashing raids on New England's isolated settlements long before the French and Indian War—because of the weather's mildness, while the white herons silently stalked for food in the tall reeds of the expansive salt marshes lining Pelham Bay. This scorching summer in New York had been dry, and the trees, especially the clumps of cottonwoods along the shoreline of Pelham Bay and the Hutchinson River, had already turned lighter earlier than usual in September. At this time, the first shades of bright autumnal colors of the leaves were already seen in the woodlands of Westchester County.

Thankfully to the thinking of the young men and boys of the four Massachusetts regiments of Glover's brigade, there was neither a need or sense of urgency to attempt to fortify the small encampment located just southeast of the small village of Eastchester. Colonel Glover realized that his key mission was not to defend this advanced position on the army's far eastern flank, but to guard the Eastchester Road that led west to Washington's army and to use his tiny brigade as a mobile strike force, or a strategic reserve, if or when the British again attempted to conduct an amphibious landing on Westchester County soil. Of course, no one in Glover's brigade knew of Howe's plan or intentions by this time. Not even a rumor of Howe's next movement had been gained by the Massachusetts men. Therefore, the Bay State soldiers slept well on the night of October 17, enjoying the cooler weather and better sleeping conditions of early autumn without knowing that they were about to become victims of a surprise invasion during the nighttime hours.

Consequently, in the early morning hours of Friday, October 18, the encampment of Colonel Glover's small Massachusetts brigade remained quiet in the predawn darkness, while soldiers of Colonel Loammi Baldwin's Twenty-sixth Massachusetts Continental Regiment rested on the ground because they had no army tents like the British and Hessians. Except for the handful of sleepy-eyed guards posted around the serene encampment situated on high ground along the Boston Post Road that was the most important strategic artery in Westchester County because it led north to New England, Glover's New Englanders slept comfortably on the ground.

Colonel Baldwin's men now lay on the ground wrapped in thin woolen blankets, dirty and insufficient for the cold fall at this latitude on a chilly New York night, trying to stay warm amid the brisk early morning coolness. In the confusion of the chaotic evacuation of

New York City and especially after British warships had moved north with impunity up the Hudson River on September 15 to abruptly end the flow of supplies and equipment from the city by water, the baggage of Glover's brigade had been left behind along the banks of the East River for eventual transport north with Washington's army during the withdrawal north. However, unlike the other three regiments of Glover's Brigade, the baggage of Colonel Loammi Baldwin's barely 225 young men and boys of the Twenty-sixth Massachusetts Continental Regiment had been captured by the British, when New York City fell. Baldwin's command represented the smallest regiment in the Bay State brigade, but its fighting spirit was outsized as if to compensate.

Consequently, like Colonel Glover's other Massachusetts soldiers of three regiments and in general, Colonel Baldwin's troops were less healthy than Washington's better-equipped troops and the command was harder hit by illness, especially with the advent of cooler weather. At this time, very few soldiers in Washington's army possessed winter clothing, including Glover's mariners, who yet wore summer garb—light, baggy, and loose in the seafaring tradition—as throughout this grueling campaign for New York. They were true summer soldiers in this regard.

For good reason, Colonel Glover was concerned about his men's welfare because of the lack of clothing and tents. In a September 18 letter, he had predicted only a short time before how "Col. Baldwins Regi[ment] is much in want of tents, there being none to be had here, nor any barns but what are taking up for the Sick. The men being So much exposed I feare [that they] will be all Sick & Very Soon unfit for duty." In the quiet encampment located along the dusty Boston Post Road, situated just below, or southeast, of Eastchester and now covered with the first fallen leaves of the arrival of early autumn, that led northeast to New Rochelle and then on to Boston, only a few of Glover's soldiers stirred in the blackness before dawn.[17]

In addition, a handful of sleepy-eyed sentinels stood guard around the tented encampment, except in regard to the men of Colonel Baldwin's regiment, which was sprawled along the grassy slope of a commanding hill, while a salty air blew west from the Atlantic. Here, beyond the outer limits of the village of Eastchester in Westchester County, almost everyone in Glover's camp remained deep in sleep in the cold darkness of what seemed like just another uneventful night. Perhaps the hooting of a great horned owl was all that disturbed the stillness of the night in the distance in the ghostly looking clusters of ancient oaks at the edge of the saltwater marshes or along the tidal waters of the Hutchinson River, which flowed in a north-south direction from its headwaters north of Eastchester and straight south into the northern end of Pelham Bay.

Somewhat ominously in the eerie darkness and perhaps versed in some details about the region's dark history from locals in Eastchester, Colonel Glover might have heard about the tragic fate of Anne Hutchinson, for whom this tidal river was named. At this time of year, the somber, black woodlands seemed almost haunted around the slow-moving and wide Hutchinson River partly because of dark past events in this part of Westchester County, which were not only mysterious but also tragic, including the recent bitter civil war against patriots and Loyalists in this area.

Anne Hutchinson had been a defiant preacher and a freethinking woman well ahead of her time. In 1638, she had been forced to flee the autocratic theocracy of Boston and the Massachusetts commonwealth from where she was officially banished beyond the strict confines of an intolerant organized religion of autocratic Puritan leaders, because she had adhered to the belief of separation of church and state by worshipping as she pleased. She and a small band of followers were unfairly considered heretics by the orthodox Church of Boston. After attempting in vain to settle down south of Boston, due to harassment from intolerant Massachusetts officers and their religious patrons, Anne was forced to continue on her search for religious freedom to around two hundred miles to the southwest. She eventually settled in the Dutch lands of New York, or New Amsterdam, well beyond Massachusetts. Here, Anne and her religious followers set down roots along this river, which only became tidal near where it entered Pelham Bay to the south. The Hutchinson River was named after Anne Hutchinson, who was a feisty fighter for individual and religious freedom who paid a high price for her unorthodoxy. She had been exiled from Boston because she had believed in freedom of worship and detested the abusive religious and government authority that had attempted to force her to conform to their autocratic dictates.

After having been the only English settlers to set down roots among the Dutch on the fertile lands around Pelham Bay deep in Indian country when Native Americans of the Siwanoy tribe were particularly angry over white encroachment of their sacred lands and had been at war with the Dutch since 1640, she and her half dozen children and a handful of faithful followers were unprepared for trouble. Anne had always gotten along well with Native Americans in Massachusetts, and she had no fear of them. She had even opposed the Massachusetts Government's bloody war on the Pequot, who were destroyed by fire and sword or taken prisoner and enslaved. Anne's belief that Native Americans were God's children had also made her an outsider. When her Dutch neighbors had advised Anne to secure arms for their own protection, she refused. As a sad fate would have it, the entire Hutchinson clan, including Anne, was massacred by Native American warriors of the Siwanoy tribe in 1643.

Or perhaps Glover and his New Englanders also might have gained an ominous feeling about upcoming events in Westchester County, if they had taken note of the fact that the peninsula's southern tip had been an old Indian burial ground, offering an ill omen to the most superstitious soldiers. Like Anne Hutchinson, who had been born in England, had been forced to settle in the dangerous region of the Pell's Point Peninsula because of Puritan persecution by the Boston theocracy, so Glover also now faced a daunting dilemma and a seemingly no-win situation, because they were basically serving as the army's shock troops of a strategic reserve to meet any suddenly emerging threat, which was sure to be a sizeable one, from Long Island Sound just to the east or Pelham Bay to the southeast. Carrying considerable risks if and when the British landed around Pelham's

Bay or any other advantageous point farther north of Washington's army, this risky independent assignment of Glover's brigade in such an advanced forward position to guard the Eastchester Road, that led west to Kingsbridge and Washington's army, and the coast around Pelham Bay while distant from General Washington's army, around half a dozen miles to the west, brought considerable responsibility to the Marblehead colonel. In overall terms, Colonel Glover's brigade had been placed in an advanced position on the far eastern flank to go into action in any suddenly developing emergency situation to ensure the army's safety and protect the withdrawal that included the evacuation from Manhattan Island.

To his credit, Washington had chosen this small command of only four Bay State regiments for the most crucial of missions, if General Howe landed farther north and thousands of enemy troops poured inland. Because this flood of British and Hessians could not be stopped because of overpowering numbers, Howe's invasion would somehow have to be slowed by only a relative handful of Massachusetts men as long as possible to buy precious time for Washington to escape and perhaps even dispatch reinforcements, if he even decided to do so, and by then it would be too late.

Most important at this crucial time, no troops in Washington's army were more likely to accomplish this impossible task if Howe suddenly landed than Glover and his men, who could be relied upon to do their best in buying that precious time so badly needed for Washington's army to escape and survive. After all, Glover and his mariners of the mostly Marblehead regiment and his three other Massachusetts regiments were seasoned Continentals and the antithesis of the Connecticut militiamen who had run like jackrabbits at Kip's Bay. This gave General Washington confidence when he was focused on saving his army by a timely retreat. Quite simply, these tough, disciplined Continentals from the Bay State "were the elite of the Patriot armies, the men whom Washington and other American commanders placed their trust" throughout the course of the New York Campaign.[18]

And now to not only guard the Eastchester Road that led west toward his army and his exposed eastern flank but also to ensure that Howe's force did not gain a toehold to trap his army on the north before it reached the safety of White Plains if he landed farther north, General Washington's complete trust lay with Colonel Glover and his small Massachusetts Brigade and what they could accomplish against the odds. Picturesque Westchester County was dotted with the old Dutch names of villages like Yonkers that was located to the west on gently rolling hills situated on the Hudson's east bank and populated by an enterprising, agrarian people whose descendants had been proud residents of "New Netherland." Westchester County was largely Loyalist like New York City. In fact, this fertile county of fine farmlands and virgin woodlands was so Loyalist that General Charles Lee, despite having been born in England, advocated harsh retaliation against the Tory inhabitants during what was America's first civil war. He had strongly urged the imprisoning and banishing of Westchester County Loyalists to Connecticut to the north, but Congress rejected these measures as too extreme. General Lee's concerns, however, were well-founded and now these had become Glover's problem. Not long after Howe had taken possession of New York City, for instance, the ships of the Royal Navy had established communications with Loyalists of Westchester County to gain support and intelligence.

A good many Westchester County Loyalists marched in the ranks of an excellent unit consisting of Westchester County Tories, the Queen's American Rangers. This Tory command was led by America's great hero of the French and Indian War, Robert Rogers. He had been America's top Ranger leader in that war for empire, and his fame had spread on both sides of the Atlantic. This Loyalist command of Americans was now an active unit in Howe's army. One Loyalist of the Queen's American Rangers was an officer named Joshua Pell, who had been born in 1710 and lived at the vast estate known as Pelham Manor, whose mansion house stood on high ground above Pelham Bay east of the Hutchinson River. It was his prosperous family in which he was the son of Thomas Pell, Third Lord of Pelham Manor, that had bestowed the name of Pell's Point to the peninsula's southern end. Nevertheless and despite its many diehard Loyalists in the area who loved the Crown as much as the Massachusetts soldiers loved their infant nation, Glover and his men were prepared to defend Westchester County, despite being a land of slavery and of wealthy Loyalist families, with their lives, whenever the landing of Howe's forces occurred, which was now only a matter of time.[19]

Far from the main army and without adequate supplies of any kind, the hardest-drinking men in the ranks from Marblehead—former fishermen and sailors—lamented the lack of liquor at the remote and uneventful encampment just outside Eastchester on the night of October 17, especially with the advent of cooler autumn nights. Displaying a wry sense of humor, Glover described in a letter about the fine wine that the general officers and other high-ranking officers—colonels and majors—drank at long dinners. He had to admit that this amount was nothing compared to what was consumed by the men of his own regiment, the Fourteenth Massachusetts Continental Regiment. He noted how much alcohol was consumed at headquarters "tho' not so much us'd to Wine as the Choir of the old 14th." Enterprising Marblehead merchants had long brought large quantities of foreign wines, especially a rich Madeira, into the thriving port and its many taverns like the Three Codd's Tavern, The Little Jug Inn, the Bunch of Grapes, and Aunty Bowen's Tavern on Gingerbread Hill.[20]

Meanwhile, Howe continued to gather strength for the move north from Throgs Neck to Pell's Point. Ever meticulous, he waited for his thorough preparations to be completed and for the arrival of the Hessian troops from Staten Island before ordering the advance by water toward Pell's Point. As he wrote: "The army remained [stationary] until the stores and provisions could be brought up, and three battalions [First Division] of Hessians drawn from Staten-Island, which, together with some bad weather intervening, occasioned a delay of five days."[21]

Finally, Howe made his next bold move to the north in the chess game to determine the fate of Washington's army and the revolution itself, after receiving reinforcements sent by Lord Germain on October 12. As explained in a letter from one of Washington's men, who possessed the latest intelligence that proved accurate:

> We hear 60 sail of vessels, with troops on board, went up [north] the east river from New-York last Monday, in order, no doubt, to effort a landing the some other quarter [to the north and] Accounts from head-quarters as late as yesterday are that nothing material had happened there, or at Throgs Neck, for some days past, but that an attack is hourly expected.[22]

Much like Howe's redcoat and Hessian troops in neat blue uniforms during this campaign when the stakes could not have been higher for the infant American nation that was literally fighting for its life, the Massachusetts soldiers were highly motivated on Friday October 18. From either the rural countryside or small towns from across the Bay State, these men consisted of primarily a moral soldiery, who were deeply religious and Bible-reading since as long as they could remember. As explained a New Yorker in regard to the less-sophisticated, more-homespun New Englanders, who were mostly farm boys from western and central Massachusetts: "They have all the simplicity of ploughmen in their manners, and seem quite strangers to the vices of older soldiers," especially British and Hessian troops.[23] And perhaps the best compliment that revealed the resolve of the American fighting man, especially the New Englanders of Glover's brigade, was the fact that they were motivated by a simple equation that they readily understood: "Independence or slavery is the only alternative."[24]

Here, on the chilly morning of October 18 and encamped around two miles southeast Eastchester, the young men and boys of Glover's brigade were now prepared to defend Westchester County, because the threat might come at any moment from Long Island Sound or Pelham Bay—both were wide open without a single obstacle to oppose the approach of the entire British Navy—if Howe suddenly ordered it north up the East River from Throgs Point. Just beyond Glover's encampment lay the Boston Post Road that led northeast to New England and Boston and the Eastchester Road, which branched off from the Boston Post Road that led west to Kingsbridge and Washington's army. And Marblehead lay on the coast just beyond Boston. It had to be tempting to some of these Massachusetts men to just leave camp some dark night and make their way north up the road to their homeland and families. But here at the Eastchester encampment and like throughout this campaign, in contrast to most other commands in Washington's army, none of Glover's men deserted from the ranks despite the temptation, although Marblehead lay just over two hundred miles to the northeast. Most of all, these men knew that they had a job to do and they would do it, just like they had a job to do when they had worked in the lucrative waters of the Grand Banks in hauling in boatloads of cod; no one could desert when at sea.

Now situated in the depths of Westchester County and far from home, the Massachusetts soldiers believed that their presence was essential in defending their native New England, families, villages, and farms, because their crucial mission called for protecting Washington's army at all costs. Indeed, if Washington's army was destroyed in this campaign, then the patriots and their families would be persecuted by the Loyalists in the home port, especially if victorious British troops entered Marblehead. Capturing the powerful spirit of Toryism that continued to exist, a Loyalist minister from Connecticut had rejoiced at the news of arriving British troops "coming from England and sultry men of war. So soon as they come, hanging work [of rebels] will go on, and destruction will first attend the seaport towns" of New England, which of course included Glover's beloved Marblehead.[25]

A lifelong resident of Marblehead and a longtime seafaring man, Ashely Bowen, who possessed Loyalist sentiments like a small minority of other citizens of Marblehead, lamented the divisions in the community caused by the war, writing in his journal: "Poor, poor, oh poor Marblehead!"[26]

Revealing the prevailing sentiment was the fact that "if New York and the Hudson River fell to the enemy, the line between New England and all the provinces to the south," it would be catastrophic by cutting the colonies in half, because in Washington's words, the maintaining of this vital strategic linkage was "upon which depends the Safety of America."[27]

The loss of such a key linkage would spell the doom of New England, which had long been the earliest center of this people's rebellion against the Crown. In addition, these Massachusetts soldiers knew that General Howe's invasion had to be stopped for another reason as well. Like French leaders during the French and Indian War, New Englanders were concerned that the British would unleash the wrath of their Native American and Canadian allies to once again ravage New England with a vengeance. For the many French and Indian War veterans now serving in the ranks for Glover's Bay State brigade, this fear was ever-present, nagging at minds and consciences, reminding them of an especially brutal killing time. However, the fear of a British and Hessian soldiery occupying the homeland was as frightening as the threat of unleashed Native American warriors. During the spring of 1775 not long after the revolution had erupted at Lexington and Concord just outside Boston, these Massachusetts soldiers had been first called to arms "to defend our wives and children from the butchering hands of an inhuman soldiery" from England.[28]

Consequently, knowing that he might have to oppose a full-scale British landing at some point along the sprawling shore of the Long Island Sound or from Pelham Bay, Glover had placed his small brigade of Massachusetts Continentals on the commanding high ground to protect the Eastchester Road, which led west to Washington's army, and from which they could descend to meet a threat to the southeast at Pelham Bay. He could quickly rush down the descending ground east of the Hutchinson River that led south to Pelham Bay, where the river entered on low-lying ground dominated by an expanse of salt marshes. Holding the extreme eastern flank of Washington's army,

Colonel Glover's position along the Boston Post Road was located just northwest of Pelham Bay and in a place southeast of Eastchester to be able to rush either east (Long Island South) or southeast (Pelham Bay) to meet any threat. Most important, Glover had placed his men and established his encampment close to Eastchester and connecting roads to increase his options and flexibility, because he could move in any direction and wherever the threat might emerge. But in looking at a map, Glover would have seen that wide Pelham Bay, which was a better landing site than at New Rochelle farther northeast up the Long Island Sound, offered the best possibilities for the landing of Howe's army.

The Pell's Point Peninsula, spanning north-south and about three miles in length, was located only

a few miles to the east of Kingsbridge, which was the most important position of the American lines, being [Washington's] only means of passage from the Island of Manhattan [and a] successful landing at this place would turn the left of the American Army and deprive them of their only means of escape.[29]

Situated at the northern tip of Manhattan Island about fifteen miles north of New York City, Kingsbridge linked the northern tip of Manhattan Island with the mainland. This strategic crossing point with the Dutch name of Spuyten Duyvil Creek, a short tidal estuary with strong currents (hence, the name devil) connected the Harlem River to the Hudson. Here, Kingsbridge crossed the Harlem River along the strategic road that led north to the Bronx and Westchester County on the New York mainland. But, more important, this wooded bridge across the Harlem River at this point where the Boston Post Road crossed the tidal estuary provided the "only good exit from Manhattan [Island] to Westchester" County and the New York mainland: Washington's avenue of escape.[30]

As early as July and before the first fighting of the campaign for New York, the civilian powers of New York had been correctly concerned that because New York was surrounded by water, and the British Navy possessed total mastery of these waterways, then the British could easily "cut off Communication between the City and Country by landing above Kingsbridge": a very good tactical concept embraced by Howe at this time, although belatedly.[31]

By this time, no doubt few, if any, of these young men and boys from Massachusetts expected a serious fight of any kind to suddenly erupt in the pastoral setting of Westchester County early on October 18, because it had been excessively quiet for days, although they had been assigned to watching the strategic Eastchester Road that led west toward Kingsbridge and Washington's army. Commanding the Twenty-sixth Massachusetts of Glover's brigade, Colonel William Baldwin had retired to a private house for the night of October 17 because of a lingering illness, or "a flux" as he penned in a letter and the seemingly incomprehensible fact that, in his own words, "the enemy lay still all this time." Although, Baldwin was entirely "unfit for duty," he had refused a medical discharge when it was easily obtainable, after Howe's landing at Throgs Neck, as if prophetically sensing that a far greater threat was about to erupt farther north.

If anything, Colonel Glover and his men contemplated a nice respite near the quaint town of Eastchester and not far from the expansive Long Island Sound that reminded them of Marblehead so far away, while enjoying the balmy weather of an Indian summer. Now distant from the main army and subsisting upon a bland diet of salty pork or beef and bread baked on sticks over fires and few, if any, vegetables to break the monotony of an non-nutritious diet, perhaps these New Englanders contemplated a tastier and more healthy diet from oysters and fish that could be easily taken from Long Island Sound and Pelham Bay with an extended stay in guarding the far eastern flank of Washington's army, if all continued to remain quiet on this far-flung front.[32]

But as seen throughout this grueling campaign for possession of New York City, service in General Washington's army at this time meant enduring close calls and harrowing experiences, because of its losing ways. As demonstrated repeatedly throughout the ill-fated summer of 1776, General Washington possessed an almost incomprehensible penchant for allowing his troops to be repeatedly outflanked and out-generaled, while consistently risking encirclement, surrender, or annihilation in one showdown after another. Even now Washington expected Howe's next move might not come at all north of Throgs Neck at Pell's Point, but around five miles southwest of Eastchester at Morrisania, which was located in the Bronx west of Throgs Neck, where another British landing could be conducted. By this time, some Massachusetts soldiers of Glover's Brigade must have felt that it was actually much safer to serve as far away from General Washington and his army as possible by mid-October 1776, because of so many recent setbacks and disasters.

Glover's Massachusetts soldiers experienced relief now that they were on their own in a remote area of Westchester County and seemingly far away from the main theater of operations. In the early morning blackness of early October 18, consequently, these young Bay State soldiers slept the deep sleep of men who felt relatively little concern and anxiety for immediate danger or about the future. After all, if there was any hard fighting to be done, then it would certainly be back on Harlem Heights far to the south or to the west if the British ascended the Hudson. If everything continued to go right for these veteran troops of the Massachusetts brigade as they hoped and prayed, then this assignment near Pelham Bay might in fact prove to be little more than an unofficial rest period—although officially Glover's brigade now served as a strategic reserve to rush to any newly developed emergency situation, especially if it came from the Long Island Sound or Pelham Bay. Fortunately for them, Glover's soldiers were at least now spared the anxiety of knowing that they were about to see some of the most desperate fighting of the war, when everything was at stake, because Howe was already moving north with a mighty invasion force under the veil of darkness on the night of October 17–18. About to spring still another surprise on Washington, General Howe's invasion force was about to land at Pell's Point in a bid to gain the Eastchester Road and then push west to Kingsbridge to trap Washington's army on Manhattan Island. At this time, only Colonel Glover and his undersized brigade stood in General Howe's way from fulfilling his lofty ambition of gaining solid ground and moving inland, while guarding the Eastchester Road that led west to Washington's army during a chaotic retreat—the sole obstacle, and an extremely minor one, in the face of a mighty invasion.

Glover's Greatest Shock, Spying Howe's Invasion on October 18

Either because of custom, habit, or from the fact that he could not sleep this night when his brigade was isolated and on its own during an independent assignment far from support, Colonel Glover was up earlier than usual on the morning of Friday October 18. All the while on this most peaceful of nights, the moon's sheen placed a shimmer of light that sparkled over the nearby waters of Pelham Bay and the Long Island Sound. Perhaps dogged by a premonition of brewing trouble on the eastern horizon like a storm rising over the Atlantic and haunted by the realization how easily the British Navy could land troops anywhere at will, the colonel from Marblehead might have possessed an ominous feeling about events to shortly come.

Without any prior warnings of Howe's plans or next tactical moves, the last thing that Glover expected at this time was the arrival of a full-scale British invasion targeting this remote narrow neck of land called the Pell's Point Peninsula that extended southward out into the wide waters of Pelham Bay, around three miles north of Throgs Neck. No pickets or guards had been dispatched from Washington's army to watch the coast of Pelham Bay and give Glover a timely warning with a smoke signal from accumulated piles of dry brush or a prearranged signal from the firing of muskets, even though the bay lying just off the Long Island Sound was spacious and sufficiently deep for a fleet of British warships.

Almost incredibly, there was no thin line of watchers, either military or civilian, now guarding the coastline or the expansive bays

(Pelham Bay and Eastchester Bay just to the south) to give timely warning to Glover of an impending danger. However, for a man-power-short army, the sprawling coastline of Westchester County was simply too vast to watch with so few troops under Washington's command when now in retreat and, of course, Glover's undersized brigade of four regiments. Thinking optimistically as usual, Glover reasoned that by relying on aggressive tactics he could march his troops toward Howe's landing site along the coast in an effort to keep the British from establishing a toehold on the American mainland north of Washington's army, if the enemy struck.

Not long after he awoke in the chilly darkness of early morning on October 18, Colonel Glover was about to receive the surprise of his life. Nagged by a strange restlessness that was inexplicable and as mentioned, Glover was up early at headquarters. Even more, he was fully dressed in his finest uniform almost as anticipating trouble. As brigade commander, Glover evidently was completing some paperwork in his tent by candlelight before the first light of dawn. At this time, he also might have been thinking about the fact that his forty-fourth birthday, on November 5, was only eighteen days away, and about the unpredictable course of his life that had been one of an amazing rise from rags to riches. But most likely on this early morning, the former Marblehead cobbler was thinking of his beloved wife, Hannah, because of his love for her and the fact of her failing health. Glover perhaps now felt somewhat guilty that he was not by her side when she needed him after nearly a quarter century of a blessed marriage now that she was keeping the home front at Marblehead together and raising the family in his absence. Worn and exhausted from life's burdens, Hannah was destined to die of disease on November 13, 1778, at age forty-five and just days after her husband's forty-sixth birthday, which inflicted a devastating loss on him and more than the ravages of any battle.

Colonel Glover also might have wondered about what he had accomplished during all those years of hard work, including mostly at sea, and business dealings in Marblehead and if it was all worth it.

Certainly, the year of 1776 had been the most eventful one of his life, when he and his men had saved so much of Washington's army, around a third, from entrapment and a cruel fate on Long Island near the end of August. Or he might have contemplated the fact that October 30—only twelve days away—was the twenty-second anniversary of his marriage to Hannah Gale of Marblehead, who had brought him so much happiness and peace in this life. But in fact, the colonel was now more focused upon what Howe might do next in October.[33]

With the first faint gray streaks of light of this Friday of another beautiful early autumn day in Westchester County beginning to lighten the eastern horizon as the sun started to peek over Long Island Sound to the east, Glover had already been up for some time, long before the drummer boys—usually teenagers yet to shave, take their first drink of alcohol, or have their first lover—beat the morning reveille at dawn. As usual, Glover had dressed in his finest uniform, which was his custom when in the field. Meticulous and fastidious by nature, Glover knew that it was important to look the part of a Continental brigade commander for his men. He now wore a Dutch shirt, a fine blue uniform, a brace of silver pistols, and his favorite Scottish broadsword, a traditional Claymore. He did not wear boots but stylish shoes with silver buckles. When the infant American army had first formed at Cambridge during the summer of 1775, Glover had gained the reputation as the best-dressed officer in the army, and this fact was a source of personal pride.[34]

While his boys slept in the early morning hours at the quiet brigade encampment seemingly in the middle of nowhere on the other side of a grassy hill just west of the Hutchinson River and southeast of Eastchester to provide concealment just in case the enemy landed, Glover was busily working in his headquarters tent. He was yet watching over this troops in protective fashion like a veteran sea captain in a voyage during their repose. The early morning air of October 18 was cool, almost cold to a Virginian but not a New Englander, especially one who had long journeyed through rough waters all the way to the Grand Banks. The cooler weather reminded the men from the

Massachusetts Brigade that another hard winter was on the way—the second winter of this war that was already longer than they had originally imagined from those heady days in the spring 1775, when it had seemed that the war would be short, especially after the Battle of Bunker Hill.

However, in the chilly half-light of October 18, it was yet too dark and shadowy to ascertain that the leaves of the oaks, hickories, and maples around the serene American encampment of white tents, except for Colonel Baldwin's men, situated along the west side of the Westchester County hill were already wearing first bright autumnal colors of yellow and red. Indeed, the first hint of winter's relentless approach was already in the air, lingering like the night's dark shadows in the early morning coolness. By this time, V-shaped formations of Canada geese had filled the sky, heading south for warmer weather and better feeding grounds beyond the distant southern horizon and ever-farther away from Marblehead to the northeast.

The dim light of early morning slowly began to reveal the ghostly outlines of nearby St. Paul's Episcopal Church of Eastchester just to the northwest, standing at the edge of the Eastchester village green. Objects surrounding Glover's silent encampment west of the Hutchinson River, southeast of town, and along the Boston Post Road grew more distinct in the grayish first light just before dawn, when the Massachusetts men were so far from home.

Fueled by the parishioners' desire for freedom of worship in the Episcopal faith, this church had been first established by the pious settlers of Westchester County in 1665. But now, the old wooden church was in the process of being replaced by a new and much more magnificent structure that was ensured to last for hundreds of years and to this day. On October 18, the church was now only about half completed, a dedicated work in progress. By any measure, this house of God would be a stately, permanent place of worship for generations of come. Ambitious plans by visionary church fathers called for a stately stone structure of an impressive height to replace the old wooden meetinghouse. The new church was to be fronted by a large tower, topped by a decorative cupola, to present an impressive facade. However, the war had put an abrupt end to the ambitious plans for the completion of the stone house of worship.[35]

In symbolic terms, Colonel Glover's encampment on Washington's far eastern flank seemed to mock the house of worship of the Episcopal faith, which had origins in the Church of England or the Anglican Church, dedicated to peace on earth. Meanwhile, in the cold darkness just before the dawn, the quiet Massachusetts encampment still lay undisturbed in the early morning hours of October 18, as if the war was somehow thousands of miles away. Hundreds of Bay State soldiers continued to sleep, including on the ground, in peace and the relative warmth of their thin blankets in the chilly half-darkness, while still wearing ragged summer uniforms or civilian clothes on their backs. All the while, the moon lingered low on the horizon, looking larger to the eye in an optical illusion, at this time just before the dawn of another pleasant autumn day.

Like Colonel Glover, a handful of Massachusetts soldiers were also up early as well on this Friday morning in Westchester County. Either they could not sleep for whatever reason or it was their turn to collect wood for starting fires to cook the early morning breakfast. Other soldiers prepared a meager supply of salt pork and bread rations, getting ready for the morning meal and then the routine of drill, because the colonel was always obsessed with making these men even better soldiers.

As usual, the ever-active Colonel Glover was not thinking about sleep or breakfast at this early morning hour before the sunrise of October 18. Instead, he was looking ahead toward what might happen in the immediate future in regard to Howe's next tactical move in a seemingly ill-fated campaign full of surprises. So far, the American army had just narrowly escaped with its life because of the effectiveness of Howe's tactical surprises by steadily moving north. In this key assignment in Westchester County, Glover had been attempting to do whatever was necessary to be as fully prepared and as much as possible just in case he was surprised by Howe like Washington had been so often in the recent past. An introspective man with a good deal of pent-up energy and restlessness that only increased because of his precarious situation now on his own in a dangerous advanced position to meet any threat that might be forthcoming from Pelham Bay and the Long Island Sound.

As a precaution or out of habit, Colonel Glover walked leisurely out of the silent encampment with the approach of the first light of day, while feeling the refreshing early morning breeze that swept across the Hutchinson River just to the east. Seemingly on a routine walk of little consequence to get some fresh air after leaving his stuffy headquarters tent, he headed to the hilltop on the encampment's other side that over-looked the waters of Pelham Bay to the south. The hill commanded the Boston Post Road, which was now the most strategic road in New York.

Long used to acting on his own and making his own quick, but on-target, decisions without time-consuming deliberation or debate like a time-consuming conference at Washington's headquarters just like when he had been at sea out of urgent necessity in emergency situations, Glover was now without a trusty staff officer, like Surgeon Isaac Spofford and Surgeon's mate or assistant Nathaniel Harrington, or another top lieutenant by this side at this time, when he walked alone up the grassy hill. Although on his own, Colonel Glover was in his element, because he was basically a solitary man when it came to holding leadership positions. He was the kind of commander who did what so many other leaders would only order others to do in regard to leading the way for his men into the midst of the hottest fight or in crossing a river. This was one source of Glover's immense popularity among his troops. Glover had neither politically focused priorities or a fawning personality toward superiors that were necessary for effective social climbing in this increasingly-politicized army, because he had always allowed his actions to speak louder than his words, as during the miraculous escape from Long Island near the end of August.

All the while, Colonel Glover continued to move deliberately up the grassy slope to the nearby hilltop that dominated not only the Boston Post Road but also the encampment of his Massachusetts brigade a short distance to the west. He carried a mug of hot coffee to warm him on this chilly early morning. Almost as if on a morning walk on a lazy Sunday afternoon across the rocky peninsula that overlooked the beautiful harbor of Marblehead so far away, Glover reached the commanding crown of the eminence in the early morning coolness and fading early morning darkness.[36]

With the warming rays of the first sunlight of Friday October 18 making the eastern horizon grow lighter and reddish in color while the waters of Pelham Bay and the Long Island Sound slowly began to become visible in the early morning light, Colonel Glover felt the slight sea breeze and the smell of salt air blowing in from the east. The usual early morning chorus, the noise of gulls squawking overhead and songbirds in the foliage could be heard in the distance east toward Long Island Sound and from the murky saltwater swamps around where the Hutchinson River entered the head of Pelham Bay to the south. The Marblehead colonel perhaps thought of his wife Hannah and their brood of children and their home overlooking the town's harbor, while wondering if he would ever see them again. While bathed in the refreshing breeze and the cool half-light near the commanding point of the grass-covered hilltop clear of trees that would have blocked the view to the east and south, Colonel Glover suddenly stopped at the elevation's highest point.

Wearing his finest Continental uniform of blue, Glover stood atop the dominant high-ground perch. This hilltop overlooked Pelham Bay to the south toward where the Hutchinson River flowed lazily into the northern head of wide Pelham Bay and the Long Island Sound to the east. Colonel Glover now possessed an unobstructed view of these extensive bodies of water in multiple directions. He might have not known that this narrow point of land slightly to the southeast and now made strategically important by the war was known as the Pell's Point Peninsula. Glover also could view the shallow and narrow Hutchinson River Valley, the swampy ground of salt marshes in the lowlands, which were covered in tall cordgrass, virgin timber, and thick underbrush, to the southeast from his high-ground perch.[37]

All the while, the Bay State colonel, who was older than almost all of his men, prepared to take a close look at the expanse of coastal lowlands, salt marshes, and the broad stretch of water—Pelham Bay and then Eastchester Bay farther south as they were adjacent to each other—that he and his around 750 Massachusetts troops had been assigned the kind of daunting challenge that might well have unnerved a less-determined brigade commander. With General Washington without a navy to stop an armada of British warships, the most powerful naval force in the world possessed the luxury of conducting amphibious landings of large numbers of troops at any point to the north. This undeniable fact was the exact reason why General Washington, demonstrating tactical wisdom in this heart-breaking campaign that had been nothing short of disastrous, had made one of his smartest decisions to send one of his most dependable lieutenants, Colonel Glover, and most versatile troops, especially for sea-based operations befitting the Continental Marines of that infant corps, in his army to closely watch Pelham Bay, an ideal landing site for the British and Hessians. The mostly seafarers from Marblehead of the Fourteenth Massachusetts Continental Regiment were a natural fit for meeting a seaborne operation of the enemy, as if they had been born for this all-important mission in the autumn of 1776.

With additional early October sunlight descending upon the autumn-hued land around Pell's Point and Pelham Bay's wide waters near the southern end of the Hutchinson River, Glover placed his eyeglass to his eye with the early morning's first visibility, which iron-ically was now nothing more than a routine precaution because there had been no sounds or hint of any enemy activity. With the sky on the low-lying eastern horizon finally beginning to lighten up, the col-onel then peered south toward the wide bay from where any British invading force would surely come, as he had reasoned, if Sir Howe was sufficiently wise to launch an amphibious strike as at Kip's Bay and Throgs Neck to once again catch Washington by surprise.

At the moment he peered south from the hilltop toward Pelham Bay, which now looked like a big, shimmering lake in the half-light of early morning, Colonel Glover, a tough and hardened man who did not shock easily, was stunned by what he saw looming before him. In fact, he now received the greatest shock of his life, because Pelham Bay was filled with the towering masts of seemingly countless British warships until it appeared that the entire bay was filled with a forest of tall trees—even more sailing ships than he had ever seen filling Marblehead Harbor.

As he explained with a great deal of understatement, which was one of Glover's personal trademarks: "I rose early in the morning and went on the hill with my glass, and discovered a number of ships in the Sound under way." Catching the Americans completely by surprise, General Howe's invasion of Westchester County north of Throgs Neck had already begun in the night. Colonel Glover was absolutely stunned by an incredible sight that must have taken his breath away. He had never seen such a sight in his life, because Pelham Bay was filled with an armada of Vice Admiral Howe's warships that seemed to have no end. The Marblehead colonel was now absolutely stunned upon spying so many British vessels lying in the tranquil waters of Pelham Bay to the south.

As throughout this campaign, General Howe had once again caught the Americans by surprise, having already landed his foremost troops on Pell's Point (known today as Rodman's Neck) at the peninsula's western side to gain the southern end of Shore Road, which led to Split Rock Road (then called Pell's Lane), which ascended north up the peninsula to the Boston Post Road. What Glover had just seen was nothing less than a full-scale invasion by Howe to gain a point north of Washington's army and trap and then destroy it, if unable to force its surrender to end America's resistance effort. To his credit, Howe's gaining of the element of surprise and Washington's rear so easily was masterful. Indeed, after having sailed north from Throgs Neck toward Pelham Bay with the benefit of a strong "wind [that] was now fresh at south-west," in General William Heath's words, the first British warships had pushed three miles north from Throgs Point, after having embarked thousands of troops from that strategic point at 2:00

a.m., in the crisp October darkness, after the British light infantry-men and grenadiers in scarlet coats had been awakened at 1:00 a.m. in the first phase of the secret invasion. This contingent of well-trained light troops was the initial wave that led the invasion force north by water toward the stillness of Pelham Bay. Indeed, at 3:00 a.m., the First Brigade of British troops and the Royal Scottish Highlanders had piled into another wave of flatboats at 6:00 a.m., while the chilly night's blackness had provided an ideal screen for a mighty invasion force. And only now with the first light of day, the arrival of an entire British invasion force—flat-bottom troop transports filled with thousands of men—had been revealed to Colonel Glover for the first time. Since his reeling army was now in the midst of a chaotic retreat north to White Plains, the fact that Washington had ordered no pickets or signalmen to man posts along the extensive shoreline had ensured that Glover received the surprise of his life, because he had gained no warning whatsoever.[38]

For such reasons, General Howe was obviously confident of success, feeling that he had finally landed sufficiently far north on his opponent's easternmost flank to trap Washington's entire army. In a matter-of-fact manner, he described the bold movement that had been masterful in so easily gaining the strategic advantage: "On the 18th, several corps re-embarked on flat boats, and passing round Frog's-Neck, [and headed toward] Pell's Point," which was reached without incident or obstruction, because nothing had been done to impede the British movement north by Washington.[39] In his journal, Thomas Sullivan, Forty-ninth Regiment of Foot, described how the flatboats had made good time during the stealthy push north in the darkness, "passing round Frog Neck, landing on Pell's Point, at the mouth of the Hutchinson's River, which joins the main-Land."[40]

But as the esteemed commander of the Fourteenth Continental Regiment—along with the Twenty-seventh Massachusetts Regiment under Colonel Israel Hutchinson, who had been born in Salem like Glover but in 1727—who had orchestrated the ferrying of nearly ten thousand of Washington's best troops from inevitable destruction off

Long Island and across the wide East River to Manhattan Island's safety on the foggy night of August 29–30 by the narrowest of margins, Glover was not unnerved by the stunning spectacle that Pelham Bay now presented to him. Nor did Glover panic from the sudden realization that he was now facing an entire British invasion that might decide America's fate like would have been the case with many brigade commanders on their own. Although it is not known, the imposing sight of the mighty British-Hessian invasion on his doorstep might well have initially taken Glover's breath away, which would have been fully justified.

In the tranquil waters of Pelham Bay to the south, the tall masts of British warships towered high, which made the wide bay look almost like a small city instead of a natural harbor in a remote part of Westchester County. Worst of all, Colonel Glover knew that these dark, menacing warships of General Howe's invasion force were escorting thousands of finely trained and well-equipped troops in the hope of entrapping and destroying Washington's entire army in a tactical masterstroke. And without defenses or artillery positioned around Pelham Bay, Glover realized that it would now be only a matter of time before large numbers of these highly disciplined troops would descend upon the American mainland for the first time in this campaign, because they could not be stopped.

General Howe planned to march swiftly inland to gain the strategic Boston Post Road and the town of Eastchester to then strike General Washington's army, which was in overall bad shape, just to the west, by taking the Eastchester Road that led west to strategic Kingsbridge. Washington's dispirited command was now strewn out for miles along the Albany Post Road, while steadily withdrawing north toward White Plains during a nightmarish retreat that had begun on the previous day. Clearly, this was a key crisis situation not only for Washington's army but also for the revolution, because the lives of both were now at stake. Wearing a scarlet uniform with immense pride like his Scottish heritage and feeling that an imminent decisive victory would now be relatively easy, Captain Frederick MacKenzie basked in General Howe's ambitious intentions that promised to not only end the campaign but also crush the intoxicating dream of an independent nation: "The grand point in view is certainly to beat and disperse [Washington's] army, which, if once effected, little more will remain to be done."[41]

After successive defeats, what little remained of Washington's army could hardly have been more vulnerable at this time. Glover realized that far more redcoats than he could count would now shortly gain the shore near the mouth of the Hutchinson River, where it entered Pelham Bay, with effortless ease and then they would march north up Split Rock Road, after the vast armada of troop transports unloaded thousands of troops with impunity. As at Long Island and at Throgs Neck, General Howe had once again caught the Americans napping, but this time he was even more determined to exploit his supreme advantage to the fullest, which was now greater than at any time in the past.

Again catching Washington by surprise was not only easy but all but inevitable once Howe had decided that outflanking the novice revolutionaries was the best possible tactical solution that called for moving farther north. Because General Washington possessed no navy on these waters around Manhattan Island and had stationed too few pickets along the shoreline to give a timely warning about Howe's next move north when he was in the midst of a confused retreat not far to the west, nothing could stop a British invasion force from landing at any point farther north in Westchester County. Howe had now grasped the golden opportunity.

Far from help of any kind, Glover and his tiny brigade of Bay Staters were on their own and the Marblehead commander naturally feared the worst if he and his band of men failed to rise to the occasion. As Glover, a mature man who was also a self-made one who had long relied on his well-honed instincts, wrote in a letter how "at this critical moment [I] looked around, but could see none [of the reinforcements and support necessary to halt a mighty invasion], they all being three miles from me."[42] But fortunately, Colonel Glover now possessed excellent top lieutenants in his four regimental commanders for the daunting challenge that lay ahead. Colonel Loammi Baldwin, who commanded the barely 225 men of the 26th Massachusetts Continental Regiment, could be counted upon to provide spirited resistance and tactical skills in the upcoming defensive effort, if he returned in time from a nearby private residence in Eastchester because of "being unwell," in the colonel's words, and spent the cool night recuperating. Glover possessed other fine regimental commanders in Colonel Joseph Read, who led the 264 men of the Thirteenth Massachusetts Continental Regiment, and Colonel William Shepard, who led 292 solders of the Third Massachusetts Continental Regiment.

By this time, one of Glover's top lieutenants had joined him on the hilltop. Without saying a word, Glover passed his eyeglass, which no doubt was a nautical instrument from his old seafaring days, to either Read or Shephard. One of these colonels had just arrived on the high ground at the break of dawn. Either one of these fine regimental commanders only had to take a quick look at the incredible sight of what appeared to be the entire Royal Navy now filling Pelham Bay to the brim. Consequently, nothing was said between the two astounded colonels. One of these trusty colonels, either Read or Shepard (Colonel William Baldwin was now abed sick), merely looked at Glover, who only nodded because these experienced leaders instinctively knew exactly what they now had to do under almost impossible circumstances and against the odds. To their credit, neither colonel thought a second about withdrawing before the massive onslaught to save their own skins and the lives of their men. Instead, they would fight to the finish if necessary. Glover and one of his top lieutenants, therefore, then dashed down the hill and back to the encampment on the hill's other side (a hidden strategic reserve on the west side of the high ground) to rally the four regiments of the Bay State brigade. Despite the odds, they were about to meet the invaders head-on by way of their own surprise attack to buy precious time for Washington, the entire Continental Army, and America, in the greatest of crisis situations.[43]

Clearly, under such disadvantageous circumstances, an officer of less ability and iron determination than Glover would have ordered a withdrawal in the face of such a mighty invasion. But Colonel Glover was not that kind of leader, because he was most of all every inch of a fighter when it came to a crisis situation of the first order. He immediately reasoned that he could neither wait for reinforcements or orders from headquarters, but must boldly act on his own in the manner that he deemed best in order to buy as much time as possible. The only reason that Washington's army would not be intercepted and destroyed was because of Glover's audacious decision to take the tactical offensive on his own on October 18.

General Washington Again Caught Napping

As if he did not already hold enough high cards in the strongest of hands against the inexperienced revolutionary army's commander who little knew how to play this kind of poker in a high-stakes game, General Howe possessed yet another advantage besides having achieved complete tactical surprise on October 18. To disguise the embarkation of thousands of troops from Throgs Point to the Pell's Point Peninsula to orchestrate his tactical masterstroke in a bid to end this war and Washington's upstart career, Howe had smartly created a masterful diversion that had proved effective in focusing the attention of not only General Washington but also other Continental leaders in the wrong direction. This aggressive demonstration by British troops came at the causeway near the town of Westchester, around three miles slightly southwest of Eastchester. Howe's clever diversion had caused Washington and other commanders, who had yet to ascertain that Howe had pushed farther north into the lower edge of the Long Island Sound, to believe that a serious offensive threat yet existed from Throgs Point on the morning of October 18.

When appraised of this surprising development, General William Heath led a Continental brigade from Valentine's Hill, which was located southwest of Eastchester about midway between Westchester and Eastchester, to meet the anticipated British advance along another causeway that linked Throgs Point to the mainland. When the reinforcing American brigade finally took position at the causeway's head, it was only then learned "that the whole British army were in motion and seemed to be moving towards the pass at the head of the creek."[44]

This advantageous strategic situation caused by Howe's clever diversion seemed so critical at the causeway that General Washington arrived on the scene in an attempt to ascertain if the entire British army was advancing west and farther inland. Washington ordered General Lee's (former Heath's)

> division formed ready for action, and to take such a position as might appear best calculated to oppose the enemy, should they attempt to land another body of troops on Morrisania [at the southern tip of Westchester County in the Bronx about halfway to the Hudson River, directly west of Throgs Nest, and about five miles southwest of Westchester], which he thought not improbable.[45]

Therefore, Washington yet expected an immediate threat from Throgs Point on October 18 because the army's northward withdrawal, just to the west, to White Plains had made the army even more vulnerable, while Howe began to land troops on the Pell's Point Peninsula that very morning. Most significant, this clever demonstration by the tactically astute Howe and perceived threat to the southwest guaranteed that Glover and his band of men would not receive support, assistance, or advice on the army's far eastern flank for all of October 18, just as Howe had planned. For a wide variety of reasons, consequently, Colonel Glover was even more on his own to do or die than he could possibly imagine, when he now possessed perhaps the war's most impossible mission to date: somehow thwarting the invasion of thousands of British and Hessian soldiers in the rear of Washington's retreating army, whose offensive capabilities had been vastly diminished, after so many defeats, withdrawals, and widespread desertions. Indeed, because of Howe's tactical wizardry,

Washington and his commanders believed that what was happening on the Pell's Point Peninsula was only a feint and that the real threat was at Morrisania, located directly west of Throgs Neck and just across the Harlem River from Manhattan Island. Clearly, Washington and his top commanders once again had been badly fooled about Howe's well-conceived strategy for invading the New York mainland.[46]

As mentioned, the main Continental Army was now busily engaged in a chaotic retreat north from Harlem Heights to White Plains to escape: basically, a noose that Howe hoped to tighten and Washington hoped to slip out of before it was too late. General Charles Lee was now in charge of the long withdrawal to White Plains, where high ground offered safety. He was busily attempting to protect the reeling army's movement north up the Albany Post Road as much as possible by erecting a network of earthworks on high ground at White Plains to shelter the ragtag army from harm.[47]

This tactical situation and steady withdrawal north largely explained why Generals Washington and Lee, both focused on the disorganized retreat, would send no support to Glover on October 18. By the time that Washington would have received information about what was happening at Pell's Point and then took some kind of action if he decided to do so, it would be too late. Consequently, there existed a variety of reasons for Glover not to expect any assistance because army leadership was focused on the long withdrawal north and because his immediate superior (division commander Lee) was headquartered at Valentine's Hill, which was located several miles away slightly to the southwest. For a host of reasons, therefore, General Lee would fail to dispatch "any orders, or sent any troops to Glover's support, but spent the day inactively," leaving "Glover and the brave men under his command" completely on their own to do or die in one of the most important situations and battles of the American Revolution.[48]

Meanwhile, as revealed in a letter from one of Washington's soldiers, who was caught by surprise like everyone else by the massive British and Hessian landing at Pell's Point: "While we were making this grand movement [toward White Plains and] into the country, the enemy were not idle; having collected their troops from all quarters at Frog's point, and on board their ships, which were ranged along shore, off against the point, and opposite East-chester," and had then pushed to Pell's Point unopposed.[49]

On this Friday of destiny when so much was at stake, Glover understood that it would now be up to him and his small brigade of only four Massachusetts regiments to somehow halt Howe's mighty invasion and that everything would be based upon his own personal judgment and decision-making. But, of course, this tactical objective would be impossible, because the Marblehead colonel commanded only 750 troops of an understrength Continental brigade that would not be reinforced. However, Colonel Glover was going to try his best regardless of the cost. Of course, this unnerving reality now presented Glover with his greatest challenge to date and one that could not have been more daunting. To his credit, Glover never lost his nerve. However, he was now left to readjust to the crisis situation to the best of his ability. Not a soldier, scout, or officer had arrived in camp to give Colonel Glover any scrap of intelligence that even hinted that a powerful British invasion force was headed his way and about to land on Westchester County soil and he was now determined to do his best.

Located on Shore Road, a small "outpost near the shore" of Pelham Bay, one or two untrained soldiers, including Abel De Veau, of the local New York militia had no time to give warning to Glover, who by then had already seen the invasion armada in Pelham Bay from the grassy hilltop. To conceal it from enemy eyes and as noted, Colonel Glover had prudently set up his encampment southeast of Eastchester behind a hill as a strategic reserve. In consequence, he had hoped that an advanced sentinel or picket of the handful of New York militiamen on Pelham Bay's shore would sound a timely warn-ing if they had viewed British warships entering the bay. But the stealthy nature of the British landing in the night had negated the meager advance warning system, setting the stage for Glover's star-tling discovery of a mighty armada's arrival to give him the shock of his life.

After firing only two token shots at the first British troops who boldly stepped ashore on the American mainland—the west side of the Pell's Point Peninsula—for the first time and after British warships began a bombardment on the shore near where the Hutchinson River entered Pelham Bay on the north, these Westchester County militiamen then fled back north up Split Rock Road and toward Glover's encampment west of the Hutchinson River. Not trusting the inadequate warning system and as noted, Glover had already taken the initiative to gain the nearby hilltop and take a look at Pelham Bay for himself. Clearly, the colonel was not taking any chances because too much was at stake for not only Washington's army but also for America to base everything on a handful of New York militiamen doing their duty, as they had been ordered: a most prudent, adroit decision by Glover.

After all, in such a no-win situation, this farsighted Marblehead colonel could not afford to rely on anything or anyone other than his own abilities, if he was to succeed in his crucial mission of somehow delaying the massive invasion force and buying precious time to ensure the safe withdrawal of Washington's army to White Plains. The morning of October 18 was one of the few instances in the annals of American military history when the commander of an isolated task force on his own decided to confront a large-scale invasion with far too few troops, after having actually first spied the arrival of the invasion force himself.

It is not known if Colonel Glover was a student of ancient history, especially Greek history, because of his humble origins. However, if he had read about the dramatic showdown at Thermopylae between East and West at some point, then Glover would have readily identified with the analogy of his unenviable situation with the arrival of the mighty Persian invasion of "barbarians," as the Greeks called them, under King Xerxes in 480 BCE, which had been faced by only three hundred Spartans under King Leonidas at Thermopylae. Before they made their famous last stand in defending the strategic Thermopylae Pass to protect the Greek city-states that needed time to make preparations for meeting the invaders, the relative handful of Spartans of the king's bodyguard had watched in awe when first spying the size of the great Persian fleet. Like King Leonidas 2,500 years ago in a comparable no-win situation when he had to buy time, Glover had also felt much like the ancient Spartans when they had viewed the immense size of Xerxes's massive fleet—the largest the world had ever seen—when the colonel knew that he also had to buy precious time.[50]

But not all was lost. The farsighted Colonel Glover had wisely ordered the handful of New York militiamen on Pelham Bay to do something that was especially crucial because it was calculated to buy time: to cut down trees to impede passage of British artillery along Shore Road and then Split Rock Road while retiring north up the peninsula. Of course, the thoughtful colonel had already made sure that these militiamen carried axes with them to perform this critical job of impeding Howe's advance inland just in case the enemy landed. As revealed in the journal of a young redcoat: "The Enemy fired but two shots during the time of [our troops made their] landing, and then ran away from the shore with great Precipitation, cutting down the Trees across the Road as they went."[51]

The fallen trees lying across the road would have to be removed by the invaders, which meant that they would have to obtain axes and other equipment from the boats which would take time. Glover had already managed to buy precious time, while also ensuring that the British could not initially use their abundant artillery because of numerous trees felled across the road, while allowing his Massachusetts infantrymen a chance to initially meet the invaders on more even terms without facing massive firepower. For the first time this morning, Glover was certainly heartened when he first heard the echo of axes striking tree trunks, telling him that he had gained more time. It is not known but the colonel might have smiled to himself upon hearing the sweetest sound that he could have now heard at this time, which was the buying of precious time as he had envisioned with clarity.

However, because of their advanced position on the army's extreme eastern flank, Glover now realized as never before that he and his small band of men were entirely on their own and that they would have to make the best of a very bad situation. No doubt having given Glover an initial sinking feeling upon first sighting the vast armada, a mere handful of Massachusetts men had been left to fend for themselves as best they could, because of the lack of Washington's foresight in anticipating that Pelham Bay was Howe's next target when it was the most logical next move, when the reeling American army was most vulnerable during its lengthy retreat. Now alone on the army's far eastern flank, Glover and his brigade of four regiments were in an isolated position around half a dozen miles east of General Washington's withdrawing army slowly making its way to the new position at White Plains far north along the Bronx River, which flowed through Westchester County about midway between the Hudson and Long Island Sound.

Colonel Glover was now well beyond supporting distance of the Continental division of General Lee, who commanded the withdrawal to White Plains. Glover's immediate superior, General Lee, was located some three miles to the west, or rear, at his headquarters on Valentine's Hill and with Massachusetts-born John Nixon's New England Bay State Continental brigade (the Third, Fifth, Sixth, Seventh, and Eighth Massachusetts Continental Regiments) of his division. During this emergency and crisis situation when absolutely no extra time remained, such a dire situation meant that Washington's units were too far distant to the west for Colonel Glover to request or even to receive specific orders from Generals Lee or Washington now that he was alone with an undersized brigade to face a mighty British and Hessian invasion, when he had to respond immediately to the growing threat because time was of the essence.[52]

Colonel Glover understood that support from General Lee was desperately needed for any realistic chance of stopping—and perhaps even slowing to buy precious time—Howe's invasion from pouring inland like a flood. At this time, Glover could count on only around 750 troops, which was closer to the strength of a newly formed Continental regiment than an entire Continental brigade of

New Englanders, because of the heavy attrition and spread of disease during this campaign.

But Glover felt somewhat optimistic despite the no-win situation. Again, Colonel Glover's determination to succeed against the odds only grew greater when the challenge was the greatest like now on the morning of October 18. Fortunately, he commanded some of Washington's finest troops, which they had repeatedly demonstrated throughout the course of this grueling campaign, while so many other troops had failed the commander in chief, as at Kip's Bay. By far the premier regiment, or the shock troops, of the Massachusetts Brigade was the Fourteenth Massachusetts Continental Regiment, even though its strength had been reduced to only 180 soldiers by this time, which made it the brigade's smallest regiment. When the Continental Congress had designated the formation of Continental regiments during the autumn of 1775, it prescribed regiments to consist of 728 men in the ranks. However, the high-quality and feisty fighting spirit of the crack fighting men of Colonel Glover's regiment made up for numbers and other shortages.[53]

This undeniable factor was all-important, because the strength of the Fourteenth Massachusetts Continental Regiment was now only one-fourth of what it should have been, especially in a crisis situation in which every man counted and every musket was needed on the firing line. On October 12, the regiment consisted of eight companies, which were led by Captains William Courtis (senior captain), James Grant, John Glover Jr. (the colonel's son), Nathaniel Bond, Joseph Swasey, William R. Lee, Moses Brown, and Gilbert Warner Speakman. The Fourteenth Massachusetts was one of the few regiments of Washington's army not cursed with plagues of desertion, because its members were more determined and committed to the cause of liberty to an inordinate degree.

Other Bay State regiments of Glover's brigade was almost as thoroughly reduced by disease, battlefield deaths, and desertions as the Fourteenth Continental Regiment. Colonel Baldwin's Twenty-sixth Massachusetts was the second-most-depleted unit with only 226 men, which was followed by the Thirteenth Massachusetts, under the command of Colonel Joseph Read, who had been born in 1732 at Uxbridge, Massachusetts and fought at Lexington and Concord, with only 264 soldiers in the ranks. Regardless of exact numbers, Colonel Glover simply did not have enough men for the crucial mission assigned to him, but that fact failed to make any difference to him.

Do or Die in Westchester County

Consequently, Colonel Glover would now have to accomplish virtually the impossible in meeting the formidable task of somehow halting or slowing the invasion of the thousands of British and Hessian troops who were now pouring into Westchester County. But Glover felt that he had no choice because he knew that this was shaping up to be a day of destiny. He, therefore, eagerly accepted the most daunting of challenges without hesitation. Only one tactical solution in this crisis situation entered the mind of Glover when he was on his own to do or die: the time-proven axiom that the best tactical defense was the tactical offensive.

Naturally aggressive, tough-minded like his mariners from mostly Marblehead, Glover understood instinctively that he had to make a steadfast defensive stand on the army's extreme eastern flank against impossible odds to buy as much time as possible. Most of all, he planned to take the tactical offensive at the first opportunity, which was always the best defense in a no-win, crisis situation. Such an audacious tactical decision came easily and naturally to Glover, reflecting his never-say-die personality and positive attitudes about not only war, but also about what it took to survive in life, including on the turbulent high seas. Unlike so many other Continental field-grade officers and to mirror his self-made man status in Marblehead, Glover was the rare kind of commander who did not need any specific orders or instructions from either Washington or Lee to know what he had to do and what was best for meeting this crisis situation, when so much was at stake: an almost businesslike and workmanlike attitude that was all about getting the job done on land or sea as best as he could regardless of the circumstances, including in the most adverse situation as now presented to him on October 18.

During the long fishing expeditions for cod every season from Marblehead, even the worst Atlantic storms had long failed to cause intrepid mariners to return back to their home port before reaping the rich, bountiful natural harvest of the Grand Banks, the world's greatest and most productive fishery. Such stoic determination was a duty-bound obligation and issue of simple survival, because Marblehead families had to be fed, and incomes from fishing had to be earned despite the risk, because no other means of subsistence, including farming, existed on the rocky Atlantic coast of Massachusetts.

And now on the cool morning of October 18, the situation was still not all different in fundamental ways for Glover, because there was a job to be done and it needed to be accomplished as expertly as possible and at all costs. Like during a lengthy fishing expedition to the Grand Banks hundreds of miles from Marblehead, Glover was about to boldly take the initiative because he actually had little choice and it was now an issue of simple survival for an army and a nation. In addition, there was now no time to receive permission or orders from Generals Washington or Lee to either make a defensive stand or attack the invaders in a desperate attempt to slow the invasion. In such a situation, less-capable brigade commanders would have hesitated or have been rendered impotent without having any specific orders until it was too late, allowing thousands of British to march inland unopposed and ever closer to Washington's reeling army.

But not the irrepressible Colonel Glover. He hesitated for not a moment and immediately flew into action, despite facing impossible odds of around seven to one. The very last that he considered doing was to order a tactical retreat when by-the-book leaders, like General Charles Lee, almost would have done so under the same circumstances. However, Glover, a natural and experienced problem-solver who embraced challenges, was very different. And it was such rare qualities that endeared the Marblehead colonel to Washington and the thousands of thankful men who had escaped capture or death on Long Island, because of the strenuous efforts of the mariners who had ensured their escape from a death trap. Quite simply, Glover was cut entirely from a much different cloth compared to Washington's top lieutenants, especially those scheming men who were political players and best suited to be desk officers: a reality that guaranteed that he would rise to any and every occasion, especially on October 18, 1776. To bestow a measure of comfort, Washington could depend upon the resourceful Marblehead colonel to do whatever was necessary regardless of the situation, knowing that Colonel Glover would do his very best.

Indeed, Glover was as individualistic and unorthodox as the rugged land from which he hailed and the rolling sea upon which he had long roved in providing for his family year after year, reflecting his character and personal values that were hallmarks of his distinctive fishing community situated on a picturesque harbor. Out of necessity and habit, he always thought for himself in an innovative manner and relied on his own resourcefulness and ingenuity, while making his own decisions because they were usually the best ones available during the most difficult circumstances: lifelong habits forged out of years of hardship and adversity, including from the challenging seafaring experience. If anyone could buck the traditional eighteenth-century ways of fighting and the conventional military mindset so detrimental to success during this campaign by hastily improvising to create a better way of fighting on the fly in a crisis situation by using a rare blend of savvy and ingenuity, it was the ever-resourceful Colonel Glover.

Indeed, these heightened qualities made Glover perhaps the most independent-minded and resourceful brigade commander in Washington's army to ensure that he was absolutely indispensable to the commander in chief: when needed the most, personal characteristics that were destined to rise to the fore on October 18 like the proverbial phoenix to pay immense dividends in a crisis situation in which the army's life was at stake. To his credit and revealing that he was a good judge of character, General Washington's faith in Glover could not have been better placed, representing one of his most shrewd, insightful judgments based on the moral fiber and overall quality of this tough-minded New Englander during this most ill-fated of campaigns.

Time was now of the essence, and this key factor was the crucial element upon which the fate of America precariously rested. And, of course, Colonel Glover realized as much from the beginning, and ever since having first sighted the armada of warships of the invasion fleet filling the placid waters of Pelham Bay. Embracing the daunting challenge, he would now act out of a desperate sense of urgency necessary with sound judgment and wisdom like the Hebrew King Solomon long ago, because this was the ultimate emergency situation. Somehow a powerful British invasion had to be slowed as long as possible and Glover was going to do his best, as General Washington knew he would.

As mentioned, Glover's top priority was now to somehow buy as much precious time for Washington's army as possible. The fact that he had previously ordered trees to be felled by the New York militiamen across Shore Road and Split Rock Road was a very good start, negating an immediate swift advance of the enemy's artillery without having lost a man. However, to really slow the opponent, a price in blood had to be paid, as Glover realized. Most of all, this situation meant that he would have to fight as long as he could against impossible odds with almost zero chances for success, sacrificing the lives of his men and perhaps even his own to purchase additional time so that an army and new nation could live: an especially daunting prospect and the most impossible mission yet faced by a Continental colonel and a single brigade of fighting men during the New York Campaign. Consequently, Glover now would have to formulate a well-designed tactical plan of an extremely innovative nature to fully exploit his few strengths, because the overall situation on October 18 excessively magnified his considerable weaknesses and vulnerabilities.

Only one slim chance now existed to slow Howe's march inland. And the most drastic of tactical options that existed for Colonel Glover now called for hitting the foremost British troops as soon as possible in the hope of somehow blunting the momentum of the amphibious invasion in a desperate bid to steal the initiative that had been so easily won by the surprise amphibious landing. Therefore, Glover understood that he would have to strike a blow as soon as possible, because he instinctively knew that the best defense with a small force in a dire situation was a bold offense. And this meant meeting the British invasion force head-on with what he had available in the most desperate of situations. And Colonel Glover was just the kind of man—hard-nosed, stubborn, and tough as nails—to lead such an audacious strike in a seemingly no-win situation. Most of all and as the colonel fully realized, he had to take the offensive immediately, before even more of General Howe's troops poured ashore and up the peninsula to gain a permanent toehold on the New York mainland.

What was now at stake was not as much the lives of 750 soldiers of the Massachusetts brigade, but the very life of General Washington's army and the revolution itself. In this regard, the lives of Glover and his men were insignificant because they had been put into a truly dire position and emergency situation, which now made them expendable for the greater good of the Continental Army and the infant republic. Without stopping or even slowing the British invasion force at or around Pell's Point, then quite possibly General Washington's army, a ragged mob of around thirteen thousand men now withdrawing slowly north and in disorganized fashion toward White Plains for nearly a dozen miles, would be destroyed in the midst of a messy retreat from Harlem Heights and other strategic points on Manhattan Island.

The British-Hessian Tide Continues to Pour Inland

Under the cover of darkness and even before the first light of day, scores of small wooden flatboats—the day's best landing craft—had already unloaded a good many troops on the New York mainland just north of Pell's Point. By this time, the first British troops had already begun to move north by the time that Glover had seen the mighty armada from the hilltop. This landing site was well-chosen, allowing the first redcoats and Hessians to pour out of their flatboats and onto the empty shoreline of Pelham Bay. This perfect landing site was not at the very southern end of the Pell's Point Peninsula in Hutchinson's Bay, or Eastchester Bay, which lay below, or south of, Pelham Bay, but farther north and farther up the peninsula's west side adjacent to Pelham Bay. The unopposed landing took place on the peninsula's west side near the mouth of the Hutchinson River, which was sometimes called Eastchester Creek. All the while, seemingly endless numbers of flatboats continued to spill their colorful contents from the mass of British warships on the west side of Pelham Bay, where the roads—first Shore Road and then Split Rock Road—could be quickly gained by the invaders for the march up, or north, the peninsula to then secure the high ground and a permanent grip on the mainland. A small mill stood along the bay at this point. Westchester County farmers had long transported their goods along this road, known locally as Shore Road, to the gristmill and then for shipment down, or south, the East River to the merchants of New York City.

Escorted in guardian fashion by the British warships of Admiral Howe, hundreds of the flat-bottomed boats—the British secret weapon that had bestowed them with the tactical advantage of maneuverability and guaranteed the easiest of landings on the shore—had already been used successfully in having transported British troops during the amphibious landings on Staten Island, Long Island, at Kip's Bay and Throgs Point. Of course, this vital advantage of maneuverability on the waters had been the key to the sparkling British successes around New York City throughout this campaign, ensuring that Washington had been repeatedly caught by surprise. And now, this key advantage had been used once again in masterful fashion by General Howe, who demonstrated his full appreciation of the principles of the art of amphibious warfare in landing on the Pell's Point Peninsula.[54]

Howe described how he "landed at Pell's Point, at the mouth of the Hutchinson river, after which the main body crossed the mouth of that river to the same place, advanced immediately" along Shore Road in a bid to gain higher ground along Split Rock Road (Pell's Lane) and a permanent toehold on the New York mainland.[55] Clearly, General Howe held all the advantages and possessed no weaknesses whatsoever in this winner-take-all game. To achieve the crucial element of surprise like at Long Island and Kip's Bay, this bold amphibious landing had first begun while Glover's troops and the Marblehead colonel had slept peacefully in the Eastchester encampment seemingly without a care in the world. Therefore, the initial advanced troops, the fast-moving light infantrymen, or grenadiers, of General Howe's invasion force had already moved north from Pelham Bay even before Colonel Glover had ascertained that a seemingly endless number of British warships had filled Pelham Bay: an almost incredible failure of American intelligence-gathering.

Some time had passed before the increasingly light of early morning fully revealed to Glover the full vastness of the invasion force, which might have been reminded him about when the ancient Spartans of King Leonidas had first looked upon the massive armada of King Xerxes, who commanded the largest army from across Persia and ever seen on European soil, before the Battle of Thermopylae in 480 BCE during a heroic age like which many revolutionaries, who were imbued with Enlightenment ideology, now viewed their righteous struggle against England. Glover never forgot the most unnerving sight that he had ever seen: "upwards of two hundred sail, all manned and formed in four grand divisions" in preparation for the conquest of America. By that time when the first faint sunlight of morning reflected off the waters to make them sparkle, it had seemed to him as if all of the blue expanse of Pelham Bay had been overflowing with British warships and transports as far as the eye could see. Colonel Glover had prepared himself for action, knowing that Howe planned to land "several corps" of his army right under his nose.[56]

But most menacing of all for Glover had been the sight of hundreds of flat-bottom boats with their sides reinforced with planking for protection against musket fire—a most effective and innovative landing craft now full of experienced troops. These menacing-looking flat-bottomed boats, overflowing with British and Hessian solders, continued to be rowed by strong-armed British seamen all the way to the shoreline, where they continued to land large numbers of soldiers without meeting any opposition, in successive waves.[57]

All the while, this mighty flotilla of seemingly countless flatboats disembarked thousands of infantrymen from Great Britain and Germany on the sandy shore. As Colonel Glover realized, this massive tide of men in red and blue uniforms coming ashore unimpeded consisted of some of the most experienced and best disciplined soldiers in General Howe's army. For these invaders, the colorful sight of the massive invasion that could not be stopped was intoxicating. An infantryman from the green hills of Ireland, Thomas Sullivan, described the sensation gained from the imposing sight of the Royal Navy's might that he had experienced during this campaign: "The whole Army was ready together in Flat-boats, the sight of which was very beautiful and delightful to any English soldier or Subject, to see near twenty four Thousand men ready to land in a moment."[58]

From the beginning, these hardened professional soldiers from Britain and Germany had tasted nothing but victory on American soil, never knowing a single setback, and they were now determined to continue their amazing winning streak in Westchester County. Another Irishman in King George III's pay, Captain William Glanville Evelyn, was one of those fine officers who had already come ashore, touching the soil of America's mainland for the first time. A proud member of the Fourth Royal Regiment, he embodied the overconfidence and sense of invincibility that existed among the members of General Howe's invading force.

Like so many British and German soldiers in Howe's command who were fully justified in their unbounded confidence after what they had witnessed throughout the course of the New York Campaign,

Captain Evelyn held nothing but contempt for the American "rabble" in arms. This longtime prevalent attitude had first stemmed from his experiences in having faced untrained American militia, which had so often failed to rise to the challenge, during the French and Indian War. After all, the colonial fighting man was a citizen-soldier who compared most unfavorably with British professionals. In a long letter to his father, for instance, the dashing, young captain from the Emerald Isle explained: "I believe there does not exist so great a set of rascals and poltroons" than the Americans.[59] And on April 23, 1775, in yet another letter, Evelyn denounced the rustics in rebellion as "Yankey scoundrels" at a time when Yankee usually referred to New Englanders by both friend and foe—a fact certainly not lost to Colonel Glover and his men, who were determined to overturn the tarnished reputation of New England soldiers stained at Kip's Bay. The handsome captain from the Green Isle across the sea was convinced without a doubt that the "rebels are the most absolute cowards on the face of the earth."[60]

Additionally, Captain Evelyn, now leading a light company of highly disciplined grenadiers in pushing north up Split Rock Road, believed beyond a shadow of a doubt that the Americans in arms were "the most despicable Enemy" and "the greatest cowards" in the world. Like so many soldiers in General Howe's army, both Hessians and British, the young Irishman was about to pay a high price at Pell's Point for his arrogance and utter contempt for his opponent before the sun set on his early autumn day in Westchester County, because they were about to meet some of the best troops in the Continental Army under the most talented and versatile brigade commander in Washington's army.[61]

Never in this campaign for possession of New York were prospects brighter for British success than now when Howe had finally landed sufficiently north above Washington's army to trap and destroy it. All that Howe had to do was to march west to gain strategic Kingsbridge at the northern tip of Manhattan Island to trap a portion of the Continental Army on Manhattan Island and also to hit Washington's army in retreat on its eastern flank. All the while, General Howe's great invasion and amphibious landing went as planned and without meeting any obstacles except for the trees that had been felled across the Shore Road and then the Split Rock Road, which led north, by the New York militiamen. For hours, confident enemy troops continued to pour inland like a red and blue flow of ants that were too many to count. Because the Pell's Point Peninsula was actually part of the mainland, Howe now faced no bottleneck, created by either geography or American troops, at the landing place like at Throgs Neck. And now because of still another massive American failure in the art of intelligence-gathering, "nor would there be a large force [only Glover's brigade] to stop Howe from knifing inland to strike at straggling American columns" not far to the west along the Albany Post Road near the Hudson River.[62]

In consequence, it seemed as if Glover and his tiny Massachusetts brigade did not have a prayer on this cool morning, and that they were now on the verge of being destroyed. But these were some very good fighting men, and they had a chance to succeed in their most dangerous of missions partly because they so passionately believed in the great dream of America and the promise of independence and they were led by an exceptional brigade commander. Despite the small number of the Massachusetts brigade members, such formidable challenges only inspired, rather than deflated, the resolve and fighting spirit of one of the toughest colonels in Washington's army, the diminutive Glover, and his men. As if still a captain at sea who had no choice but to weather a severe north Atlantic storm like so often in the past, the colonel now embraced the most formidable of challenges almost without thinking.

In fact and as noted, Glover's determination only grew with the heightened danger and risks. Indeed, the colonel was at his best when the odds against success were the stiffest, which revealed that he was a true contrarian by nature. In a striking paradox, out of the ashes of one miserable defeat and gloomy retreat after another during the New York Campaign would shortly emerge a tactical masterpiece of Glover's own creation at this remote location in Westchester County.

Fortunately, in depending upon his own abilities and not counting on the judgments and dictates of superiors who were out of touch with the situation, Colonel Glover had quite a few tactical tricks of his own up his sleeve. This resourceful Marblehead colonel's tactical innovation and cleverness were about to come to a great surprise to Howe, who had become the master at repeatedly surprising Washington and his generals, especially on the morning of October 18.

Rallying to the Beating of the Drums in Westchester County

Of course, Glover had been severely sobered, to say the least, by the realization that a major British invasion was in the process of descending upon Westchester County in overwhelming might. Colonel Glover, however, simply ignored the fact that he possessed too few troops and too little time to stop the invasion that had caught everyone by surprise, deciding that he would do the best he could under impossible circumstances. A positive thinker, he took no notice of any dark omens or portents as would have an ancient Roman in a comparable situation, because he was a man on a mission and an extremely important one. Colonel Glover was determined to undertake the desperate attempt to slow down the juggernaut as much as possible, taking immediate action in the hope of somehow reversing the day's fortunes. To spread the alarm and as mentioned, Glover had almost immediately raced down the slope from the top of the hill to arouse the quiet encampment of Massachusetts men.

Not long thereafter, drummer boys, who had yet to shave, soon sounded the call to arms. The beating of the long roll brought the Massachusetts soldiers to life. They spilled out of the neat rows of white tents amid a field covered with autumn grass that had already turned brown. Every Continental soldier of these four Massachusetts regiments, consisting of seasoned men who represented not only the legacy of the frontier democracy like in the western Massachusetts hills but also the seafaring world of the east coast, knew that the steady cadence of the beating drum called for assembling on the double and rushing into formation. Without speaking, these veterans hurriedly pulled on clothes, strapped on accouterments, wooden canteens, and leather cartridge boxes. Men spilled out of their canvas tents, only a few at first, then in greater numbers with each passing minute, with everyone moving as quickly as possible. They then grabbed their flint-lock muskets from the long row of neat stacks that were aligned before white tents and hustled into formation as they had practiced so often in the past.

All the while, Glover and other Bay State officers barked out orders for their men to prepare to march in preparation for meeting the enemy on Westchester County soil. With the British invasion of the Pell's Point Peninsula underway and with the foremost British and Hessian troops meeting no opposition of any kind in pushing steadily north and toward the higher ground to secure a toehold on the New York mainland, the Massachusetts soldiers knew that there was no time to waste. Of course, there was now no time to cook breakfast and eat a morning meal, which caused some disgruntlement among these hungry fighting men, who knew that they were facing a crisis situation.

As if once again homespun minute-men in civilian clothes back in their home communities across Massachusetts only last year when some of these citizen-soldiers had rallied to severely punish the British retreat from Concord, hundreds of Glover's soldiers prepared to meet the hated professional soldiers, who had invaded the American main-land for the first time. But the Bay State men now had no way of knowing that they were about to engage the most detested opponent of all, the Hessians from Germany. On the double, meanwhile, the veteran soldiers continued to hurriedly fall into line to face their great-est battlefield challenge to date, while knowing that Howe's army was in the process of landing not far from their tented encampment.

Within minutes, around 750 of Glover's men had assembled to meet the first successful British offensive, whose members were steadily moving north up the Pell's Point Peninsula as if nothing in the world could stop them, on the American mainland. Glover was now acting on his own without orders from General Washington or anyone else, which only fueled his determination to succeed against the odds. Most of all, this was going to be Colonel Glover's battle, and it would be entirely in his capable hands, just as he liked it. With time critical because the advance elements of British and Hessians continued to swarm into Westchester County, Colonel Glover wrote of the critical situation while he was hurrying his soldiers into formation: "without orders [I] turned out the brigade I have the honor to command, and very luckily for us I did" as soon as possible. But in truth, luck would have nothing to do with Glover's upcoming achievements, and he was only being modest. Without a professional military education before the war because of his humble origins and the fact that his life had been primarily devoted to peacetime pursuits, Glover was once again relying on common sense and his own well-honed instincts—which had paid dividends for him and his men so often in the past—to face a formidable, if not impossible, challenge on his own. Colonel Glover was destined to demonstrate considerable tactical insights and abilities far beyond his peers and which were extremely rare in Washington's army at this stage of the war.

Almost as soon as the New Englanders formed into a lengthy line in a grassy field before the neat rows of tents aligned just west of the hill and the Hutchinson River, Glover ordered his men into a tight marching formation just like they had practiced hundreds of times at Marblehead. Aligned in column, the Massachusetts boys were in high spirits and eager for action to prove their value to one and all. After all, these were hardened veterans who not only knew how to fight but also relished a good clash with this "wicked enemy" and the "butchers belonging to the tyrant of Great Britain," who they viewed as attempting to deprive them and their families of God-given liberties and freedoms. Some of the more jaunty Continentals wore sprigs of evergreen in their cocked hats attached next to revolutionary cockades, which revealed the fighting spirit and esprit de corps that still existed in Glover's brigade, despite all of the past defeats and setbacks.[63]

Hatred of the enemy, especially the hired mercenaries from Germany, fueled the fighting spirit of the Massachusetts soldiers on this day of destiny. A young British soldier from Ireland, Roger Lamb, had been early amazed how: "The people of New England appeared to indulge a deadly hatred against the British [and] rejoiced at any occasion to gratify it."[64] While this observation was true, a greater reality was emphasized by a Maryland politician in a letter when he explained the situation that now applied to Colonel Glover and his men: "It is our Duty, however, to struggle against the tide of adversity, and to exert ourselves with vigour . . . We are not to expect the purchase our Liberties at a cheaper rate than other nations have done" throughout history.[65]

Glover's aggressiveness and the upcoming dramatic confrontation on this early morning in Westchester County would present the Massachusetts men with ample opportunity to inflict as much harm upon the enemy as possible to fulfill their most crucial mission of saving Washington's army. In preparation for meeting the greatest challenge of their lives, the Bay State soldiers' cartridge boxes at their sides were crammed full of paper cartridges that fit tightly in wooden slots. Ironically, some round lead balls, with charges of black powder, that were inside these paper cartridges possessed symbolic meanings, even though those exact origins were most likely unknown to Glover's soldiers at this time. Indeed, the primary source of this lead supply of Washington's men had been cast into more than forty thousand round balls at Ridgefield, Connecticut. Some of this supply came from the lead gutters and downspouts of the houses of New York City, but it primarily derived from the huge, gilded lead equestrian statue of King George III on Bowling Green at the southern tip of Manhattan. This massive statue had been torn down by the city's patriots on July 9, 1776, the memorable day that General Washington had ordered the inspiring words of the Declaration of Independence to be read to the Continental troops to explain exactly why they were fighting for their infant country. So short was Washington's army on supplies of lead shot that they had been early forced to melt down all available lead and pewter, including plates used on the dinner table.[66]

In addition, Colonel Glover almost certainly had already taken the wise precaution of ensuring that the wooden canteens of his soldiers were filled with good fresh water from a nearby spring before his men had gone to sleep on the night of October 17. This was but one sage precaution made by the forward-thinking colonel to ensure that the entire brigade would be ready to march and engage the enemy on a moment's notice, if an invasion force had suddenly come ashore. Soldiers could not fight hour after hour on a hot day—this mid-October in Westchester County would be hot by early afternoon when yet blessed with delightful Indian summer weather—for long without fresh water, when so much water, including the Hutchinson River where it entered Pelham Bay, was tidal, brackish, and salty. Long Island Sound and the grassy marshes surrounding it offered only salt water, which Glover already realized from his familiarity with the Essex County, Massachusetts, coast and he had acted accordingly.[67]

Most of all, Colonel Glover felt confident in the fighting prowess and overall superior quality of his tough Continental troops and for good reason. Like their commander, the men of the mostly Marblehead regiment possessed the uncanny ability to arise to the challenge during crisis situations, which had been recently seen during the miracle nighttime evacuation from the Long Island trap. Friday October 18 would be no different, although the challenge was now even greater this time, because the stakes could not have been higher. Even under a host of disadvantageous circumstances of an impossible situation, this firm conviction that the colonel held in the superiority of his fighting men, who were almost all younger than him, encouraged Glover that the likelihood of at least some degree of success could be reaped this morning despite the odds.

However, Colonel Glover was much less confident about the combat prowess of the other troops of Washington's army at this time compared to what he knew his men could accomplish. Prophetically, in a no-nonsense October 7 letter to his mother Tabitha, written barely eleven days before the decisive showdown in Westchester County,

Glover had complained about the disturbing reality that existed for Washington's army, which was simply

> no match for the enemy in the open field; but at present we dare not meet them there, our army being composed of flying Camp, four months Levy men, and one month Militia, who are always uneasy and cannot go through the fatigue and hardships, which soldiers are necessarily called to, like those troops [like his Continentals] that have been seasoned to it. We have a few old Regiments, if detached by themselves, I believe would do honour to their Country, [which included the four regiments of his undersized brigade of Bay Staters].[68]

In this estimation, Glover would prove most prophetic on this autumn day in Westchester County. And this was despite the fact that he now possessed only a small "detached" brigade in an independent assignment and mission far beyond supporting distance of the main army in a chaotic retreat and his superiors in the face of a mighty invasion, which was an impossible situation that afforded this enterprising colonel exactly what he needed to excel because he was entirely free to implement the key to success: tactical flexibility and an unrestricted opportunity to conduct this upcoming battle as he saw fit in a highly innovative and original manner, while continuing to prove that he was the ultimate problem-solver with well-honed tactical skills. Most important, Glover could count on four excellent and experienced regiments of Continental troops, who now possessed the opportunity to "do honour to their Country" on a true day of destiny. These young men and boys were not only regulars in Continental service but also tried veterans who could be depended upon in a crisis situation, because they were highly motivated and durable—the very "flower of American youth."[69]

Such comforting realizations gave added confidence to Colonel Glover, whose own motivation was fueled by the extent of this daunting challenge precisely because he and his men were alone and on their own.

Even at this time, consequently, Glover fairly basked in the freedom of independent command which presented an opportunity for him and his men, who were basically Washington's Grenadier Guard, to excel beyond the usual level because of the usual time-consuming tangles of army red tape, traditional protocols, and incompetent superiors.

What has been generally overlooked was the fact that even sectional differences played a role in motivating Glover and his mariners, while ensuring that the fighting spirit and esprit de corps of the Massachusetts soldiers were high partly because of the intensity of sectional rivalries—not only between east and west, but also between north and south—and the burning desire to serve with honor for Massachusetts and their people back home. To many New Englanders, General Washington was still viewed as "a newcomer from another colony [Virginia]—a slaveowner moreover, and therefore doubly suspect to the New England conscience [and men] from Connecticut or New Hampshire or Massachusetts did not wish to be ordered about by Southern nabobs."[70]

As they fully realized, these Massachusetts soldiers were completely on their own in Westchester County, and they accepted their fate stoically as they had when struggling against pounding waves and high winds during the fierce storms in the Atlantic coast, while sailing vessels had been rocked like toys tossed around on the sea. Ironically, they now prepared to fight and die for an unfamiliar region of New York where most of its own people refused to defend their own homeland as patriots, because Loyalist sentiment was so high. The New York's Convention Committee of Safety had earlier warned Washington of the unsettling reality that worked at such a disadvantage to Glover at this time to ensure that his Massachusetts men would fight and die on their own without any support even from sizeable numbers of the local Westchester County militia, because this region was Loyalist: "We suppose Your Excellency has taken the necessary Steps to prevent the Landing of any Men from [British] Ships, should they be so inclined, as no Reliance at all can be placed on the Militia of Westchester County."[71]

Consequently, with a sense of urgency and a surprising degree of confidence that contradicted the seriousness of the tactical situation, Glover led the small column of Massachusetts soldiers from their tented encampment situated just southeast of Eastchester and across the grassy hill that overlooked Long Island Sound to the east and Pelham Bay to the south. With gear clattering that echoed through the silent woodlands, bathed in early morning light and autumnal colors, on both sides of the road that led southeast toward the Hutchinson River, the Bay State soldiers pushed downhill at a brisk pace. Nearby Eastchester villagers watched the New Englanders march farther away from their town and across the lower ground to the southeast. In contrast in a land torn by the horrors of civil war, patriots in the town might have cheered the sight of Glover's men, with muskets on shoulders, moving steadily onward to meet the enemies of their country, while Loyalists remained silent. Almost certainly, some of Glover's fast-moving troops now recalled how the routed Connecticut militiamen had fled down this same dusty Boston Post Road during the Kip's Bay disaster. If so, then they no doubt hoped that this recent fiasco at the wide bay located just north of New York City was no dark portent about what was shortly to come on the morning of October 18.[72]

On the double, the Massachusetts Continentals pushed down the all-important Boston Post Road and toward the distant eastern horizon where Pelham Heights could be seen just east of the Hutchinson River. Glover deployed the right of his Fourteenth Massachusetts on the high ground lining the river's west bank to stand guard over the three regiments in case they suddenly fell back and guard the three artillery pieces aligned on the high ground overlooking the river, while the regiment's left would shortly be aligned by Glover on the high ground east of the Hutchinson. After crossing the small wooden bridge, described as the "Causey" or causeway by one Massachusetts soldier who also emphasized how this was the "the only passage" across the river, Glover was determined to fiercely contest the ground on the river's east side. Here, the Boston Post Road crossed the sluggish

Hutchinson River just below the westernmost edge of the highest ground of Prospect Hill.

Then, once east of the river, Colonel Glover's troops of the other three regiments advanced east to gain Split Rock Road, located below, or south, of the Boston Post Road (which was strategically important because it led to the Eastchester Road that then ran west to Kingsbridge and Washington's rear) on the river's east side. This narrow, dusty road led south along descending ground that eased down the peninsula's length to Pelham Bay and Shore Road. By this time and before gaining Split Rock Road, which paralleled the north-south-running Hutchinson River on its east side, Shore Road was the key avenue by which Howe's troops had initially swarmed inland from Pelham Bay like a flood, before they gained the southern end of Split Rock Road, which the British and Hessians had already secured without opposition after having departed Shore Road. All the while, Colonel Glover was leading his men steadily south and toward this key artery that led from Pelham Bay, after having secured the high ground of Pelham Heights, where he had deployed the left of the Fourteenth Massachusetts east of the river, that Howe needed to secure as soon as possible.

For this upcoming clash of arms upon which so much now depended, Split Rock Road—which ran north-south down ever-descending ground, like the Hutchinson River just to the west, that led to the northern head of Pelham Bay—had been widened and sunken in the soft soil by years of travel by generations of colonists from the original Indian Trail. This dirt road led almost southeast to the southern end of the Pell's Point Peninsula. Here, along the bay, a Native American village of the Siwanoy people had existed in the distant past. And before this artery had become an Indian trail, this narrow avenue that ran through the hardwood forest had been merely a game trail made by the hooves of white-tailed deer that had long daily moved up and down the slight ridge to feed and bed down, especially on the high ground of Pelham Heights which offered a vantage point for them to keep an eye out for predators. Leading toward Pelham Bay located just to the southeast, the dirt road followed a slight north-south ridge east of the Hutchinson River, which flowed just west of Pelham Heights that stood to the north. This narrow ridge was the last high ground before the land dropped sharply to the south toward Pelham Bay and also west into the shallow, tree-filled lower valley of the north-south-flowing Hutchinson River, which paralleled Split Rock Road. Covering with thick underbrush and tall virgin timber, the river valley of low-lying land to the west was dominated by an expanse of wetlands and salt marsh. This flat terrain was often flooded by the heavy rains of spring and summer and the heavy winter melt-off each year.

In pushing south down Split Rock Road and even though following the slight ridgeline that dominated the eastern edge of the shallow Hutchinson River Valley and a plateau of mostly level ground to the east that also descended south, the Massachusetts soldiers moved along the sloping ground along Split Rock Road southeast of Eastchester. Like the river now just to the west on their right, Glover and his men of his three regiments marched across ground that continued to gradually descend ever lower with the land dropping toward the flat coastal plain that surrounded the blue waters of Pelham Bay.

Normally a means by which to inspire confidence and to enhance morale for the hard day's work that lay ahead for the Massachusetts troops in confronting an invasion force on their own and with almost no chance for success, Colonel Glover wisely refused to order the regimental fifers and drummers to play at the column's head to ensure as stealthy of an approach as possible while pushing south, because the foremost British light troops were now headed north up Split Rock Road, as if nothing could stop them. Likewise, regimental banners were not flying from the hands of Massachusetts color bearers above the fast-moving ranks for the same reason. Fully understanding the importance of the psychological element in warfare, Glover wanted most of all to retain the element of surprise by striking a blow to catch Howe and his most advanced light troops off-guard, because the British were not now expecting any opposition since the landing had been so easy and painless. Meanwhile, if General Howe had realized exactly how few American soldiers were now headed his way, then he would have thought them crazy: a small column of only three regiments of New Englanders, mostly men out of uniform who looked more like farmers than veteran soldiers, descending from the high ground and heading relentlessly south down Split Rock Road toward Pelham Bay with confidence to face an overpowering invasion force, which seemingly could not be slowed, much less stopped by so few men, especially when without artillery.[73]

Indeed, at this time and after a good deal of active campaigning in the struggle for New York this summer, the young Massachusetts soldiers looked like anything but crack troops to belie their lofty reputations as can-do and versatile fighting men. Even at this relatively early date, the elite Continentals under Colonel Glover hardly appeared like highly disciplined soldiers, wearing "breeches that put decency to the blush."[74] General Howe and his troops, both British and Hessian soldiers, were about to discover that looks could not be more deceiving when it came to the American fighting man, especially hard-fighting soldiers from the faraway port of Marblehead.

Indeed, for its dramatic showdown with the surging tide of Howe's invasion force, Glover's brigade of citizen-soldiers "was not immaculately attired; indeed, many had no [blue] coats at all, and those that had were generally out-at-elbow [and] One British report has it that 'in a whole regiment [in Washington's army] there was scar a pair of breeches'."[75]

But this early chilly morning in Westchester County what most of all distinguished the former seafarers of Glover's Fourteenth Continental Regiment was their striking appearance as ordinary seamen, as if they had just stepped off fishing vessels that had been sailing the North Atlantic. When Colonel Glover's regiment had first reached General Washington's army at Cambridge in the summer of 1775, the mostly Marblehead men had worn "uniforms" that "consisted of a blue round jacket and trousers, trimmed with leather buttons"— the common garb of seamen, sailors, and fishermen of New England, especially Massachusetts.[76]

If Howe and his troops, finely uniformed in woolen coats of scarlet for the British grenadiers and dark blue for the German Hessians, had previously seen these men from the odd-sounding port of Marblehead, then they would have thought that they were seeing nothing more than common fishermen, who only wanted to cast their lines and nets in the Long Island Sound this morning instead of having been specifically ordered by Washington to guard the army's far eastern flank, because they were his most trustworthy soldiers. These Massachusetts soldiers were as tough as nails and natural fighters just like the spunky Glover: a perfect match for what had to be accomplished against the odds on October 18 and destined to pay high dividends in the end. In fact and regardless of the vast disparity of numbers, they would shortly fight the British and Hessians to a standstill and like few other Continental troops in the army. And Washington fully realized as much from the beginning.

No one more than Colonel Glover, ever realistic and pragmatic on land as he had been when sailing the Atlantic, realized just how slim were the odds of achieving any kind of success whatsoever on this early morning. While Glover had been amazed by the sight of "upwards of two hundred sail" that filled Pelham Bay, he had been more astounded by the sight of the steady flow of the large number of flat-bottom boats that transported thousands of troops ashore. With an advanced contingent of light troops and grenadiers in scarlet uniform now rapidly pushing north up Split Rock Road, hardworking British sailors of Rear Admiral Richard Howe's fleet continued toward the shore with fresh loads of troops, manning oars of the small flat-bottomed boats that covered the wide bay. While Glover led his men south down Split Rock Road and toward Pelham Bay filled with tall masts covered in the white canvas sails of seemingly countless warships, the seamen of King George III steadily rowed their flat-bottomed boats in unison, keeping a steady rhythm that indicated their experience.

Ironically, these British seamen were much like the seafaring soldiers of Glover's regiment in some fundamental ways. As in the past, Howe's masterful plan of conducting an amphibious landing was a well-conceived stroke that paid high dividends by posing a threat to the life of Washington's army, which Glover was determined to prevent at all cost. With the advanced enemy troops pouring inland, in Glover's frustrated words, the invaders had early gained an advantage by having now "stole a march . . . on us," which filled them with greater confidence, while heading north up the Pell's Point Peninsula along Split Rock Road. Off in the distance to the southeast, the dull booming of naval artillery fire from British warships had earlier reminded Glover's advancing troops of the seriousness of the hard work that lay ahead for them this morning. From a letter, one soldier described Howe's masterstroke:

> On the 18th they began a cannonade from their shipping early in the day, and landed some men [of the advanced party of grenadiers in red uniforms] on a point or neck of land near East-Chester meeting house, and their main body advanced [north] from Pell's neck out towards the great [Boston] post road from Connecticut to New-York.[77]

Since having first led the way from Shore Road on Pelham Bay and then gaining Split Rock Road, meanwhile, the small advance party of Howe's light troops pushed rapidly north and deeper inland up the steadily ascending ground without meeting any opposition. Keeping a sharp lookout in case of an ambush from wily Yankees hiding in the woods, these foremost British soldiers observed the lay of the land and felt greater assurance by seeing no opposition of any kind, while moving in a tight column north up Split Rock Road. Essentially, Howe's most advanced troops now acted basically as scouts to reconnoiter and draw American gunfire by springing any ambush before the arrival of Howe's main body.

Confident of success and eager to whip the ragtag colonials as so often in the past, Howe's top lieutenants conducted this initial phase of the invasion of the American mainland with skill. Talented Sir Henry Clinton was second-in-command of the invasion task force.

The aristocratic son of a British admiral who had then served as the Royal governor of New York, Clinton was in immediate charge of this initial phase, including the landing, of this all-important operation into the American mainland. Clinton's strategic and tactical insights were right on target. He had earlier correctly advised the Howe brothers that Kingsbridge, which connected the northern tip of Manhattan Island to the New York mainland, should be targeted instead of Kip's Bay, but his timely and sound tactical idea—striking at the upper end of Manhattan Island instead of at Kip's Bay farther south on lower Manhattan Island—was rejected by Howe.[78]

A veteran leader of hard-fought battles on both sides of the Atlantic who had been wounded in Germany, Clinton had also served among his fellow aristocrats in the House of Commons. The greatest personal pain of his life had been the loss of his wife Harriet Carter-Clinton, who died during childbirth in 1772. General Clinton, who was Howe's top lieutenant and second-in-command at Pell's Point, was no ordinary British commander, before the dramatic rise of his subordinate later in the war, Lord Charles Cornwallis who presided over the Yorktown disaster in October 1781, when luck and fate had turned against him. Cornwallis, who was destined to play a key role at Pell's Point before October 18 came to an end, was "the most capable of Britain's generals in America in 1776 [and perhaps] the best strategic planner on the British side."[79]

By far, Lord Cornwallis was Clinton's most capable and best lieutenant. A rich aristocrat like Clinton and hailing from a distinguished aristocratic family with connections to King George III, Cornwallis had voluntarily pulled himself away from his lavish estates and influential family in a bid to win glory and laurels in America, even though he had felt sympathy toward the American rebels and their cause, which he openly voiced as a member of the House of Lords. Ironically, he had opposed the use of military force against the unruly colonies until the first shots were fired in anger on Lexington Green in April 1775. Now at age thirty-eight, Lord Cornwallis served as the third-highest-ranking officer in Howe's army and deservedly so.[80]

Foreign Mercenaries, the Hessians

The vast majority, around three-fourths, of Howe's invasion force consisted of Hessians. From the higher ground along the slight ridgeline upon which Split Rock Road ran south down the descending terrain toward Pelham Bay, Colonel Glover at this time was not yet able to ascertain that the majority of the fast-moving enemy soldiers heading north were not wearing the expected scarlet uniforms. Most invaders now pouring inland wore splendid uniforms of blue that were based on the legendary Prussian model. Of course, these well-disciplined soldiers wearing the Prussian-style uniforms were the Hessians, and they mostly hailed from Hesse-Kassel, Germany. The most advanced Hessians now served in Major General Werner Von Mirbach's Brigade of the First Division under Lieutenant General Leopold Philip de Heister.

Indeed, General Howe now led not only a British Army but also an Anglo-German one, commanding the Hessians of the First Division. Ireland-born Thomas Sullivan had been overjoyed by the timely arrival of German reinforcements to bolster the Briton's ranks, writing in his journal how: "The Landgrave of Hesse Cassel gave his Majesty 12000 Men, to serve in America." By this time, more than one-fourth of Howe's army consisted of Hessian troops, who were well-trained and highly disciplined. The Hessians who fought at Pell's Point were part of the First Division (ten regiments, three grenadier battalions, one Jager company, and two artillery companies), which was led by General-Lieutenant Leopold Philip von Heister. The First Division had arrived at Staten Island on August 12, 1776, after having crossed the Atlantic from the primary British naval base of Portsmouth, England, and just in time to engage in the Battle of Long Island.

Most of these disciplined fighting men of the First Division hailed from the Hesse region, or Hesse-Kassel, in southwest Germany, which bestowed their popular nickname. With its capital of Hesse-Kassel, Kassel was the mercenary capital of the world. King George III had paid a high price for the services of twelve thousand

Hessians, who were mostly conscripted farm boys, in a cynical deal to kill American citizen-soldiers. To be fair to the king, England had begun using Hessians as early as 1715, including in the crushing of Jacobite rebels, when these Celtic warriors, who were armed with Claymore broadswords like Glover, from both Scottish Highlands and lowlands had threatened to invade England. Ironically, the vast majority of Hessians were Protestants, and they had been hired to fight fellow Protestants, which made no difference to them because they were mercenaries.

As fate would have it, the Hessians of the First Division were part of the mass of well-trained fighting men who were now marching forward and north up Split Rock Road to do battle with Glover's men, who were now simultaneously pushing south along the same road partly because the war in America was so unpopular in Great Britain. Sufficient numbers of British recruits, therefore, could not be secured in England to fight the war in America also because England had a vast empire to protect which had spread the British Army extremely thin around the world.

Therefore, to the absolute disgust of Washington and his men, including Glover's Massachusetts troops who had gained another powerful motivation to defend the invaded homeland, King George III had taken a necessary step by having resorted to contracting out for soldiers from Germany's western and southern princes because of extensive global commitments of empire. The king had made expensive deals in having purchased mercenary troops from the duchy of Hesse-Kassel, but German soldiers also came from Hesse-Hanan, Ansbach-Bayreuth, and Anhalt. For instance, Brunswickers and Waldeckers, who hailed from the Duke of Waldeck, also fought for the British Crown during the New York Campaign. However, they were all called Hessians and worse by the Americans, who could not have been more outraged by having to fight foreign mercenaries because of King George III's determination to crush the rebellion and snuff out its short life like the light of a candle in Windsor Castle.

At this time, there was no large Germany as we know it today, but many small Germanies divided into separate principalities. The Teutonic nation that would one day become modern Germany was an ancient land dominated by a conglomerate of several hundred city-states, including Brandenburg and Nuremberg and other principalities. Such alliances were only natural because the rulers of these minor Germanies were royal Hanoverian cousins of King George III, who was a Hanoverian. Additionally, the Germans and Great Britain—Protestants all—had been allies in the Seven Years' War against Catholic France, when British troops, including Lord Charles Cornwallis, had fought in Germany. Even General William Howe and his admiral-brother, Vice Admiral "Black Dick" Howe, were half-German, indicating the extent of the Hanoverian bonds that ran deep among the ruling British upper class and the elite.

After British leaders learned of the surprising fighting resolve of the embattled farmers of the feisty Massachusetts militia at the Battle of Bunker Hill in June 1775 and realized that a far more serious war was in store than anyone had originally imagined, the first British alliance treaties with the German principalities had been signed in January 1776. Even though less than half of all German soldiers in this war hailed from the duchy of Hesse-Kassel during this war from beginning to end, all German troops in America earned the despised name of Hessian, which became synonymous with evil in American minds. Not only did Great Britain pay a high price for each German soldier who served in America, but also paid extra if Hessians were killed or died of disease (which was far more likely the case) while serving in America or became disabled with a battle injury. In the end, the Elector Frederick II, the ruler of Hesse-Kassel, reaped the highest payment from Great Britain's coffers. Even many Britons, including leading politicians in both houses of Parliament, condemned the employment of German "foreigners to subdue British subjects" in America.[81]

In general, the German people, especially those individuals who had sons, fathers, and brothers pressed into military service by their princes, were horrified by the thought of German troops fighting against their own people, including relatives, who had migrated to America by the thousands during the colonial period. What resulted, including during the New York Campaign, was a German civil war on American soil and one that sadly has been either forgotten entirely or badly neglected by generations of historians, who had too often overlooked the American Revolution's racial and ethnic complexities in this regard. Therefore, because of this mini–civil war among the German people in America since large numbers of Germans had settled in America and now served in Washington's army, Germany's Frederick the Great lamented: "I pity the poor Hessians who end their lives unhappily and uselessly in America."[82]

The first news that Great Britain had employed tens of thousands of German troops played a key role in radicalizing the colonists not only to take up arms but also to declare for independence: a turning point moment that had made it clear to Americans that there was now no turning back. The hiring of so many German mercenaries had revealed that this was now going to be a war to the bitter end, with the hardening of positions on both sides. As never before, Americans had then been convinced that King George III was a sworn enemy of the American people and freedom, which he sought to extinguish by any means and by the most extreme measures. The hiring of tens of thousands of mercenary troops had also fostered the illusion among many Americans that King George III must have been misled by his conniving and corrupt ministers in the ultimate delusion.[83]

These Teutonic fighting men in blue uniforms proudly called themselves "Hulfstruppen," and they were determined to prove their combat prowess in America, after having sworn service to King George III and a distant island nation that they had never seen before. Ironically, like Glover's Massachusetts soldiers, the Germans were also fighting for a piece of this bountiful and rich land. Mostly landless peasants, these young men and boys from Germany had been promised one hundred acres in America for their faithful service against the rebels who had defied the king's divine authority with an unprecedented audacity.[84]

But more important, for the forthcoming clash of arms in Westchester County, the Hessian troops were even considered more effective fighting men than the much-touted British regulars, because of their ferocity in combat and no mercy tendencies when they met rebels on the battlefield like on Long Island. This was a well-deserved reputation, especially with using the bayonet for which they had been well-trained. While charging forward under the "golden lion of Hesse [painted] on their blue flags" of silk in pursuit of routed troops under General John Sullivan, who was the son of Irish immigrants from County Cork, at the disastrous Battle of Long Island, the Hessians had unmercifully bayoneted a good many hapless Americans, including wounded men lying on the ground and those who attempted to surrender. Even British officers were shocked by what they saw during the slaughter on Long Island, including American soldiers pinned to trees by German bayonets.

In fact, British officers were to blame for this unbridled ferocity that was demonstrated by the Germans on Long Island, which was unmatched on the battlefield by any other troops. Fearing that the Germans might fall victim to Washington's clever propaganda and desert in droves to secure their own American Dream, especially bountiful amounts of land, the British had cleverly spread the false rumor that the Americans planned to wage a brutal no-quarter policy on the Hessians. Therefore, a good many young Americans were slaughtered unnecessarily at Long Island, when they were outflanked and attacked from the rear, leaving them at the mercy of the German soldiers, who could not be controlled by their officers or even British soldiers who intervened on behalf of the helpless Americans. By October 18 and like during the Battle of Long Island, Howe's Hessian troops continued to believe much the same about the alleged no-quarter policy among the Americans. In consequence, these professional fighting men from Germany were sure to continue their special Teutonic brand of ruthlessness upon meeting the Massachusetts men in Westchester County.[85]

Colonel Glover's men, consequently, faced the grim prospect of facing thousands of German troops, which were the majority of Howe's men who landed just north of Pell's Point in what would certainly be an especially ugly and bloody confrontation, after what the Hessians had demonstrated at Long Island. If Glover's upcoming defensive stand was overwhelmed, then not only would the Massachusetts soldiers be defeated, but they also would receive no quarter from the Hessians like at Long Island: the nasty prospect of an especially grim fate that ensured grisly deaths from plugging and jabbing bayonets at the hands of a vengeful opponent, especially if additionally incensed by having suffered combat losses from Bay State bullets.

However, for these Massachusetts veterans and despite the odds, their fighting resolve and spirit remained solidly intact partly because they knew that Glover was the best possible commander in such a no-win situation. In fact, the motivations of the Massachusetts men were only heightened with the prospect of meeting the hated Hessians with whom they had scores to settle, including what had happened to a good many of their unfortunate fellow Americans on Long Island. By any measure, the Germans were now the most hated troops in America because they were foreign and because the American people were convinced that their express purpose was "to rob them of their Freedom" in the New World.[86]

Indeed, the Massachusetts soldiers knew that Hessian troops on American soil had already brought some of the most nightmarish aspects of warfare to the people of America, both soldiers and civilians who had also become victims of the German's wrath. Indeed, as if waging a vicious brand of waging war in Germany seen during the nightmare of the Hundred Years' War that had devasted large portions of western Europe, these tough Hessians not only showed no mercy to colonials in arms, but also dealt harshly with civilians far from the battlefields. Eventually, murders, looting, and rapes of civilians came with the arrival of the German soldiers, ensuring that the harshest aspects of European warfare had descended upon America.[87]

By relying on so many Hessian troops on October 18, Howe was also carefully husbanding the lives of his British redcoats, because this would largely be the Hessians' battle, which would be the first on the American mainland. Ironically, William Howe had been a hero of America during the French and Indian War, when he led an advance party of Britons up the steep cliffs of Quebec to gain the Plains of Abraham before the strategic city's gates on the night of September 13, 1759. Howe's amazing feat had paved the way for General James Wolfe's army to reach the top of the heights and then defeat the French Army under the Marquis de Montcalm, who was mortally wounded like Wolfe, in the climactic battle on the Plains of Abraham that won Canada for Great Britain: a remarkable success that had doubled the size of British possessions in North America and all but eliminated the French presence in North America except in Louisiana, where they held the strategic Mississippi River port of New Orleans, and in the Illinois country along the "Father of Waters."

More than any person in his privileged, aristocratic world as a member of the upper-class elite and like the British nation, General Howe had long idolized the oldest of the Howe brothers, George Augustus Howe. He became Great Britain's and America's hero during the French and Indian War, having been killed by a French bullet on a scouting expedition near Fort Ticonderoga, New York, in early July 1758. Howe's tragic fall had been an unnecessary death of one of the British Army's rising stars, because he had foolishly raced toward the sound of the guns when shortly fatally cut down just after having been urged to be cautious. In a rather remarkable development of the day, he was famous for having demonstrated none of the usual British contempt for Americans, who loved him as much as Britons. Howe had also possessed a rare "popularity with the average man," both British and American. In consequence, the Colony of Massachusetts had erected a stately monument in Howe's honor at the magnificent Gothic church in London, Westminster Abbey. Even now General William Howe admired the citizens of Boston for the honor that they had paid to his beloved brother, who had fallen in an obscure wilderness region near Lake Champlain, which was the strategic waterway leading to Canada. And now to deliver a death stroke to Washington's army, Howe needed to first smash a tiny brigade of Massachusetts Continentals who hoped to somehow stop a mighty invasion of his best troops on the Pell's Point Peninsula.[88]

Howe now possessed around three thousand Hessians (and about the same number of British regulars) of four regiments and a crack German light unit known as the Third Grenadier Battalion of around five hundred disciplined and well-trained men, who were among those troops leading the way north. All in all, a total of more than six thousand troops were on the move and about to secure the Pell's Point Peninsula with ease, or so it seemed. After all, these professional fighting men were now on the march north up Split Rock Road without meeting any opposition, while steadily ascending up a gentle slope toward Pelham Heights, which was about to become one of the keys to the upcoming battle that might well decide America's fate.[89]

A Classic Case of Now or Never

Like throughout the ill-fated New York Campaign, this war had already proven to have a will of its own, shifting and changing the dynamics of the tactical chess game for possession of Great Britain's former thirteen colonies. Obscure places with strange-sounding names like Kip's Bay and Throgs Neck had suddenly and unexpectedly become all-important on a moment's notice and without warning, so it had been the same in regard to this remote peninsula northeast of New York City called Pell's Point, which few people had heard about before. As fate would have it, destiny had brought Colonel Glover and his Massachusetts to this obscure corner of Westchester County on a crucial mission upon which the fate of Washington's army and America now hinged.

Not only vastly outnumbered by the combined invasion force of British and Hessians, Glover also faced a great disadvantage because no strong defensive works had been constructed along the shoreline or between the coast and the Massachusetts encampment southeast of Eastchester. As a strategic reserve playing its traditional role in a crisis situation, Glover's brigade would have to go wherever the fight would suddenly erupt in what would become a dangerous open-field fight with an overpowering opponent. Quite simply, there had been no time for Washington's troops to erect defenses along the coast to protect the wide expanse of Pelham Bay or Pell's Point that thrust southward like a sharp dagger. In addition, with the British Navy enjoying complete control of the waterways around New York City, the erection of defenses would have been easily negated like on Long Island and Kip's Bay by landing an invasion force farther north. Indeed, with an almost effortless ease, the British could have simply continued north up the Long Island Sound and then land at some undefended point had strong defenses been constructed to defend Pelham Bay.

In addition, for Washington's New Englanders, the winning tactics and the glory days of Bunker Hill were no more, vanishing like what had once seemed like the certain promise of America easily prevailing in this war. Even at Kip's Bay, a far larger number of New Englanders had possessed what seemed to have been the ultimate advantage of a lengthy line of earthworks and all the reasons to have held firm. Nevertheless, a disastrous rout had occurred of a magnitude not yet seen in this war, with hundreds of Connecticut militiamen, without firing a shot, fleeing from their defenses in a widespread panic, when the big British naval guns had opened up. For some Bay State men, the enduring memory of this shameful rout might have now well given more than one Massachusetts soldier of Glover's brigade pause for thought, especially now when so few troops were facing Howe's invasion pouring inland like a flood.

Colonel Glover fully realized that he would have to face an overwhelming force of British and Hessian troops in a most disadvantageous situation that offered the least possible chance for achieving any kind of success, because the tactical situation certainly appeared truly hopeless, especially a stand-up open-field fight in which General Howe's vastly superior forces could overwhelm the Massachusetts men in relatively short order, if Glover committed this tactical folly of fighting in a conventional manner. Indeed, this daunting prospect and undeniable reality nagged at Glover's consciousness while he led his men south down Split Rock Road, reminding him of his precarious situation and the fact that he would have to develop intelligent and masterful tactics to thwart the advancing juggernaut by any means possible.

In this war and as demonstrated repeatedly, a stand-up fight between the patriots and redcoats and Hessians was virtually a certain guarantee for an American defeat, because British regulars were considered the best fighting men in the world. What had been proven repeatedly in this war was that American troops, especially untrained militia, were unable to stand up to the British and Hessians in an open field fight, when facing the bayonet charge for which Howe's men were most famous. The first demonstrated exception to this rule—followed by the first hurling back of British troops at Harlem Heights on September 16—that contradicted the usual British winning formula was seen in the fierce counterattack of the Maryland and Delaware Continentals on Long Island, which had saved the day and a large portion of Washington's army that was given time to retreat unmolested. On August 24 and led by hard-fighting Major Mordecai Gist who was destined to emerge as one of Washington's finest officers, the Marylanders had performed exceptionally well against Lord Cornwallis's attackers, taking shocking casualties of 259 men, while demonstrating "Roman virtue," as one soldier penned in a letter.

A Desperate Plea for Help

Since having first sighted the scores of flat-bottomed boats that had spilled forth from a vast armada of more than two hundred ships and headed toward the undefended shoreline of Pelham Bay at the southern end of Shore Road, Colonel Glover realized that he desperately needed assistance to say the least. Of course, Glover knew that only 750 Massachusetts men would have no realistic chance in the world of stopping this powerful invasion of thousands of British and Hessian troops, who were better equipped than the Marblehead colonel's men. Therefore, Glover had almost immediately dispatched a desperate message on a fast horse to General Charles Lee at Valentine's Hill. Colonel Glover knew that he had to secure assistance before it was too late. Again, there was no way this mighty invasion force could be stopped. Glover, therefore, knew that he had to buy time by delaying the invasion as long as possible.

In the words of Colonel Glover about the desperate last-ditch effort to gain reinforcements not long after having first caught sight of the British armada: "I immediately sent off Major [William Raymond] Lee's express to General [Charles] Lee, who was about three miles distant."[90] At this time, General Lee had made his division headquarters at Valentine Hill and Valentine's Tavern, situated about halfway between Eastchester and Westchester but more to the west and about halfway from the Long Island Sound to the Hudson River, which were near Kingsbridge, which connected the northern tip of Manhattan Island to the New York mainland.

Born in Manchester, Massachusetts, in 1744, Major William Raymond Lee was a handsome, jovial-looking man and highly competent officer. The former merchant's family lived on a commanding hill that overlooked Marblehead's harbor. He had commanded Glover's old Fourteenth Continental Regiment when Lieutenant Colonel Gabriel Johonnot, a French Huguenot who was not from Marblehead and had been educated at the Boston Latin School, was absent or sick. Lee now served as the dependable "Brigade Major," in Glover's words. Most important, Lee also served as the colonel's top staff officer. An esteemed officer of the Fourteenth Massachusetts before becoming the "Brigade Major" of the four Bay State regiments, Lee was an officer who Glover thoroughly trusted and could count on through thick and thin partly because he was a Marblehead man.[91]

Of the most urgent nature, this desperate message for help had been hurriedly carried on a fast horse by Major Lee, who shortly informed General Lee of the extent of the crisis situation at Pell's

Point. But even if General Lee decided to reinforce Glover's lone brigade when focused primarily on the army's retreat to White Plains, it would be too late because it would take too long to arrive. And Colonel Glover had realized as much from the beginning, knowing that he had the fight of his life on his hands, which only fueled his determination to succeed at any cost.

Steadily Advancing into Harm's Way

Despite the ever-increasing slim chances of not only defeating the swarm of invaders but also even slowing them down sufficiently to allow General Washington's army to safely complete the long withdrawal to White Plains, Glover continued to lead his band of men of three regiments south down the leaf-littered Split Rock Road and along the descending ridgetop, that pointed toward Pelham Bay, to face impossible odds, after having deployed the right of his Fourteenth Massachusetts on the high ground on the Hutchinson River's west bank and the left of his old regiment on Prospect Hill, or Pelham Heights, east of the river, before pushing farther south down the road. With flintlock muskets on shoulders and with the discipline for which they were well known, the Massachusetts soldiers pushed ever-southward toward Pelham Bay, while moving parallel to the Hutchinson River just to the west and below, or southeast, of where the Boston Post Road crossed the river by the small bridge, or causeway, whose planks had been removed on Glover's orders. Meanwhile, the Bay State men were warmed by the exercise of marching at a fast pace on this cool autumn morning, while Glover felt the weight of the burden of command.

Like in having defended New York City in vain, the Massachusetts Continentals hoped for the best in a no-win situation like their commander, who had been presented with his greatest challenge that far exceeded the nighttime evacuation from Long Island. Moving hurriedly south down the narrow Split Rock Road with uncertainty about exactly what they were about to confront, Glover's troops of his small column of three regiments eased ever-closer to Pelham Bay, the seemingly countless British warships, and the encroaching tide of General Howe's army, while the early morning sunshine had yet to warm the land made colorful by the magnificent hues of early autumn.

In Colonel Glover's words that masked his tactical audacity—or almost insanity to more conventional military men—of a relative handful of Continental troops advancing to meet a powerful invasion force, whose relentless advance had gone uncontested so far: "I marched down to oppose their landing with about seven hundred and fifty men, and three field pieces" of light artillery, which had been left on the high ground on the river's west side to anchor the right of the Fourteenth Massachusetts, to face the greatest challenge ever imagined by Glover and his Massachusetts soldiers.[92]

Despite the large number of British warships and troop transports that he had seen filling Pelham Bay as far as the eye could see, Glover had not been dissuaded in the least by the fantastic odds that he would have to face. Indeed, with only "a few field pieces [three brass twelve-pounders] and 750 men Colonel Glover, without a higher command post for guidance, was faced with British artillery and troops that outnumbered his, five to one."[93] But the odds were actually higher and about seven to one. Like other times during the war to determine America's destiny, no doubt Glover wondered, perhaps even doubted, at this time while leading his troops south down Split Rock Road if he would survive this day to ever again see his wife, Hannah Gale who he had married in 1754, family, and his beloved Marblehead.[94]

In his first independent command and entirely on his own with no reinforcements nearby or destined to arrive on this day, Glover was about to demonstrate that he could be exceptionally innovative and resourceful in tactical terms to a degree not yet realized by anyone. Colonel Glover simply accepted the most daunting of challenges like in having successfully risen up in life as a self-made man who had always struggled against the odds and worked as hard as he prayed at the Old North Church, which stood on high ground overlooking

Marblehead Harbor in protective fashion. Here, the good Reverend John Barnard had delivered fiery sermons from 1715 to 1770, inspiring the good townsfolk to pray for salvation, while imploring the Marbleheaders of his flock to remain moral and God-fearing to reap the rewards of Christian blessings. In many ways, Glover was now motivated to fight for God, Massachusetts, and country on New York soil and in an area that he had never seen before. The colonel knew that he would be shortly battling to the death for his home community by the sea, his church, and his family and friends of his home port so far away.

One man who was present never forgot the extent of the stiff challenge now faced by Colonel Glover and his small band of New Englanders on October 18. As he later wrote in the third person from an October 23 letter that described the no-win situation faced by the Massachusetts men: "The brigade under the command of Colonel Glover, consisting of about seven hundred men, one regiment being absent for guard, marched down towards the place where the enemy were advancing with a body of sixteen thousand and a very large artillery" arm.[95]

Indeed, as penned in his journal, redcoat Thomas Sullivan described the swarm of Howe's troops pouring inland with impunity, because after "The Brigade of Guards and Hessians landed at the same time at 8:00 o'clock; after which, they immediately advanced" into Westchester County without meeting any opposition whatsoever before gaining Split Rock Road and then pushing north toward Pelham Heights.[96]

Because they had faced no opposition in surging north up Split Rock Road, the level of confidence had grown ever higher among the invaders who already felt triumphant. After all, it now seemed as if there were no American defenders nearby or for miles around or they would have defended the landing site. In a strange paradox, the seemingly insurmountable obstacles faced by Glover actually presented an advantage of sorts to him. Now far away from the main army on his own and in command of the army's elite troops, Glover now possessed the freedom of action and tactical flexibility to work his tactical magic, relying on his own abilities and not orders from above by a less able superior. In an October 6, 1776, letter to his brother Jonathan, Glover emphasized a reality that would become true only twelve days later on October 18, lamenting the dismal situation of Washington's army, which was "in its present Confused State [and] at present Dare not meet" the British Army, because defeat would be all but inevitable in an "Open field" fight in no small part because of the overall poor condition and the high level of inexperience of so many troops, especially the ill-trained militia. Continuing in his letter, Glover then wrote about an undeniable truth that only fueled the colonel's growing sense of frustration: "We have a few old Regi[ments] if Detacht [detached] by themselves I believe would do Honour to there [sic] Country, but we are Obliged to intermix them with the raw troops which is by far the Gratest [sic] part of the army."[97]

And now on the morning of October 18 morning and fortunately for America, Glover now possessed in his head the ever-elusive and much sought-after magical formula that for him was the key to tactical success, because it bestowed him with an unprecedented degree of freedom of decision-making and movement now that he was completely untethered to incompetent superiors and restrictive orders. In this context, he could not have wished for a better overall situation to exercise extreme tactical flexibility for which to be entirely free to manufacture his own battle plan in real time. The key to Colonel Glover's upcoming remarkable success in orchestrating his own defensive masterpiece lay in a number of factors in a symbiotic development: commanding elite troops from his own state; noninterference from higher-ranking officers who were not familiar with the ground or situation; completely untethered which allowed to make his own leadership and tactical decisions on the fly that allowed the cerebral colonel to be entirely tactically flexible to an unprecedented degree; and possessing the luxury of leading his men on his own and of his own command, while free to make his leadership decisions to hurriedly adjust to any tactical situation that might suddenly be presented.

He had not brought this three twelve-pounders with him east of the Hutchinson River because they would have impeded the swiftness of his advance down Split Rock Road to meet the enemy head-on as soon as possible. These guns had been left on the commanding ground on the west side of the Hutchinson River with the Fourteenth Massachusetts's right to overlook the north-south-running watercourse that steadily descended to the northern end of Pelham Bay. Of course, this was a smart decision that bestowed not only speed to his column but also tactical flexibility. Meanwhile, the three small-caliber guns bolstered his final fallback position just in case the three regiments now to the southeast met with disaster east of the Hutchinson and were forced to withdraw. Now Glover would not have to worry about protecting the three cannon, now safely positioned on the river's west side, upon meeting the enemy, who would have easily outflanked his thin, stationary defensive line shortly to be established east of the Hutchinson, if he had remained solidly anchored in place by the priority of protecting his artillery, which was tactically necessary. As mentioned, Glover had ordered his brigade's elite regiment, the Fourteenth Massachusetts, which was now divided with the regiment's left on the Pelham Heights and the regiment's right on the river's high west bank, to remain behind on high ground on both sides of the Hutchinson River in the key role of a strategic reserve—the colonel's invaluable ace in the hole that could be hurled forward, if necessary, to rescue the three advancing regiments from any crisis situation, if the three regiments got into any kind of trouble, then they could fall back on a dependable strategic reserve bolstered by three cannon on commanding ground above the river.

All the while, Colonel Glover continued to lead his troops rapidly down Split Rock Road under the increasingly bright sunshine of a beautiful fall day in Westchester County. Colonel Read's Thirteenth Massachusetts was in the van leading the way, followed by Colonel Shepard's Third Massachusetts, and then Colonel Baldwin's Twenty-sixth Massachusetts. Although these Continental regiments were small (264, 292, and 226 men, respectively), morale and esprit de corps were sky-high. In regard to numbers, it could have been worse because fortunately the Massachusetts regiments, especially Glover's command, had some of the lowest desertion rates in the army. At this time, the eight companies of the Fourteenth Massachusetts Continental Regiment, now acting as a strategic reserve along with the three cannon poised on the high ground above the Hutchinson to the northwest, were commanded by Captains William Courtis, James Grant, John Glover Jr., Nathaniel Bond ("the fighting surgeon"), Joseph Swasey, William R. Lee, Moses Brown, and Gilbert Warner Speakman. Seasoned Captain Courtis now commanded the Fourteenth Massachusetts—Glover's strategic reserve and most dependable fighting men of the entire brigade.

While the sound of gear clattered through the autumnal woodlands on both sides of the narrow dirt road that continued to descend across ever-lower terrain toward Pelham Bay, the fast-moving column of Massachusetts soldiers continued to push south with confidence. They moved ever closer to a huge egg-shaped glacial boulder—split in the middle and sufficiently large for small trees to grow up from the soil at the bottom of the crevice that was eighteen inches wide and with enough room for a child to play in—of gneiss rock. Almost severed in half as if by a giant meat cleaver, this was the landmark known as the split rock that stood beside the road. Located in today's northwestern section of Pelham Bay Park, this large rock stood on fairly high ground almost half way to the strategic crossroads of Split Rock Road and Shore Road to the south. Meanwhile, Glover's men, with muskets on shoulders and deep in thought when about to meet the enemy in a deadly showdown in an area that they had never seen before, continued to move steadily south in silence. Some Massachusetts soldiers almost certainly thought of home and families in New England, wondering if they would survive the upcoming clash of arms and ever see them again.

But the impossible task that now lay ahead must have reminded these men from the Bay State brigade, especially of Glover's pet regiment which was his own, of having faced dark situations in the past.

General John Glover of Marblehead, Massachusetts, in his prime: The enterprising former sea captain was the tactical mastermind behind one of the most brilliant defense stands in the annals of the American Revolution, when he had been left on his own and saved the day on October 18, 1776. Glover and his Massachusetts men thwarted the mighty British-Hessian invasion force that had targeted General George Washington's Army for destruction, while the reeling Continental Army retreated north in confusion from Manhattan Island to White Plains, New York. *(Wikimedia Commons;* Appletons' Cyclopædia of American Biography, *v. 2, 1900, p. 666)*

Statue of General John Glover on Commonwealth Avenue in Boston, MA, near the intersection with Berkeley Street *(Wikimedia Commons; Photo by Daderot)*

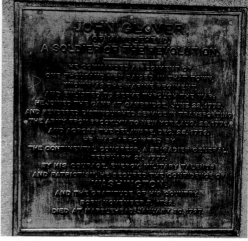

The statue's inscription *(Wikimedia Commons; Photo by Ydi99)*

Colonel William Shepard, seasoned commander of the Fourth Massachusetts Continental Regiment, Glover's Brigade, served as one of Colonel Glover's top lieutenants at the Battle of Pell's Point. Shepard was severely wounded in orchestrating his regiment's defensive stand, but gamely returned to his hard-fighting command to lead his troops during the final phase of the battle and provide inspired leadership. *(Wikimedia Commons)*

Colonel Loammi Baldwin, who commanded the Twenty-Sixth Massachusetts Continental Regiment, Colonel Glover's Brigade, was a key player in Glover's magnificent defensive stand on October 18, 1776. *(Wikimedia Commons)*

General George Washington commanded the retreating Continental Army when Glover's masterful defensive stand bought precious time for the Virginian's successful retreat to White Plains to fight another day. *(Wikimedia Commons; Westervelt Warner Museum of American Art)*

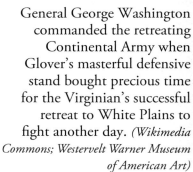

General Charles Lee, the England-born immediate superior of Glover on October 18, 1776, left Colonel Glover and a relative handful of Massachusetts men on their own to do or die in the face of an overpowering British-Hessian invasion. *(Wikimedia Commons; National Archives and Records Administration)*

The HON.ᴮᴸᴱ Sᴿ Wᴹ HOWE.
Knight of the Bath, Commander in Chief of his Majesty's Forces in N. America.

General William Howe's golden opportunity to destroy Washington's disorganized army in full retreat was missed when Glover and his Massachusetts Continental Brigade stopped his push inland and plan to strike a lethal blow in a forgotten turning point of the American Revolution. *(Wikimedia Commons; Anne S. K. Brown Military Collection at Brown University)*

General Henry Clinton was Howe's immediate commander of the powerful British-Hessian invasion force that conducted a successful ambitious landing and poured into Westchester County to catch Washington and Glover by surprise on the morning of October 18, 1776. *(Wikimedia Commons)*

Lord Charles Cornwallis was Howe's most aggressive and capable top lieutenant who nearly succeeded in cutting off Glover and his crack brigade of tough Continentals before they could safely withdraw from the field of strife. *(Wikimedia Commons; National Portrait Gallery)*

Early photographs of the Split Rock Road on the Pell's Point Battlefield
(Photos courtesy of the Westchester Historical Society, New York)

The Pell's Point battlefield today *(Photos courtesy of Joe Bischoff, Pelham Bay Split Rock Golf Course)*

These stone walls are the defensive structures used by Glover and his men to slow the British/Hessian advance inland. *(Photos courtesy of Joe Bischoff, Pelham Bay Split Rock Golf Course)*

A modern photo of the Split Rock Boulder in Pelham Park, New York
(Wikimedia Commons; Photo by Sarnold17 at English Wikipedia)

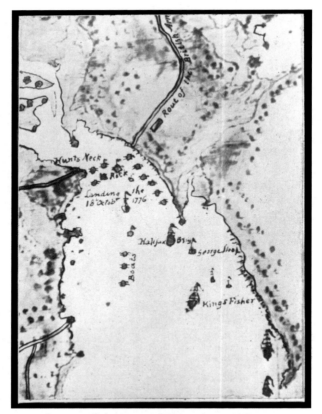

Period map of the area of Westchester County, New York, where the Battle of Pell's Point raged throughout October 18, 1776 *(Photo courtesy of the Westchester Historical Society, New York)*

Although now held back as a strategic reserve, the highly disciplined soldiers of the Fourteenth Continental Regiment bestowed added confidence that strengthened the resolve of the troops of the other three Massachusetts regiments while they marched south, because these men knew that they could always fall back on the last line, if they suddenly found themselves in trouble in the upcoming showdown east of the Hutchinson River. After all and as had been obvious to the thousands of Washington's when stranded troops on Long Island during the Dunkirk of the American Revolution, the hardy Marblehead soldiers stood out as "the lads that might do something," especially in regard to saving the day. And now these same young men and boys, most of whom had the sea in their blood, had been presented with still another crisis situation in which the life of Washington's army was at stake.[98]

In consequence, the legacy of past successes now fueled the can-do determination of the Massachusetts men. In his forthcoming attempt to slow down the invaders' steady advance north up the Pell's Point Peninsula, Glover perhaps could somehow perform yet another miracle as he and his followers had accomplished during the stealthy withdrawal in all manner of boats from Long Island on the hot, foggy night of August 29–30. The New Englanders in Glover's command felt that they had much to prove not only to themselves but also to the rest of Washington's army. This dark blemish that stained the valor of all New England troops came when hundreds of rookie Connecticut militia had run away at Kip's Bay even before the British soldiers had swarmed ashore in southern Westchester County. In a letter, a Virginia Continental officer, Captain Gustavus Wallace, who led a company of the Third Virginia Regiment from King George's County, Virginia, wrote of his disgust about the sad conduct of the "cowardly Yankeymen," who never fired a shot during the Kip's Bay debacle. Southerners in Washington's army damned New England soldiers in general because of the fiasco.

And now less than ten miles north of Kip's Bay, Glover and his steadfast New Englanders were facing a far less favorable situation—less troops and no defensive works like at Kip's Bay, which was one of the war's worst disasters to ever befall Washington's army. If the men of the Middle and Southern colonies of Washington's army believed that Glover and his Massachusetts soldiers would run before Howe's sizeable invading force on the morning of October 18 like the hapless New Englanders at Kip's Bay, then they were sadly mistaken. In fact, Glover and his Massachusetts soldiers were determined to prove that they were entirely unlike—in fact, the very antithesis—of those fainthearted Connecticut militiamen who had run for their lives at Kip's Bay. Consequently, the Massachusetts soldiers were motivated to demonstrate that they could rise to any challenge and no situation could be more formidable for them than their current situation during still another crisis for Washington's army.

First and foremost in overall tactical terms, Colonel Glover fully realized that he would be unable to reach the shoreline of Pelham Bay, even with his small force moving at good speed south, in time to contest the British landing, which had begun in the predawn darkness. By this time, the British had already advanced north along Split Rock Road about a mile and a half inland and ever-closer to Pelham Heights, which Howe needed to secure. Therefore, Glover was concerned and for ample good reason—that he would be forced to fight upon meeting the enemy's advance out in the open at some point on the gradually sloping terrain along Split Rock Road between his encampment and the landing site. After all, it was only a matter of time before his troops moving down Split Rock Road suddenly ran headlong into the British and Hessian onslaught in an accidental collision at a point not of his choosing, before he could develop his master tactical plan. Without having the time to orchestrate his thoughtful and innovative plan of a flexible defense in depth, Glover's audacious effort would be all but doomed to failure if such a situation played out before he was ready.

Most of all, Glover knew that he had to make a defensive stand on some good position on high ground along Split Rock Road to block the open avenue leading northwest to Eastchester, and, most important, the strategic Eastchester Road that led west to Washington's vulnerable army in withdrawal along the Albany Post Road and also the key position at Kingsbridge that connected Manhattan Island to the New York mainland to trap American troops and stores left behind on the island. In addition, Glover also realized that he must make a defensive stand before the equally strategic Boston Post Road, which led northeast all the way to Boston and his own Massachusetts homeland.

Of course, Glover knew that he possessed far too few troops to launch an offensive thrust in the hope of hurling the invaders back to their warships, because the landing had been going on for some time now and too many enemy troops were already shore and had pushed up Split Rock Road. For all practical purposes, the British very nearly already gained a firm toehold, thanks to the lack of prior preparations, including an adequate intelligence and warning system, from Washington's headquarters, despite Pelham Bay having been the next and best place north of Throgs Neck for landing troops.

Knowing that he had to somehow slow down the British juggernaut as much and as soon as possible in some innovative manner in overall defensive terms and as noted, Glover had already prudently ordered a detail of soldiers to dismantle the wooden bridge, or causeway, spanning the Hutchinson River, that flowed south into Pelham Bay, just to the west. And like Colonel Hand's Pennsylvania boys had accomplished at Throgs Neck with the blistering fire of their blazing long rifles, this key mission of presenting a serious obstacle to the enemy advance had involved the Massachusetts soldiers pulling up the wooden planks of the small bridge to deny a passageway to the invaders. Indicating tactical foresight and revealing a wise precaution, Glover's decision was a good one, which protected his rear and gave his strategic reserve (the right of the Fourteenth Massachusetts located on the river's west side) an improved defensive stance on high ground overlooking the brownish Hutchinson River. If his little Massachusetts brigade of four regiments was defeated or routed, then at least the dark-hued river, thanks to the sabotaged bridge, could then serve as an obstacle to impede the British and Hessian advance to buy time to escape west toward Washington's forces.[99]

As everything was shaping up, Glover understood that the upcoming battle in Westchester County would be in large part all about possession of Split Rock Road, which led to the Boston Post Road, which then led to the all-important Eastchester Road, which ran west to the vulnerable rear of General Washington's army, because it is yet in the midst of a chaotic withdrawal to White Plains. Without exaggeration, historian John R. Alden wrote how a "swift advance by the British from Pell's Point might still have interrupted the retreat of the Patriots as they straggled toward White Plains [which presented Colonel Glover with an opportunity to add] to his laurels."[100]

In this regard, General Howe already held decisive victory firmly in his grasp, after his successful landing and unopposed march inland on the mainland for around a mile and a half. After all, the confusion that now consumed Washington's army along the Albany Post Road near the Hudson could not have been greater by this time. In an October 7 letter to his mother, the commonsense Tabitha, in Marblehead, Glover wrote how an overwhelmed Washington, who had the most chaotic of withdrawals on his hands, "observed that the business of the Army in its present confused state was more than he could possibly attend to."[101]

This widespread disorganization had only increased by October 18 to new heights during the long northward withdrawal to White Plains, after the army had suffered so many past defeats, setbacks, and retreats during this disastrous campaign. No army in America had ever been more vulnerable than at this crucial time, appearing less like an organized military force than at any time in the past. With great difficulty, General Washington was attempting to organize a proper withdrawal of what was described as nothing more than a disorganized "rabble," as long derided by the enemy. Throughout this Friday morning in October, the lengthy column of retreating men, who were plagued with losing ways and excessive weariness, consisted of a jumble of wagons loaded with supplies, wounded and sick soldiers, and "stores & baggage."[102] For such reasons, one confident

Briton in Howe's army bragged about an undeniable reality in an October letter:

> Every time [the British and Hessians] attack the rebels they rout them with great loss; they fly before our victorious army on every onset; and I don't doubt but in a very little time this daring rebellion will be crushed . . . and I hope by the next letter to give you an account of an end being put to a government that have dared to call themselves the Independent States of America.[103]

Here, on October 18, the Massachusetts brigade of four regiment now possessed the crucial mission of protecting an often-beaten army in its most vulnerable state, when the lives of America's army and young republic were at stake. The retreat was so chaotic partly because troop deployments had been extended over a wide area had been by Washington at different points "till we extended from the [Long Island] sound [on the far right] up to White Plains, and over to King's Street, not far from [the] Connecticut line" during this autumn of decision.[104]

Therefore, the fast-paced tactical decisions made by Colonel Glover on this day would determine the fate of the rest of Washington's army, and he knew it, realizing that everything was now at stake for him, his brigade, and his infant nation. Meanwhile, and ignoring the fact that he faced a no-win situation of the first magnitude in which he had suddenly found himself at no fault of his own, Glover continued to lead his band of only three regiments of Massachusetts infantrymen south along Split Rock Road. All the while, he drew ever closer to Pelham Bay to the south while the ground descended straight toward the onslaught of thousands of British and Hessian troops now steadily pushing north up Split Rock Road. Like a Jacobite fighter from the Scottish Highlands who had battled the hated England and their allies on the soggy moor of Culloden in 1746, Colonel Glover now carried his old Scottish broadsword since the days of the French and Indian

War, with the same pride as when he had served as an ensign of the Third Military Foot Company of Marblehead. A fastidious dresser who reflected a meticulous exactness that paid dividends as a brigade commander, Glover was now attired in his finest Continental uniform of navy blue and wore a brace of his favorite flintlock pistols by his side.

With time especially crucial in which he was racing against fate itself and since having reached Split Rock Road, Glover's soldiers continued to move south at a brisk pace in the hope of meeting the invaders before too many of Howe's troops had landed. But by this time, far too many Britons and Hessians had already poured inland from their landing site on the west side of the Pell's Point Peninsula. Aligned four abreast in column, Colonel Read's Thirteenth Massachusetts still led the way south followed by the swiftly moving ranks of Colonel Shepard's Third Massachusetts, and then Colonel Baldwin's Twenty-sixth Massachusetts. As noted, the three Massachusetts artillery pieces—which were pulled either by hand or oxen and not by horses—remained behind with the right of the Fourteenth Massachusetts: the strategic reserve positioned on the high ground overlooking the Hutchinson that was Glover's ace in the hole, whenever (it was only a matter of time) the three Bay State regiments were hurled rearward by the invading tide that could not be stopped because of overwhelming numbers.

In addition, to retain the element of surprise with General Howe's troops so near and steadily moving ever-northward as if nothing in the world could stop them, Colonel Glover at some point directed some of his soldiers off Split Rock Road to take advantage of advancing under cover of timber on the west side of the road. He ordered this portion of the advancing command through a patch of woodlands, where most leaves had not yet fallen from the hardwood trees so early in the autumn that had not been as dry as in the past, which would partly disguise the movement south. In this way, the Massachusetts soldiers moved stealthily south through the timber on this part of the higher ground, the southern end of Pelham Heights, that had not been cut down for crops or pasture because it was too rocky and infertile. In a letter, one of Glover's men wrote with pride how "we advanced under cover to receive the enemy, marching out towards the country" to the south.[105]

Perhaps Colonel Glover recalled either oral or written instructions from General Washington that were comparable to what he had recently written to Colonel Joseph Trumbull, the army's commissary general, with conviction: "If the enemy advances from the [Long Island] Sound, so must we. They must never be allowed, if it is possible to avoid it, to get above us and possess themselves of the upper country" at any point north of Washington's army: the exact disastrous tactical situation that Glover now faced and was determined to stop at all costs.[106]

Because of the distance involved, Colonel Glover realized that long before his small force of only three regiments even neared the flat lands of the coastal plain surrounded by saltwater marshes, it would be much too late to not only impede the pouring of Howe's troops inland, but also to make a good defensive stand on the advantageous terrain of high ground. Geography now favored Howe, whose advance troops had already gained a toehold on higher ground above Pelham Bay more than a mile and a half inland unlike at Throgs Neck, where low-lying terrain had immeasurably favored the defenders. Therefore, without a choice, Glover was determined to make the most of what little advantages that geography had to offer him and his relative handful of men on the Pell's Point Peninsula, exploiting every possible aspect of the terrain, which included stone fences, patches of woods, rocky outcroppings, and boulders left behind by receding glaciers millions of years ago. Colonel Glover knew that he had to somehow create a masterful defense based upon these relatively few natural assets located on the sloping ground north of Pelham Bay.

For any realistic hope of any kind of success of delaying Howe's overpowering onslaught, the middle-aged colonel from Marblehead soon came to the conclusion that a defensive stand now had to be made on the existing high ground in the area around Split Rock Road northwest of the Pell's Point Peninsula, before the terrain leveled-out and before it was too late with the enemy close by this time. And, fortunately for Glover and his quickly developed tactical plan, some of the best defensive terrain northwest of the Pell's Point Peninsula was the high ground at the southern edge of Pelham Heights, or Prospect Hill, located on the east side of Split Rock Road.[107]

So far and with time of the essence, Glover had made the most prudently correct tactical decision in regard to not waiting for any orders from General Lee at Valentine's Hill and especially not remaining in position around his encampment in an indefensible position located just southeast of Eastchester. Not wasting any precious time, the Marblehead colonel had instead continued to boldly march his troops south down Split Rock Road to meet the invaders on the lower ground southeast of Eastchester. Washington, an excellent judge of character, and Lee knew that Glover was not only a fighter, but also a tactical innovator in a crisis situation and he could accomplish what no other brigade commander could do. Indeed, Glover was just the kind of officer who could be counted upon to act with a rare combination of aggressiveness and tactical skill to the exact kind of an emergency situation that now existed, when everything was now at stake. In fact, Glover was already angry—which acted like a tonic that only fueled his already-heightened motivation and determination—because "as it turned out afterwards, the enemy having stolen a march one and a half miles on us." This cantankerous and tough-minded seafarer of feisty spirit had taken Howe's surprise amphibious landing as a personal affront to his reputation and honor, especially because, like everyone else, had been caught by surprise.

No one, not even General Howe or his brother Vice Admiral Howe, was going to make John Glover look bad or incompetent to the Marblehead colonel's way of thinking. This strategic part of Westchester County had been assigned to Glover and his Massachusetts men, and he was determined to manufacture the best possible defense. Therefore, Glover took this crisis situation as a personal affront which now called for a settling of the score on the battlefield, despite the harrowing overall tactical situation that he now found himself in at no fault of his own.

Against the odds, he was determined to rise to the challenge even though the dense columns of disciplined professional soldiers from Britain and Germany were fast advancing toward him up Split Rock Road. At this time, the invaders were already a good way up the narrow peninsula and about halfway to the town of Eastchester. The Massachusetts Continentals steadily pushed south through the cool of early autumn, while the enemy continued to move north up Split Rock Road in the early morning sunlight with impunity, advancing north with silk battle flags flying in the slight breeze sweeping off the Long Island Sound. The British and Hessian drums continued to beat loudly from the pounding of drummer boys, echoing through the fall woodlands of Westchester County. But long familiar with what kind of unexpected trouble that an angry, ever-unpredictable sea could throw his way at any moment and thanks to Glover's unorthodox personality and keen instincts that had been thoroughly molded by the seafaring experience and an authentic people's revolution, what loomed before the colonel was not a completely impossible tactical situation in his mind that he could not handle or even overcome as it seemed on paper, because he believed in the popular axiom that "if there was a will, then there was a way" in the seafaring tradition.

The rapidly evolving tactical situation in which the British had already gained a precious toehold on the rising ground called for Glover to swiftly use his most astute and careful tactical calculations to an inordinate degree to compensate, because he could not afford to make a single mistake. Only the colonel's tactical wisdom could now save the day. After all, the extent of the overwhelming success of the amphibious landing had allowed the British to already advance a good distance inland and ever closer to the strategic Boston Post Road entirely unopposed: already more than a mile and a half of free passage north. This disturbing reality now became evident to Glover, who was leading from the front as usual, when he first spied the initial contingent of British soldiers—an advance skirmish company of seasoned grenadiers in bright red coats—who suddenly appeared pushing north up Split Rock Road with disciplined step and in a

tight formation. Glover was not surprised by their sudden appearance because of the escalating noise of the pounding drums before the
dense enemy formation, which had pinpointed the progress of their
steady advance north.

General Howe's invasion could not have possibly made better
progress by this time. As mentioned, a good many of General Howe's
troops had already marched along Shore Road and then turned north,
or right, up Split Rock Road at this small crossroads located in the
middle of nowhere to advance steadily north up ascending ground
toward Pelham Heights. All the while, they continued to push forward in the bright morning sunlight up Split Rock Road as it gradually ascended up ever-higher ground, which needed to be secured by
the invaders as soon as possible. Howe's foremost troops, the British
grenadiers, then took a good position on "an eminence" in prudent
fashion when in unfamiliar territory. Thanks to the swiftness of the
southward advance of the Massachusetts men, Glover's foremost
scouts had seen the finely uniformed grenadiers about the same time
that the first British soldiers spied them.[108] In the words of the British
officer in command of the vanguard: "After moving on about a mile
[and a half north] toward Eastchester, I was ordered by the General
[Sir Henry Clinton] to the top of a rising ground in front with the
Advanced Guard of the light infantry to reconnoitre" the surrounding
area that was entirely unfamiliar to the invaders in scarlet coats.[109]

These foremost advancing British skirmishers were not only
grenadiers, but also included dismounted troopers of the Sixteenth
Regiment of Light Dragoons, which had only joined the army on
this very day. In total, General Howe possessed only 240 of these
cavalrymen, including the Seventeeth Regiment of Light Dragoons
(Dismounted) and known as the "Horse Marines," who were considered indispensable for the task at hand in reconnoitering the way north
because the British Army's great deficiency was its cavalry arm, thanks
to the extreme difficulty of transporting horses across the Atlantic.
These well-trained Britons were among the most advanced troops who
had been sent forth by Sir Henry Clinton, who was in charge of the

task force, to reconnoiter Split Rock Road. The dragoons and grenadiers were determined to fulfill the ambitious design of pushing across the rural countryside to strike Washington's army on the right flank just west of the Bronx River, which flowed about halfway between the Hudson and the Long Island Sound, and deliver the withdrawing revolutionaries an overpowering blow from which they would never recover. Considered two elite commands by October 1776, these dragoon regiments had been formed as light cavalry in 1759 for reconnaissance, scouting, and intelligence-gathering duties and these dismounted cavalrymen were experts at their craft, to the overall benefit of Howe's vigorous push inland and deeper into Westchester County.

The Sixteenth Regiment of Light Dragoons, which had been organized in Northampton, England, in 1766 became known as the "Queen's Light Dragoons." The Seventeenth Regiment of Light Dragoons had been formed in the count of Hertfordshire, England. To serve king and country, these proud troopers had arrived in Boston on May 24, 1775. The finely uniformed horsemen of this excellent regiment wore a Death's Head badge—a "sinister" skill and crossbones insignia, which verified that they now meant business in Westchester County—on their stylish black leather helmets topped with red horsehair crests to make them look more imposing. The regimental motto of the Seventeenth Regiment of Light Dragoons was "Death or Glory," and this now applied to October 18.

Because their prized mounts had either died or had been injured during the turbulent Atlantic crossing, these cavalrymen in scarlet had been dismounted for service in America. Having just arrived on America's shores on October 3, or just fifteen days before, to reinforce Howe's army, which possessed no cavalry, after a voyage of three months, the Sixteenth Regiment of Light Dragoons was ready for action, although its members were yet shaky and half-sick from the long Atlantic passage. These dismounted dragoons were now equipped as light infantry and trained to fight independently of the main body. The troopers of the Seventeenth Regiment of Light Dragoons had been in America since the siege of Boston after having departed Ireland, where they had been stationed, when they had reinforced Howe's garrison when trapped in the port city. And these crack horse soldiers, who were proud of their long and distinguished lineage, had the honor of having been among the British troops who had received an enthusiastic response when they "liberated" a portion of Long Island known for its Loyalist sentiments, while Washington had evacuated New York City and headed north to escape entrapment.[110]

Only a short time before during the thwarted landing at Throgs Neck, Thomas Sullivan had marveled at the superior performance of these elite dismounted horsemen known as

> Chausseurs which are Excellent good Marksmen, and have all Rifle Barrells, [and] They are always upon the Flanks of the Army, on the march . . . They can hit a crown Piece at 100 Yards distance; and that for a Dozen times together. The men serve 7 years, as to a trade, before they are admitted into those Companies, and are so expert in shooting, that if an Officer sees any of them miss the object he fires upon, [punishment had been forthcoming].[111]

To face the finest troops in Howe's army, Colonel Glover possessed far few troops and even fewer chances for success, but not the determination to stand firm at all costs, when so much was at stake for Washington and the Continental Army. The long lines of Washington's retreating troops were now less than a half-dozen miles to the west in attempting to escape to White Plains, before it was too late.

Chapter 4

As Usual, Colonel Glover Again
Doing the Unexpected

After having advanced south down Split Rock Road and nearly a mile southeast from his small, tented encampment on the Boston Post Road, Glover was now forced to make a hasty tactical decision upon first sighting the advancing redcoats on the open road. As fate would have it, an army's and nation's destiny now lay in Glover's hands, based on his judgments and calculations, that had to be made on the fly, which would determine the day's outcome. Instead of immediately deploying his New England troops for action at this point which would have usually been the case for a brigade commander leading such a small force against impossible odds, Glover realized most of all that he had to somehow retain the initiative under such disadvantageous circumstances, especially in regard to buying precious time. However, the Marblehead colonel knew that he possessed a key advantage because the enemy would continue to advance in column north up Split Rock Road with the usual arrogant confidence, leading the invasion force. Therefore, he quickly selected the most reliable soldiers of Colonel Read's regiment, which was leading the way south, "a captain's guard," in the colonel's words, to take the offensive against the dismounted troopers and grenadiers in red.

Eager to confront the invaders on the American mainland for the first time, this handful of veteran Massachusetts men were sent forward before the column on the double, while Glover's soldiers continued to push forward in column down Split Rock Road that led south toward

Pelham Bay. Significantly in overall tactical terms, Glover knew that it was important to advance as far south as possible down the road and toward the three-mile-long, north-south peninsula in order to bottle up the invaders as far south as possible in a desperate bid to plug the cork of the bottle on the narrow roadway that led north to Pelham Heights.

Pushing forward with flintlocks at the ready, this hand-picked forty-man "captain's guard" of the best soldiers of Colonel Read's Thirteenth Massachusetts Continental Regiment was led by an experienced, reliable captain, who knew exactly what to do under the circumstances. These seasoned men had been used as skirmishers for the Massachusetts brigade in the past. But they were now ordered by Glover to advance in a thin, extended line as skirmishers in typical textbook fashion on this cool, autumn morning in preparation of meeting the invasion force head-on. Knowing the supreme tactical and psychological importance of striking first to gain the initiative and momentum, while giving the distinct impression by deliberate design that a larger number of American troops were now marching south with confidence to disguise his small numbers, Glover knew what he had to do under such adverse circumstances. He prepared to order these foremost troops to attack the dismounted troopers and grenadiers, who were leading the way and had gained a high-ground position along Split Rock Road. Clearly, by any measure, this suddenly unleashed aggressiveness when least expected by the enemy was an audacious tactical decision by Glover and one that was meant to catch the enemy off-guard and to fool them in regard to numbers. But most important, Glover's innovative tactical decision was calculated to gain the all-important initiative and momentum to buy time during the opening first phase of the battle.

In addition, the forthcoming attack by only a handful of Massachusetts men of this "captain's guard" against crack British dismounted cavalry and grenadiers was also calculated to protect Glover's three regiments which were still moving south down the road so that they would not be surprised by the British, while ascertaining the strength, location, and dispositions of the advancing enemy up the ascending ground leading north along Split Rock Road from Pelham Bay. Colonel Glover realized that the approaching "advance guard," in the colonel's words, of General Howe's invasion force had to be hurled back and as soon as possible.

Colonel Glover Audaciously Strikes First

Clearly, under the circumstances, this unbridled aggressiveness was a smart tactical decision by the Marblehead colonel, who was about to see his finest day, which even outshined his stirring role in the evacuation across the East River from Long Island and in helping to save the day at Kip's Bay. After all as Glover fully realized in overall tactical terms, there was only one way to gain the tactical initiative to eliminate the enemy's momentum after having been caught so completely by surprise and that was by taking the offensive as soon as possible. After advancing some distance south and as ordered by Glover, who remained in front and mounted so that his men could see him and to allow for quick maneuvering upon his specific directions based on the existing tactical situation as soon as it developed, which was guaranteed to be extremely fluid, the handful of Bay Staters advanced close to the enemy and then took defensive positions behind trees and stone fences on the colonel's orders.

By this time, the "Advanced Guard" of British soldiers had just gained "the top of a rising ground," as ordered by General Clinton, who possessed a good eye and keen tactical sense well-honed from years of experience. Catching the British by surprise after Glover had deployed the Continentals of his vanguard behind the most readily available cover of woods, stone fences, and boulders along Split Rock Road, a sudden volley exploded from the muskets of around forty Massachusetts skirmishers, when the colonel shouted "Fire!" This explosion of gunfire from the handpicked soldiers of Colonel Read's Continentals sent the light cavalrymen and grenadiers fleeing south back down the road and toward their main body marching up Split Rock Road in complete confidence. As revealed in a letter, one

American described the day's first success at a time when none at all seemed possible: "The first attack was made by a small party of their advance guard, which were utterly routed and forced to retreat."[1] The British commander who had ordered the advanced guard to deploy atop "the rising ground" described how: "we were immediately fired upon from behind trees and heaps of Stones where the Rebels lay concealed."[2]

Despite only a hot "skirmish," General Howe himself described the initial British tactical setback of the day that caught him completely by surprise as envisioned by Colonel Glover: "On the march to this [higher] ground, a skirmish ensued with a small party of the enemy, posted to defend a narrow causeway."[3] Howe was already surprised by the fact that these Americans were going to fight and defend American soil with a spirited determination not seen on previous fields.

Thanks to an accurate fire unleashed by the Massachusetts soldiers at close range, the mere sight of the dismounted British cavalrymen and battle-hardened grenadiers fleeing for their lives was a rare sight, because American troops had run in almost every armed clash to date except at Harlem Heights and Throng's Neck. In fact, during this disastrous campaign that saw America saddled with one humiliation after another, the Scottish Black Watch Regiment of Highlanders, who were considered among Howe's finest troops, had been put to flight during the Battle of Harlem Heights on September 16, which had been a magnificent spectacle to General Washington and his men, who could hardly believe the astonishing sight. This small success had been a significant morale booster for the army because it was the first time during the New York Campaign that the enemy's finest troops had fled the field, after having been punished by the resurgent rebels.

However, many soldiers of Glover's Brigade, including the colonel, were veterans of the French and Indian War and they had seen redcoats previously put to flight by Canadians, Native Americans, and French regulars. In addition, men of the Marblehead Regiment, including leading officers like John Glover, Joshua Orne, Gabriel

Johonnot, and Caleb Gibbs, had arrived as reinforcements on the same day, April 19, not long after the first clash with the British at Concord and Lexington. At that time in the balmy weather of mid-April 1775, Glover and his men from Marblehead had seen the British retreat during their nightmarish withdrawal to Boston, when they harassed the retreating redcoats, when they were continuously raked with a heavy fire unleashed by hidden citizen-soldiers from behind trees, houses, and stone fences. Symbolically, Glover and the Marblehead soldiers and Major Loammi Baldwin, whose regiment of Massachusetts "minutemen" had also joined the fight, had played roles in decimating the British column headed for Boston's safety.

Nevertheless, even the stiff odds, the astronomically slim chances for any kind of success, and the fact that Glover and his New Englanders had been caught totally by surprise by the British and Hessian night-time invasion that had been completely unexpected, the first sight of these well-trained soldiers of General Howe's seemingly invincible invasion force taking flight was a most uplifting sight to the Massachusetts Continentals. Therefore, Glover and his Massachusetts men were inspired by an astonishing spectacle that was a mini-replay of Harlem Heights, when the backs of the crack Scottish Highlanders had been shown to the cheering Americans. A very good omen for the rest of October 18, this opening phase of the fighting raised the spirits of Glover's foremost fighting men on this day of destiny, bestowing greater confidence.[4]

After taking punishment from the explosion of fire that had suddenly erupted from the row of Massachusetts muskets that had been fired from good cover, these foremost soldiers of the invading force, around forty of Howe's best men, fell back down the road and then rallied on a good defensive position to the south on Split Rock Road. Here, the humbled redcoats, licking their wounds, awaited the arrival of Howe's main column, which continued to push north up Split Rock Road. Paying dividends and as noted, this advance party of Massachusetts soldiers had been hurriedly sent forward by Glover, who led the way down the road and along the sloping ground, from the main body, yet advancing south behind the plucky vanguard of chosen men, to delay the British push north to buy time. Most important, precious time had been won by Glover for him to more accurately ascertain the lay of the land in which to orchestrate a masterful defense and the exact tactical situation, especially if Howe had dispatched any flanking parties west, while in the process of formulating the best defensive plan on the fly based on existing circumstances in a fluid tactical situation.

In Glover's words about his fast-evolving and maturing tactical plan that he was already envisioning with clarity, the brushing aside of the foremost soldiers of General Howe's invading force bestowed upon the Marblehead colonel not only added confidence, but also sufficient time to "dispose of the main body to advantage" on good high ground northwest of the Pell's Point Peninsula. And this tactical advantage won by Glover's insightful decisions, smarts, and the natural instincts resulted in the beginning of the process of the careful choosing of the best available defensive positions of his three regiments situated on the high ground of the southern end of Pelham Heights near where the Pelham Manor stood to the northwest and southeast of Eastchester.[5]

By this time and thanks to having immediately reacted to the threat and then hurling back the vanguard of British grenadiers and dismounted dragoons who had been caught by surprise by the sudden volley that raked their formation at close range, Glover had advanced his troops sufficiently far enough south below Pelham Heights that he was in the process of making a determined attempt to keep the advancing British and Hessians bottled up in the relatively narrow ground of the peninsula located between the Long Island Sound to the east and the Hutchinson River to the west. The strategic crossroads of Shore Road and Split Rock Road had been early gained by Howe's troops and it was now well beyond Glover's range. Colonel Glover, therefore, had wisely not made the tactical mistake of advancing too far south and attempting to make a defensive stand on less favorable terrain that was less elevated had he continued farther south. Glover had to be exceedingly careful because the British and Hessians possessed the seemingly endless advantages of superior numbers, better equipment, more firepower, greater mobility, and tactical flexibility of an entire invasion force. If Glover had advanced too far south, then he would risk getting hit by a flank attack from the east, while also being forced to defend less favorable terrain.

Meanwhile, after the first Massachusetts volley from the forty-man advanced party had been unleashed to force the dismounted dragoons and grenadiers rearward on the double, large numbers of British and Hessian troops—Howe's foremost troops—were hurriedly pushed forward by energetic young officers, who led the push north up Split Rock Road in column like a relentless juggernaut. Almost as if Colonel Glover had never struck a blow, the invaders continued to swarm up the Shore Road and then the Split Rock Road to strengthen their already firm toehold on the peninsula and Westchester County soil of the New York mainland. After the lengthy landing process in small flat-bottomed boats just north of Pell's Point on the western side of Pelham Bay, even more of Howe's men flooded inland like a blue and red tide that was rising ever higher on this beautiful autumn morning.

Hundreds of the Crown's soldiers continued to hurriedly land, then formed in neat and tight columns for surging inland. Larger numbers of British and Hessian troops steadily pushed north up Split Rock Road to reinforce the foremost ranks farther up the little dirt road suddenly made important by this war and which led to higher ground. The farther north that Howe's troops surged north and ever closer to Eastchester to the northwest, they steadily gained a more solid toehold on the mainland from which they could never be pushed off.

Colonel Glover was yet entirely on his own in regard to having been left to make his hard tactical decisions very quickly about how to best overcome the most vexing of tactical situations that was seemingly hopeless. At this crucial moment, Glover's three top lieutenants were not available to bestow advice and wise council in a truly desperate situation. A veteran of the opening day of the revolution during the harassment of the British during their bloody retreat back to Boston's safety after the initial clashes at Lexington and Concord on April 19, 1775, Lieutenant Colonel Gabriel Johonnot was a talented officer of French Huguenot descent, who had engaged in the Boston Tea Party with typical patriotic enthusiasm. However, he was now absent. Johonnot had taken command of the Fourteenth Continental Infantry when Glover had been promoted to brigade command on September 4, but he was now ill. Nor could Glover consult Major William Raymond Lee, a fellow Marbleheader who was as determined a fighter as Glover and possessed a host of tactical skills. Major Lee was cut of the same mold as Glover, resilient, tough, and reliable. He was destined for a colonel's rank in January 1777. But the former Marblehead merchant now serving as Glover's most trusty staff officer was absent in having been early dispatched to Valentine's Hill by Glover to General Charles Lee's headquarters in a desperate plea for assistance, before it was too late. Fortunately, for Glover, the highly capable Lee was destined to return and join his fellow Marblehead comrades in the field in time to participate in the raging battle.[6]

In addition, Colonel William Baldwin, commander of the Twenty-sixth Massachusetts, was still absent from the regiment because of his lingering illness. He had spent the previous night in a private residence, located not far from the encampment, to recuperate in the hope of restoring his shattered health. But like Major Lee, Baldwin was destined to shortly reach the field to take command of his regiment, despite the fact that he was still "unwell," as he penned in a letter to his wife.[7]

By this time in his own mind, Colonel Glover had already developed a masterful tactical plan that was essentially a brilliant defense in depth, which was distinguished by a great deal of tactical innovation that maximized every possible asset of the Massachusetts men and the terrain. Although having been hastily conceived on the fly and born of a sense of desperation, this novel tactical plan was distinguished by considerable tactical insight, flexibility, and resourcefulness on the part of the Marblehead colonel. Because the overall situation was now so crucial, Glover wisely avoided the temptation to immediately launch a headlong attack with his main body of troops on the risky premise that the best defense was an offensive thrust to catch the invader by surprise. Quite simply, Glover's force was simply much too small and his mission too important to take such risky gambles. The colonel, therefore, decided on a more conservative tactical approach that masterfully used the lessons of irregular warfare from what had been learned from the French and Indian War and in battling Native Americans.

As his overall battle plan was steadily evolving in a real-time situation, Glover was demonstrating the epitome of tactical flexibility, because he was in the process of developing a more complex tactical plan than simply relying on the tactical offensive during the battle's opening phase, because he could not risk the life of his command. Such a penchant for offensive action almost regardless of the situation often included General Washington, who was aggressive by nature. He had been plagued by the curse of over-aggressiveness against a superior opponent like his planned attack on Boston to drive the British out in early 1776, which offered little opportunity for success. In addition, Glover had already resisted the temptation of immediately withdrawing his tiny force, despite being so badly outnumbered. Instead of either attacking or retreating with his entire force, he planned to stand firm and hold his advanced position on Split Rock Road not only with his vanguard but also with most of his command. Now in the development of his well-conceived tactical plan, Colonel Glover demonstrated his penchant for unconventionality, individuality, and unorthodoxy that had so often distinguished Marblehead and its people for so long.[8]

As a self-made man in both civilian and military environments, Glover embraced the opposite view of what most other commanders, especially conventional ones, would have done in a comparable tactical situation, when no hope remained. He simply refused to do what might have been expected of him in such a no-win situation and to do what most, if not all, commanders in charge of a such diminutive brigade when facing a mighty host on his own and without any nearby support or reinforcements would have ordered: immediately withdrawing his small command instead of standing firm in the face of an invasion force rapidly pouring inland.

As important under such circumstances, Glover continued to be burdened by the knowledge that he could not afford to make a single tactical mistake this morning, because there was no absolutely no margin for error in the upcoming showdown. Quite simply, the fate of Washington's army and America were at stake and the future of both would be determined by the tactical judgments and calculations in the orchestration of a land battle from a former ship captain, who had long sailed the Atlantic's cold waters. After all, defeat would have opened the door for more than six thousand British and Hessian troops to march inland unopposed to strike Washington's army during its disorganized withdrawal north to White Plains, gain the army's rear, secure the strategic point of Kingsbridge—directly due west from Pell's Point— and trap elements of the Continental Army on Manhattan Island. Without advice or orders from his superiors, Generals Washington and Lee, Glover quickly made his unorthodox, but adroit, tactical decisions on his own in orchestrating his masterful defensive stand, which was needed to save the day. He was now planning to create an innovative defense in depth which was calculated to slow the rapidly advancing British and Hessian troops as long as possible and to buy as much precious time as possible. As noted, time had to be gained by the Bay Staters to allow the complete withdrawal of Washington's army from Harlem Heights to get safely off Manhattan Island and to the high ground of White Plains.

Without cavalry, scouts, or advanced pickets to provide timely intelligence about the exact dispositions of General Howe's forces, especially if any parties of soldiers had been sent west across country to outflank his position on Split Rock Road, Glover's earlier decision to dispatch an advance force of forty Massachusetts soldiers, under a capable captain, south down the road to strike the first blow had already paid immediate tactical dividends by gaining the initiative, buying time, and giving Howe something to think about. For Colonel Glover, the recent initial clash of arms had not only indicated the exact location of the foremost advancing enemy troops, but more important, also brought an abrupt end to Howe's unimpeded confident march straight north up Split Rock Road and the narrow Pell's Point Peninsula. Most important, some precious time had been won by the advanced party of Colonel Read's men when they had unleashed their offensive strike, because Howe's forces had been forced to prepare for action, deploying his troops and bringing up artillery and this all took time. As the ever-modest Glover concluded with a gift for understatement in the tradition of the stoic, hardworking seafaring people of Marblehead in regard to his overall battle plan: "This plan [was destined to succeed] very well" and far beyond expectations. Reacting to the fluid, fast-evolving tactical situation in real time, Glover now embarked upon making a series of quick, but well-conceived, tactical decisions in record time, as if it had been deliberated at headquarters during a lengthy conference.

With a modesty that was as genuine as the self-sacrificing character of Marbleheaders and the hardness of the gneiss boulders left behind by retreating glaciers and now scattered across the Pell's Point Peninsula, Glover wrote with blunt honesty how: "I would have given a thousand worlds to have General Lee, or some other officer present [especially General Washington] to direct or at least approve of what I did. However, I did the best I could and disposed of my little party to the best of my judgement," when on his own this morning, while wrestling with lingering self-doubts about his hasty decisions. And what the Marblehead colonel developed on his own was a brilliant tactical plan of a well-conceived defense in depth based upon the nuances of the terrain, which offered few advantages. Even more remarkable, this innovative and novel plan that revealed the extent of Glover's tactical resourcefulness and insightfulness had been hastily developed on the spot when a fast-evolving battle of supreme importance was brewing in which he would attempt to do the impossible against the odds. Remarkably, Glover's tactical plan was most of all distinguished by a skillful blend of insightful tactical intricacy and delicacy based on the terrain, despite what little the ground offered to him and his men: an innovative battle plan orchestrated with a brilliance seldom seen by any American commander on either side during the American Revolution, especially during a crisis situation.

Well-Conceived Deployments of a Brilliant Defense in Depth

As mentioned, what was most remarkable about Glover's tactical decisions was the fact that he made them on the spur of the moment, when knowing that he was alone and would have to fight this battle by himself. By relying on an abundance of tactical resourcefulness and flexibility, Glover now processed to orchestrate the most brilliant and ingenious battle plan of the war to date and in record time, as if it had been planned for months by experienced general officers on a conference table. Because he faced impossible odds, the Marblehead colonel knew that the only possible way to buy precious time to save Washington's army was to fully use the few advantages offered by the terrain—the combination of gently rising ground, stands of timber, and stone fences—and his own freedom of thought to create a masterful defense in depth, which was calculated to buy time and severely bled the enemy as much as possible to make up for the disproportionate odds.

Thanks to the precious time that already had been bought by his advanced handful of Massachusetts vanguard in having successfully pushed the dismounted British dragoons and grenadiers back down Split Rock Road, Glover gained an opportunity to deploy his three foremost regiments in well-placed positions of a defensive in depth on both sides of Split Rock Road, where he reasoned that the terrain gave him the greatest advantage. And from the beginning in his mind, he instinctively knew exactly where each of his three regiments should go based not only on the ground but also upon its particular strengths and weaknesses that revealed the depth of his insights about his top lieutenants and their men—Colonel Read in the first defensive position east of the road where his right flank was anchored; Colonel Shepard in a second line west of the road where his left flank was anchored behind Read; and Colonel Baldwin's troops east of the road, where his right flank was anchored in the rear of the first two regiments situated on lower ground at a proper interval. As the overall foundation of his intricate battle plan and serving as his strategic reserve, Glover had positioned the left of his Fourteenth Continental Regiment on the highest ground near the summit of Prospect Hill. Meanwhile, to the northwest, the right of the Fourteenth Massachusetts was aligned on the Hutchinson's River's west bank while the regiment's right to the east was on Pelham Heights.

Knowing exactly what he wanted to do in this emergency situation when time had already all but run out for him, the Marblehead colonel felt more secure because he had the most reliable troops of his small Massachusetts brigade, the left of his own Fourteenth Continental Regiment, in a good defensive position along the high ground of Pelham Heights, known as Prospect Hill. Captain William Courtis, senior captain who had been a former sailmaker, now commanded the Fourteenth Continental Regiment. In the captain's capable hands, Glover's old regiment now served as the anchor of the defense in depth in two directions: not only to the north but also to the northwest.

This key defensive deployment of the Fourteenth Continental Regiment on both sides of the river had been made because the three artillery pieces could not be advanced across the river and through rougher terrain, especially after the little wooden bridge across the Hutchinson River, where the Boston Post Road crossed the wide watercourse from west to east, had been dismantled by the Bay Staters on Glover's orders. Therefore, the Fourteenth Massachusetts's right was more powerful than the regiment's left aligned on Pelham Heights, because of the three guns. But most of all, Glover knew that the artillery needed to be positioned on high ground and in a secure position on the river's west bank, which was his final line of defense and his westernmost one. In consequence, the Fourteenth Continental Regiment had been spread thin—more than any other of Glover's regiments—to cover the main road, the river crossing, and the summit of Prospect Hill, while fulfilling a grenadier guard role as the brigade's strategic reserve situated on both sides of the river.

Here, on this windswept perch known as Prospect Hill, the citizens from Eastchester and the surrounding area had often gathered under the refreshing shade of large oak trees to vote for local officials as early as 1733. At this strategic high point, Glover now could count on a seasoned and well-honed strategic reserve—his own regiment—and a strong natural defensive position located near the summit of Prospect Hill just east of the river. As noted, the regiment's strongest point was its right, bolstered by the three artillery pieces, along the high ground overlooking the Hutchinson. But more important, the Fourteenth Continental Regiment now possessed a firm grip on the most commanding terrain on both sides of Split Rock Road and the Hutchinson River, which offered protection against British flanking movements—of which Howe and his top lieutenants were masters as demonstrated at the Battle of Long Island—from the east.

Distinguished by "a spirit and resolution peculiar to the Marblehead Corps," Captain William Curtis's highly disciplined troops, who continued to wear the traditional garb of sailors and fishermen, on the left had formed a battle line that spanned along the road on the high ground at Prospect Hill, which commanded the neck of the Pell's Point Peninsula. Consisting of solid high ground compared to the marshy lowlands covered in high swamp grasses around Pelham Bay and bordering the Long Island Sound, most of Prospect Hill had been cleared of timber to serve as crop or pasture lands that were entirely free of flooding unlike the low ground around the bay. The mostly Marblehead soldiers of Glover's old regiment were aligned in fine defensive positions that had been carefully orchestrated by the innovative Marblehead colonel. Offering a protective perch, Prospect Hill anchored the left flank of the Fourteenth Continental Regiment just like the high ground along the river's west bank anchored the regiment's right flank. Significantly to ensure a stronger defensive position when combined with the high ground position, Captain Courtis had formed his Continentals behind a lengthy stretch of stone wall, which was a common feature that dominated the rural landscape east of the Hutchinson.

Therefore, just north of the natural landmark known as Split Rock, the bulk of Glover's old regiment—the brigade's strategic reserve—stood on excellent defensive ground on the road's east side near Prospect Hill's summit from where the Long Island Sound could be seen to the east, dominated the east side of Split Rock Road. The strategic summit of Prospect Hill—as both Colonel Glover and Captain Courtis, a tall man with a dark complexion, fully realized—had to be protected not only to guard against flank attacks from the east, but also to serve as a fallback position to ensure that the three regiments on both sides of the road to the south would not be surrounded, trapped, and annihilated, because no escape existed if the British gained the brigade's rear by overrunning Prospect Hill and reached Split Rock Road at some point farther to the north.[9]

In this way, the defensive alignment of the Fourteenth Massachusetts Continental Regiment took advantage of the fact that the west side of the road, or the right flank, would be partially protected below the bluff-like high ground by the swampy salt marsh of the lower lands in the river's slight valley to the south. Indeed, the slight north-south ridgetop, and hence the road, was nearest to the drop-off to the lower ground of the Hutchinson River Valley just to the west. All in all, Glover and Captain Courtis had selected a fine defensive position by which the Fourteenth Massachusetts's right flank would be protected by its high ground position because the river's west side offered additional protection since the murky watercourse provided a wide obstacle to the advancing enemy. The relatively level land of the high plateau of Prospect Hill east of the road had to be guarded at all costs. Most important in tactical terms, this high-ground perch of the Fourteenth Massachusetts on both sides of the river dominated both Split Rock Road and the lower ground of the Hutchinson below it, while the land gradually descended south to Pelham Bay.[10]

Solid as a rock, the hardy fishermen, seafarers, and sailors of the Fourteenth Massachusetts were an ideal choice for Glover to have anchored his overall defensive arrangement of a masterful defense in depth that he was orchestrating with great care on the spur-of-the-moment in the face of Howe's invasion, which was about to hit hard at any moment. Most of all, these veteran Massachusetts men could be counted on in a crisis situation and Colonel Glover fully realized as much like General Washington. Captain Courtis felt confident for success although he now commanded the Fourteenth Continental Regiment for the first time when a large fight was brewing and the storm about to break in full fury. As so often in the past, the tactically astute captain, whose former livelihood had been based on life at sea like almost everyone else in the fishing port of Marblehead, would rise splendidly to the challenge on this day of destiny.

Assisted by capable Ensign Thomas Courtis, Captain William Courtis had formerly commanded the regiment's Company Seven. Captain Courtis had taken charge of the regiment after Major Lee had been appointed by Glover to "Brigade Major" of the Massachusetts brigade. At age fifty-six, an old friend of Colonel Glover, and a worthy replacement for Major Lee and Lieutenant Colonel Johonnot, the hard-fighting French Huguenot who was now ill, for regimental command, Captain Courtis had been the senior captain of the Fourteenth Massachusetts Continental Regiment: the position that had ensured his rise to regimental command at Pell's Point. Capable and possessing plenty of experience in having led the First Company of the Fourteenth Continental Regiment, the talented captain was the right man for the job of commanding Glover's strategic reserve now located on both sides of the Hutchinson River. Aligned near the summit of Pelham Heights, or Prospect Hill, and along the high ground of the river's west side and most important, the 180 soldiers of Glover's old regiment could be relied upon in such as critical situation. Situated on lower ground that gradually descended toward Pelham Bay, the men of the three regiments before, or south of, the left of the Fourteenth Continental Regiment gained confidence in knowing that they possessed a reliable strategic reserve behind them.

Like for most of Marblehead's citizens back at the home port, life had been difficult for Captain Courtis. However, this hard-earned

life experience had toughened him for the challenge, forging character and a never-say-die quality that would shine today. Indeed, life's
misfortunes that were so commonplace in the home port had only
hardened Courtis like Colonel Glover, as if specifically preparing him
for this day of destiny in Westchester County. Captain Courtis had
already outlived two wives at a time when seafaring males usually left
widows and orphans all over Marblehead until the town appeared like
a large orphanage before the war, because of the dangers of life at sea.
Sarah Courtis had died in 1765 at age forty-three, and then Elisabeth
Courtis had died in 1771 at only thirty-eight years old: two searing
personal tragedies in barely half a decade that had molded the life and
outlook of Captain Courtis. Here, just below the summit of Pelham
Heights, Captain Courtis might have thought of his Cornish heritage
and an ancient seafaring land across the Atlantic, which his hopeful
Celtic ancestors had departed long ago for a new life in America. The
captain, the former skilled sailmaker whose ancestors hailed from the
rugged, but picturesque, peninsula located at the southwestern end of
England and had the sea in his blood, now had barely three years to
live. He would die in the service of his country and for the dream of
independence before the revolution was finally officially won in 1783
with the signing of the Treaty of Paris.[11]

John Glover Jr. was another excellent captain of the Fourteenth
Massachusetts Continental Regiment who had directed his men into
position on the high ground to anchor Glover's defensive line, while
serving as his strategic reserve. He was the oldest and "favorite" son
of Colonel Glover. At only age twenty-one, John Jr. had commanded
the Third Company of the regiment since its formation. He had been
only a lieutenant in William Raymond Lee's Company but became
company commander when Lee moved up to the coveted position
of "Brigade Major." Young Captain Glover was assisted by First
Lieutenant Joshua Orne, who had departed Harvard College to fight
for the great dream of America, Second Lieutenant Marston Watson,
and Ensign William Hawks of the regiment's Third Company. The
Third Company was under the command of the colonel's son, because

this fine unit was Glover's "favorite company in the regiment" of mostly Marbleheaders.[12]

But by this time, Glover's regiment had already lost some of its best officers to the ravages of sickness and death. One excellent captain of the Fourteenth Continental Regiment who revealed the depth of familial connections within the regiment that was a direct extension of the Marblehead seafaring community was Nicholson Broughton, who was Glover's good friend and business associate. A former sea captain from a long line of ship captains who had become legendary for their high seas adventures, he had led the regiment's Sixth Company. After the insanity of this war finally ended, Broughton was destined to marry Glover's daughter, Susannah. During the late summer of 1775, when the Continental Congress had made yet another one of its grievous mistakes by having seen no need to allocate the necessary funds for the creation of a navy and to his great credit, General Washington had developed an innovative plan: to raid British shipping that was supplying and reinforcing British forces besieged in Boston, which led to the birth of the United States Navy.

As daring on land as the sea, Captain Broughton had commanded the first vessel of what would become "Washington's fleet" of the nascent United States Navy. Broughton's ship was the schooner *Hannah*. This excellent sailing ship of seventy-eight tons had been converted into a warship at Glover's Wharf in Beverly, Massachusetts, for the express purpose of preying on British shipping in a logistical war on the high seas. Appropriately, Washington's first warship was Glover's own vessel that had sailed to the Grand Banks for a decade and it had been named in honor of Glover's wife, Hannah Gale-Glover. Among Captain Broughton's crew members had been Glover's own son, John Jr., and brother, Jonathan, who was a savvy businessman and self-made man in his own right like the dynamic Marblehead colonel. The naval service had ended in time for both of the Glover boys, son and brother, to serve with distinction at the Battle of Pell's Point like Broughton's teenage son, Nic, or Nicholas Jr.

Ironically, the former commander of the regiment's Company Nine, Captain John Glover Jr., had most of all wanted to command one of Washington's ships since having served as a lieutenant aboard the *Hannah*, following in the footsteps of his father. However, he had failed to receive the coveted position because of his young age, only twenty, and lack of experience, which now ensured that he was a key player in the showdown at Pell's Point. The ever-ambitious son, therefore, had quit the fledgling naval service, demonstrating a certain hardheadedness and an independent-minded streak, just like his father, that nevertheless made him a fine officer, while revealing that he was very much his father's son. John Glover Jr. had then rejoined his father's regiment and became the respected captain of the Third Company in place of First Lieutenant Joshua Orne Jr., an articulate and bright Harvard man, and he now benefited from the assistance of Second Lieutenant Edward Archibald at Pell's Point.[13]

Other experienced captains yet remained in charge of seasoned companies of the Fourteenth Massachusetts Continental Regiment at this time. For instance, another reliable company commander of Glover's pet regiment was yet another former sea captain who had sailed the seventy-two-ton schooner *Speedwell*, which had joined Washington's small fleet that was nothing less than the birth of the United States Navy. He was a skilled Marblehead silversmith, who owned his own shop in the thriving port, named Captain Thomas Grant. Grant now led a company whose ranks including his young son of the same name. Born on August 3, 1729, the captain now commanded the Second Company of this excellent regiment. Captain Grant, age forty-seven, was assisted by First Lieutenant William Bubier and Second Lieutenant Ebenezer Graves and Ensign John Allen.

In the ranks of the Second Company was the captain's son and fifer Thomas Grant Jr. The young man had been born on December 13, 1761, just six months after his father's marriage to his pregnant mother, which of course revealed that a considerable degree of lust had existed between the two lovers in the conservative port of Marblehead. His mother was Margaret Bubier, the daughter of Joseph Bubier and the sister of William Bubier, who now served as the first lieutenant of Captain Grant's company, along with Corporal John Bubier. Part of one of the regiment's father-son teams that bestowed a community feel to the command, the eleven-year-old fifer was the youngest member of Colonel Glover's old regiment at this time. When the battle on October 18 erupted in full fury, young Bubier would put down his fife and fire a flintlock musket with considerable enthusiasm. He was destined to become a Marblehead silversmith of note like his father, who passed down his artisan skills to his favorite son.[14]

And Colonel Glover's good friend who had served on a number of revolutionary committees with the colonel before the war, thirty-six-year-old Captain William Blackler, who was assisted by Lieutenants Nathaniel Clark and Nathaniel Pearce, commanded the Second Company soldiers in good defensive positions on the high ground. Of course at this time, Company Drummer John Thompson and fifer Benjamin Gardner had no orders to play their instruments and favorite martial tunes, because Glover was concerned about masking his intentions and defensive positions as much as possible, especially the exact location of his strategic reserve. An experienced "mariner" with the command presence and leadership skills necessary to be entrusted with such a special mission near the end of eventful 1776, Captain Blackler would transport General Washington across the swirling waters of the icy Delaware River for the December 26 surprise attack on the Hessian brigade at Trenton in barely two months.[15]

Most important and as demonstrated repeatedly on other fields of strife in crisis situations, the other soldiers of the three regiments on the lower ground before them knew that these seasoned fighting men of the Fourteenth Massachusetts Continental Regiment would stand firm when the fighting opened in full fury, regardless of the odds or the slim chances for success: a psychological advantage that fueled the determination of the Massachusetts brigade's soldiers to fight even harder to match the superior past performances of the young men and boys of Glover's old regiment. After all, these mostly Marblehead soldiers had proved themselves to have been some of the most resilient and versatile troops in Washington's army during the New York Campaign. Most of all, Glover knew that this thin line of former fishermen, seafarers, and sailors, who were now acting as the brigade's strategic reserve, of the Fourteenth Massachusetts would not break or run in the face of a British bayonet charge.

Glover's Brilliant Battle Plan

And that was the very reason why the Marblehead colonel had chosen them to anchor his last defensive line on Pelham Heights and on the Hutchinson River's west side, although divided by the river, in what was basically the last phase of his four-part defense in depth and another ambush of sorts, which was to be the fourth one, after Glover would orchestrate three more defensive lines by regiment in echelon before the last on the highest ground, where the Fourteenth Massachusetts stood fire to overlook the future battlefield: all part of Glover's masterful battle plan that called for the other three regiments to defend their assigned defensive positions before gradually falling back up ever-higher ground by innovative design in a leapfrog tactic from three separate defensive positions, whose fall was only a matter of time because of the disparity of numbers.

Before falling back on Glover's order to the next defensive position to their rear, the men assigned to the foremost position would deliver repeated fires before retiring north to the next line to the rear in a tactical relay to gain a more elevated defensive position, until the retiring troops led the British into multiple ambushes at all four positions: the central tactical feature of the colonel's masterful defense in depth. The British and Hessians would be cleverly lured ever-northward and from one defensive position to the next and ever-farther up the slope until they confronted Glover's best regiment, bolstered by three twelve-pounders, on the high defensive ground on the river's west bank, after the attackers turned west in pursuit. Quite simply, the three Massachusetts regiments retiring north in turn to new defensive positions would provide, in Glover's mind, the ideal lure for the enemy to pour uphill with enthusiasm and then straight into the fire of each separate ambush on both sides of the road (staggered defensive positions with the regiments situated in echelon and one behind the other on ever-higher ground) and then finally into the well-positioned strategic reserve on Pelham Heights and then on the highest ground bordering the river's west side.

The men of the left of the mostly Marblehead regiment had been aligned in place behind a lengthy stone wall that spanned Pelham Heights. Glover had ensured that his final, or northernmost, defensive line would be his strongest, especially by his wide placement of the three pieces of artillery positioned on the high ground west of the Hutchinson River on the Fourteenth Massachusetts's right. After having been pulled by oxen rather than horses, which were in short supply in Washington's army, these three guns were now in the right place for Glover's tactical purposes because they were the key to the plan of thoroughly punishing the attackers, because they were certain to follow on the heels of the retiring three regiments in succession in the belief that victory had been won. These three artillery pieces on the right of the Fourteenth Massachusetts that overlooked the Hutchinson River and terrain, including the open plateau, east of the river had created a killing zone to the west. Glover was in the process of creating a staggered defense in depth that alternately featured a series of ambushes (four in total) of each regiment on both sides of the road that would be sprung separately by his regiments in echelon defensive positions in relay fashion in order to buy as much time and to inflict as much damage as possible.

With considerable insight, Glover planned the tactical orchestration of his innovative defensive arrangement of a brilliant defense in depth to maximize his limited combat capabilities when every single man was needed in the ranks. Glover knew that his tactical deployments had to be carefully made, which was somewhat easier because of the colonel's meticulous and precision-oriented nature, which had been partly forged from the demanding seafaring experience. Of course, the delicate intricacy of Glover's innovative battle plan was based on the hope of somehow stemming the tide of British and Hessians pouring up the Pell's Point Peninsula: quite simply, the greatest challenge ever faced by the colonel during the war years.

And by this time, Glover felt the heavy burden of command responsibility for his tiny brigade of Massachusetts soldiers, who faced extermination if anything went wrong or if he made a single tactical mistake or miscalculation. There was now simply no margin for error and Glover acted with great care. He fully realized that every one of his soldiers "entirely depended on their being well disposed of," in Glover's words, in their multiple staggered positions of a defense in depth and in echelon to withstand the raging torrent of invaders, both British and Hessians, who would soon strike with a vengeance.[16] In consequence, what Glover orchestrated was something that was tactically unprecedented in its originality to reveal a new kind of American warfare born of desperation, resourcefulness, and ingenuity in an emergency situation: "a defense in depth to inflict as many casualties as possible despite [facing overwhelming odds and] a novel form of warfare for the time and demonstrated the evolving nature of the American way of war."[17]

Because he commanded only "my little party" of Bay State Continental soldiers who were determined to do or die, as Glover explained in a letter about the host of severe disadvantages that he now labored under, in the face of a massive invasion, he took full advantage of the lay of the land in the clever and ingenious orchestration of his defense in depth. With a good eye for terrain, the colonel's judicious placement of troops along the best defensible ground on the southern edge of the high ground of Pelham Heights on both sides of Split Rock Road and not far from the giant egg-shaped boulder named Split Rock was the only way that a relative handful of Continental soldiers in successive defensive lines would be able to hold firm under the inevitable onslaught of Howe's finest troops.

Therefore, from the beginning, Glover had carefully surveyed the lay of the land with a keen eye as it steadily descended south to lower elevations and then gradually dropped all the way to Pelham Bay and the flat coastal plain and saltwater marshes. To fully exploit the lay of the land with the keen eye of a topographer, Glover had early envisioned with clarity a series of four separate defensive lines—a defense in depth based upon his strategic reserve of his old regiment situated on the highest ground to the north (the left of the Fourteenth Massachusetts) and to the northwest (the right of the Fourteenth Massachusetts) along several different and gradually more elevated positions from south to north below the southern end of Pelham Heights. With his regiments positioned in echelon, Glover planned for his staggered defense to be established on both sides of the road and in which each separate defensive line would be supported by another defensive line or position—four in total of each regiment—located just to the rear and on ever-higher ground that led all the way up the gradual slope nearly to the summit of Pelham Heights, where the fourth defensive line was located. Here, just east of the Hutchinson River, the men on the Fourteenth Massachusetts's right stood on the highest ground to dominate this key point.

With the forty-man advance party under an experienced Massachusetts captain now in an advanced position down Split Rock Road having already bought additional precious time by keeping the invaders at bay and, most important, beyond the enemy's sight of Glover's orchestration of a masterful arrangement of a defense in depth, the former ship captain from Marblehead possessed the invaluable luxury of making tactical dispositions unseen to the north on higher ground. In consequence, these astute placements would be entirely unknown to the fast-approaching British and Hessians, who never expected to meet such a highly competent American leader in command of crack troops, especially after what had happened at Long Island and at Kip's Bay to reveal the shocking lack of experience, sound leadership, and training of American soldiers.

Colonel Glover especially liked the terrain that lay before the southern end of Pelham Heights, especially because the sloping ground was covered with row after row of sturdy old stone fences that stood on both sides of and perpendicular to Split Rock Road. Continuing a lengthy tradition from old Ireland, generations of local Westchester County farmers, including Scotch-Irish and Irish Catholic immigrant settlers along with the Dutch who had first settled the area, had spent considerable time and effort in clearing the land of the many large rocks left behind by receding glaciers millions of years ago and constructing the stone fences that covered the countryside as far as the eye could see. In addition, these walls of rock were also built to mark land boundaries between neighbors to prevent quarrels, keep livestock within property, and to separate cropland from fallow land. Like in New England, these stone fences were fairly high—from around waist high to around shoulder height—in order to keep cattle and horses from destroying the crops or keeping their pastures enclosed for safety against thieves and natural predators.[18]

Glover carefully established a series of defensive lines that stretched across the southern end of Pelham Heights. The terrain gradually descended until it met the saltwater marshes and wetlands of the lower Hutchinson River Valley on the west side of Split Rock Road, while eastward the plateau gradually sloped downward, or south, toward Pelham Bay. With the same skill as captaining a fishing vessel at the Grand Banks and with considerable tactical insight and after having positioned the Fourteenth Massachusetts, Glover first established Colonel Baldwin's position near Pelham Manor (the Joshua Pell House) with the Twenty-sixth Massachusetts in the third line and Colonel Shepard's position with his Third Massachusetts in the second line on lower ground, and he then placed the 226 soldiers of Colonel Joseph Read's Thirteenth Massachusetts Continental Regiment in the most advanced defensive position, or the first line, at the southern end of the slight north-south ridge in the lowest-lying defensive position. Read's men were placed behind a stone fence that ran to the left, or east, of Split Rock Road. These were successive defensive positions behind stone fences on both sides of the road with Colonel Read occupying a position east, or the left side, of Split Rock Road, while Colonel Shepard was on the west of the road, or the right side, and Colonel Baldwin on the east side and all in staggered positions on ever-higher ground from south to north: an innovative and masterful defensive in depth with regiments positioned in echelon and designed to cover a wide front so that the enemy, advancing from the south, would have to run a gauntlet and funnel of fire from successive ambushes on ever-higher ground and on both sides of the road.

Read's veteran soldiers of the Thirteenth Massachusetts formed last into a lengthy defensive line in the first position east of the road on advantageous high ground, located at the edge of a woods just before, or north of, the "eminence" that had been gained in hurling back the foremost dismounted cavalry troops and grenadiers of the British advance. This careful positioning meant that Colonel Read's right flank would be well protected because the ridge dropped off to the west and the swamps of the river valley of the Hutchinson to the west ensured no passage of British or Hessian troops to gain either his flank or rear.[19]

Sufficiently elevated to offer protection, the lengthy stone fence now held by Colonel Read's men of the Thirteenth Massachusetts was located on high ground that made for an excellent defensive position. Hidden in a thick stand of timber to the rear, this elevated position along the stone wall located east of Split Rock Road was an ideal defensive location for the veterans of Read's Thirteenth Massachusetts Continental Regiment to make their stand against the odds and spring the first ambush as planned by Glover.[20]

Born in the small town of Uxbridge, Massachusetts, on the Blackstone River and near the Rhode Island border, Colonel Joseph Read was a hard-fighting colonel from Worcester County, Massachusetts. His fine regiment consisted of Massachusetts soldiers who had seen service that went back to the siege of Boston in 1775–1776. The antecedent of the Thirteenth Massachusetts Continental Regiment was a command of Massachusetts State Troops, authorized in late April 1775, appropriately known as Read's Regiment, which had been commanded by Joseph Read. Later, on January 1, 1776, this unit of citizen-soldiers then had been consolidated with two other Massachusetts regiments, David Brewer's Regiment and Timothy

Walker's Regiment, to officially form the Thirteenth Massachusetts Continental Regiment. Fortunately, in holding the first defensive line on this day of destiny in Westchester County, Read's experienced soldiers had no fear in meeting either Hessians or redcoats, regardless of their numbers; this feisty and confident attitude was certainly needed on Friday October 18. Many of these men were savvy veterans who possessed both French and Indian War and minuteman experience, steeling them for the stern challenge that lay ahead.[21]

Then, after carefully surveying the ground northwest of the southern end of the Pell's Point Peninsula and how to take advantage of it to the fullest, Colonel Glover made another clever defensive decision as part of his meticulous defense in depth across the sloping ground below Pelham Heights. After ascertaining the best defensive position to align the next phase of his defense in depth just to the north of Colonel Read's position, Glover placed Colonel William Shepard's Third Massachusetts Continental Regiment behind "a fine double wall" of stone, in Glover's words, on the opposite side of the road, right or west, to the Thirteenth Massachusetts. Indeed, on the lowest ground, Colonel Read's regiment was positioned on the road's other side, or east, in a staggered defensive line located just to the south: all part of Glover's plan of placing regiments in echelon. Just over two hundred soldiers, therefore, of Shepard's regiment held this excellent defensive position west of the road behind a rock fence that was also situated on higher ground and more open terrain than Colonel Read's regiment. As Glover had early envisioned, the highly disciplined men of both regiments were carefully positioned behind the stone fences, which were concealed in thick woodlands to their rear, on both sides of Split Rock Road.[22]

By this time, Colonel William Shepard had returned to his Third Massachusetts just in time to take command, despite still being sick and having spent the night at a private home near the encampment because of his lingering illness. But he had refused to desert his beloved regiment by requesting a well-deserved medical discharge. In the defiant colonel's words from a letter: "I immediately joined the Regts. and found them posted on each side of the road [in echelon] behind a cross [stone] fence situated to annoy the enemy as they approached" from the south.[23]

In a letter, one soldier of the Massachusetts brigade penned with admiration for Glover's consummate tactical skill by explaining how the troops under "Colonel Sheperd [sic] was well covered under a wall" of gneiss stone in a good defensive position that dominated the road's west side by which the British and Hessians would have to march up in column.[24] Born in Westfield, Massachusetts, on December 1, 1737, Colonel Shepard was a seasoned and "grizzled veteran" of the French and Indian War. He knew what it was like to battle in the dense woodlands against Native Americans, French regulars, and Canadian militiamen, who all fought Indian-style in a highly effective manner.[25] But more important by this time, Colonel Shepard, in the estimation of General William Heath, was "one of the most efficient American officers" in Washington's army, which lacked comparable fine officer material that partly explained the series of disasters during the ill-fated New York Campaign.[26]

The grandson of an English immigrant and the promising son of a humble tanner and respected deacon of the Congregational Church, Colonel Shepard began his military service as a seventeen-year-old youth in 1757 during the French and Indian War, when Native Americans, including Abenaki warriors, from the dark depths of the Canadian wilderness raided far and wide, even striking by surprise near Boston. Shepard's military career continued until 1763, at which time he had gained a captain's rank by the war's conclusion. This was no small accomplishment for a God-fearing preacher's son who was nearly as devout as his father. Colonel Shepard's fight had been a holy war against the longtime invaders, especially Native Americans, who had long brought death and destruction across New England well before the French and Indian War. He was a veteran of all four colonial wars for empire and possession of the North American continent, including the French and Indian War fights at Fort William Henry and Crown Point in the strategic Lake Champlain Valley, which was the main artery that led north into Canada.

When not battling French regulars, irregular Canadians, and Native Americans, especially the Abenaki of the notorious village of Saint Francis located on the river of the same name, on the rampage, Shepard had farmed the land he loved around the picturesque farming community of Westfield, located amid the rolling hills of western Massachusetts. He then returned home to his small brown house and married the love of his life, after the war concluded. Here, he was known in the hardworking agrarian community for his simple ways, frugality, and industriousness as a humble yeoman farmer who was a decent and esteemed man of the soil. Despite being handicapped by limited education in part because he had pursued a lengthy military career out of necessity, Shepard possessed considerable political influence and the respect of Westfield. For example, Shepard served as a selectman and as a member of the Westfield committee of correspondence in 1774 in the community on the Westfield River that flowed into the Connecticut River just to the east.

With the news of the first shots having been fired in anger at Lexington and Concord, Shepard had led his militiamen to Cambridge, when he had served as a lieutenant colonel of minutemen in April 1775 in the fast-gathering New England army of mostly yeomen farmers. He then gained more experience as the lieutenant colonel of Colonel Timothy Danielson's Fourth Massachusetts during the siege of Boston, when Howe and his army had been trapped inside the city located just southwest of Marblehead. On January 1, 1776, Shepard then became the lieutenant colonel of the Third Massachusetts Continental Regiment. In part because of his faithful service in active campaigning for so long, Shepard was not in the best shape on Friday October 18. However, like Colonel Baldwin and to his ever-lasting credit, he refused to leave his men much to Colonel Glover's benefit on October 18. Shepard, always a fighter and never wanting to be away from his boys from the Bay State for long, had been wounded at the Battle of Long Island near the end of August. By dint of seniority and demonstrated ability for an extended period, he was promoted to the rank of colonel to command of the Third

Massachusetts Continental Regiment. In part because of the skill and ability he would demonstrate on this day of crisis in Westchester County and like Glover in 1777, Shepard was destined for a general's rank in a most distinguished career.[27]

Like the Thirteenth and Fourteenth Massachusetts Continental Regiments, the Third Massachusetts also could be depended upon in a crisis situation like on this Friday morning when so far from home. These soldiers of Colonel Shepard's command had gained considerable military experience beginning during the siege of Boston while serving in the Fourth Massachusetts. On January 1, 1776, this fine Continental regiment known as the Third Massachusetts had been formed from the consolidation of Theophilus Cotton's Regiment and Timothy Danielson's Regiment and an independent company of Massachusetts volunteers.[28]

Most important in overall tactical considerations and as noted, the defensive line of Colonel Shepard's Third Massachusetts had been carefully arranged in position by Glover, so as not to be parallel to Colonel Read's defensive line on the other, or west, side of Split Rock Road, in a staggered defensive arrangement to fulfill his vision of a series of successive ambushes in a defense in depth of regiments in echelon. The veterans of the Third Continental Regiment now held an excellent defensive position behind the "fine double [stone] wall to the right-rear of Colonel Read's regiment": a well-conceived staggered defensive arrangement in depth and of regiments in echelon on both sides of the dirt road that was sure to pose a both a surprise and tactical challenge to Howe's attackers, as Glover had early envisioned with clarity.

Continuing this innovative, well-thought-out tactical arrangement of a clever defense in depth of a kind not previously seen in this war, the 234 soldiers of Colonel Loammi Baldwin's Twenty-sixth Massachusetts Continental Regiment had been placed by Glover behind another rock fence running parallel to the previous defensive positions east of Split Rock Road and among the glacial boulders lying along the slope. Baldwin's veteran regiment was positioned just to the north on higher ground than Colonel Shepard's regiment to the south but on the road's other side (east), while situated below the summit of Prospect Hill held by the left of the Fourteenth Massachusetts.

While a straw-colored regimental battle flag with boldly painted words waved about them and in methodical fashion, the men of the Twenty-sixth Continental Regiment, such as the troops of Captain Thomas Mighill's Company, felt secure in their assigned defensive positions along the fence of stone on the east side of Split Rock Road. Once again, Glover was stacking up most of his strength—two of his three regiments that were positioned in echelon—on the east side (Read and Baldwin) of the road as opposed to the west side where only Shephard's men had been positioned, because of the possibility of British flankers surging forward from the east and the topography of the gradually descending plateau that made his left flank more vulnerable and, hence, most likely to be outflanked, when compared to his more secure right flank closer to the Hutchinson River and rougher terrain.[29] By this time, most soldiers of Colonel Baldwin's regiment wore a mixed lot (of course, motley attire in professional British and Hessian eyes) of Continental uniforms, civilian clothes, or fancy Grenadier uniforms of the unit's elite troops. By far, the most splendidly uniformed men in Glover's Brigade were the members of the Grenadier company of the Twenty-sixth Massachusetts. This was the regiment's elite company, and Colonel Baldwin could not have been prouder of these excellent fighting men. Better trained and more skilled than even light troops, Grenadiers had been first organized for service in the British Army in 1678 for the express purpose of throwing a new weapon of war to cause destruction in the enemy's ranks, the hand grenade. In general, the Grenadiers, therefore, were usually taller, stronger, and more durable specimens than the other men of the regiment, because of their more important role as elite regimental members. As revealed by the distinctive uniforms that indicated as much to the enemy, this Grenadier company contained the best fighting men of Colonel Baldwin's command and some of the finest soldiers of Glover's brigade. Therefore, they had led the advance of the

Twenty-sixth Massachusetts Continental Regiment at the head of the regimental column in the morning south toward Pelham Bay, but were now positioned on the regiment's left flank a good distance east of the road to protect it from any slashing attacks across the plateau from the east toward the Long Island Sound. In striking contrast to the common fishing, sailor, and seamen garb worn by the men of Glover's old regiment, the distinctive uniforms of the Twenty-sixth Massachusetts Grenadiers consisted of lengthy coats of a reddish-brown color, light blue jacket underneath the coat, and white breeches that bestowed a jaunty look.

But what really made these Grenadier Continentals of Colonel Baldwin's regiment stand out in appearance not only among other members of Glover's Brigade but also in General Washington's army was their distinctive and imposing-looking regimental Grenadier mitre headpiece, or cap, which in shape was not unlike the tall Hessian headpieces. These high caps of brown to match the uniform coat of the grenadiers made soldiers appear taller on the battlefield—important for shock value, especially during an attack—much like a British and Scottish bearskin. Created for the same purpose of making the grenadier appear taller and more formidable to awe the opponent, this high cap of Baldwin's grenadiers was brimless so as not to impede the throwing of grenades in accordance with a theory from the past. Soldiers like Corporal Ansel Pope of this Grenadier Company of the Twenty-sixth Massachusetts wore their tall caps, around a full twelve inches high, that were covered in dyed wool. The front of the hat was decorated with the insignia of two large brass letters in white, "GW" and a small sunburst design. At the base of the high Grenadier cap of Baldwin's Grenadiers was the word, "Regiment" and the Roman numerals of "XX VI," with a "flaming" grenade symbol between the two sets of letters, for the regimental designation of which its members were most proud.[30]

Of course, it was no accident that Colonel Glover, who looked to gain every possible topographical and psychological advantage possible to maximize the overall effectiveness of his carefully orchestrated defense in depth, placed his best uniformed soldiers—the tall, formidable-looking Grenadiers of Baldwin's regiment—in the third defensive line positioned before the left of the strategic reserve (the Fourteenth Massachusetts to the north in the fourth defensive line) on the higher ground of the southern end of Pelham Heights, because of the lofty reputation of the elite Grenadier soldiers. This tactical placement was a well-calculated decision by the old seafarer, who continued to exploit every possible advantage to the maximum extent, including psychological factors.

Stretching from south to north, the first two defensive lines of Colonels Read's and Shepard's troops, respectively, consisted of soldiers who wore nondescript uniforms of civilian clothes, which made them look like New England militia and farmers, which was most deceiving to ensure that the enemy would become overconfident and overaggressive, especially when pursuit when the Massachusetts men were ordered to fall back: the exact attitude needed to ensure that the foe's tactics could be fully exploited by the springing of Glover's multiple ambushes along his masterful defense in depth. This common look of Glover's foremost defenders gave the distinct appearance to any approaching enemy that these Massachusetts soldiers were certainly not the elite Continental troops of General Washington's army, but only ill-trained citizen-soldiers who could be easily brushed aside. Therefore, to Howe's British and Hessians, who were already supremely confident about their incredibly easy invasion of the American mainland, it would appear to them that only the common people of the countryside—ragtag New York militiamen—had risen up to defend their homeland against the invader: a prospect that gave Generals Howe, Clinton, and Cornwallis absolutely no doubt whatsoever about the wisdom of aggressively pushing farther inland with confidence in an attempt to outflank and gain the rear of Washington's army to win it all in one bold stroke.

Clearly, British leadership was in for a nasty surprise, because General Howe was not considering the severity of his upcoming meeting with Glover and his Continentals. And to have soldiers who looked almost like battle-hardened regulars in their tall Grenadier mitre caps and reddish-brown uniforms was calculated by Glover to give an added shock value in the overall element of surprise—like when these hidden Massachusetts men would finally unleash their first volley—in a masterful game of psychological warfare, which was a vital ingredient of his brilliant defense in depth: a shrewd tactical development not unlike General Morgan's brilliant tactical thinking in later creating a third defensive line of crack Maryland and Virginia Continental troops, the Southern army's elite troops, at the Battle of Cowpens in January 1781, after the overconfident enemy of Lieutenant Colonel Banastre Tarleton's British Legion (a Loyalist command) had already faced militia and state troops in nondescript uniforms in the first and second defensive lines and easily pushed them aside, as they had been ordered to fall back by design to serve as bait, to become immensely overconfident in believing that the day had already been won—a big mistake of immense proportions. The soldiers of the first two lines had been informed by Morgan to offer only light resistance before falling back to a stronger third defensive line to encourage the enemy's over-aggressiveness to be fully exploited by the men of the strongest defensive line to the rear. In much the same way in overall tactical terms, so Glover had used his innovative plan of three strategic defensive lines of men behind stone fences, trees, and boulders on the high ground and then a fourth defensive line of the Fourteenth Massachusetts in a series of ambushes of a masterful defense in depth. Therefore, while Morgan would use three lines of a defense in depth at Cowpens, Glover employed four defensive lines in the same manner by adhering basically to the same brilliant strategy that he had developed on the fly long before the Battle of Cowpens: the art of irregular or asymmetrical warfare at its finest.

Indeed, at this time, the British believed that in all of Washington's army, except for Colonel John Haslet's Delaware Continental Regiment and Colonel William Smallwood's Maryland Continentals, who had tenaciously battled Cornwallis's attackers to a standstill at the Battle of Long Island and certainly not now in Westchester County, "there were no grenadiers" that they would have to face in battle. Therefore, this eventual realization about the presence of Baldwin's grenadiers in their fine uniforms was guaranteed to come as a great shock to the Hessians and British, who believed they would be only facing a few ill-trained Westchester County militia on October 18.[31]

Indeed, with Colonel Baldwin in command, the Twenty-sixth Massachusetts Continental Regiment was more dependable and solid than the other regiments of Glover's Brigade with the exception of the Fourteenth Massachusetts: hence, its position in the third defensive line that served as a sturdy anchor for the first two lines that had been ordered to retreat when Glover gave the order at the right time. Like Captain Courtis, who now commanded Glover's Fourteenth Massachusetts, and Colonels Shepard and Read, Colonel Baldwin could be relied upon as he possessed plenty of experience and a good tactical sense. Most of all, Baldwin was every inch of a fighter of a never-say-die quality. Now wearing a London brown uniform coat with epaulettes on each shoulder and stylish white breeches, Baldwin was still ailing at this time. But he was determined to do his best, despite his fading health. However, the colonel's days as regimental commander were already numbered. Colonel Baldwin was destined to retire in early 1777 from service because of his wrecked health. However, he would rise magnificently to the fore today as if perfectly healthy and in good shape, which was certainly not the case.

Born in 1744 in Woburn, Middlesex County, Massachusetts, located just northwest of Boston, of English heritage, and descended from the forward-thinking pioneer who had been the town's founder, Baldwin was not only a capable citizen-soldier, but also a soldier-scholar and a true Renaissance man. Versatile and talented on multiple levels, he had soon tired of a mundane life as a lowly cabinetmaker during the years before the war. With a passion for mathematics and physics, eagerness for acquiring even more knowledge, and ever-ambitious to move upward in life, Baldwin had excelled at Harvard College in Cambridge, Massachusetts.

As a younger man, Baldwin had fulfilled his great dream of becoming a civil engineer, rising up from humble status as a self-made man much like Glover. He also became a respected political leader of Middlesex County, Massachusetts, and he represented his beloved community at the county convention in 1774. As a major with pre-war militia experience dating back to 1768, Baldwin had led three companies of minutemen from the town of Woburn in the spring of 1775. After the fateful unleashing of those shots "heard around the world" at Lexington Green on April 19, he had demonstrated considerable tactical ability gained from the French and Indian War by setting up a deadly ambush of the retreating British at the so-called "Bloody Angle" on the road to Boston. Motivated not only to defend homes and families but also to avenge the shooting down of a handful of militiamen on Lexington Green, Baldwin had aligned his 197 Woburn militiamen along the stone walls and rocks at the angle, or double bend, along the road full of retreating British on April 19. Baldwin and his citizen-soldiers had decimated the enemy's ranks with their close-range musket fire to inflict the highest casualties on the withdrawing British during this bloody day. So many British regulars were cut down by the hot fire of Baldwin's militiamen that the redcoats thought that the entire column might well be "annihilated," before it reached Boston's safety.

Leading a holy crusade against the invaders in scarlet uniforms with a righteous vengeance, Baldwin's first name of Loammi, the third son of Hosea, appropriately came straight from the pages of the Old Testament, which he revered. God had commanded Hosea to marry a prostitute to have children to send a stern message of disapproval to the Israeli people in an attempt to convince them to repent for their sinful ways. The name Loammi meant "not my people," which was a severe rebuke from the Lord, who had given Hosea the mission of transforming the Hebrew people, which represented God's hard judgment against Israel for their sins against the Lord.

Baldwin also had seen service during the siege of Boston, when Howe and his garrison had been forced to evacuate and sail to

Halifax, Canada, on St. Patrick's Day, March 17, 1776. After Howe and the British garrison departed the strategic port just southwest of Marblehead, Baldwin had then commanded Colonel Samuel Gerrish's Massachusetts Regiment, which was later designated as the Twenty-sixth Massachusetts Continental Regiment on January 1, 1776 when the colonel retired. Baldwin then became the first colonel of the Twenty-sixth Massachusetts Continental Regiment, molding his command into a close-knit group of excellent fighting men with thorough training and discipline, a fact that was about to be demonstrated in full during the dramatic showdown at Pell's Point.[32]

Selected carefully by the formidable team of Glover and Baldwin, the defensive position of the Twenty-sixth Massachusetts Continental Regiment was located behind yet another sturdy stone fence during Glover's orchestration of his masterful defense in depth. Situated in an ideal position on high ground, Baldwin's soldiers on the east side of the road were at the left-rear of Colonel Shepard's regiment on the road's west side. Colonel Glover's stratagem of a staggered defense in depth with regiments in echelon was now complete: the third defensive line under Baldwin, which was located on the east side of Split Rock Road, behind the left-rear of the Third Massachusetts Continental Regiment, in the second line, and on the opposite side of the road (west) from the Thirteenth Massachusetts Continental Regiment, the first line on the road's east side, and just below the left of the Fourteenth Massachusetts of the fourth defensive line, which was aligned behind a stone fence on the southern slope of Pelham Heights, farthest north.

Most important, Glover had ordered the hundreds of men of his regiments to lay low behind the stone fences so that they could not be seen by the British and Hessians, setting the stage for multiple ambushes (four in total, counting the left of the Fourteenth Massachusetts farthest north) to catch the enemy by surprise, when the Bay State men would be ordered to rise up and fire as one. All in all, Colonel Glover had orchestrated nothing less than four successive ambushes in four multiple lines of regiments in echelon in a brilliant defense of depth.

Therefore, with much tactical foresight and innovation, Glover continued to perfect his tactical arrangements of a staggered defense in depth by adding his final touches, while making sure that everyone was in exactly the right position. Much as at the future Battle of Cowpens in January 1781, this clever tactical arrangement of a staggered defense in depth meant that two regiments—the Thirteenth and Twenty-sixth Massachusetts Continental Regiments in the first and third positions from south to north—were positioned behind the stone fences on the road's left side, or east, while only a single regiment—the Third Massachusetts Continental Infantry in the second position under Colonel Shepard—was situated behind a stone wall on the right, or west, side of Split Rock Road: the clever staggered defensive, or ambush, positions of regiments in echelon from which multiple fires could be unleashed from four different elevations, including the left of the Fourteenth Massachusetts, at four different points that became ever-higher and across the broader front to make up for small numbers, especially after the enemy deployed in lengthy lines in a general assault.

Solidifying all three defensive lines on ever-descending ground before it and serving as the central foundation of Glover's unique defensive arrangement along the gradually sloping ground below the summit of Pelham Heights stood the left of the mostly Marbleheaders of the Fourteenth Continental Regiment of the strategic reserve in the fourth defensive line. These troops of Glover's old regiment were stretched across the heights—the highest ground position held by the Massachusetts men during the battle—to the rear on Split Rock Road to anchor Glover's entire defensive arrangement east of the Hutchinson River. As mentioned, Glover had masterfully devised not only a staggered defense in depth along ever-rising ground because each rearward defensive position was located on higher ground than the previous one, but also a series of clever ambushes with his regiments in echelon, thanks to the advantage of the stone fences and terrain. These stone fences now concealed hundreds of veteran defenders of the first three defensive lines in ambush positions, after they had been ordered by Colonel Glover to crouch low, stay silent, and not rise above the stone barriers that concealed them from prying enemy eyes.

To the advancing British and Hessians when they came forward, therefore, it would appear that, as Glover had planned, only a single American line opposed them once Colonel Read's men in the first line rose up and unleashed their first volley. Colonel Glover had ordered the men of the left of the Fourteenth Massachusetts situated just below the summit of Pelham Heights not to hide behind the stone fence, because by exposing them in the last, or fourth, defensive line on the highest ground of the three previous hidden lines, they would have served as an effective bait. Such a clever strategy would have helped to perfect the three ambushes on lower terrain along the gentle slope below the Fourteenth Massachusetts's left. Perched just below the summit of Prospect Hill east of the road, it would appear to General Howe's troops that *only* the mostly Marbleheaders of the Fourteenth Massachusetts's left stood before them on the most elevated terrain to the north. After all, Colonel Glover had ordered the troops of the other three regiments of the first three line to remain hidden and concealed behind the three parallel rock fences that spanned the open slopes below Pelham Heights and on both sides of Split Rock Road, which would have perfected such a tactic.

Indeed, the just more than two hundred soldiers of the Third Massachusetts, the 226 men of the Thirteenth Massachusetts, and the 234 infantrymen of the Twenty-sixth Massachusetts now lay low silently behind the lengthy stone fences, without revealing a single head of a man above this natural breastwork that stretched across the open countryside. Even the officers of the first three regiments were laying low in hidden positions, ensuring that they remained out of sight until the enemy got close to them. To the rear of the three deployed Bay State regiments on the lowest ground in elevation along the slope, the smallest number of men—about half of the total of 180 soldiers of the Fourteenth Massachusetts Continental Regiment— on the regiment's left stood in the last defensive line on the highest ground as not only a strategic reserve, but also as a sturdy tactical foundation for Glover's entire defense in depth, which had been set up to the south with extreme care.[33]

Making Colonel Glover's defensive arrangement of a series of ambushes in depth most formidable was the fact that the first three defensive lines were now cleverly masked positions behind stone walls that stretched across farmer's fields unseen by Howe's troops. Indeed, and most important, Glover's hurried tactical deployments and careful placement of his troops had been entirely unseen by the advancing British and Hessians. This key tactical advantage of an unseen deployment of an entire brigade of Bay Staters had been gained by the time that had been won because of Glover's swift movements to meet the enemy since departing his encampment and his earlier decision of having sent forth the advance party, under an experienced captain, of skirmishers down the slope to strike a blow to successfully keep the invaders at a distance and well beyond the eyesight of his stealthy deployment on the multiple defensive lines in the morning light.

In addition, Glover had thoughtfully established his regiments in the first three defensive positions based upon their combat prowess and fighting ability, ensuring that each successive defensive line was stronger and consisted of better fighting men, who were the most reliable in a crisis situation: much like the masterful battle plan of a comparable defense in depth developed years later by General Morgan to reap a sparkling victory at Cowpens. The honor of the foremost Bay State unit about to face the onslaught of British and Hessian invaders—the Thirteenth Massachusetts Continental Regiment—was followed by the Third Massachusetts Continental Regiment and the Twenty-sixth Massachusetts Continental Regiment and then the left of Glover's old regiment on the highest elevation of these multiple defensive lines. Colonel Glover's well-conceived and skillful tactical arrangement of an ingenious defense in depth was also calculated to enhance morale and bolster esprit de corps of his men at a time when it was most needed when facing such unfavorable odds. The Continentals of each Bay State regiment also desired to do their best for their unit's name and honor, and, of course, to outfight its sister regiments in a traditional rivalry that would pay high dividends on October 18.

Most important, Glover's masterful defensive arrangement of his staggered defense in depth had two regiments—the Thirteenth and Twenty-sixth Massachusetts Continental Regiments—on the left side, or east, of Split Rock Road: a guarantee that the enemy would be hit with fires from regiments in echelon from both sides of the road at the time when they would be expecting a fire from the same side of the road that they had just received, when they encountered Glover's next ambush position of hidden troops.

As calculated, this double defensive strength of two regiments on the east side of the road protected Glover's weakest flank, the left, because of the lay of the land, especially the open plateau, and the fact that the Long Island Sound was just to the east, just in case General Clinton sent detachments of flankers overland and west. Therefore, the heavier defensive strength situated east of the road was calculated to buy time to allow for the greater possibility of escape for the Massachusetts men from the area just northwest of the Pell's Point Peninsula and then for slipping away west by the right flank across the Hutchinson River to link with the right of Glover's Fourteenth Massachusetts, if the defensive lines were smashed before the men could withdraw north to the next defensive position or a flanking movement from the direction (east) gained Glover's rear, while they battled the attackers surging north up Split Rock Road to the south.

Colonel Glover's wise placement of the three artillery pieces in the fourth, or last, defensive line on the right of the Fourteenth Massachusetts, situated on high ground above the river, of his complex defense in depth, especially the Fourteenth Massachusetts's left at the highest point on the north, only enhanced a tactical illusion to disguise the trap that had been so cleverly set up by Glover to give the false impression that the defenders only possessed a single battle line, and a very weak one at that, on the southern end of Pelham Heights, because the men of the three defensive lines were now hidden by the stone fences of gneiss stone. Therefore, before Glover's ambushes were sprung, to professional British eyes, it seemed that this feeble defensive stand was only that of a small band of soldiers—only 180 men of what was actually the fourth defensive line—under Captain Courtis spread across the high, open ground of the lower end of Pelham Heights and also on high ground west of the Hutchinson River: as planned by the colonel, the appearance of only one defensive line at first glance before the men of the first three defensive lines opened fire to reveal their hidden positions on lower terrain. And the tactical misconception was exactly what Colonel Glover wanted the enemy to think, hoping such a mistaken impression would fuel an overconfidence and cockiness that could be their undoing. Clearly, Glover had set up a tactical scenario in which the advancing enemy would be surprised by each defensive line: the first three hidden ones and then the strongest one—the fourth and last consisting of the brigade's best men—bolstered by artillery to the northwest on the river's west side.

Indeed, as the enemy was about to learn the hard way in advancing north with unbridled confidence, the stealthy tactical arrangement of Captain Courtis's Fourteenth Massachusetts was not only the last defensive line, but in fact only the fourth defensive line along the slope that rose ever-higher and the defense became even more staunch by deliberate design: a fact that would be unrealized by the advancing British and Hessians until it was too late. To completely surprise Howe's troops, Glover had established four separate defensive lines of each of his regiments in echelon and at intervals on both sides of Split Rock Road and at ever-higher elevations along the slope leading up to the highest ground at Pelham Heights in not only a staggered defensive arrangement, but also a defense in depth that was masterful in its tactical originality: an unprecedented and sophisticated defense of a brilliance not yet seen in this war in what was essentially the first Cowpens of the American Revolution.

Most important, Glover now held good high ground on the west side of the road, where Colonel Shepard's regiment was hidden behind its own stone fence, before the land descended south toward an expanse of low-lying saltwater marshes and swamp meadows that were impassible, especially when flooded at high tide, before the wide expanse of Pelham Bay. The geography to the south below Pelham Heights ensured that Howe's attackers would not only have to advance primarily up Split Rock Road but also to the road's east side where the land, the plateau, was mostly covered grassy fields or pastureland of local farmers: ideal for enemy flankers to advance. Colonel Glover had wisely chosen his defensive positions not only because they dominated the main road leading north from Pelham Bay but also effectively used the high ground at multiple ascending levels, which was mostly open and cleared since it had been cultivated for generations by Westchester County farmers unlike the marshy lower ground to the south that often flooded, as much as possible. Like a true Marbleheader who was frugal and resourceful by nature, Glover's innovative tactical arrangement made the most of what little the ever-economical colonel was available to him, while he had exploited everything possible to his maximum advantage when the stakes were high.[34]

With considerable understatement that disguised the reality that Glover had orchestrated the most clever and well-conceived of defensive arrangements—the exact details would not even become known to Washington by the time that he reported on the battle because he was not on the field to see Glover's brilliant defense in depth, one of Washington's officers described in a letter how Glover, "who had been watching their motions, had posted [his Massachusetts troops] in a very advantageous manner to annoy them."[35]

Ironically, Marylander Tench Tilghman, of Washington's staff, had written a most insightful and almost prophetic letter on October 13, 1776 to a politician friend in which he revealed a winning tactical formula, as now fully embraced by Glover although there was no connection between the two men, emphasized how in the areas of Westchester County from Throgs Neck west toward Kingsbridge and the Hudson River

are as defensible as they can be wished. The roads are all lined with stone fences and the adjacent Fields divided off with stone [fences] likewise, which will make it impossible for them to advance their artillery and ammunition wagons by any other Rout than the great roads, and I think if they were well-lined with troops, we may make a Considerable Slaughter if not discomfit them totally.[36]

Fortunately, for Glover and America on October 18, this exact same situation that had earlier practically made Tench Tilghman salivate because of the availability of bountiful defensive opportunities now existed farther north and inland from Pell's Point, where Colonel Glover had completed his tactical masterpiece on just such an ideal defensive arena to set the stage for the upcoming battle. In a most masterful way that was as innovative as it was ingenious, Glover had maximized every inch of the lay of the land to his advantage and every possible feature to enhance his defensive positions along Split Rock Road: a tactical plan that also maximized the overall effectiveness of his small numbers and his soldier's fighting prowess in terms of marksmanship, training, and discipline. All in all, the colonel from Marblehead had masterfully combined the lessons of the French and Indian War, Indian warfare, and the New York Campaign in regard how best to defeat European troops by irregular and unorthodox, or frontier, tactics for which the English and Hessians would be entirely unprepared.

By the same token and most important, Glover had also significantly minimized his considerable weaknesses, especially in regard to numbers, by cleverly concealing his small number of Continentals by way of a unique blend of stealth and deception, except the forty-man advance party that now stood atop the small eminence—according to plan, the initial bait that would have to fall back on the double and lead the attackers to the stone fences for the hidden veterans of Colonel Read's Thirteenth Massachusetts Continental Regiment to then rise up and open fire at close range to punish the overconfident pursuers, who believed that they were on the verge of another one-sided victory as throughout this campaign: Colonel Glover's first ambush of his defense in depth. Only one of Glover's four regiments—the left of the Fourteenth Massachusetts Continental Regiment now posed near the summit of Prospect Hill, which was cleared land for farming or pasture and in a defensive line that overlooked the Split Rock Road—would be seen by General Howe's men, when they approached from the lower ground to the south, but only after pushing through three previous defensive positions, or ambushes, based on sturdy stone fences and a defense in depth. In record time and with pinpoint precision, Glover had placed more than three-fourths of his brigade east of the Hutchinson River in multiple concealed defensive positions, and these crack Continental troops now lay in ambush positions that had been cleverly devised to inflict maximum damage.

And demonstrating even more tactical and psychological insight that would pay dividends in the upcoming fight when so much was at stake, Glover had placed his most reliable soldiers—the left of the Fourteenth Continental Infantry—exactly where they needed to be to bestow confidence to the men of the three regiments in front by serving as the solid anchor for the defense in depth: in the fourth and last defensive line poised across the best defensive ground. Ironically, even though they were the brigade's most dependable troops, the soldiers of Glover's old regiment were also the least experienced in the use of firearms compared to the men of other regiments, which explained Glover's exact positioning of his regiments in his defensive scheme. Unlike the soldiers of Glover's other three regiments, who were mostly farmers from among the rolling hills and fields of western and eastern Massachusetts and were long familiar with the use of firearms, most Marbleheaders of the Fourteenth Massachusetts had spent their lives on the sea as sailors, seafarers, and fishermen.

As Glover fully realized, therefore, this unique defensive arrangement that he had created in record time based upon varying strengths and weaknesses of his troops recognized the fact that the Fourteenth Massachusetts soldiers were less experienced in regard to marksmanship than his other men. In consequence, it would be mostly farm boys for the foremost defensive lines who would be the shooters and killers today. Nevertheless, the Fourteenth Massachusetts troops were the most steadfast and reliable men, especially when bolstered by artillery, who were ideal for a strategic reserve on the high ground of the Hutchinson River's west bank, while Colonel Glover counted on the other three regiments to inflict the most damage on the enemy in defense of Split Rock Road.

Even though the Massachusetts men of Glover's old regiment were now familiar with firing muskets with accuracy and knew how to use them as lethal implements of war in case of hand-to-hand combat, they still in general possessed less marksmanship skills than the mostly yeomen farmers of the Thirteenth, Third, and Twenty-sixth Massachusetts, which were positioned from south to north, respectively. Consequently, Glover had placed the troops of these three veteran regiments in the first three defensive lines, where marksmanship would be most required in facing Howe's advance to inflict as much damage and buy as much time as possible, while the less-proficient marksmen were to the rear. Indeed, Glover had constructed his entire defense in depth partly with the best riflemen in the first line, the second best in the second, etc. However, the seasoned fighting men of the Fourteenth Continental Regiment were ideal for anchoring the final defensive line, because they would fight with bayonets, fists, and musket-butts, if the redcoats and Hessians reached their line and attempted to overpower them.

Most important, Glover had developed a most innovative and flexible tactical plan that was based not only on the enemy's weaknesses but also on the relatively few strengths of the Massachusetts men to achieve the element of surprise in the form of a series distinct ambushes established on ever-rising ground where his regiments were deployed in echelon, with the first on the lowest ground, the second on the second lowest ground, etc. from south to north. By relying on a complex mix of asymmetrical or irregular tactics stemming from the French and Indian War and Native American combat not found in textbooks and not taught at any military schools in Europe, Glover had created a new American kind of waging war by setting the tactical stage for the springing of multiple surprises on the advancing enemy with a carefully established network of separate tactical ambushes. During centuries of warfare, Native Americans had perfected the art of the ambush, and the New England colonists, especially the men from Massachusetts, had learned their lessons well. And, most of all, Glover knew that the key to spring these successive ambushes was feigning a series of retreats not unlike when King Leonidas had feigned retreats before he ordered his Spartans to suddenly turn on the pursuing Persians to inflict devastating losses.

Besides the stone fences that now entirely hid hundreds of Massachusetts soldiers in the staggered defensive positions, among scattered boulders and in stands of thick woods just behind the stone fences also helped to conceal some of Glover's troops. This triple network of tactical surprises orchestrated by Glover was now ensured by the three hidden seasoned regiments, while hundreds of veteran Continentals were sheltered behind the high stone fences, remaining perfectly still and quiet in the cool of this sunny autumn morning. Clearly, with a good deal of resourcefulness and innovation because of limited manpower and because he had no choice, Glover had orchestrated a tactical defensive masterpiece second to none in overall brilliance, which was impressive for its originality, clever qualities, and innovation—basically, the first Cowpens of the American Revolution. As he revealed the source of his novel tactical thinking derived from personal experiences in a letter, Glover based his well-conceived plan upon an ancient tactical principle that he understood well by this time: "It's one of the first principles in war to deceive."[37]

The multiple surprise ambushes that Colonel Glover had set in place would achieve this crucial goal in masterful fashion. But as important, Glover understood the axiom about the psychological advantage that resulted in the high motivations of his men, which was more appropriate under the circumstances:

> By all means meet them if possible at their first landing [and]
> If a general battle comes on, one or the other must be conquered. If it should be our unhappy lot, (which God forbid)

we must be slaves, which is worse than death. We can but die
in conquering them, which will be dying gloriously.[38]

As mentioned, Glover had based his ingenious tactical design on the
supreme importance of inflicting as much damage and buying as much
time as possible because Howe lusted for the opportunity to cut off
and trap Washington's army, if he quickly pushed the Massachusetts
men aside. The requested reinforcements at General Lee's headquarters by Major William Raymond Lee would fail to arrive in time,
which Glover had already anticipated to ensure the careful and meticulous orchestration of his defense in depth upon which everything
now depended: "Pray let no time be lost, a day's delay may be fatal to
America."[39]

Forgotten Top Lieutenants on a Day of Destiny

On this day of decision in a picturesque area of Westchester County,
Colonel Glover benefited immensely from the fact that he could rely
on a high quality of leadership ability among his veteran regimental
commanders, because most of them had seen arduous service during
the French and Indian War, when Massachusetts had waged war
against its most hated opponents—Native Americans and the French,
which had so often descended upon New England from Canada
in devastating raids year after year: Captain Courtis and Colonels
Shepard, Baldwin, and Read.

Past conflicts, especially the French and Indian War, had created a source of pride in the accomplishments of these Bay State soldiers during arduous service that helped to bestow confidence in this
upcoming confrontation with Howe's army, while solidifying their
distinctive identity as Massachusetts men from faraway places like
Marblehead and Woburn. Like Glover at age forty-three and who
was less than three weeks away from his next birthday, these tried
senior officers of the undersized Bay State brigade were mature, savvy
in the ways of war, natural leaders, and experienced fighting men who

possessed an abundance of leadership abilities and tactical skills. These citizen-soldiers who had risen to high rank were highly respected by their followers: Captain Courtis at age fifty-six; Colonel Baldwin at age thirty-two; Colonel Read at age thirty-four; and Colonel Shepard at age thirty-nine. Glover's trusty right-hand man who he would depend upon was Major William Raymond Lee, who was about to return to the command from his headquarters mission to request assistance before it was too late. He had been promoted as the senior captain of the Fourteenth Massachusetts by the time of the evacuation from Long Island to a major's rank, and he was now Glover's top staff officer and the "Brigade Major."[40]

The highly capable Major Lee hailed from one of the most distinguished and richest merchant families of Marblehead, whose revered patriarchal head was Henry Lee. He had founded the Lee family in Marblehead, and it had long thrived to become prosperous and highly esteemed. Samuel Lee, Henry Lee's son, became one of Marblehead's leading merchants. He owned some of the largest commercial vessels of Marblehead, growing rich from lucrative trade with not only the West Indies, but also around the world. Despite enslaving people as domestic servants who worked in his stately mansion, Samuel Lee was a pious man, serving as a deacon of the Congregational Church and justice of the peace. His son, Justice Samuel Lee, continued the long-established traditions of Marblehead's so-called "codfish aristocracy," becoming a community leader and wealthier as a prosperous merchant and shipowner of the town. Justice's son, David, was the first member of the Lee family to demonstrate a deep love for the military. He served in the combined British and American siege of France's mighty fortress of Louisbourg, Nova Scotia, which protected the entrance to the St. Lawrence River that led west to Quebec and then Montreal, during the French and Indian War. Another promising son, John Lee, who was born in 1716, owned even more ships and mercantile enterprises and enslaved more African people than his ancestors. He married Joanna Raymond, who was the granddaughter of a local hero of the French and Indian War, Captain William

Raymond. From this happy union, William Raymond Lee had been born in 1745. With the outbreak of the crisis with England, John Lee had served as a member of the Essex County Convention of 1774 and the committee of correspondence in 1775. Then, he become the colonel of the Marblehead regiment, and helped to defend the port of Salem, where Glover had been born in 1732, against a land threat and then played a role in the defense of port of Beverly against a naval threat.[41]

William Raymond Lee was as enthusiastic about the patriot cause as John Lee and his other relatives, including Jeremiah Lee, of Marblehead. William Raymond Lee began his prosperous career as a businessman in his uncle Jeremiah's counting room and then eventually managed all of the widespread shipping concerns of the wealthy Lee family. Lee also excelled in his personal life, making a wise choice in marrying Mary Lemmon of Marblehead. Also a member of one of the three great merchant families of Marblehead, Jeremiah Lee had offered his "fortune, influence, and himself" to fulfill the great dream of independence.

He became a Continental Congress delegate in Philadelphia, embarking upon a distinguished political career. By the time of the American Revolution, the enterprising William Raymond Lee family lived in the beautiful sprawling mansion built by his grandfather at 185 Washington Street in the most prestigious section of Marblehead, while Glover lived at 11 Glover Street on the square. In a short time, William was destined to play a key role in ferrying thousands of troops of Washington's army across the Delaware River for the unleashing of the surprise attack on Trenton near the end of December 1776, when the tide of the revolution was turned with the defeat of an entire Hessian brigade of three regiments. And in the future, Lee would gain the coveted rank of colonel in part for what he accomplished at the Battle of Pell's Point before the sun set on October 18.[42]

Representing the distinguished military tradition on both sides of the family, Major Lee now officially served as the "Brigade Major," and, more important, as Colonel Glover's top adviser on his personal staff. Glover and Lee were kindred spirits and fighters, who worked together as an especially highly effective team on October 18. This development was most appropriate because Lee was also an in-law of Colonel Glover to ensure that military bonds and commitment to the cause as strong as familial ties. The colonel's son, John Glover Jr., had married Fanny Lee, the sister of Major Lee. Captain John Glover Jr. now proudly represented the crack fighting men of his company, his father, and his beloved community of Marblehead.[43]

Urgent Need to Buy Precious Time

It was well that Glover had now demonstrated that he was not only tactically innovative and resourceful but also tactically gifted, because the element of surprise that could be gained by a relative handful of Massachusetts soldiers was now practically all that stood between the patriots and the overpowering might of the British-Hessian invasion force, General Washington's disorganized withdrawing army, and perhaps the revolution's dismal end.

As the sun rose higher in the autumn sky of Westchester County and shined across the Pell's Point Peninsula nestled between the Long Island Sound to the east and the Hutchinson River to the west gradually began to warm up on the morning of October 18, after the cool night that reminded them that winter was on its way, barely 750 Massachusetts soldiers were finally ready for action at their assigned defensive positions just northwest of the Pell's Point Peninsula, after Glover had completed his dispositions. As noted, the left of Glover's regiment stood in line along the last, or fourth, defensive line on the highest ground on the Hutchinson River's east side, while their comrades lay quietly on lower terrain behind the lengthy stone fences of the first three staggered defensive lines to the south.

With thousands of Howe's best troops, with their well-oiled Brown Bess muskets on shoulders and gear clattering in conjunction with their disciplined step in time with the beating drums while their brass buttons, breastplates, and accouterments reflected the soft sunlight of early fall, marching relentlessly north up Split Rock Road and the Pell's Point Peninsula after having turned off Shore Road to gain Split Rock Road and then pushed north, Glover and his small band of men now faced odds of more than seven to one. Meanwhile, a smug Lord Howe, confident of success because of the lack of serious opposition, was at the landing site, supervising the arrival of more troops on shore and busily directing them inland as quickly as possible. The last thing that General Howe imagined at this time was that his surprise landing in Westchester County was about to be trumped by one of the war's most resourceful set of tactical surprises of a masterful defense in depth that stemmed from the fertile imagination of a former Marblehead seafarer, who more properly belonged on water rather than land.[44]

In total, more than six thousand confident British and Hessian troops would come ashore and march north up the Pell's Point Peninsula on October 18, ensuring that the odds were more than seven to one against Glover and his brigade: certainly a sufficient force to cut off Washington and trap his badly disorganized army on Manhattan Island with ease or destroy it during the gloomy withdrawal to White Plains, after the diminutive seafaring colonel and his equally undersized Massachusetts brigade were quickly hurled aside with inevitable ease or so it seemed. As a cruel fate would have it, this impressive total of enemy troops was greater odds for Glover and his small brigade than any American soldiers had ever faced on their own in any major battle of the American Revolution to date, including at Bunker Hill.

Despite being a veteran commander well known for nerves of steel and a toughness born of the seafaring experience, Glover was outwardly calm but anxious deep inside. He was uneasy, and his nerves were taut because so much was at stake this morning, and he knew that Howe had to be thwarted at any cost to ensure the escape of Washington's army and its very existence. In his own words from a letter, the small and stocky Marblehead colonel, who was in the process of rising magnificently to the challenge, continued to experience considerable "anxiety of mind [because] I was then in for the fate of the day.—the lives of seven hundred and fifty men immediately at hazard . . . besides this, my country, my honour, my own life, and every thing that was dear, appeared at that critical moment to be at stake."[45]

In many ways, this upcoming fight just northwest of the suddenly strategic Pell's Point Peninsula was shaping up to be a dramatic show-down that was remarkable by any measure—the Thermopylae of the American Revolution in a number of ways. Not unlike the Spartans under King Leonidas defending the strategic pass in the Greek moun-tains until no Greek of the elite bodyguard remained alive in their desperate bid to protect the Greek city states from the invading Persians of Xerxes's great army, the Massachusetts troops occupied the high ground and defended New York soil to block the key road that led to the rear of General Washington's withdrawing army and west to Kingsbridge at the northern tip of Manhattan Island, where the Continental Army, including at Fort Washington, could be cut off, trapped, and destroyed. Indeed, the upcoming contest for possession of Split Rock Road, which led to the strategic Eastchester Road, was all about saving Washington's army and the revolution on the morn-ing of October 18, and this feat could only be accomplished by hard fighting and if Colonel Glover's masterful defensive plan worked as well as he envisioned.

The Irresistible Bait

With his innovative tactical dispositions complete and the multiple ambushes firmly set in place along the ever-rising slope of excellent defensible terrain after having established a brilliant defense in depth, Colonel Glover then galloped forward to inspire his most advanced party of men and lead them farther south down the dusty road, ignor-ing the danger of Howe's approaching troops, who were still heading straight toward them. In Glover's own words, he now "rode forward to the advance guard, and ordered them to advance" upon the foremost enemy troops advancing up Split Rock Road. Most of all, by ordering this bold move forward that was sure to receive a vigorous response, as he fully realized, Glover was attempting to buy additional time by retaining the initiative while also making the invaders think that they were facing more troops than was the case. This was all calculated to steal away the enemy's confidence and momentum as much as possible. Colonel Glover now had one final plan to draw the overconfident opposing soldiers into his tactical trap—dangling a most tempting bait before the enemy's eyes. He was convinced that the small advance party of Massachusetts men would act effectively as an irresistible lure that the British and Hessians would not be able to resist: one of the oldest and most effective tricks of Native American warriors in a tactical bag of many such tricks born of the frontier and wilderness experiences.

Obeying Glover's orders, the around forty Bay State veterans of the "captain's guard," departed their secure "eminence" near Split Rock Road, surging a good distance down the slope along the road to

within forty yards, and received their fire without the loss of a man [and] we returned it and fell four of them, and kept the ground until we exchanged five rounds. Their body being much larger than mine, and having two men killed and several wounded, which weakened my [advance] party, the enemy pushed forward not more than thirty yards distant [and therefore] I ordered a retreat which was masterly done by the Captain that commanded the party

wrote Glover, who had carefully planned the baiting of the confident enemy into attacking with abandon into the very midst of his intricate maze of his elaborate ambush and defense in depth.

Just as Glover had foreseen, the sudden falling back of this small party of the foremost Massachusetts soldiers from a sheltering rock fence caused the advancing British and Hessians to believe that they had the cowardly Americans once again on the run in another Kip's Bay–like rout. Consequently, General Howe's troops, wrote Glover, "gave a shout and advanced" with heightened enthusiasm and a sense of bravado, while yelling "Huzzah!" and believing that another victory was theirs as so often in the past during this most ill-fated campaign to date that had brought sagging American fortunes to new lows.[46]

But most important, Colonel Glover's overall tactical plan, based upon the springing of multiple ambushes from behind a series of three consecutive stone fences situated on ever-higher ground, was in the process of working to perfection and right on cue, after his masterful design had been carefully set in place. As one of Washington's officers described the Marblehead colonel's primary tactical thinking and clever plan of a small band of men serving as bait in a letter: a "small party of our troops were sent forward to fire on the large advanced body of the enemy, and divert and lead them on to a wall, behind which the [where Colonel Joseph Read's Thirteenth Massachusetts were ready and waiting in the first line] were principally secreted."[47]

British soldier Thomas Sullivan, who wore the scarlet uniform with pride, wrote in his journal how the initial band of Massachusetts men, who Glover had used as bait, "were pursued for a mile" in the morning and ever closer to Glover's well-developed tactical trap and multiple ambushes that were about to be sprung on ever-higher ground.[48] Because of the lay of the land and with a belt of timber covering the lower finger of ridge on the road's west side and eager to gain the ridge's higher ground as it ascended toward Eastchester to the northwest, the Hessians and British troops advanced north up Split Rock Road in column with the exhilaration that another smashing victory had been won at little cost. Therefore, no British flankers or scouts were sent ahead by overconfident officers, who had nothing but contempt for the Yankee fighting man, especially when on the run. At this time, the entire "King's Own" regiment, or the Fourth Royal Regiment of Foot, and other British regiments were not yet up or were still moving north farther to the south.

Therefore, only the two elite light companies, normally employed on the flanks of the Fourth Regiment of Foot when deployed in line of battle, of this fine British regiment, which proudly had the British lion on its regimental badge, led the advancing Hessian column. The bluecoat column of Hessians was led by the five hundred men of the

Third Grenadier Battalion of Germans. The attackers felt that another splendid victory was in the air like at Long Island, where the Fourth Regiment of Foot had been punished and lost heavily, but had prevailed in the end. By any measure, the Fourth Regiment of Foot was a tough, reliable regiment. This excellent unit had played a leading role in the slaughter of the Scottish Jacobites at bloody Culloden, where the Celtic dream of the capture of London and Scottish independence had died ugly deaths together in mid-July 1746. By this time, regimental members had no fear of charging fortified high ground because they were veterans of the victory at Bunker's Hill and had emerged victorious in the end, despite having suffered severe punishment.

With an absolute faith in their superiority and combat prowess to easily push aside any ragtag opposition, especially if only local Westchester County militia, the British and Hessians merely advanced in a solid column up the road in complete confidence. After all, the patriots had seemingly missed their best opportunity of stopping them by having not defended the shoreline of Pelham Bay to oppose the landing. The tactical folly of Howe's men pushing forward in an unprotected advance straight up the dusty road that led north from Pelham Bay was just what Glover had been hoping for, because it would allow Colonel Read's hidden men of the Thirteenth Massachusetts to spring their surprise and deliver a concentrated fire on easy targets that they could not miss, just as the Marblehead colonel had envisioned. Glover had demonstrated that he knew intimately the strengths and weakness of each regiment, which had allowed him to carefully customize his masterful defense to every possible advantage of his Massachusetts men in a thorough manner. The Marblehead colonel, who was about to enjoy his finest day as a brigade commander, reasoned that because the enemy expected little, if any, resistance and because of their own lofty sense of superiority on every level, the British and Hessians advanced carelessly up Split Rock Road in column in head-on fashion: the tactical situation that he had already planned to exploit to the fullest.[49]

Therefore, General Howe's most advanced troops, British regulars of the Fourth Regiment of Foot and Hessian grenadiers of the Third Grenadier Battalion, in having pushed so far north up Split Rock Road were now in for a thorough shock as great as when General Glover had first looked over Pelham Bay's waters to see it overflowing with an armada of British warships and troop transports. Confident of yet another victory over the colonial amateurs who seemed to be only playing at the game of war, the crack British troops of the Fourth Royal Regiment of Foot and Hessians continued to surge up Split Rock Road with fixed bayonets glistening in the sun, after having already unleashed a cheer that echoed over the Hutchinson River Valley to the west, when they had pushed Glover's foremost men rearward up Split Rock Road.[50] This cocky attitude of the attackers represented exactly the kind of overconfidence Glover reasoned that he could exploit to the fullest to make his multiple ambushes and defense in depth succeed as he had early envisioned with a sparkling clarity.

At this time, even Colonel Glover did not know that these were no ordinary British troops who were now advancing north with discipline upon the foremost, or southernmost, Massachusetts position, the Thirteenth Continental Regiment, at their assigned stone wall. Leading the Hessian column were the two crack British flanking companies of light troops who were regulars in red coats, Captain John Holmes's company and Captain William Glanville Evelyn's company and some dismounted cavalry, who Howe described as "chasseurs," which was the French term for hunters. These reliable veteran Britons were all under the command of Lieutenant Colonel Thomas Musgrave, who commanded the First Battalion of Light Infantry, which was part of the same brigade as the crack Fourth Regiment of Foot and the "chasseurs."

At the head of the British-Hessian column, drummer boys in stylish red uniforms continued to furiously beat their drums that grew ever-louder and echoed across the slope where Colonel Read and his silent men were hidden and crouched behind their first line of stone.

These finely uniformed soldiers from across England were the shock troops of the "King's Own" Regiment and the Hessians, who wore Prussian dark blue uniforms trimmed in red, of the Third Grenadier Battalion, or the Regimental Guard, which was commanded by a capable German colonel of light troops. Of all the units in General Howe's army, no command held a more esteemed place at "the head of the list" of elite regiments than the Fourth Regiment of Foot. In fact, no regiment in the invasion force contained men who were more proud or confident for success against the despised rebel "rabble" than the young men and boys wearing the bright red uniforms of the "King's Own." This well-trained regiment was composed of eight companies, consisting of around forty to seventy men in each one, and every soldier was a veteran: a highly capable strike force that had to be reckoned with by the outnumbered Continentals this morning in Westchester County. Two companies of this crack British regiment now marched straight for Glover's first hidden ambush position held by Colonel Read, while leading the Hessian column. Clearly, hard fighting was about to erupt in full fury.

Colonel Glover and his men would certainly have been more worried had they known about the lengthy and impressive history of the "King's Own" regiment. Wearing the coveted Lion of England insignia on its cap badge, these British soldiers in resplendent red uniforms with blue facings and sliver lace considered themselves invincible partly because the Fourth Royal Regiment of Foot, or the "King's Own Royal Regiment," possessed a most distinguished lineage. This excellent combat command was one of the oldest regiments of foot in the entire British Army. The regiment traced its rich history all the way back to 1680 during the reign of Charles II. Regimental members had battled against the ever-hostile Irish Catholic rebels, who fought as much against the relentless march of Protestantism as against England from 1690 to 1695. The Fourth Regiment of Foot also served in the Netherlands to establish William of Orange on the throne of England. They had been converted to marines who had served aboard English warships in 1703. The regiment had been the first to land ashore at Gibraltar in 1704 in a conquest that had ensured British naval dominance in the Mediterranean Sea. Reverting back to its former role on land, the regiment had then officially become "King's Own" in the summer of 1715.

After fighting at the Battle of Falkirk, Scotland, the regiment then assisted in crushing the last Jacobite Rebellion in 1746 at Culloden (a Gaelic word) that abruptly brought the Jacobite cause to a blood-soaked conclusion on this infamous grassy moor in northcentral Scotland. During this decisive encounter, which was the Jacobite high tide, the Fourth Royal Regiment had held the left flank of the main Hanoverian battle line of the Duke of Cumberland on April 16, standing firm against the Celtic Highlanders' fierce onslaught and "borne the brunt" of the Scottish Jacobite attacks, which were not only reckless but also foolhardy in the face of superior weaponry, including rows of cannon. Consequently, the disciplined British regulars had decimated the Scottish attackers with an accurate fire that resulted in a slaughter. Despite inflicting severe damage, the Fourth Royal Regiment had paid a high price in losses—one third of its strength and its cherished colors—for helping to save the day at Culloden with other Hanoverian troops. Despite having been outflanked and shattered by the headlong attack of the Jacobites, the Fourth Royal Regiment had later rallied in splendid fashion, which became part of regimental lore. Regimental members had then fought on, buying precious time with its sacrifice to set the stage for the launching of a Hanoverian counterattack that carried the field and won the day. Clearly, the "King's Own" was an elite regiment, as demonstrated throughout the past and during the showdown at Pell's Point.[51]

What had now made these redcoats especially fearsome was the fact that they had long embraced a special hatred of the people of Massachusetts, especially Boston, and held an utter contempt for Massachusetts soldiers, especially militia, just like regimental members had once possessed in abundance for the Scottish Highlanders, while continuing the stereotypical arrogant attitude about America's citizen-soldiers that had been dominant since the French and Indian

War. When the Provincial Congress had declared a fast day for Wednesday, March 15, 1775, the people of Boston had flocked to their churches that cold, late winter morning to pray and give thanks to God. At this time, the soldiers of the "King's Own" had devised their own personal plan to disrupt the solemn worship in giving thanks to God by the common people. With the full approval of the regiment's colonel, the redcoats had proceeded to pitch their white canvas tents just outside the most heavily attended church located in Boston's west end. Then, the drummers and fifers of the Fourth Regiment of Foot had played jaunty martial airs as loud as they could, which almost certainly included the derisive "Yankee Doodle," for the express purpose of disrupting religious services.[52]

Now on the autumnal morning of October 18, the Fourth Regiment's soldiers continued to display their well-known contempt for colonials, both soldiers and civilians, by advancing recklessly up Split Rock Road as if they were invincible. Along with the red-coats of the "King's Own," the dismounted British cavalrymen of the Sixteenth Light Dragoons and the lengthy lines of blue-coated Hessians of the Third Grenadier Battalion of Major General Werner von Mirbach's Brigade, Heister's First Division, steadily pushed north in column under the bright fall sunshine and faint hint of early fall in the air, while drummer boys enthusiastically pounded drums with all their might. All the while, Colonel Read and his 226 silent men of the Thirteenth Continental Regiment remained well-concealed in their defensive positions, while hidden behind their lengthy fences of stone and by stands of timber on the east side of the road and behind their rocky shelter. These tough Massachusetts soldiers were about to demonstrate General "Old Put" Putnam's wise maxim in regard to the Bay State troops, which was right on target and had been early demonstrated in full during the three successive redcoat charges up the grassy slopes of Bunker Hill: "Cover them [with defenses] and they will fight until doomsday," if necessary. Meanwhile, not a Massachusetts soldier of the Thirteenth Massachusetts said a word, coughed, or sneezed, keeping perfectly quiet and still so as not to reveal their secreted positions and the series of ambushes set firmly in place by Glover.[53]

General Washington had even more specific advice than General Putnam in regard to what was the key to making his troops more formidable. He had emphasized in a June 29, 1776 order:

> He recommends to them to load for their first fire with one musket ball and four or eight buck shot [buck & ball], according to the size and strength of their pieces; if the enemy is received with such a fire at not more than twenty or thirty yards distant, he has no doubt of their being repulsed.[54]

No one more than Colonel Glover embraced this sound advice of both Generals Washington and Putnam, and it was about to wreak havoc among the attackers to a degree almost unprecedented. In fact, Glover's entire defensive arrangement and tactical plan of multiple ambushes and a defense in depth were based in part upon this wise advice about how best to maximize American firepower to the fullest. General Washington's and Colonel Glover's wisdom in regard to this proven lethality was about to be employed in full with so much now at stake in Westchester County.

Indeed, contrary to common stereotypes, Glover's Massachusetts Continentals were far more formidable in firing their large-caliber smoothbores, like the "Brown Bess" carried by the British and Hessians, rather than the Pennsylvania long rifle largely because of the sage usage of "buck & ball"—the day's most effective round because of its shotgun-like effect that was devastating to attacking infantry, especially at close range. Unlike the common smoothbore flintlocks that had been issued by the State of Massachusetts, which were now carried by Glover's men, no bayonet could be attached to the legendary long rifle, which was a slim, delicate, and finely crafted weapon of mostly the western frontier. Most important when it came to close combat, the long rifle took at least twice as long to reload as the smoothbore flintlock musket, because of its rifled barrel and small caliber. These were precious seconds when the British could strike in a fierce bayonet charge before the defender's weapons could be reloaded in time to unleash the next volley.

At close range and compared to the small-caliber long rifle, nothing was more deadly than the large caliber smoothbores loaded with "buck & ball," which basically transformed the weapon into a lethal shotgun, whose spray of lead balls of multiple sizes caused fearful damage to human bodies, especially when packed together. In this way, "buck & ball," which now filled the smoothbore muskets of Glover's men, was most effective counter to the British bayonet charge when unleashed at close range. And in hand-to-hand combat, the heavy, old smoothbore was sturdier than the fragile long rifle, and less likely to have its wooden butt or stock shatter upon impact upon an enemy's head or shoulders during deadly hand-to-hand combat.[55]

A strange fate had seemingly now placed Glover and his Massachusetts men at a key position and moment of the American Revolution which had begun in Massachusetts primarily because of the folly of British leadership, both military and civilian, and statesmen who could have headed off open conflict with wisdom and flexibility. British mismanagement and seemingly endless mistakes had led to an unnecessary and unavoidable conflict and Glover and his Continentals now stood at center stage of the struggle for liberty, as if ordained by destiny.

Punishing the "King's Own" Regiment and the Hessians' 3rd Grenadier Battalion Without Mercy

Closer and closer, meanwhile, the well-trained light troops—British, Hessians, and dismounted English cavalry—approached Colonel Read's Cambridge boys of the Thirteenth Massachusetts at a rapid pace to exploit what seemed to be yet another success when they were now already unknowingly well within firing range of the unseen Massachusetts soldiers hidden behind the stone fence on the road's east side. By this time, the "King's Own" Regiment, dismounted cavalry of the Sixteenth Light Dragoons, and Hessians of the Third Grenadier Battalion had not deployed in a regular battle line, continuing to carelessly advance in column based upon the Split Rock Road. This situation meant that the two elite British companies of light troops had not formed on each flank in guardian fashion as usual from their tight, narrow column because of woodlands on both sides of the road, which forced them to surge up Split Rock Road that constricted alignment and reduced tactical options. In addition, the supreme confidence of Howe's troops ensured that necessary precautions of the most basic kind were not taken during the steady advance north.

But relying on a natural soldier's tactical instincts and years of experience, Colonel Glover knew that his most advanced position was vulnerable on the right, or east, of the road, because this area of a wide plateau was more open and due to the lack of easily maneuverable ground for the British to advance across on the road's west side, where more rugged terrain of the eastern edge of the heavily timbered Hutchinson River Valley lay. This astute tactical realization had early come to Glover as soon as he had seen the lay of the land that he had immediately exploited in full. Consequently, he had wisely established his first ambush position, which was held by Colonel Read and his Thirteenth Massachusetts men, on the east side of the road to counter the terrain vulnerabilities.

As the disciplined ranks of scarlet and dark blue ranks drew ever-nearer under the morning sunshine, meanwhile, Glover continued to resist the temptation of ordering Colonel Read and his soldiers to stand up from behind the stone fence as one and open fire with a volley. Glover knew that he had to wait until almost the last moment before giving the order to fire to ensure maximum damage and shock value. Meanwhile, Read's anxious men became increasingly nervous, wondering when their officers would finally give the eagerly awaited word to fire, while they crouched low behind their stone fence. After all, a good many eighteen-inch British bayonets were getting ever-closer to Colonel Read's hidden position behind the stone fence, while the beating of the British and Hessian drums grew ever-louder and sounded like thunder because they were so close. To the Massachusetts soldiers out of sight and hidden behind the stone wall, the pounding of the drums became more unnerving as they grew louder as they were meant to accomplish to unnerve an opponent. Under Glover's strict orders, no one in Read's command poked their head above the stone fence to see exactly how close the attackers were to them, because they obeyed orders to the letter to verify the regiment's high level of discipline.

Colonel Glover, whose horse was now tied to the rear and out of sight among the trees, was relying completely on the dual elements of surprise and shock that he planned to suddenly inflict in a massive dosage once he gave the word for Colonel Read's men to open fire. Of course, Glover knew that such sound tactics would help to make up for the small numbers of troops that he commanded in the face of a mighty invasion force: the tactical situation called for allowing the enemy to get as close as possible to Colonel Read's boys before he ordered the Cambridge regiment to open fire. All the while, the colorful, silk regimental flags of the "King's Own" regiment and German regiments waved in the salty sea breeze sweeping west from the Long Island Sound on this pleasant October morning, while the tension continued to mount among the Massachusetts men. The British troops of Captains Holmes's and Evelyn's light companies of grenadiers had been long inspired by the sight of their precious battle flag, which was yet back with the regiment's main body and not up front with the vanguard of light troops. Symbolizing old England and its constitutional monarchy that the redcoats in the ranks viewed as the freest government in the world while the Massachusetts soldiers saw it as the most tyrannical, these silk colors were distinguished by a painted image of "the lion of England"—the Fourth Regiment of Foot's official emblem.[56]

Meanwhile, on the colonel's orders when he had felt the time was right, the forty members of Glover's advance guard had earlier retired on the double from the shelter of their stone fence atop a slight knoll and headed north up the main slope near Split Rock Road in what looked like another panicky American rout: the irresistible bait that had thoroughly emboldened the attackers and set the stage for Glover's first ambush to be sprung with deadly effectiveness by Colonel Read. As noted, this was an old Indian trick learned by Glover and other veterans of the French and Indian War and a most effective one. All the while, Colonel Glover hoped for the dense scarlet ranks of the "King's Own" and the dismounted dragoons, the English "chasseurs," and the Hessians to continue relentlessly advancing with unlimited confidence like during a lazy Sunday afternoon review in London's Hyde Park and to get as close as possible to his first ambush position, before barking out orders for Colonel Read and his veterans of the Thirteenth Massachusetts to stand up from behind the stone fence and open fire, when the enemy's dense ranks were now well within the kill zone.

Perhaps Colonel Glover recalled how the key to the British victory in winning the climactic battle for possession of Quebec and all Canada on the Plains of Abraham in mid-September 1759 had been the fact that General James Wolfe, before he was mortally wounded like his adversary the Marquis de Montcalm, had allowed the disciplined French regulars in Bourbon white uniforms to advance to within less than forty yards before ordering his British regulars to fire at point-blank range, which destroyed the front rank and dissolved their attack formation with one fatal explosion of gunfire.[57]

All the while, the anxiety continued to mount among the ranks of the silent Massachusetts soldiers, who remained remarkably calm because these veterans knew that they were about to punish the enemy as never before. Glover remained patient while allowing Howe's men to ease closer under the soft October sunshine, while the pounding of the British drums grew louder until it seemed that they had practically reached the stone wall. Not losing his nerve, Glover was biding his time until the moment was exactly right, because each second mattered. The peaceful-looking autumnal woodland along the slope behind the stone wall, behind which crouched Colonel Read's men who were all bunched up together with their flintlock muskets cocked and ready, added to the deceptiveness of the ambush, while remaining eerily quiet to give no indication of their presence. But thanks in part to no British scouts or skirmishers having been thrown out in front to lead the column up Split Rock Road in a repeat of Major General Edward Braddock's folly—he had even arrogantly declined to use invaluable Indian allies in the summer of 1755—of having walked straight into a French, Native American, and Canadian ambush not far from Fort Duquesne that this proud former member of the Coldstream Guard had believed that he could easily capture, the advancing overconfident redcoats of the Fourth Royal Regiment and Hessians failed to notice the strange calmness that dominated the land on both sides of Split Rock Road below Pelham Heights.

Even as the push north proceeded farther up the road that led up steadily ascending terrain, no advanced parties of British skirmishers had been yet gone forward to ascertain that a clever ambush of these seasoned Continentals had been set in place. Instead, the five hundred Hessians of the Third Grenadier Battalion, dismounted British cavalrymen of the Sixteenth Light Dragoons, the British "chasseurs," and "King's Own" troops continued to surge up the road with confidence, as if marching on parade at Windsor Castle, before the smug approval of King George III and his aristocratic ministers of the upper class or in the Rhine River country before one of the haughty German princes of an ancient Teutonic land.

Incredibly, the highly disciplined Hessian and British troops were marching north in column completely blind along the road and taking no precautions whatsoever in their hubris, as if nothing had been learned from the ambush that had led to the destruction of General Braddock's army and countless other such comparable bloody examples of the French and Indian War. At that time, the redcoats had been especially vulnerable when jammed close together along a narrow forest trail, while marching straight into one of the great disasters of the French and Indian War. What had resulted from Braddock's folly was the loss of nearly one thousand British and colonial troops on bloody July 9, 1755. And now in marching north up the Pell's Point Peninsula and the terrain to the northwest covered more in woodlands than fields, the Hessians and redcoats were about to make the same tactical mistake, especially in regard to underestimating their opponent and feeling that victory had already been won.

All the while, the steady tramp of hundreds of marching feet of a disciplined step and the clatter of gear of the encroaching enemy grew louder to Colonel Read and his hidden Massachusetts soldiers, who had yet to see a Hessian or redcoat this morning, while they remained silently behind their sturdy fence of stone while maintaining an iron discipline. But these Bay State veterans did not have to see the foe, because the ever-increasing noise emitting from the pounding of the British and Hessian drummers and the steadily advancing column told them that the enemy was not only drawing nearer, but now practically atop them. However, what Colonel Read's men did not know was that these foremost British troops of Captains Evelyn's and Holmes's light companies were members of General Howe's finest regiment now leading the way north.

Perhaps, under the circumstances, it was best that Glover's men did not know the fact about the well-deserved lofty reputations of Howe's tough fighting men who they were about to engage at an exceptionally close range. After all, it was unnerving enough, even for Read's tried veterans, to have to wait patiently behind a stone fence without seeing the approaching foe while knowing beyond all doubt that large numbers of redcoats, who knew how to use their bayonets with deadly efficiency against hapless Americans, were now getting exceptionally close. Only iron discipline kept Colonel Read's soldiers quietly in position while awaiting their commander's word to stand up and open fire. Read and his soldiers knew that Glover's ambush was now working to perfection, after the most advanced small party of Massachusetts men had earlier raced back to Colonel Read's concealed position and they were now lay concealed with their comrades behind the stone fence: the intoxicating sight of more fleeing Americans, which had emboldened the attackers to make them even more vulnerable than ever before, as planned by Glover, while they neared the hidden Thirteenth Massachusetts soldiers.

All the while, the Marblehead colonel, who held firm under the mounting pressure because of his desire to wait until the last possible moment, resisted the temptation to order a premature volley, which would have negated the ambush's overall effectiveness. Most of all, Colonel Glover knew that the shock value of unleashing close-range volleys to catch the enemy by surprise was one of the keys to success. Glover wanted the steadily advancing British and Hessians to ease as close as possible to Colonel Read's position before he gave the word to open fire to inflict the maximum amount of damage.

Most of all, Colonel Glover was determined that this upcoming fight would not be the usual long-range exchanges of musketry and trading volleys in formation during a traditional stand-up fight against a superior opponent, as if on some distant European battlefield or like when General Washington had too often attempted the impossibility of matching up to well-trained professionals: a certain recipe for disaster at Pell's Point because of the heavy odds. With the scarlet and blue column approaching the stone fence of the Thirteenth Massachusetts and with the autumnal woodlands along the road giving way to gradually more open ground—ideal fields of fire—leading to the stone fences crowded with concealed crack American fighting men, Howe's troops finally deployed in a battle line from their tight column on Split Rock Road, but yet along a relatively narrow front because the woods prevented a wider front. As customary in such a tactical situation, the two British light companies quickly hustled into position on the right and left flank upon reaching the more open ground, while the Hessians of one command, the Third Grenadier Battalion of around five hundred men and at least one German regiment, perhaps two, formed in the middle between the two groups of redcoat flankers on each end of the assault formation. Then, Howe's advance continued north up Split Rock Road but along a wider and more menacing front, with a lengthier line of the British king's and the German prince's soldiers pushing forward in the attempt to gain more ground to secure a permanent toehold on the mainland.

Even while he admired their discipline and fine uniforms of red and blue, Glover was no longer mounted, having taken a hidden position like his men. He, therefore, was now under cover in a belt of woods immediately behind Read's stone fence, maintaining his nerve under the overwhelming onslaught of nearly too many attackers to count. All the while, he allowed General Howe's Hessian and British troops to approach even closer to the lengthy stone fence in what had become a game of nerves at this point. How long could Colonel Read's men maintain their discipline and silence in such a stressful situation, and when would Glover give the word to open fire? As yet, the foe had no idea that behind the lengthy stone fence were the concealed soldiers of Colonel Read's regiment on the east side of Split Rock Road. In Glover's words, the entire regiment of "Colonel Read's, laying under cover of a stone wall [were] undiscovered till they came within thirty yards" of the hidden position of the Thirteenth Massachusetts. This was now the moment that Glover had been awaiting with an amazing level of patience and a burning desire to punish the enemy.

Glover Springs His First Masterful Ambush

At last and sensing that he could now reap the maximum advantage and inflict the most damage, Glover now knew that the long-awaited time had finally come. When the British and Hessians were within only sixty feet of the stone wall hidden immediately before a belt of woodlands, Colonel Glover finally gave the long-awaited order to open fire, when the soldiers of the Hessian regiments, with the Third Grenadier Battalion leading the way, and the "King's Own" were at their most vulnerable: climbing over the last stone wall unoccupied by Massachusetts soldiers just to the south, which ensured they were out of formation and unable to fire a volley in their usual manner.

For all to hear, Glover shouted at the top of his lungs for Colonel Read's soldiers to stand up from behind the stone fence as one and unleash their buck and ball loads into the scarlet ranks of the Fourth Royal Regiment of Foot and into the dark blue Hessian ranks of the Third Grenadier Battalion. Admiring the discipline of Colonel Read and his soldiers, who were mostly from Cambridge, Glover wrote how the entire regiment of the Thirteenth Massachusetts Continentals, who already had been joined by the forty-man advance guard of chosen men after they had swiftly retired to the cover of the stone wall, "then rose up and gave them the whole charge" of musketry at close range that stunned the attackers.[58]

To the shock of the British and Hessians, the seasoned fighting men of the Thirteenth Massachusetts suddenly rose up as one like ghosts from behind the stone wall on the road's east side, as if performing a routine drill maneuver on a Sunday afternoon parade ground of a small Massachusetts town. Only a moment before completely hidden by a belt of woods behind the stone fence and the protective cover of the wall of rocks, Read's veterans unleashed a close-range volley into the faces of the advancing foe, who never knew what hit them. Erupting in unison after hundreds of dark-colored flints from each musket struck the steel of the firing pan to create the spark that ignited black powder charges, a solid sheet of flame erupted from a simultaneous explosion of gunfire, which poured from the length of the stone wall like a volcano.

The shock of the first devastating volley fired by Colonel Read's men was as complete as it was thorough in decimating the hard-hit enemy. Swept by a perfect storm of "buck & ball" that unleashed more than one thousand projectiles at close range, General Howe's Hessian troops of the Third Grenadier Battalion and the British soldiers of the two light companies of the "King's Own" and the dismounted horse soldiers of the Sixteenth Light Dragoons were swept by the point-blank volley. After all, before the entire Thirteenth Continental Regiment stood up and fired as one, Howe's advancing troops had their eyes fixed on the higher terrain and road ahead that showed no signs of rebel soldiers, not even a scout or picket, to ensure that no one expected an entire regiment of Bay State veterans to suddenly rise up from seemingly out of nowhere.

Therefore, the amount of surprise that swept the attackers was complete, when more than 226 Massachusetts soldiers of the Thirteenth Continental Regiment fired as one to thoroughly riddle the ranks of the foremost British and Hessian troops, who had been confidently streaming up Split Rock Road with fixed steel bayonets and the open ground of a field just to the east. Large numbers of enemy troops, especially from the more numerous Hessians of the hard-hit Third Grenadier Battalion, dropped like stones from the hail of buck and ball that swept the ranks at close range without mercy. The advancing ranks of red and blue were simply shattered. In fact, this explosion of musketry was the closest and most devastating fire yet experienced by General Howe's troops during this campaign—a mini–Bunker Hill of sorts. Most important, to reap the highest dividends and as noted, the ever-astute Colonel Glover had ordered the first ambush to be sprung at exactly the right time when Howe's troops were at their most vulnerable: clamoring over the stone wall that had been formerly held by the band of Glover's foremost skirmishers, before they had hustled back to seek cover with their comrades of Colonel Read's regiment.

A Grim Harvest in October

This first volley was extremely accurate because the Massachusetts men rested their flintlocks atop the stone fence for a steady aim that ensured that "dozens of Redcoats and Hessians dropped." Some of the best British officers, who were bravely leading the way, were cut down in the hail of lead. Of the "King's Own" regiment, fine leaders were hit in the deadly spray of "buck and ball," including handsome Captain William Glanville Evelyn. He was leading his light company of the Fourth Royal Regiment of Foot forward when shot down before his men. A natural leader of highly-disciplined grenadiers, Evelyn was a dashing Irish officer of much ability, who was as obsessed with his Irish mistress named Peggie as in vanquishing the hated rebels. When he had "vaulted" over the wall of stone on a knoll once held by Glover's small band of skirmishers who had effectively served as bait to draw the enemy closer to Read's hidden men by having fueled an overly aggressive pursuit, the Celtic-Gaelic captain from County Meath, northeast Ireland, was struck with three bullets, including a spray of buckshot.

One projectile from a Massachusetts musket grazed the Irishman's left arm and another one ripped open his left thigh, while yet another round smashed the captain's right leg above the knee. An Irish hero of the late August victory on Long Island, where he had led the advance guard of a flanking column of light troops that turned the American's exposed left flank to rout thousands of Washington's men and ensure a one-sided victory, the thirty-three-year-old Captain Evelyn had now met a cruel fate. He was the oldest son of Reverend William Evelyn, who was the vicar of Trim, which was located on the River Boyne. Evelyn had met his tragic destiny far from his County Meath home. He fell to the ground along with other redcoat soldiers of his hard-hit company, who were killed or wounded by the close-range volley from the Thirteenth Massachusetts. The courageous Emerald Islander, who had faced Glover and Baldwin and their minutemen during the disastrous British retreat to Boston after the first clashes at Lexington and Concord, had fallen mortally wounded, ensuring that he would never again see his beloved Emerald Isle homeland. And now nothing that his alluring Irish mistress, Peggy Wright, who had once been one of the wealthy Celtic family's servants, could do could possibly save her dashing Irish captain, who had "gone for a soldier" in a faraway foreign land to break her heart because of his ambitions to reap glory, which he had followed like a siren's call. This most "gallant officer" from the Green Isle in General Howe's estimation would be dead in less than a month.[59]

Additionally, Lieutenant Colonel Thomas Musgrave, who commanded the light troops at the head of the sweeping advance up Split Rock Road and who led the First Battalion of Light Infantry, was also cut down in the hail of lead from the thunderous volley unleashed by Colonel Read's troops. Like Captain Evelyn, he fell badly wounded to the ground before the stone fence. However, Musgrave would eventually recover in time, unlike the mortally wounded Evelyn, whose life's blood now nourished the ground of Westchester County far from his native homeland.[60]

The shock of the close-range volley that resulted in the fringe of fire exploding along the length of the stone wall was so completely unexpected that no troops could withstand such terrible punishment. What was especially horrifying for the Hessian troops, dismounted cavalrymen of the Sixteenth Light Dragoons, and soldiers of the "King's Own" Regiment was that brothers, fathers, sons, cousins, uncles, and nephews had been cut down around them. Ironically, like the Massachusetts men, they had long served together in companies that were as much of a close-knit community as military units. In fact, these soldiers who fought, marched, starved, and died together were family and their units served as surrogate familial communities, especially when it came to the Irishmen in red uniforms. Indeed, a good many of Howe's soldiers were related by blood, and most had served together in the same unit for decades. Therefore, the horrifying sight of so many of their friends and relatives being slaughtered at such close range before their eyes was a severe shock to the lucky survivors of Glover's first volley that had exploded in their faces from the Thirteenth Massachusetts.[61]

In his journal, Thomas Sullivan, a British soldier from Dublin on the Liffey River, described the stunning surprise of the first fire of Colonel Read's regiment that riddled the ranks without mercy, because Howe's men believed that they were only yet in pursuit of only a handful of an advanced party of "Yankee Doodles" who had fled before them in terror. But then, all of a sudden a "Considerable body [had risen up,] appearing in front behind Stone walls, and in woods" opened fire at close range.[62] What Sullivan failed to write about was the raising of the regimental colors of Read's command on the stone fence, consisting of a light-colored silk banner decorated with a hand-painted pine tree and head of Indian corn that symbolized the agrarian culture of these mostly yeoman farmers and then the words of the regimental model, "For Posterity I Bleed."[63]

But the death and destruction that wreaked havoc among the scarlet and blue ranks had only begun at the hands of the determined fighters of the Thirteenth Massachusetts Continental Regiment.

Hurriedly reloading their flintlocks after using ramrods to push down their "buck & ball" rounds, another volley by Colonel Read's veteran Continentals was unleashed with muskets again resting atop the wall of stone to ensure a high degree of accuracy, adding to the horror and confusion of General Howe's foremost troops. More soldiers, mostly Hessians, were cut down in the second volley that swept their ranks. Then, not long thereafter, a third murderous volley exploded at close range from the muskets of the fast-firing men of the Thirteenth Continental Regiment. This was the third fire that unmercifully raked the ranks which finally broke the back of the Hessian-British attack. Consequently, those surviving soldiers fortunate to have escaped the most scorching close fire that they had ever encountered had lost all fighting spirit by this time. Despite their pride and lofty reputations that were considerable, hundreds of British and German soldiers now turned and ran for their lives, heading down Split Rock Road and the nearby field with abandon. With pride, Glover described how "the enemy broke" under the repeated explosions of gunfire at close range, which were simply too much for any soldiers to bear, regardless of how well-trained, experienced, and disciplined.[64]

In a letter, one American soldier described the repulse that turned into a rout, after the third murderous volley riddled their ranks: "The enemy came near the wall, and received a general fire from our troops, which broke, their advanced party entirely, so that they ran back to the main body" of advancing troops.[65]

A chorus of cheers spontaneously erupted from Colonel Read's men, while a cloud of sulfurous smoke blew across the fields of autumn to the west and the regimental silk flag, which was decorated with the words "For Posterity I Bleed" and waved proudly, after having been unfurled with great pride at the first fire. Clearly, this was a special moment for the triumphant Bay State men. This was the first time that the Massachusetts soldiers had ever seen Hessian soldiers, who had already acquired a fearsome reputation, run for their lives on the battlefield: a psychological victory in its own right. Upon first rising to fire, they might have been surprised to have discovered that they were now facing mostly German troops in navy blue uniforms, because American propaganda had predicted that the Hessian soldiers would "desert in great numbers" once they served on American soil and so far from the Teutonic homeland rather than face the legendary lethality of long smoothbore muskets loaded with "buck & ball."[66]

Hardly believing his eyes, one of Glover's men penned in a letter of the dramatic moment when Colonel Read's soldiers "well covered under a stone wall, and at thirty or forty yards gave their Grenadiers and Infantry an unexpected heavy fire, then a second, and third, which broke the enemy so much that they ran away as fast as they could, in confusion."[67]

What Colonel Glover, who had never seen such an astonishing sight before, and other Massachusetts soldiers meant by "broke" was that the Hessians—of at least one battalion, the Third Grenadier Battalions, and perhaps an entire German regiment—two British light companies, and the dismounted British troopers of the Sixteenth Light Dragoons were routed and hurled back by the blistering fire of Colonel Read's Thirteenth Continental Regiment. While the Massachusetts men erupted in a chorus of wild cheering, hundreds of Hessians and redcoats fled rearward in panic, retiring in confusion of a rout. Hard-hit by the point-blank fire from multiple volleys, they headed down the slope without a hint of order or discipline, running along Split Rock Road and the more open ground to the east from where they had come with so much confidence and certitude. The Bay State defenders had expected a series of determined bayonet charges like at Bunker Hill, but such was not the case. Never before had any of Washington's troops so thoroughly routed such a large number of combined British-Hessian attackers during this ill-fated New York campaign of 1776, exceeding the rough treatment received by the famed Black Watch regiment of crack Scottish soldiers at the Battle of Harlem Heights in September.[68]

Meanwhile, the thick layers of sulfurous smoke that slowly raised higher into the autumn sky from the lengthy stone fence revealed to Colonel Read's men the extent of the horror and damage dealt to Howe's troops, because before them lay a carpet of bodies in blue and red uniforms, dead men and wounded soldiers groaning in pain and begging for water. Invigorating spirits and fueling the cheers that erupted from the throats of the jubilant Bay Staters was the sight of "along the roadway [of] the [enemy] dead and wounded [which were] seen lying in heaps, while the broken columns are falling back in disorder."[69]

For the redcoat soldiers of the "King's Own" who proudly wore their lion crest insignias, they had always been the ones in the past who had routed rebels of popular people's revolts in Scotland and Ireland, killing with impunity and without remorse, including infamous slaughters and massacres. For instance, the soldiers of this legendary regiment, the Fourth Regimen of Foot, had fought with distinction at the turning point Battle of the Boyne, which raged along the River Boyne, County Meath, in northeast Ireland, on July 1, 1690. Here, they had played their part in decimating the Jacobite rebels in this bloody engagement fought not far from Dublin, which guaranteed permanent British domination of the Emerald Isle.

Then, on April 16, 1746, and as in Ireland throughout the past during the smashing of another Celtic people's bid for freedom against foreign oppressors, the troops of this famous regiment had slaughtered a seemingly endless number of Scottish Jacobite rebels, including wounded men, on the windswept flat lands of water-soaked Culloden Moor, while breaking the back of the final great Jacobite rebellion in history. In scarlet coats as now during the showdown at Pell's Point on October 18, the regulars had played a key role in defeating the ferocious Highlander attack of young Celtic men and boys who had charged impetuously across the moor, while waving Scottish broadswords—like the only carried by Colonel Glover at Pell's Point that partly reflected his own Celtic roots in Cornwall situated in southwest England—which symbolized this decisive mismatch of a premodern army with outdated tactics against a modern army backed by rows of cannon.

For the men of the "King's Own" regiment, therefore, this first tactical setback on New York soil dealt by Colonel Read's Continentals was their most unexpected and inglorious fate of all—to the thinking of the common soldiers in the ranks—ever to befall the Fourth Royal Regiment: to be routed by the contemptable American rebels, who were not even wearing proper uniforms and fought behind cover in cowardly fashion like Indians unlike in the open like true fighting men, in open rebellion against their king and country. In consequence, this sharp and unexpected setback was a most humiliating experience that equally mortified the hard-hit Hessians, who so proudly represented their princes and Teutonic homeland so far away. Like Howe's Britons, the highly disciplined Germans had not yet previously tasted such a severe reversal in this war against the American rebels and it was something that was simply unimaginable to them, because they knew that they faced mostly rustic ex-farmers in open revolt.[70]

As throughout his brief written account of the battle, Glover was exceedingly modest about the remarkable success that he reaped in this hard-fought battle based on his clever orchestration of the most brilliant defensive tactics yet seen at this point in the American Revolution: a misplaced modesty that was entirely in keeping with his taciturn nature and Congregationalist faith. Therefore, the talented colonel was guilty of considerable understatement when he described the battle in the stoic Marblehead and seafaring tradition in which even the greatest of Atlantic storms and dangers at sea were routinely minimized, as if they were nothing. More accurately placing exactly what happened to the severely punished "King's Own" regiment was revealed in a letter written on October 23, 1776, by an American soldier in the ranks who never forgot the sight as long as he lived: "People may think what they please of the regular and spirited behavior of the British troops, but I that day was an eye-witness to the contrary [because] The fourth regiment was the one that had run."[71]

This was no idle American boast based on provincial pride. One Hessian officer described the rout of two light companies of the Fourth Royal Regiment and other companies, the dismounted men of the Sixteenth Light Dragoons, and the foremost Hessian troops of the Third Grenadier Battalion and evidently at least one other command, a German regiment. Captain Andreas Wiederholt, who served in the ranks of the Wilhelm von Knyphausen Regiment of Major General von Mirach's Brigade of the Hessian Division commanded by Lieutenant General Leopold Philip de Heister, wrote how,

> we marched toward the hill, since a battalion [regiment] of riflemen [Colonel Read's 13th Massachusetts] lay closely concealed on the road in the woods behind so-called stone fences and poured a heavy and unexpected fire on an English Light battalion marching at the head [of the column] which was careless and had no flanking parties out and thus fled at a full run.[72]

Advancing in the rear ranks farther south down Split Rock Road, this finely uniformed German officer had not seen the full deployment of Howe's first battle line and only the initial alignment during the first stages of the advance north up Split Rock Road, however. In addition and as usual displaying the rivalry that existed between British and German troops that was intense for obvious cultural and national reasons, he also conveniently overlooked the fact that Hessian soldiers had been as hard-hit by Colonel Read's Continentals as the Britons and that they also had been swept aside, taking to their heels like the British during the rout.

No one in Glover's ranks had seen such a panic among the enemy before, not even during the British retreat on the road from Lexington and Concord to Boston on April 19, 1775, because the severely punished redcoats and Hessians now fled for their lives just like the Connecticut militiamen at Kip's Bay during one of Washington's most humiliating days. No doubt, while the heavy palls of white smoke drifted slowly west across the Hutchinson River by the salty-smelling breeze that swept over the slopes from the Long Island Sound, the Thirteenth Massachusetts men continued to cheer their one-sided success for an extended period of time like when the July news of the Declaration of Independence's signing had been read to the army in July on Washington's orders, while waving their hats like madmen at the exhilarating sight of the rout of some of Howe's best troops.

The shock and surprise of the attackers had been so complete and the punishment delivered had been so severe that Glover, as he had planned, gained an invaluable respite from the first major repulse of the attackers, who had so boldly surged up Split Rock Road and the ground to the east. Therefore, in Glover's words, the hard-hit British and Hessians fell back with great rapidity and "retreated for the main body to come up." Exactly what Colonel Glover and his brigade now needed most of all, precious time, had been gained by the murderous volleys of the Thirteenth Massachusetts Continental Regiment delivered at close range. Thanks to his clever stratagem of having Colonel Read's regiment fire volleys from a concealed position at almost point-blank range to maximize not only punishment so suddenly unleashed upon the opponent, but also to inflict the key elements of shock and surprise won Glover extra time needed by Washington's retreating army.

Then, during the respite from the time won, Colonel Read's soldiers caught their breath and began to quickly reload their muskets just in case another attack suddenly surged up Split Rock Road or across the more open ground to the east in an outflanking movement. From leather cartridge boxes that were worn and cracked from the hot summer weather and the downpours of rain, the Thirteenth Massachusetts soldiers grabbed paper cartridges, bit off the top, and then poured the black powder down the barrel of their smoothbore flintlock muskets. Wooden ramrods were used to then ram down the round lead balls with loads of buckshot, which was wrapped in paper with the lead ball, into long musket barrels. The remaining black powder in the paper cartridge was then placed in the firing pan. With new flints in place to ensure that a spark would be generated in the firing pan when the steel hammer struck, the muskets of Colonel Read's men were ready for the next onslaught of Howe's troops up Split Rock Road and the gently sloping ground to the east. After having hurriedly reloaded with the burning desire to inflict additional punishment upon a hated foe, the respite also bestowed a chance for men to take sips of water from wooden canteens of oak and cedar and refresh parched throats grimed with black powder from having just repeatedly loaded muskets to blaze away at the enemy.

But, contrary to expectations of the immediate launching of another attack by the formidable team of Howe and Clinton, an hour entire passed without any hint of another assault, while the tension in the ranks of the Bay State men continued to gradually increase in the strange, unexpected silence in anticipation of what might come next. Was Colonel Read's advanced position to the south in the process of being outflanked on the left toward the Long Island Sound? The lack of any evidence of General Howe's next move only made the odd stillness along Split Rock Road seem eerie to the Massachusetts men, because everything remained quiet for too long to the thinking of Glover's savvy veterans. All the while, the October sun rose higher in the autumn sky and the day grew warmer until it felt more like late summer than early autumn. In consequence, the young men and boys of the Third, Thirteenth, and Twenty-sixth Massachusetts basked in the calm because they knew that the storm was about a break anew at any moment, while they anticipated the next attack that was sure to come. With stomachs growling, hungry soldiers now thought of the breakfast that they had missed back in camp on this hectic morning in their haste to meet the invaders because Glover had wisely determined that no time could be wasted.

As the minutes continued to tick by during the strange stillness that was haunting, Colonels Glover and Read and their men wondered when the British and Hessians would launch their next attack, despite the ground now littered with sickening clumps of scarlet- and blue-clad bodies. But most important, Glover knew that he was continuing to buy precious time with each passing minute, which was a victory of sorts because protecting Washington's army was the top priority. The sweat-stained defenders hoped that the next assault would again come north primarily up Split Rock Road, which was bordered by rock fences that paralleled the road as well as the stone walls that branched off from the road perpendicular to the road, because Glover's series of ambushes had been created for that tactical eventuality. If so, then a heavy fire from Colonel Read's men from the same stone wall east of the road could be concentrated at a single point to inflict even more severe damage upon the attackers, while Colonel Shepard's men were in Read's rear west of the road: the first phase of the staggered defense in depth based on regiments situated in well-conceived echelon positions. However, Glover and his top lieutenants knew only too well that the tactically astute Howe had plenty of tricks up his sleeve and that they themselves could be surprised at any moment by the clever Briton.

But more time passed and still no attack and Glover and his men started to worry a good deal more. What was the enemy now planning and doing? Was General Howe even now in the process of swinging wide in a bid to outflank the stone walls along Split Rock Road to completely sabotage the orchestration of Glover's brilliant defense in depth, before it had a chance to work? Of course, no member of the Massachusetts brigade knew for sure, so they just hoped for the best, kept fingers crossed, or prayed to God for a favorable outcome. But knowing the depth of British arrogance and like Glover, who had already planned accordingly, the seasoned Bay State men in the ranks were betting that the next enemy assault would once again come straight up the road. Nevertheless, Colonels Glover, Baldwin, Shepard and Read, and Captain Courtis were still concerned that the long quiet respite meant that some of General Howe's troops now planned to outflank their defensive positions along the lower, or southern, edge of Pelham Heights on the left, or east. After all, the defender's right flank was protected by rough and heavily wounded terrain of the Hutchinson River Valley, especially the high ground on the river's west bank, where the right of Glover's old regiment and the three artillery pieces stood on commanding terrain.

But in fact, the mounting concerns of Colonel Glover and his veterans were now well-placed and right on target. Having met with more determined resistance than expected in a land covered with stone fences that spanned in every direction, General Clinton had already wisely ordered Lord Charles Cornwallis to conduct a flank movement east. To cover the landing on the Pell's Point Peninsula, Cornwallis and his troops had earlier pushed west toward the plateau east of the Split Rock Road with a large force of handpicked grenadiers and light infantry to protect troops pouring ashore. Lord Cornwallis relied on light troops and the dismounted dragoons of the First Dragoons to lead the way in an advance of this "corps" calculated to outflank Glover on the left, or east.[73]

This flanking formation of Howe's reserve corps, consisting mostly of light grenadier battalions (four in total) and the Thirty-third and Forty-second Regiments of Foot, could not have been in better hands. Major General Cornwallis was one of the most tactically gifted members of Howe's army. He also hailed from the British aristocracy and he possessed close connections with King George III. Despite his prestigious position in Parliament as a member of the House of Lords before the war, rewarding marriage to a beautiful woman named Jemima and a loving family that included two children, his seemingly endless wealth and estates, Cornwallis had enthusiastically departed home when he volunteered to fight for king and country in America because he saw it as his sacred duty. Ever-ambitious and a relentless pursuer of glory because of his abundant skills and sense of duty Cornwallis had seen abundant opportunities to be gained by him in America. He had ignored the advice of his friends and his sympathies for trampled colonial rights in part because he was a friend of the king, who was determined to subdue the wayward colonies at any cost. The talented Cornwallis had gained a fine education at Eton and Cambridge and then compiled a distinguished record during the Seven Years' War in Germany. By the time of the American Revolution, consequently,

Cornwallis had possessed plenty of solid experience, having joined the military at age seventeen. In part because he had attended a prestigious military academy at Turin, Italy, Lord Cornwallis was the best tactician in the entire landing force at Pell's Point, posing a most serious threat to sabotage Glover's masterful tactical plan before it could be fully employed.[74]

But while Cornwallis's flankers steadily moving west across mostly open ground without the sun in their eyes, Colonel Glover still continued to stand firm in his advanced position, gambling that the main threat would continue to come from the south and up Split Rock Road. He, consequently, continued to resist the temptation of sending out parties to the east to protect the left flank of his first defensive line held by Colonel Read's regiment, which was hanging in midair in the direction of the Long Island Sound, especially now that his most advanced position to the south had been revealed by the first fire in repulsing the enemy—he needed every single fighting man on the firing line. Such a hasty knee-jerk tactical decision by Glover based more on emotion than solid judgment would have seriously compromised the overall strength—already severely limited—of his masterful defensive arrangement in depth along Split Rock Road and based on the successive lines of stone fences at a time when he already possessed too few men to oppose a mighty invasion force. Clearly, this all-important showdown was now a game of nerves and Glover was not the kind of man who could be easily panicked or lose his nerve even in a crisis situation, which had been well-honed from his seafaring experiences over the years. He, therefore, continued to stand firm with a spirited defiance, relying on his defense in depth to buy precious time to not only save the day, but also Washington's army.

Most of all, Colonel Glover knew enough about British tactics and that the top priority of an amphibious landing was to gain a secure toehold on high ground and land as many troops as quickly as possible, which guaranteed that the enemy's main effort would continue north up Split Rock Road. Indeed, by reading his opponent's finely-educated mind, Glover realized that General Howe would be less likely to take the longer time in conducting flanking maneuvers because of the crucial nature of the time element. Indeed, Howe knew that he had to gain the high ground to secure a permanent toehold as soon as possible, and this ensured that Clinton would push straight forward with the bulk of his troops to force a passage of Split Rock Road rather than depend upon a more time-consuming flank movement, because it would take too much time. These undeniable tactical realities had served as the primary foundation of Glover's creation of his series of multiple ambushes of a defense of depth based on Split Rock Road. As Glover had seen with tactical clarity, the fact that the right of the Fourteenth Massachusetts, bolstered by three pieces of artillery, held high ground on the Hutchinson River's high west bank would act as a strong deterrent for a sweeping British flank movement by Lord Cornwallis to gain the rear of Glover's four undersized regiments.

Despite the first bloody repulse, Colonel Glover knew that the British and Hessians were exceptionally cocky and overconfident, despite the initial setback that would do absolutely nothing to humble them. Even more, Glover also realized that the enemy and their leaders were now upset, if not angry, by their unexpected repulse and eager for revenge, and, hence, more likely to commit tactical errors in their arrogance and impatience in facing these particularly stubborn Americans, who seemed so unlike Washington's other troops who had so often taken to their heels: perfect situational requirements that were guaranteed to generate carelessness and draw the enemy deeper into Glover's clever defense in depth and multiple ambushes.

Earlier, General Howe had considered the American fighting man so inferior that he had been convinced that flanking maneuver would not be needed during their initial advance into Westchester County. Such arrogant attitudes ensured that the British and Hessians would continue to direct their main efforts up Split Rock Road in column on this day of destiny. For all that Howe knew and if the Virginian from Mount Vernon awoke to recognize the extent of the new crisis on his far eastern flank, then Washington was now rushing troops (which was not the case) on the double to Glover's aid, before it was too late. Consequently, like for Glover, time was of the essence for General Howe and his army of confident invaders.

All the while, the advantages of geography continued to benefit Glover's defensive stand on multiple high ground perches. Fortunately for Colonel Glover's defensive arrangement on the lower end of Pelham Heights, the Hutchinson River and the swampy ground to the west continued to provide good protection for the right flank of his defenders of Split Rock Road. Therefore, as Glover anticipated, General Howe's troops, at least initially, still had little choice up but to attack once again straight up Split Rock Road and across the land to its east, where Read's men east of the road were ready for the next onslaught.

At the first defensive line behind the stone fence during this lull before the storm, meanwhile, Colonel Read's Continentals waited with cocked muskets and prepared for the inevitable next assault in their concealed position behind the stone fence, while the muscles of legs and feet of the older men in the ranks felt increasingly cramped and sore with each passing minute. As before the first attack, they now remained perfectly quiet and laid low behind the fence of stone in obeying Glover's and Read's strict orders to maintain silence.

In high spirits and confident that they could once again repeat their success, Colonel Read's young soldiers, including teenagers who had yet to shave, of the Thirteenth Massachusetts perhaps violated orders by trading a joke or bragged about their recent marksmanship in hushed tones, while the more serious men read silently from small pocket Bibles about Old Testament lessons that focused on the "Sword of the Lord," while awaiting the next onslaught that they knew was sure to come. The large number of bodies of dead and wounded from Hessian units and the "King's Own" from the first attack lay across the ground just before the stone fence held by Colonel Read's band of soldiers. The dead and wounded men of the German units and the crack Fourth Royal Regiment of Foot were scattered in the roadbed and along the slope to the road's east like freshly fallen autumn leaves.

Some wounded Hessians and redcoats of the "King's Own" lying before the stone wall called for help or water; one or two, or perhaps more, of Colonel Read's more compassionate men jumped over the rock fence against orders to give the wounded enemy water from wooden canteens to ease their intense suffering. Meanwhile, more time passed and still no sign of an impending attack up Split Rock Road or to the east, which continued to raise additional questions among these veterans. Was Glover now foolishly endangering the lives of his men by standing firm instead of retreating, while the enemy maneuvered to gain his rear while most of his troops remained idle in ambush positions along Split Rock Road to the south? Therefore, was the Marblehead colonel now making a costly tactical mistake that might result in his regiments getting cut-off east of the Hutchinson River and then destroyed? Of course, only time would tell. But Glover had no choice but to gamble because this fight was all about buying time to save Washington's army: a crisis situation that made the men of the Bay State brigade not only highly motivated but also expendable on October 18.

Most encouraging to the increasingly anxious Massachusetts soldiers was the fact that no sign of a British flanking movement or effort to gain Glover's rear had been ascertained to the east at this point. Thanks to Glover's way-of-thinking upon which his entire strategy was based, the more time that went by without an attack, then the more that he was succeeding in his crucial mission of buying time. All the while, the nervous anxiety and sense of apprehension among the Massachusetts men grew under the warming sunshine of early fall. However, these men continued to feel a sense of solace mixed with pride because no sign of the enemy advancing now equated to victory, because they were succeeding in buying precious time for Washington's army to escape north with each passing minute.

During this thankful respite while crouching on grass behind the fences of stone, the older Massachusetts men, as opposed to the teenagers in the ranks, had plenty of time to think about wives, families, and lovers back home in the Bay State, wondering how everyone, especially children, was doing without the family's head. Some soldiers found time to say quiet prayers to themselves, sensing that the day's hardest fighting lay ahead and knowing that a good many more lives would be lost before the sun went down. And, of course, like fighting men for centuries, Glover's veterans said prayers for victory and divine deliverance so that they would be able to return home one day.

Meanwhile, the less optimistic Massachusetts soldiers wondered if they would survive this day and if they might be fated to find a final resting place far from home and families. Colonel Glover's men speculated about their chances of ever seeing their beloved families and small farms ever again, while placing their faith in God and the leadership ability of the former sea captain, who was now fighting the most important land battle of his career on his own. Would a large number of Massachusetts men meet their Maker on October 18 with the next British and Hessian attack, which was now guaranteed to be far more severe? These Bay State veterans knew that they were in an exposed, vulnerable forward position a good distance away from General Washington's army in the midst of a long retreat, looming dangerously alone on the army's far eastern flank. Indeed, these small regiments were still on their own in this remote part of Westchester County and these veterans were only too aware of that disturbing fact, almost sensing that no reinforcements would be sent by Washington in time to bolster their ranks when most needed. Therefore, the Massachusetts men realized that they must aim carefully and make every shot count while firing as rapidly as possible, because this key situation in protecting Washington's army was literally a case of no tomorrow for the arm and infant nation.

Ever-the-realist, Glover realized that the message which had been earlier sent to General Lee's headquarters at Valentine's Hill, which was located several miles to the southwest, by the reliable Major Lee would take some time for him to return to the command during a nearly a seven-mile round trip. But, fortunately, Lee had ridden a fast horse and he eventually rejoined Glover in record time to reunite a hard-fighting and highly capable team with the Marblehead colonel. And, of course, Glover knew that General Charles Lee's reply and that the arrival of reinforcements, if they were even dispatched at all, would take much longer. Indeed, General Washington or Lee might well decide not to send support to this remote edge of Westchester County, electing to meet General Howe's invasion at some point farther inland to protect Washington's army or simply continuing to hurry north in retreat, if Glover's brigade was brushed aside which was all but inevitable. Instead of supporting the last stand on the southern end of Pelham Heights and on the army's far eastern flank, the generals might simply order Glover and his troops rearward to rejoin the withdrawal to White Plains instead of being destroyed by the tide of Howe's invaders, since these were Washington's indispensable men. Glover and his men almost certainly correctly sensed that no reinforcements would be forthcoming.

Nevertheless, Colonel Glover also reasoned that it might be necessary to hold out as long as possible so as to allow the arrival of General Lee's reinforcing units, if dispatched at all, down the Eastchester Road for what might well become a major action in a larger effort to halt Howe's push inland. But of course and most of all, Glover took comfort in the fact that the longer he held firm to keep the tide of British and Hessians at bay, then he was buying precious time to increase the possibility of the survival of Washington's army: the top priority of extreme importance on October 18, which was a realization that never departed Colonel Glover's mind and defined his decision-making from beginning to end on this bloody Friday.

Fortunately in this crisis situation, Glover's veterans could be relied upon to stand their ground as long as possible and face one British and Hessian attack after another as long as their ammunition remained dry and plentiful, because they would obey Glover's orders and fight to the bitter end if necessary. Therefore, because he was continuing to buy invaluable time for the army's survival, Glover felt increasingly confident because he was successfully fulfilling his key mission by simply maintaining his position and standing firm, despite his no-win situation. Quite simply and as mentioned, buying additional time now equated to saving the life of Washington's army on what was truly a day of destiny for America.

To their credit, these experienced Bay State veterans were not in the least frightened by the daunting prospect of facing overwhelming odds or the certainty of serious fighting that lay ahead, when everything was at stake. Like Generals Washington and Lee, Glover knew that there was no chance that these Massachusetts boys would take to their heels like the panic-stricken New England militiamen, who had without having fired a single shot, during the fiasco at Kip's Bay. Despite not looking like elite soldiers, except for Colonel Baldwin's Grenadiers, because of the lack of smart and fancy uniforms like the British and Hessians, these young men and boys of Glover's command were once again proving that they were crack troops, when it counted the most. Practical and pragmatic in the New England tradition rooted in their strong Congregationalist faith, these mostly middle class farmers from Massachusetts knew that being a soldier of true merit was really more about shooting straight and accurately rather than impressing the home folk and pretty girls with the perfection of drill and parade ground exhibitions. By this time, these Bay Staters realized that what was more important than anything else was fighting hard with a stubborn determination. All in all, these were tough and hardy fighting men who would hold firm regardless of the odds.

Of course, Colonel Baldwin and other top officers of Glover's brigade fully understood as much and they respected the average fighting man in the ranks in consequence. Therefore, the Harvard-educated Colonel Baldwin looked upon his steady, dependable soldiers with a sense of admiration and respect almost as if they were fellow classmates at Cambridge, because his Twenty-sixth Massachusetts consisted more of a community of fighting men with strong ties and bonds to each other, including familial ones, that ran deep. As he later penned in a letter to his wife, Mary Fowle-Baldwin, back home in Woburn, Massachusetts, Colonel Baldwin was proud of the fact that despite facing the greatest challenge of their lives, the Massachusetts soldiers on October 18 were remarkably "Calm [almost] as though [they were] expecting a Shot at a flock of [Passenger] Pidgeons [sic] or Ducks" on a placid New England pond nestled in a quiet patch of woodlands.[75]

Meanwhile, the stillness and silence continued to dominate the field of strife like a heavy shroud—the lull before the storm. With the next assault certainly about to come, Bay State officers made sure that no one made any noise, not even a whisper, while everyone was either sitting, crouching, or lying behind their stone fences in preparation for successfully springing an entire series of Glover's staggered ambushes of his clever defense in depth as the Marblehead colonel had so carefully planned. During the respite after the first repulse, officers of the three regiments concealed behind the stone walls—the Thirteenth, Third, and Twenty-sixth Continental Regiments, respectively—also made sure that none of their men smoked from their long-stemmed white clay pipes, because any hint of tobacco smoke would betray their hidden positions in echelon on both sides of the road. Meanwhile, the Massachusetts soldiers of Glover's three hidden regiments—one behind the other in staggered positions from south to north—gripped their loaded muskets, awaiting the orders to rise up and fire whenever the invaders ventured forth up Split Rock Road. These hardened Continental veterans instinctively realized that it was now only a matter of time, before the British and Hessians launched another offensive effort to force their way through the position at the lower edge of Pelham Heights and northwest of the Pell's Point Peninsula by barreling up the road with fixed bayonets and colorful battle flags of silk flying in the breeze coming off the Long Island Sound.

Chapter 5

A Systematic Slaughter of Hessians in Westchester County

All the while as the hour and a half passed since the first failed enemy attack, General Howe's troops had been preparing for a much stronger onslaught that was calculated to smash through resistance that had decimated and caused the rout of the hard-hit foremost Hessian units, the grenadiers of the two light companies of the Fourth Royal Regiment and other commands, including the dismounted men of the Sixteenth Light Dragoons. Upon Howe's orders, the British were now busily bringing up their artillery—the Hessians possessed only two companies of artillery in the entire First Division—to pound the obstinate Americans into submission, if these unexpectedly stubborn men behind the little stone fence had not run away by this time as in the past as fully expected by a smug British leadership.

Finally, an hour and a half after the first attack had been cut to pieces by Glover's first ambush that had been sprung so effectively by Colonel Read's soldiers who had suddenly risen up like ghosts to blast away with enthusiasm, once again "they appeared about four thousand, with seven pieces of artillery; they now advance," wrote Glover about the onslaught. Indeed, this much more powerful advance consisted primarily of Hessians, who made up the largest portion of Howe's invasion force, who were determined to establish a permanent grip on the American mainland and to gain the strategic Boston Post Road and then the Eastchester Road to intercept Washington's retreat to White Plains and cut off his withdrawing army.[1]

In a letter, one of Glover's men described the vigorous British and Hessian response to the first sharp setback suffered by the attackers: "They returned with field-pieces" to renew the fight once again, as if seeking revenge for this first repulse and the fact that the bodies of so many their men still lay in bloody clumps before Colonel Read's stone fence.[2] And as before, this upcoming struggle was still all about gaining possession of Split Rock Road, which led to the high ground that would give Howe a solid and permanent toehold in Westchester County. Manned by well-trained British artillerymen who worked their guns with an accurate precision, the seven cannon began to bellow away like there was no tomorrow, bestowing a stern warning to the band of defenders about what was to come.

The booming British guns sent a steady rain of shot in the area around the lower slopes of Pelham Heights, pounding the area where the first attackers had been repulsed and in the hope of battering down the stone fence that had recently spat a sheet of flame. Iron projectiles smashed off the rock fence and through the trees to the rear, falling like hail around the men lying low behind their rocky shelter that protected them from harm. Some British guns had been turned to the northwest to fire on the right of Glover's old regiment, which was aligned on the high ground just west of the Hutchinson River to overlook the north-south flowing watercourse that entered the northern end of Pelham Bay.

Meanwhile, just below the summit of Pelham Heights, Captain Courtis looked over the ranks of the former seafarers and fishermen on the left of the mostly Marblehead regiment, who still served as the steadfast strategic reserve of the three Bay State regiments on the lower ground before them to south. All the while, these Massachusetts men of Glover's old regiment farthest north were under "a constant fire of artillery," complained Glover, when the artillery fire intensified and became more accurate. Thankfully, most of the bombardment spared the men of the Third and Twenty-sixth Massachusetts Continental Regiments, yet fully concealed behind the stone walls in the second and third defensive lines, respectively, because their defensive positions, except for Colonel Read's Thirteenth Massachusetts in the first line which took artillery punishment, were yet unseen by the British artillerymen. However, some British field pieces also turned on the men of Captain Courtis's Fourteenth Massachusetts since they could be seen on the high ground unlike their hidden comrades farther south on the east side of the Hutchinson River: all part of Glover's defense in depth to continue to catch the enemy by surprise by only exposing the Fourteenth Massachusetts to British and Hessian eyes.

With his Massachusetts boys of three regiments still laying low under a heavy pounding of artillery that angrily swept the stone wall fence occupied by the Thirteenth Massachusetts and the heights farther north held by the Fourteenth Massachusetts's left while hurling clods of dirt and rocks in every direction, Glover once again allowed the dense ranks of British and Hessian troops to surge north up the slope without ordering a long-range fire to impede their relentless advance. At this time, Glover now faced thousands of Hessians of Major General Werner von Mirbach's Brigade, Lieutenant General Heister's First Division, during the second major assault.

Most of all, an undaunted Glover was determined to employ the same successful strategy and rely on the same tactics that had earlier proved so successful, because his defense in depth had been created for the express purpose of buying as much time as possible. To his credit, he had refused to panic in the face of the day's most overpowering enemy onslaught and order a withdrawal west back across the Hutchinson River—since the wooden bridge had been disabled to impede Howe's crossing, the British and Hessians would now have to ford the watercourse to gain the west bank. When he had served as the captain of his own sailing ship, Glover had faced plenty of threatening storms on the turbulent Atlantic, which helped to steel him for this current manmade storm that he faced on land. The sheer power of this next onslaught and the lay of the land meant that large numbers of General Howe's troops advanced not only along Split Rock Road but also over the plateau on the road's east side—hence, Glover had two of his regiments (Read and Baldwin) positioned east of the road—in an attempt to outflank Colonel Read's position. Clearly, this time, however, it would take far more accurate volleys from the soldiers of the Thirteenth Massachusetts Continental Regiment to slow this upcoming heavier and more determined assault than during the first attack.

Determined to maintain his ground at his most advanced defensive position upon which he had orchestrated his defense in depth, Colonel Glover never forgot the imposing sight of the massive onslaught, now much larger than the first one, while German drummer boys, whose drums were embossed with the Hessian lion, furiously pounded their instruments. In their smart-looking Prussian-style blue uniforms and carrying muskets that had been manufactured at the Pistor factory at Schmalkalden in Thuringia, Hesse, the dark-hued mass of approaching Hessians looked magnificent in the morning sunlight. The Hessians were eager for revenge not only because of the first repulse but also after having been informed by British generals in August that the Americans planned to unmercifully shoot down Hessian officers, who were distinguished from their men by their fancy hats and uniforms. In consequence, the approaching Hessian officers were now less discernable to the naked eye, after having removed fancy insignia, tassels, gorgets, and white lace from uniforms in the hope of escaping harm. Above the surging Hessian ranks of blue that stretched for a lengthy distance, a larger number of battle flags fluttered than in British ranks, because every German fusilier and musketeer company carried their own distinctive colors of silk in the Prussian tradition. Meanwhile, the regimental flags of the Hessians were distinguished by the Latin motto, "NESCIT PERICULA," or fearless of danger.

Colonel Glover wrote of the greatest crisis of the day so far: "when they appeared about four thousand, with seven pieces of artillery; they now advance [while] keeping up a constant fire of artillery." The second attack was not only of overwhelming strength, but also the artillery fire had been closely synchronized with the relentless advance of the waves of Hessian infantry—the pride of Germany—pouring up the slopes with fixed bayonets that reflected the soft sunlight of fall in New York.

Around four thousand or more attackers marched north in disciplined step toward the lower end of Pelham Heights, ascending ever-higher ground hued in bright autumnal colors, including patches of brown grass that had been green in springtime and summer. Clearly, General Howe and his top lieutenants, determined that a Throgs Neck-like fiasco, which could now be entirely avoided by the British thanks to more favorable geography at Pell's Point, would not be repeated, had thrown everything that they had into this second attack to gain the high ground of the lower edge of Pelham Heights to ensure that the amphibious landing of the invasion force had successfully secured a permanent toehold in Westchester County.

All the while, the tense Massachusetts soldiers of Colonel Read's regiment and the two regiments farther north that were hidden behind the stone fences, under Colonels Shepard and Baldwin respectively and from south to north, remained perfectly still and quiet. In the ranks of the crouched men of Colonel Read's Thirteenth Massachusetts, meanwhile, no one made a sound, while the anxiety could not have been higher. Tightly gripping their flintlock muskets, everyone in the ranks remained amazingly patient, which revealed the extent of the excellent training and heightened discipline of Read's fine regiment, while they patiently waited for the order to raise up as one, rest their muskets atop the stone wall, and open fire at close range, whenever Glover gave the signal.

In consequence, the seconds passed like hours to the anxious Massachusetts men of Colonel Read's regiment, while they sweated in the rising fall heat and their nervousness grew with each passing minute. Colonel Glover described the dramatic moment when the escalating tension reached a new high until it was practically boiling over by this time: "we kept our post under cover of the stone wall . . . till they came within fifty yards of us" with rows of gleaming steel bayonets sparkling in the October sun. In a letter, one American soldier described how Howe's troops had again "formed and came on again, in large numbers, keeping up a heavy fire with field pieces on the walls and men."[3]

At this time, Glover continued to make adroit tactical adjustments that revealed the extent of his tactical flexibility and dexterity in a fluid battle plan that continued to evolve. Because thousands of Hessian soldiers—the bulk of Howe's invasion force of more than six thousand men—now surged forward up Split Rock Road with flags flying and drums beating, Glover knew that he could not allow them to get as close as he had allowed during the first attack because of the greater numbers now advancing against him, when he had ordered firing to begin when the attackers were only thirty yards distant. He correctly worried that a simultaneous flanking movement, under the irrepressible Lord Cornwallis, might strike the stationary defenders before the attackers got that close again like during the first assault, because Colonel Read's position already had been revealed by the first fire.

Now in consequence, at a range of fifty yards, or 150 feet, Colonel Glover planned to order his men of Colonel Read's command to open fire with their lethal loads of "ball & buckshot." When he felt that the time was exactly right, therefore, Glover barked out orders for the Thirteenth Massachusetts veterans to raise up and open fire as one, when the Hessians reached this targeted point and well within close range to wreak havoc. In Glover's words, when General Howe's legions reached a point fifty yards distant, the Thirteenth Massachusetts soldiers once again "rose up and gave the whole charge of the battalion," while the nearby Third Massachusetts, under Shepard behind the stone fence on the road's west side at the second ambush in a staggered position just to the rear, or north, gave Colonel Read's men added confidence to hold firm under the onslaught, because they also opened fire on the more extended enemy battle line: the ideal way by which to protect Colonel Read's vulnerable right flank anchored on the road that was hanging in midair.[4] One Continental soldier wrote in a letter of the dramatic moment when all hell was unleashed upon the throng of attackers, when "they advanced now very near and received a second fire" at point-blank range.[5]

Glover's well-developed battle plan of a staggered defense in depth with his concealed regiments in echelon on both sides of the road now paid even higher dividends. As carefully planned and as envisioned from the beginning, he now had not one but two regiments—the Third and Thirteenth Massachusetts Continental Regiments—firing from stone fences that stood on both sides of Split Rock Road. The men of both veteran Continental units had been completely hidden behind stone fences before the eager troops rose up to fire, catching the enemy by surprise with a heavier fire from two separate higher ground positions (Shepard's command on the right—or west—was on higher ground than Read's regiment on the left—or east) from both sides of the road. Clearly, to the foe's thinking that had been gained from a new awareness and a bloody one, these fast-firing soldiers were definitely not militiamen or they would have already retired west across the Hutchinson River by this time. But as important, the fire of Shepard's regiment that poured from the west side of the road was completely unexpected by the enemy, because the Third Massachusetts's position was now revealed for the first time to the attackers, who had been only aware of Colonel Read's more advanced position farther south. Howe's men now realized that a far larger force of patriots was now contesting Split Rock Road with tenacity than previously thought. From the west side of the road, this heavy concentrated fire from Shepard's men, therefore, tore into the attacker's left formation and flank while they were pushing north and ascending Split Rock Road farther west. Consequently, Howe's Hessians now faced not only a frontal fire, but also a flank fire, which resulted in higher losses and the delivering of greater shock value, as Colonel Glover had envisioned in the tactical calculations.

Like during the previous assault, this blazing frontal fire from the Massachusetts men at close range was simply too much for any advancing troops to withstand. Both Hessians and British soldiers wavered and then broke under the torrent of spray of lead musket balls and smaller pellets of buckshot from fiery blasts of "buck & ball." But the enfilade fire caused the most damage and heaviest loss of lives among the enemy, when it rippled down the attacker's exposed left flank from the fire of Shepard's men west of the road. One American soldier described the slaughter caused by the sweeping flank fire from two Bay State regiments, after the attackers

> received a second fire, which entirely routed them again, and they retreated in a narrow lane by a wall, in a confused hud- dled manner, near which were posted a large body of riflemen, and some companies of musket men, who at this favourite [sic] moment poured in upon them a most heavy fire once or twice, before they could get out of the way; and they were seen to fall in great numbers

to the combined frontal and enfilade fires.[6]

Indeed, the narrow lane beside the stone wall became a deadly trap and slaughter pen, where a good many Hessians met their Maker around four thousand miles from the Rhine River country, falling to both the flank and frontal blasts of musketry that reaped a grim total. As mentioned, it was the blistering flank fire that inflicted the greatest damage, which was evident from the pile of finely uniformed German fighting men, who would never see their homeland again, on the ground before the fences of stone.[7]

To the delight of the Massachusetts men of these two regiments of more than 550 members (264 of Read's regiment—minus light losses that stemmed from having repulsed the first assault—and 292 of Shepard's regiment) and in consequence, this time the Hessian attackers suffered more severe losses, with officers and men dropping from the ranks in large numbers. But this time more than twice as many attackers went down than from the fire that unleashed during the previous assault because of the larger number of Bay State defenders now blasting away from both sides of the road. Unlike the first attack in which mostly British troops were hurled back by a number of frontal volleys from Colonel Read's men, it now took both frontal and flank fires of two commands to force the Hessians rearward in the bloodiest repulse of the day.

And the element of surprise and shock value had not been lost in the least, even though the Hessians (the stunned survivors of the two battered light companies of the Fourth Royal Regiment, which had suffered twenty-three casualties, had also tried to warn them) had attempted to inform their redcoat comrades in broken English of what to expect upon nearing the stone wall on Split Rock Road. The unexpected rising of Colonel Shepard's hidden troops who had unleashed a murderous fire—not just Colonel Read's men this time—from the road's west side at close range had retained the element of surprise, as Glover had planned in the beginning to deliver a double shock by a close-range fire streaming from both sides of the road. Therefore, the key elements of shock and surprise now had a far greater impact than during the first attack, because the last fire had been unleashed by the men of two veteran regiments, when they had simultaneously opened up as one with their flintlocks resting atop the stone fence to ensure an accurate and especially lethal fire.

And unlike the first assault, even larger numbers of Hessian troops of additional German units now moved forward to replace those men who had been cut down. Colonel Glover described how the blue-clad attackers from Germany now "halted and returned the fire with showers of musketry and cannon balls" fired from the seven British cannon. The neat, disciplined ranks of the Hessians to their credit held firm despite mounting losses under the severe punishment, blasting away with regular rolling volleys at Colonel Read's regiment east of the road and Colonel Shepard's regiment west of the road, while Glover's other regiment—the Twenty-sixth Massachusetts—under Colonel Baldwin—remained in its concealed position higher up the slope behind their stone fence farther to the rear east of the road: the third ambush position of Glover's intricate defense in depth and where the foremost Massachusetts men, both Read's and Shepard's regiments, had been ordered to eventually retire when given the command to fall back to a higher ground position at exactly the right time.

At close range, Colonel Read's men continued to gamely hold firm in Glover's first defense position during the rolling volley exchanges, despite taking punishment of their own. However, the sturdy stone wall provided good protection, except for clean head and shoulder shots from the enemy that brought down a handful of exposed defenders. As quickly as possible, the Thirteenth Massachusetts soldiers loaded and fired as fast as they could, ensuring a heavy fire because they were well-trained veteran Continentals in a crisis situation. These Massachusetts soldiers were determined not to give way under the increasing pressure, because they knew what was at stake and that Washington's withdrawing army had to be protected at all costs, despite facing overwhelming numbers and receiving a heavy return fire.

Under a severe fire of repeated Hessian volleys and the fire of British artillery, Colonel Read's and Colonel Shepard's veterans retained their composure in what had become a conventional stand-up fight by this time, after the Massachusetts men had been ordered to stand up from behind their respective stone walls for easier and quicker loading for volley firing. Now these Continentals displayed their discipline and the extent of their thorough training. No Massachusetts soldier was now firing at will like during the first attack, indicating Glover's tactical master plan of delivering the most concentrated fire from a series of volleys of musketry for maximum effect—basically, the British and Hessian way of conventional tactics, while also taking advantage of irregular warfare by fighting from behind cover and from higher ground. All the while obeying their commander's orders, Read's Thirteenth Massachusetts soldiers and Shepard's Third Massachusetts men loaded and fired as rapidly as possible, unleashing additional volleys upon the dense Hessian ranks, which remained tight and well-formed despite handfuls of comrades falling dead and wounded out of formation. In total, Colonel Read's veterans fired seven thunderous volleys that raked the enemy's line with a blistering fire, riddling the ranks and dropping large numbers of General Howe's soldiers.[8]

As in repulsing the initial assault, the Thirteenth Massachusetts men continued to steadily and systematically decimate this next formation of Hessian attackers of an overpowering onslaught, which was far more massive and threatening than the first one. Eyewitnesses never forgot the lethal effectiveness of the close-range volleys of Colonel Read's soldiers which poured down the slope from the stone fence to sweep the lower-lying terrain before it like a scythe, because these withering volleys, fueled by a storm of "buck & ball" projectiles of multiple sizes, including what was known as "swan shot," for hunting ducks and geese, "brought many of them to the ground."[9]

However, additional Hessian regiments of highly disciplined men were quickly moved up to replace fallen soldiers and those once-neat formations that had been cut to pieces, entering the escalating fray that was taking on a life of its own, with both sides standing firm in unleashing one volley after another. To their credit, the men of both sides defiantly stood their ground and fought bravely in the face of death, which was exchanged with enthusiasm. In a letter, one soldier described the might of a mostly German onslaught that seemingly could no longer be stopped: the "whole body of the enemy then advanced in solid column, and large flanking parties advanced different ways to surround our men; they however kept the wall, till the enemy advanced a third time."[10]

Time For the First Fallback

After unleashing seven volleys into the surging ranks of the Hessians, who continued to advance with fixed bayonets and discipline, Glover correctly reasoned that Colonel Read's Thirteenth Continental Regiment had accomplished all the damage that it could inflict, because ammunition in leather cartridge boxes was running low and the odds were simply too great and the threatening flanking movements that were meant to stealthy ease around the small band of Massachusetts men on their right flank, which rested on the road. And most important, the Thirteenth Massachusetts men had successfully bought as much time as possible.

Even more by this time, this ever-intensifying contest had become an unfair fight for Read's boys who had never fought so long or so hard on any previous battlefield, and Glover knew that he could not afford to lose any additional soldiers to the concentrated fire of so many Hessians and British soldiers and also from the fire of Howe's artillery that continued to roar. Unlike during the first attack, Colonel Read's Continentals had taken more punishment from the relentless pounding of Howe's artillery, falling under "showers of . . . cannon-balls," wrote Colonel Glover of the steady bombardment. In addition, the flanks of Colonel Read's small force, now too far advanced and too far south before the next two regiments in their staggered concealed positions to the rear or north, were vulnerable to the east on the left flank. By this time, Cornwallis's soldiers had steadily advanced east of the road through the open fields of the plateau without obstacles or defenders to impede their march west. Clearly, now was the time to retire before Read's advanced defensive position behind the stone fence east of Split Rock Road was outflanked or overpowered from the front, or both. But more important, Colonel Glover was about ready to spring still another clever ambush—with two regiments (Shepard's Third Massachusetts west of the road was about to be joined by Read's retiring men) from two separate hidden positions on ever-higher ground that were staggered in this masterful defense in depth—to exploit the defensive arrangement that he had so carefully established for just such a threatening situation.[11]

Indeed, most important in regard to buying precious time and having taken a toll on the enemy, Colonel "Read's work was done" by this time and the splendid defensive stand of the Thirteenth Massachusetts men east of the road had been magnificent in hurling back two assaults. Read had performed his vital mission of standing firm and punishing the attackers as long as possible until the cartridge boxes of his men were growing low on rounds. And it had been a job extremely well done by Read's soldiers because time had been bought to help save Washington's army in the midst of a dismal withdrawal to the west.[12]

Consequently, based upon a preplanned tactical design and because Cornwallis's troops "outflanked our party" on the west, or right flank which rested on the road, wrote one soldier in a letter with time having run out for the most advanced defensive position of the Thirteenth Massachusetts, Glover finally ordered Colonel Read's soldiers to retire rearward, or north, across Split Rock Road from east to west partly under cover of a stone fence and to the rear and left of Colonel Shepard's Third Continental Regiment (a larger command than that of Colonel Read's regiment) located on the other side, or west, of the road, which was positioned behind another stone wall on the road's west side just to the north.[13] As revealed in a letter, one soldier described how "after giving them several fires, they retreated by order from their officers," especially Glover, with skill and discipline.[14]

Then, because the return fire, including from the British artillery, had become more intense, Colonel Read's men prudently rushed rearward on the double while crouching low to escape the hail of gunfire and cannon balls streaming through the air. Naturally, the riskiest part, at least in theory, of the tactical withdrawal was in crossing Split Rock Road from east to west, or from left to right. But because the disciplined Hessian soldiers in formation only fired by volleys upon their officer's orders, little, if any, musket fire caught Colonel Read's men when they scampered across the little dirt road to form in the rear and to the left of Colonel Shepard's regiment, which was poised to the rear, or north, behind the stone wall on the road's west side. Most important, the timely reinforcement of Colonel Read's soldiers extended Colonel Shepard's vulnerable left flank of his Third Massachusetts across the road for protection on the east to gain a better defensive position to counter the possibility of the arrival of Cornwallis's flankers, who were now rapidly moving west to exploit their tactical advantage as much as possible.[15]

All the while, Major William Raymond Lee, Glover's top lieutenant and acting "Brigade Major," who had returned from having reported the invasion to General Charles Lee at Valentine's Hill, played a key role during the risky movement of the Thirteenth Massachusetts to the rear, or north, under fire to gain its new defensive position and in stabilizing the overall defense as conceived by Glover by helping to extend the second line's left flank east across the road. One eyewitness who saw Major Lee, evidently not on horseback at this time because of the close-range nature of the contest since such exposure was now far too dangerous, in action wrote that he "behaved gallantly" on this day of destiny in Westchester County.[16]

In the words of one of Glover's men, who was not aware of the tactical complexities and nuances of Glover's brilliant battle plan based upon a series of multiple ambushes and a clever defense in depth, from a letter, Colonel Read's soldiers were "outflanked which occasioned our people to retreat to a short distance, where they rallied well."[17]

Confident in the continued smooth tactical orchestration of his staggered defense in depth based on multiple ambushes that had been established on ever-higher ground, Glover continued to place utmost faith in the overall excellence of his intricate defensive plan to not only repeatedly ambush the attackers, but also punish them with multiple fires—flank and frontal—from additional successive elevated defensive positions, while extending the most-threatened flank to protect against the greatest threat where it had suddenly developed to the east from Cornwallis's flankers.

Indeed, the key tactical arrangement of the second line of defense was that Colonel Read's men were aligned not only behind Colonel Shepard's Third Continental Regiment but, most important, to extend the regiment's left, or east, to extend the defensive line behind the stone wall and to protect the open eastern flank, because General Howe's battle line now extended farther east than when attacking the first defensive line and because of Cornwallis's outflanking threat. The fact that Colonel Read's regiment had been outflanked on the east by Cornwallis had resulted in the Thirteenth Continental Regiment retiring to the second defensive line behind yet another stone fence, which was still part of Glover's plan that had continued to evolve in the heat of battle depending on the overall tactical situation and the enemy's actions. On the spot and demonstrating tactical flexibility in a fluid of battlefield situations, Colonel Glover and Major Lee made sure that the next defensive line was properly extended to the east to protect the vulnerable left flank from the threat posed by the advance of Cornwallis troops, by which Glover's entire defensive arrangement could be easily compromised, if no prudent tactical precautions had been taken. Having learned about the British penchant of launching effective flanking maneuvers, Glover knew that this second defensive line would have to be longer than the first defensive line, or it would be easily outflanked by Howe's master flankers led by officers, especially Lord Cornwallis, who were tactically astute and ready to exploit any opportunity.[18]

Clearly, Colonel Glover was making the necessary skillful tactical adjustments to solidify his overall defensive arrangement on the fly during the crisis situation. In masterful fashion, his staggered defense in depth and of regiments positioned in echelon had been quickly strengthened by Glover into a single defensive line of double strength on the next defensive line (the second), which stood before, or south, of Colonel Baldwin and his Twenty-sixth Massachusetts at the third ambush position, situated on higher ground than Shepard's line and east of Split Rock Road. Most important, Glover continued to demonstrate a remarkable tactical flexibility and adaptability in a crisis situation, making astute tactical decisions and adjustments that were necessary for this band of Bay State soldiers to do the impossible at a time when any other commanders would have either long ago withdrawn or having never attempted to slow the invasion in the first place: the crucial mission of not only standing firm against overwhelming odds, but also thwarting flanking movements to purchase even more time for Washington and his retreating army.

As noted, Colonel Glover gained a key advantage when he ordered Read's command to retire north to Shepard's position west of the road to extend the left flank of the Third Massachusetts to the east and it was an all-important one in fulfilling his primary mission of buying time. Predictably, as Glover fully realized, the attacking Hessians and British believed that they had routed the Americans, when Colonel Read's boys of the Thirteenth Massachusetts had raced off in what was seemingly another panic or rout, when more than two hundred men fled north up the gradual slope leading to Pelham Heights. But, as planned by Glover, they were only presenting the facade of a panicked rout of beaten soldiers before they quickly took up a new defensive position and a strong one farther to the rear by leapfrogging to an even better defensive position on still higher ground to the north: all part of Glover's planned relay team of moving from one good defensive position to an even better one on even more defensible terrain. Once again, General Howe's hired mercenaries from Germany had surged north up the slope with fixed bayonets and cheers upon the sight of Read's men on the run, sensing that a complete victory was theirs. For ample good reason, Glover now realized that his plan was working to perfection and that he possessed the ultimate tactical advantage, when he now saw that the Hessians and British troops had taken the bait because now "they then shouted and pushed on" up both sides of Split Rock Road.[19]

Incredibly, forgetting all about the nasty surprise that they had suffered with the first bloody repulse in attacking Colonel Read's line, the overconfidence of the elite Hessian troops again rose to the fore, as Glover had fully understood would certainly be the case since having first devised his innovative defensive plan, which was tailor-made for repeatedly surprising an arrogant opponent by exploiting his self-imposed weaknesses. An already-powerful German contempt, which was mirrored by the British regulars and their aristocratic leaders, for the average American soldier dominated Hessian attitudes and thinking, after so many easy victories in the New York Campaign and the common sight of large numbers of Americans running for their lives before a row of German or British bayonets coming straight at them. Therefore, the blue-coated soldiers from Germany surged ahead with much less discipline, believing that victory already had been won in their deepening hubris, "having learned nothing from their previous experiences and believing the Americans were repulsed, advanced in solid masses in pursuit."[20]

Indeed, Colonel Glover's clever tactical plan of a staggered defense in depth continued to smoothly proceed like clockwork just as he had early envisioned. Therefore, General Howe's Hessians had once again eagerly taken the bait that Glover had created for them and it was one that was simply too tempting to resist, causing them to rush forward up Split Rock Road and the surrounding area with fixed bayonets, while consumed with the elation of victory. What made this intoxicating feeling more plausible among the Hessians was the fact that Glover had placed the non-uniformed men of Colonel Read's regiment in the first defensive line by deliberate design. After all, the Hessians had only seen Massachusetts fighting men in civilian and farmers' clothes, which had given them the distinct impression that they were facing ill-trained militiamen from the surrounding countryside of Westchester County, when Read's Continentals had fallen back in what looked like a rout—Glover's well-designed ruse—instead of a well-timed planned redeployment. In truth, the Hessians had no idea that they were facing some of Washington's finest troops, both uniformed and ununiformed, under one of the most gifted colonels of the Continental Army, Glover. This deliberately orchestrated development of a rapid retreat of Read's men north was one of the key prerequisites for the setup of the next tactical ambush, as Glover knew to be the case.

Therefore, in the frantic rush of victory in what was a determined bid to win glory, the charging Hessians swarmed forward in the belief not only that the day was won, but also that a rout was on in full force. Because they obviously believed that Colonel Read's uniformed men were only local militia because of how fast they had suddenly abandoned their first position and headed north in flight, the Germans were once again relying upon the most winning of all tactics that had always proved so successful in the past, especially against militia and including recently at the Battle of Long Island, where the Hessian use of the bayonets had been as effective as it had been unmerciful whenever they trapped American soldiers: charging swiftly forward with the bayonet because of the defender's expenditure of ammunition after having fired numerous volleys to catch the Americans before they could reload, when the bayonet would shatter all remaining resistance to reap a decisive success.[21] And now after these Continental troops of the first defensive line had expended so much ammunition with repeated volleys, it appeared to the onrushing Germans that Colonel Read and his boys had been forced to retreat because they had expended all of their rounds and their fighting spirit had been extinguished, which was certainly not the case in either regard as the pursuers were about to discover.

Still Another Deadly Ambush

Because of the thick layers of smoke lying over the field from the repeated heavy volleys that had poured from Colonel Read's first line and the fact that the Thirteenth Massachusetts soldiers had partly retired north with stealth under the cover of a stone fence, the second line of Colonel Shepard's soldiers, who were crouched and unseen behind the stone fence west of the road that served as Glover's second ambush position, especially its extension to the east by Read's men, was not ascertained by the Hessian attackers until it was too late: the guarantee of a bloody repeat of the first assault. Glover's masterful ambush at his second defensive position now utilized not one but two regiments: Colonel Read's regrouped command east of the road and all of Colonel Shepard's Third Massachusetts west of the road to cover both sides of Split Rock Road and a wider front than previously. Another Hessian and British victory seemed to be inevitable until the great mass of attackers, aligned in long neat formations like on a drill field, "pushed on till they came on Shepard" in position with his concealed Third Massachusetts and Thirteenth Massachusetts men, in Glover's words.[22] Then, all hell suddenly broke loose when the three colonels, Glover, Read, and Shepard, barked out orders for their men to open fire. Glover explained how Colonel Shepard's crack Continentals "posted behind a fine double stone wall" responded instantaneously and the entire regiment west of the road "rose up and fired by grand divisions" into the faces of the attackers only a short distance away.[23]

Only now did the concentrated mass of Hessians realize that they had not only run into yet another lethal ambush but also that they were facing elite Continentals, who could have only been dispatched from General Washington's army. It was clear that these audacious Americans, who loaded and fired so quickly on command in unison and in a disciplined manner to unleash one accurate volley after another were certainly not untrained Westchester County militia who could be easily pushed aside with a show of flashing bayonets. Indeed, all the while, Colonel Shepard shouted orders for his soldiers to repeatedly load and fire their loads of "buck & ball" as rapidly as possible, keeping up not only an accurate but also a "constant fire, and maintained his post," before the tide of Hessians and redcoats, who just continued to keep bravely coming forward despite the punishment.[24]

Despite men falling from the ranks like autumn leaves on a stormy fall morning in Boston, the disciplined Hessians remained in tight formations as they returned fire with Colonels Shepard and Read's soldiers who blasted away in exchanging volleys. By this time, so many of General Howe's troops had surged forward that no amount of volley firing could now make them break or force them rearward. Nevertheless, the disciplined volleys pouring from Colonel Shepard's Third Massachusetts and Read's Thirteenth Massachusetts continued to inflict extensive punishment among the Hessians, who had never faced such a murderous fire. This time, the punishment was more severe, with both Massachusetts regiments now firing as one, as if to avenge fallen comrades. Consequently, the Hessians now received a dual shock with the doubling of their losses compared to attacking the first defensive line: not only from the springing of the ambush but also by the fact that they faced such disciplined troops of not one but two full regiments of veteran Continental soldiers, who continued to unleash one volley after another in mechanical fashion.

Each scorching volley pouring forth from Colonels Shepard's and Read's regiments knocked down even more men and officers, until some German units began to waver for the first time in their experiences in America. One American wrote with some amazement how the Hessian ranks had been cut to pieces, with so many men having fallen out of the blue-colored formations, dropping dead and wounded in bunches to cause panic: "I saw as great irregularity, almost, as in a militia; they would come out from their body and fire single guns."[25]

In striking contrast, the Bay State soldiers of Colonel Shepard's and Colonel Read's commands stood firm in disciplined ranks without flinching, with hundreds of men steadily loading and firing from behind their stone fences that provided good protection, despite taking return musketry in the form of regular volleys at close range. Glover was awed by the sheer destructive power of "buck & ball" ammunition unleashed at close range by the Third and Thirteenth Massachusetts men. The spirited stand of Colonels Shepard and Read against the superior might of Howe's elite Hessian troops clothed in a distinctive Prussian blue was impressive by any measure, especially in regard to continuing the steady process of inflicting heavy losses on the mostly Lutheran Germans, who now littered the ground before the stone walls in twisted clumps of red. Other soldiers of Glover's New England brigade to the north marveled at the tenacity of Colonels Shepard's and Read's defiant defenders against the odds, and the brave Hessians who just kept coming toward them with fixed bayonets and grim determination, as if there was no tomorrow.

In a letter, one of Glover's soldiers, who proved prophetic, described with a sense of awe at the overall high quality of Shepard's disciplined troops, because the Continentals of the Third Massachusetts defiantly "kept their ground against their cannonade and numbers [and] Our men behaved with remarkable spirit and coolness, and I think are in a good way to do great things" on this day of destiny in Westchester County.[26]

Eventually and for ample good reason, high-ranking American leaders shortly would highly "commend [and admire] the conduct of the men" for what they accomplished on October 18, when the stakes could not have been higher, including for not only the life of Washington's army but also that of the infant republic.[27]

After the Massachusetts soldiers had delivered one disciplined volley after another to wreak havoc among the riddled German ranks, Glover never forgot the dramatic moment, when the foremost heavily punished Hessian regiments fell back in confusion and then the next formation moved forward to suffer the same bloody fate, when unable to withstand the murderous fire any longer. In Glover's words from a letter in which he praised the conduct of Colonel Shepard and his men, who forced "them to retreat several times."[28]

Indeed, the disorderly retreat of the decimated Hessian formations, which had broken when discipline collapsed and losses escalated to unsustainable levels, was not an issue of simply falling back, although their attempts to overrun the blazing stone fence were courageous. With some contempt for a long-recognized invincible opponent who now proved vulnerable on an unforgettable Friday under the fire of relentless volleys, one American observer of what was almost unbelievable to American eyes wrote in an October 23 letter: "As to their courage, their whole body of sixteen [around four thousand] thousand were forced to retreat by the fire of a single regiment [mostly Shepard's 3rd Massachusetts but also Read's men with remaining ammunition in leather cartridge-boxes], and many of them old troops."[29]

In truth and mentioned, this series of bloody repulses had been caused by the fire of not one but two regiments, the around 550 well-trained and disciplined troops of Colonels Read and Shephard. After a brief interval that allowed for flintlocks to be hurriedly reloaded, Colonel Read's Thirteenth Massachusetts men had inflicted additional damage, after they had rejoined the fight with a spirited enthusiasm. Here, they unleashed numerous volleys into the Germans from beyond, or east of, the left flank of Colonel Shepard's regiment that rested on Split Rock Road. Not surprisingly, the crack Hessian troops had retreated from the blistering fire of two Massachusetts regiments well-positioned "behind a fine double stone wall": an almost impregnable defensive perch that dominated the open lower ground on the descending grassy slopes that offered the defenders an excellent field of fire.[30]

After the entire front of the dense Hessian formations collapsed from yet another repulse to utterly astound British and German officers who could not believe that their well-trained troops could not push through the stubborn defenders who looked like farmers, Colonel Shepard's men finally gained a much-needed breather that allowed for heated Massachusetts musket barrels to cool. Glover wrote in a letter how this last "retreat [of the attackers was continued] so far [south down the slope] that a soldier of Colonel Shepherd's leaped over the wall and took a hat and canteen off of a Captain [mostly likely a German officer] that lay dead on the ground they retreated from."³¹

With the pause in the fighting, however, the enemy now tried another tactic out of desperation. As if acknowledging that the defensive positions of the stone fences situated on ever-higher ground could not be overwhelmed, the frustrated British commander, Sir Henry Clinton, directed that all seven of their artillery pieces to concentrate their fire solely on this second stone wall to batter it down and to eliminate the obstinate defenders, who simply would not budge after his best efforts. Delivered by expert artillerymen in scarlet uniforms, the British artillery fire was severe, despite the Massachusetts men possessing good cover provided by the stone fences. All the while, a steady rain of round shot pounded the area around the isolated position held by Colonels Shepard and Read, who were located far from the right of the Fourteenth Massachusetts to the west on the Hutchinson River's west bank—truly out on a limb. One American wrote in a letter how "the shot from their artillery flew very thick about our heads," which they wisely kept down under the intense bombardment.³²

Finally, however, the British and Hessian artillery pieces grew ominously quiet, and the hail of projectiles ceased. The seasoned Bay State men, especially Colonel Glover whose fighting blood was up, instinctively knew what this meant: the lull before the storm. Sensing as much, the hardened veterans of Glover's brigade knew what this eerie silence foretold and made preparations accordingly. Seemingly in a repeat of Howe's folly at Bunker Hill, General Henry Clinton was about to launch an even more powerful attack once again in still another attempt to drive the stubborn Massachusetts soldiers off their perch and from behind their walls of stone, which had already thwarted the best Hessian and British efforts on this bloody day.

After regrouping and replenishing cartridge boxes with rounds and as expected by Glover because he knew that his supremely confident opponent was also concerned about the crucial time element, the Hessian formations once again poured forth up the slope. As before, the Hessians came up both sides of Split Rock Road with their usual splendid discipline and bayonets, eighteen inches of steel, gleaming in the sun and regimental battle flags flapping in the autumn air. Even more, this greater mass of German troops was now marching forth partly because of the war's cruel realities: these mercenaries, who received good pay from King George III and had only recently arrived in America, were cruelly expendable to a cynical British leadership. With the Hessians continuing to bear the brunt of the fighting and losses on October 18, General Howe now possessed the luxury of not having to report massive losses to his superiors in London, which was a boon because of the maturing political opposition to the war, including in the House of Commons: a certain guarantee not to raise any domestic discontent or criticism had the British bore the brunt of the casualties.

So many of General Clinton's troops aligned in dense formations now moved forward that it seemed as if nothing in the world could stop them—not unlike the tactical situation at Bunker's Hill, but the attackers were now Hessians instead of long lines of British regulars like on June 17, 1775. After all, General Howe's most pressing requirement at this time was for his invasion force to gain a permanent toehold in Westchester County as soon as possible. This key tactical requirement meant driving off Colonel Glover's men as soon as possible so that General Washington's army just to the west and moving north up the Albany Post Road and not far from the Hudson River could be trapped, outflanked, and destroyed: the situation that would be determined on this bloody Friday.

The Eruption of Seventeen Thunderous Volleys
Rising to the challenge and ignoring the sight of impossible odds that had been directed against them by the seemingly vindictive and

capricious gods of war, Colonel Shepard's nearly three hundred soldiers gamely held their advanced position under the Hessian onslaught, refusing to budge like Plymouth Rock. Iron discipline and determination meant that no Massachusetts soldier was seen to run away to the rear in panic, which had been an American specialty in almost every single battle of the disastrous New York Campaign, because Glover's men knew that they had a job to do and what was at stake.

In consequence, Shepard's veterans of the Third Massachusetts continued to stand firm and eventually unleashed an amazing total of seventeen volleys into the encroaching attackers at close range. Each punishing volley reaped a grim harvest, sending more Hessian soldiers falling in bunches until their "dead lay thick before the walls" of stone. Unlike less than a year and a half before at the Battle of Bunker Hill where the grassy slopes just outside Boston became red with the bodies of scarlet-uniformed British soldiers who had been cut down by the fast-firing New Englanders from behind earthen defenses perched atop Breed's Hill, Split Rock Road and the immediate area on each side was now covered in a sea of dark blue of the dead and wounded Hessians who had been sacrificed far from home.

Clearly, like other British and Hessian leaders, General Clinton fully realized that his troops had run into a hornet's nest like not previously seen in this war: a cruel irony because it had all appeared so easy after having landed without opposition on the Pell's Point Peninsula and then marched inland, mostly north up Split Rock Road, for a mile and a half with impunity. Clinton was extremely frustrated by this time, because he had been "certain that [the Americans] were not in any great force" to defend the Pell's Point Peninsula, especially after the landing had been conducted so smoothly without opposition in the early morning light. Therefore, as he later admitted of a situation that had bestowed a false sense of security after the incredibly easy disembarkation process on Westchester County soil, Clinton had originally expected the worst at the landing site, only to be lured deeper inland to march straight into multiple ambushes in what was essentially a tactical trap of a kind unimaginable to him, thanks to Glover's brilliant defense in depth: "I know not a more dangerous landing than Pell's Point . . . as I [was committed to] forcing a landing under fire."[33]

In a determined bid to surround Glover and his hard-fighting New England boys, the next advance of the combined might of the Hessians and British would be so lengthy and overpowering that the defensive position of Colonel Shepard's regiment, despite the extension of its left to the east by Colonel Read's regiment to cover both sides of the road, would be in serious trouble. Lord Cornwallis's flanking movement of light troops, dismounted cavalry, and chasseurs to the east was in the process of applying greater pressure and this sound tactic was destined to pay high tactical dividends on this day. As in the tactical situation of his first defensive stand, Glover's second defensive line was in the process of being outflanked by the British Army's most agile light troops under Cornwallis to the east. In addition, by this time, both Massachusetts regiments, after having unleashed so many repeated volleys, were running extremely low on cartridges. Nevertheless, firing from the meager remaining supply of their last cartridges from near-empty leather cartridge boxes, the soldiers of the Third and Thirteenth Massachusetts Continental Regiments continued to blast away with an accurate fire by this time, while resting muskets on the top of the stone fences for better aim—one of the keys to the devastation among the Hessians' ranks—and then reloading as fast as possible.[34]

Now to the east to protect his weak left flank, despite the reinforcement of Read's men, and keeping the enemy at bay in front, Colonel Shepard and his Third Continental Regiment continued to unleash rolling volleys that swept over the killing fields, while standing firm against the odds. With a voice that could be heard above the battle's roar, Colonel Shepard steadied his powder-streaked soldiers who continued to gamely hold firm, blaring out orders to encourage his men and to implore them to maintain their positions under the onslaught and continue to load and then fire as fast as possible, which was performed with discipline by these crack Continental troops. One of Glover's men wrote in an October 23 letter how this defensive line behind the stone fence was so strong because these "two regiments [Colonels Read and Shepard were] advantageously posted by Colonel Glover and Major Lee (who behaved gallantly), which brought many of them to the ground."[35]

As in the case of Colonel Read's Thirteenth Massachusetts but less so which explained why Glover had originally chosen this fine regiment to have held the first defensive position in a Cowpens-like strategy of then falling back to a secondary line of even more dependable fighting men just to their rear, the Third Massachusetts troops had originally stood so firm in their backup position under the mounting pressure and blasted away with such precision partly because the high quality of leadership that rose to the fore. Indeed, Colonel Shepard was a forgotten secret behind the successful defensive stand of the Third Massachusetts Continental Regiment, just as Glover had envisioned in having chosen this excellent regiment for its assigned position, while orchestrating his masterful defense in depth from the beginning. At this time, no Massachusetts regimental commander on the field was as tough and hard-nosed as Colonel Shepard except for Glover himself. Indeed, Colonel Shepard inspired confidence and resolve among his men to fight to the bitter end, if necessary. Standing at least six foot tall, muscular, and stout, the determined colonel from Westfield, Massachusetts, appeared as immoveable as the stone wall from which he was directing his men to deliver one volley after another into the densely packed Hessian ranks.

By any measure, Shepard was no ordinary regimental commander, although only a farmer, the son of a tanner and deacon of the local Congregational Church, and lover of the soil. Shepard's agrarian background was no disqualification from sterling military service like he now fully demonstrated on October 18. At only age seventeen, he had first gone to war in 1755 at the beginning of the French and Indian War. Most of all, Shepard was every inch a fighter and just the kind of gifted natural leader and hard-nosed commander who Glover could count on to hold firm against the odds. Although having been wounded during the fighting at Long Island on August 27 barely a month and a half earlier and having only been promoted to colonel on October 2 in a well-deserved advancement, Shepard was now seeing his finest day.

All the while, Colonel Shepard continued to demonstrate inspired leadership, yelling his directives and encouraging words to his men. Additional volleys were unleashed by his followers into the attackers, and even larger numbers of Hessians went down to rise no more. Not a soldier of the hard-pressed Third Massachusetts flinched or gave ground, standing firm and delivering punishment in a manner that filled Colonels Glover and Shepard with a great deal of pride. Still, despite the heavy pressure, none of these experienced Continentals ran off like raw militiamen because they knew that they had a job to do and went about their work with a businesslike diligence. After all, they were fighting not only to save Washington's army, but also themselves in the end. These Bay State men knew that they could not allow the Hessians to break their heavily pressured defensive line, which would mean facing a good many steel bayonets in hand-to-hand combat and grisly deaths in Westchester County, while placing the life of Washington's army and the revolution itself in the greatest peril.

All in all, the spirited defensive stand of Colonel Shepard's troops merely reflected the never-say-die qualities of their talented commander, who was like a father to his men, especially the beardless teenagers in the ranks. Shepard's reputation for tenacity in combat had already become legendary by this time. Appropriately, because he was now helping to protect the long withdrawal of Washington's army from Harlem Heights to the safety of White Plains, Shepard was determined to make the most of the opportunity.

Colonel Shepard's role on October 18 mirrored his earlier contributions in helping to save Washington's army during the evacuation from Long Island, where much of the Continental Army had been trapped and about to be destroyed by Howe's forces. In guarding the mass of withdrawing Americans, who had been ferried with muffled oars across the turbulent waters of the East River by the men of Glover's Fourteenth Massachusetts and another seafaring Bay State regiment, Colonel Shepard had lingered far to the rear on that late August day. Here, the tireless colonel had been wounded, falling from his horse. But fortunately for the regiment, he had only recently recovered from his injuries to once again take command of his beloved Third Massachusetts of around 292 good fighting men for its finest day on October 18. And now barely a month and half later during the struggle raging with an unbridled fury on this bloody Friday, Colonel Shepard was back on his feet and once again rising magnificently to the challenge like at Long Island. Clearly, this was the kind of example of inspirational leadership which now guaranteed that his Thirteenth Massachusetts soldiers held firm under the onslaught, while firing one volley after another into the Hessian ranks without flinching or losing their determination to defy the odds.[36]

While encouraging his troops behind the lengthy stone wall and exposed in standing tall from behind its cover to inspire his men, Colonel Shepard was hit by a bullet in the throat during the hail of projectiles from a Hessian volley. It is not known, but Shepard might have been loading and firing his own weapon since everyone was needed in the stone fence's defense west of the road, because every single fighting man was needed in the ranks. Blood splattered all over the fine blue uniform of the dashing Continental colonel, creating a horrifying spectacle to shock those individuals who were busily loading and firing immediately around him. Aides instantly rushed to Shepard's assistance, after he had fallen to the ground like a sack of potatoes. The lead bullet's impact was so powerful that the colonel was knocked unconscious, falling without speaking a word or making a sound. Fortunately for morale's sake at this critical stage of the battle, the thick palls of smoke obscured Colonel Shepard's fall from the eyes of his men, who were spread out behind the stone fence for a long length. Indeed, it appeared as if the Massachusetts colonel from Westfield, located in western Massachusetts and founded in 1660, had received his death stroke. Given the amount of blood lost and the severity of the wound, the fact that the colonel, who was a healthy man and as strong as a bull, survived at all was a minor miracle in itself. Later, Major

General William Heath, who marveled at Shephard's tough resilience, explained how: "Col. Shepard [was hit] in the throat, not mortally, although the ball came well nigh effecting instant death."[37]

The badly bleeding colonel, who presented a grotesque sight to those shocked men around him, was hurriedly carried rearward by a handful of his soldiers, while bullets streamed overhead in torrents. Shepard was taken to a Massachusetts regimental surgeon, perhaps Doctor Nathaniel Bond, who was the regimental surgeon of the Fourteenth Massachusetts and had assisted injured Massachusetts militiamen after the Battle of Bunker Hill, to the rear. The unknown medical man probed for the bullet from either behind the shelter of a stone wall or at a makeshift field hospital at some point rearward perhaps with the Fourteenth Massachusetts's left in the last defensive line on higher ground, almost certainly located in a protective wooded area, to the north. The sheer pain of this crude medical procedure caused Shepard to regain consciousness from the agonizing wound.

Fearing that his throat had been cut by the bullet from a German-made weapon after seeing blood splattered all over his chest, Colonel Shepard immediately requested a wooden canteen to conduct his own test case. He then drank gingerly from it, as if expecting the worst. Only then ascertaining that his throat had not been severed as feared, the colonel defiantly informed the surprised surgeon, who must have marveled by the sight of a blood-covered man seemingly all but dead suddenly coming to life and then issuing specific orders directed at him in stern fashion, as if he was nothing more than a lowly private: "It is all right, doctor, stick on a plaster and tie on my cravet, for I am going out again" to rejoin his hard-fighting soldiers of the Third Massachusetts to ensure that they held firm under the onslaught. Incredibly, and in "spite of the remonstrance of the surgeon, and to the amazement of the attendants, Shepard then went [back] into" the midst of the raging battle once again with renewed enthusiasm, proving to his men that he had not been killed to raise spirits and fighting resolve at a time when everyone had to stand firm, when most needed because pressure on the thin defensive line had intensified in his absence.[38]

Indeed, the Third Massachusetts soldiers were additionally emboldened by the inspiring sight of Colonel Shepard, with a plaster now on this throat, once again appearing like magic to embolden his boys to continue to hold firm, as if the colonel had risen from the dead. It is not known, but very likely Shepard's soldiers raised a loud cheer at the sight of their rejuvenated colonel going back into action. Once again on the battle line of fast-firing soldiers behind the stone wall, Colonel Shepard continued to encourage his men to stand firm in facing the Hessian attackers, as if nothing had happened.

The Horror of Being Outflanked!

Meanwhile, the talented commander of the Twenty-sixth Massachusetts in command of the third line was rising to the fore, despite still not engaged in the fight. In a letter, Colonel William Baldwin described how he took the initiative, because of earlier developments to the east that had boded ill for Glover's defensive stand when

> news was brought to Col. Glover . . . that the enemy was surrounding us which I mistrusted and went out [to the east] with about 30 men to post as sentries to give us information [about the enemy's movements]. Ensign Wood was with me being anxious to know the situation of the enemy; [he] advanced [east] toward them and found that they were approaching fast [and west] toward [the Hutchinson River] bridge [to the northwest] over which we had to get back . . . Ensign Wood on his return to the Regt. Was wounded in the left arm.[39]

Of course, the men on the firing line had no idea of these stunning developments to the east that threatened to cut them off or worse. After firing a total of seventeen volleys and with his men nearly out of ammunition and with his position about to be outflanked on the east like had been the fate of Colonel Read's regiment in defending the first line and then forced to retire north to the second defensive position, Colonel Shepard had no choice but to order his soldiers to fall back and head north with only a few rounds remaining in leather cartridge boxes. With his men so low on ammunition and losses starting to mount in insidious fashion, Colonel Glover described the increasing serious tactical quandary that his brigade now faced in what had become a crisis situation of the first magnitude: "the ground being much in their favour, and [with the firing of] their heavy train of artillery, we could do but little" at this point in the raging battle.[40]

With their last rounds from nearly empty cartridge boxes, the tough fighting men of the Third and Thirteenth Massachusetts Continental Regiments stoically accepted their fate of being forced to withdraw because of Cornwallis's flankers to the east, after having made a magnificent stand against the odds that bought precious time. Before departing their stone fence that had provided them security, the Bay State men fired some of their last cartridges, after accomplishing more than anyone—including themselves and especially General Howe's troops—had thought possible under the circumstances.

By this time, Glover could no longer deny the inevitable—being outflanked by large numbers of troops under Lord Cornwallis who was now advancing ever-closer from the east at the "double-quick across the neighboring fields with bayonets fixed"—under the most unfavorable of circumstances: "However, their [main] body [of troops] being so much larger than ours, we were for the preservation of the men forced to retreat," but most important the defenders had succeeded in their crucial mission of buying time for Washington and the army. Appraised that few rounds in cartridge boxes remained among the survivors of the two regiments and that the advanced defensive positions of both the Third and Thirteenth Massachusetts Continental Regiments were about to be outflanked not only on the east by Lord Cornwallis troops, but also on the west, Glover finally gave the word for both regiments to pull back according to his tactical plan before it was too late.[41]

With discipline, the Continentals of Colonels Shepard's and Read's regiments pushed north and hurriedly took position to the rear of Colonel Baldwin's Twenty-sixth Continental Regiment, which held the third defensive line behind still another sturdy stone fence, rocks, and boulders on the highest ground yet defended by the Massachusetts men. Here, in their new position east of Split Rock Road, the worn Continentals, who were dirty and smeared with black powder from having torn off paper cartridges with their teeth before cramming loads down smoking musket barrels with wooden ramrods, regained a much-needed breather and time to reload smoking flint-lock muskets. Most significant and as Glover had envisioned as part of his overall tactical plan from the beginning, Baldwin's regiment in the third ambush position on the east side of Split Rock Road (the regiment's right flank rested on the road) of a defense in depth was still hidden and concealed behind yet another stone wall, safe from prying British and Hessian eyes, while offering greater protection against Cornwallis's flankers in a defensive position that extended farther east than the previous defensive position.

With pride, Glover watched his well-trained troops fall back north up the slope in order and discipline, and then quickly "formed in the rear of Baldwin's regiment," with drill ground precision with a sharpness that brought him a sense of pride. Then, a dark, blue sea of Hessians surged up the slope and "then came up to Baldwin's" stone wall in overwhelming numbers with fixed bayonets and with a determination to hurt the last group of rebel defenders, who had already fled in what appeared to have been a panic like so often in the past—all part of still another ruse. Then, all of a sudden to once again catch the Hessians by surprise, the entire Twenty-sixth Continental Regiment rose up as one and blasted away as one into the dense ranks of the German attackers, whose blue formations stretched almost as far as the eye could see, when they were exceptionally close like during the previous assaults. Like Read's and Shepard's veterans, who had only partly replenished cartridge boxes from shared rounds with comrades by this time, of its two sister regiments whose members also opened fire, Colonel Baldwin's men loaded and fired as rapidly as possible, dropping larger numbers of Hessians, who would never again see Germany or their loved ones. But by this time, the odds simply became too great for the ever-dwindling band of Massachusetts troops and their relatively few remaining cartridges, except in the ranks of Baldwin's regiment and the strategic reserve—Glover's regiment to the north and northwest. All the while, dead and wounded Massachusetts men had continued to be carried rearward by survivors, leaving no signs, other than blood on the ground, of those who had been fatally cut down. All the while, additional pressure increased on the ever-dwindling band of defenders with seemingly countless numbers of German soldiers advancing to add additional weight to a massive assault that could no longer be stopped.

With his brigade now about to be outflanked by Lord Cornwallis's troops on the east and by still another formation of another group of flankers to the west to now face annihilation when ammunition had run precariously low, Glover had no choice but to order a general withdrawal for the first time. But the colonel only did so with great reluctance, because his fighting blood was up, and he knew that buying additional time was still of vital importance. However, at this moment of decision, Glover felt quite correctly that sufficient time—most of October 18—already had been bought with Massachusetts blood and now having the brigade wiped out would serve no practical purpose whatsoever. And the analytical colonel, who was at his best when the pressure was greatest, was right, because a sufficient amount of invaluable time already had been purchased by the Marblehead colonel's masterful defense in depth and a good deal of hard fighting by the Massachusetts boys.

After battling so hard and achieving so much against the odds, the Massachusetts soldiers received Glover's order to retire west and back across the Hutchinson River with some disgust and anger. After all, they were winning this intense fight by almost every measure when so much was at stake, inflicting high casualties while taking few losses, thanks to the brilliance of Glover's tactical masterpiece. If they had been reinforced by some good Continental units from Washington's army like Colonel Hand's Pennsylvania riflemen who had performed so magnificently in having kept Howe's legions at bay at Throgs Neck, then they might have even hurled the British and Hessians all the way back to the landing site, or so they believed and hoped, if they had been unleashed on the tactical offense, because the British and Hessian disembarkation process was still continuing unabated.

No one was more frustrated or angry about the withdrawal order than the fiery Colonel Baldwin, despite having suffered his recent serious wound when he had been shot in the neck but was now patched-up in an ad hoc manner. His fighting blood was up and the last thing that Baldwin wanted to do was now to withdraw to the west side of the Hutchinson River, because he knew what was at stake, and his men had a lot of fight left in them. In Colonel Baldwin's words that caught the mood of the members of his regiment, when they received Glover's directive to fall back, which "was obeyed with the greatest reluctance imaginable though with as much good order and regularity as ever they marched off a Publick [sic] Parade" back in Massachusetts.[42]

Clearly, the fighting spirit of Glover's men was yet sky-high, despite the relatively low number of cartridges remaining in cartridge boxes, except in regard to Baldwin's Twenty-sixth Massachusetts. Among the regiment's members disgruntled at the withdrawal order was Nathaniel Bond, the capable "fighting surgeon" of the Fourteenth Massachusetts and who now commanded the Fourth Company of Glover's regiment. Some Bay State soldiers were outright angry. After all, these seasoned Massachusetts men had not been defeated by overwhelming numbers, and they were yet full of fight because America's fate was at stake. The day's repeated tactical successes against thousands of German and British troops had only fueled their resolve to continue to punish the British and Hessian invaders at any cost, because this meant protecting not only Washington's army and the infant nation, but also New England, the land of their homes and families.

Nevertheless, under the circumstances, a general withdrawal west by Glover's undersized, but feisty, brigade was absolutely necessary by this time, because of the overall tactical situation because the three Massachusetts regiments now risked getting caught in a tightening vise. In curt fashion that diminished the stirring accomplishments of Glover and his men who had frustrated his best efforts for most of the day, General Clinton explained the decisive tactical developments that forced the general withdrawal of the hardest-fighting Americans that he had ever encountered in this war: "As we advanced, we found the enemy strongly posted behind stone walls, from whence they might have greatly obstructed our march had it not been for the corps [of flankers under Lord Cornwallis] I detached to the right."[43]

Escaping Entrapment and Certain Destruction

After having been outflanked on both sides, but especially on the east by Lord Cornwallis and his light troops, with the enemy having gained higher ground to the disadvantage of the Massachusetts men, and simultaneously unable to withstand any additional heavy pressure in front along the road, Glover simply had no choice, and he stoically accepted his fate. He, therefore, led his men, who only now fell back in a sullen manner, in their withdrawal west down an obscure country lane after leaving Split Rock Road. They now pushed toward the Hutchinson River Bridge and the Boston Plank Road, while heading in the direction where the sun was beginning to lower on the tree-lined horizon. Because the wooden planks of the small bridge had been earlier removed on Glover's orders to impede the enemy's advance, the fast-moving Massachusetts men forded the cold waters of the Hutchinson River, which the colonel incorrectly described as a creek, at a recently discovered shallow point. In Glover's words,

> we retreated to the bottom of the hill, and had to pass through a run of water, (the bridge I had taken up before), and then marched up a hill [on] the opposite side of the creek, where I left my artillery [with the right of the 14th Massachusetts on

the high ground on the west bank], the ground being rough and much broken I was afraid to risk [crossing] over it

with the British and Hessian formations closing in on his diminutive brigade for the kill.[44]

Now once again to continue to come to the rescue of Washington's army during its lengthy withdrawal to the west, the Fourteenth Continental Regiment rose to the occasion to buy additional time. This strategic reserve (the right of the Fourteenth Massachusetts on the west high bank of the Hutchinson) had held firm on the highest ground of Glover's multilayered battle line of a defense in depth—on the northwest rather than in the rear to the north (where the left of the Fourteenth Massachusetts had been positioned before the battle had erupted) by this time, after the regiment's left had already retired west from the river's east side with their comrades—since the engagement's opening. Now fresh, rested, and with full cartridge boxes on the high ground on the west bank of the Hutchinson River, Captain Courtis's soldiers from mostly Marblehead were now in the right place at the right time. A well-placed strategic reserve that was more than ready to renew the contest to save their withdrawing comrades from a host of attackers from multiple directions, these crack soldiers of the Fourteenth Massachusetts were in an ideal position to protect the retiring three regiments moving west.

Here, on the commanding higher ground just southwest of Prospect Hill, Glover once again deployed his hard-fighting soldiers of Colonel Read's, Shepard's, and Baldwin's regiments in defensive positions above the Hutchinson River on its commanding west bank. As before, he carefully took full advantage of the topography to assign his troops on the most defensible terrain that commanded the watercourse and the entire area to the east to counter Lord Cornwallis's growing threat, while blocking the strategic Eastchester Road that had verged off the Boston Post Road and led west to Washington's army. After making his adroit defensive deployments, Glover now awaited the arrival of General Howe's troops, who were sure to come forward with their usual confidence and arrogance.

Indeed, it was only a matter of time before the enemy's arrival, and the Massachusetts men knew what this meant in overall strategic terms, because Washington's army to the west was still extremely vulnerable in the extreme during its lengthy retreat north. Therefore, the crucial mission was not yet over for the Bay State brigade, especially in regard to blocking the Eastchester Road that led west to Washington's army. After all, General Howe needed to gain a more secure hold on the New York mainland and it was now only necessary for him to push farther inland to the west. And first and foremost, the destruction of Washington's army still called for first hurling Glover's brigade back by driving farther west to gain the all-important Eastchester Road that led west to the Washington's vulnerable army steadily retiring north up the Albany Post Road not far from the Hudson River.

Stained with dirt and black powder, the Massachusetts soldiers caught their breath in their new defensive position atop the high ground on the Hutchinson River's west side. After so much biting open of paper cartridges and loading and firing one volley after another for what seemed like an eternity, the New Englanders were thirsty and bone-weary, having fought for most of the day under the hot mid-October sun. What little fresh water was left in wooden canteens was drank, and these veterans were now parched from the heat and the day's intense combat. Even the water from the Hutchinson, a tidal watercourse, was too brackish and salty for them to drink.

But now and most important, Glover's Continentals of all four regiments were once again together—no small tactical achievement in itself and one of the many fruits of the Marblehead colonel's tactical master plan that had bought them time—ready with muskets loaded and primed, when large numbers of Hessians and British appeared once again to threaten them with certain destruction. Colonel Glover explained how the "enemy halted, and played away [with] their artillery at us, and we at them, till night, without any damage on our side, and but very little on theirs."[45]

In a letter, one American soldier described how: "The enemy advanced on to a high point or neck of land, not far from East-Chester meeting-house, from whence they were able to command the road with their field pieces, but they kept very much in a body, so that our people" could move about freely and without opposition. Clearly, General Clinton, like Howe, was now wary and cautious of the menacing fences of stone that could be defended because they crisscrossed all over the countryside, after having been effectively chastised by Glover and his small Massachusetts brigade on this day of destiny that saved Washington's army, taking the fight completely out of the enemy until no aggressiveness remained.[46] Most important, Glover had won the invaluable "time . . . gained for the removal of the stores and the evacuation of [Manhattan] island."[47]

From the commanding high ground, Colonel Glover watched silently while thousands of British and Hessian troops deployed in lengthy lines, facing west to confront his diminutive brigade. However, Glover felt a sense of pride for what he had accomplished. He had succeeded in getting his command safely off the field without a high loss of life, after they had pushed north up Split Rock Road and then turned left to the west to cross the river and headed northwest toward the Eastchester Road that led to the small town of the same name. Meanwhile, the invaders, especially the Hessians, had been sufficiently bloodied for most of the day that no more aggression remained.

And, of course, no one was more delighted than Glover himself by Clinton's decision to end the fighting by remaining in place on the east side of the Hutchinson River. Indeed, after having fought tenaciously for most of the day, the Massachusetts soldiers had successfully thwarted the lofty ambitions of their mighty opponent, while Washington's withdrawing army continued north for White Plains in safety. Howe's invasion force was now in absolutely no condition to push west to strike Washington's army, after having been severely mauled for most of the day.

General Clinton's decision to remain stationary and end the battle made perfectly good sense to Glover and the Massachusetts soldiers in the ranks, because they had slaughtered the enemy like never before. Quite simply, the heavy losses inflicted upon the attackers, especially the Hessians, had taken all of the aggressiveness and fight out of them, to Glover's delight. Indeed, Clinton and his hard-hit men were now licking their wounds, wanting only a much-needed respite from the murderous New England volleys to recover from hour after hour of having suffered severe punishment. All the while, Glover and his men remained in a defensive stance on the high ground of the river's west bank, just in case the team of Howe and Clinton dared to attempt to force a crossing, while ensuring that the invaders failed to gain the Eastchester Road. After all, the Massachusetts soldiers were still responsible for saving Washington's army and that meant continuing to hold firm to counter any aggressiveness.

Hundreds of wounded Hessians, far fewer than the British injured, were carried to makeshift field hospitals, where busy German and British surgeons and their assistants attempted to save as many lives as possible, along Split Rock Road. After the slaughter in the killing fields of Westchester County, the invaders now turned to more pressing concerns than attempting in vain to destroy Glover and his command: thankfully for Washington and his vulnerable army, Clinton had been effectively stopped in his tracks from continuing to advance west, where easy victory lay just over the distant horizon, if he intercepted and struck Washington's drawn-out retreat, ensuring little, if any, resistance would be offered by the disorganized Americans.

Large numbers of dead and wounded Hessians—and a far lesser number of Britons—now had to be attended to, and that process would take considerable time and effort. Hundreds of bodies were collected for either burial or for the regimental and brigade surgeons from Great Britain and Germany to attempt to save. Meanwhile, with the Hessian formations aligned out in the open in the fields east of the Hutchinson providing ideal targets, the fire from Glover's three cannon perched on the high ground of the river's west bank inflicted additional casualties, adding insult to injury and the almost unbelievable reality of a thwarted major British-Hessian offensive effort that had once possessed the potential to win it all. The angry American cannon continued to bark in defiance. One British soldier standing next to General Howe, who had a close call himself on this occasion, was killed by a direct hit by a cannonball.

During the noisy artillery duel that raged across the Hutchinson and because the dead and wounded Massachusetts men—far fewer than the enemy in a great disparity that also revealed the effectiveness and sparkling brilliance of Glover's tactics that had minimized losses—also had already been collected and taken rearward during the withdrawal toward the sun lowering on the western horizon after an all-day masterful resistance effort, Glover's regimental commanders now had time to count the dead, the number of injured men, and who was missing. Incredibly, to his astonishment, Glover learned that only eight Massachusetts soldiers had been killed and another thirteen wounded from all four regiments of his small brigade: a remarkable testament to the wisdom of the colonel's masterful tactical plan of a defense of depth that had so effectively incorporated multiple ambushes based on the element of surprise, thanks to a series of stone fences situated on ever higher ground.

Clearly, when it was most needed and when everything had been at stake like during the timely withdrawal of most of Washington's army across the East River from the Long Island trap last August, Colonel Glover had won a truly inspiring tactical success in thwarting General Howe's invasion into Westchester County and keeping it from striking Washington's retreating army, which was all but defenseless in its chaotic retrograde movement to White Plains. One of those wounded soldiers of October 18 was Colonel Shepard, who had gamely remained in the fight beside his boys after his neck injury had been hastily patched by a physician. For Glover, the wounding of Colonel Shepard represented the day's greatest loss among his top lieutenants. Rather remarkably, Shepard was the only officer wounded of the entire Bay State brigade. But the colonel's setback was only temporary, like in regard to his wounding on August 27 on Long Island, because the irrepressible Shepard, a tough and sturdy farmer in the years before the war, shortly recovered from his wound. Clearly, the talented colonel of the Third Massachusetts possessed a remarkable penchant for quick recoveries because of his imposing size, health, fighting spirit, and strength.[48]

To the surprise of everyone and after Glover's men had seen so many Hessians cut down by one volley after another at close range, casualties among the Massachusetts brigade had been kept at minimum, which was all part of the colonel's plan of a highly effective defense in depth that had been so carefully planned. However, some Bay State soldiers had been hit when exposed while firing and in retiring rearward across open ground to the next defensive position to the north in adhering to Glover's clever leapfrog tactics. As penned in a letter, one soldier wrote how: "We had but very few killed, and, as far as I can learn, not more than fifty or sixty wounded."[49] In a letter to his mother Tabitha in Marblehead, Glover wrote how his four regiments lost only eight men killed and another thirteen wounded, thanks to his brilliant tactics and highly effective defense in depth, which characteristically the modest colonel failed to mention or explain to his mother, who would have been most proud of her son's heightened tactical skills.[50]

With the redcoats and Hessians now held at bay and not wanting to sacrifice what remained of his brigade with the day ending, Colonel Glover again ordered his four regiments into formation in preparation for moving out from his defensive position along the west bank of the Hutchinson River and heading northwest for Eastchester. In record time, the soldiers of Colonel's Read's, Shepard's, and Baldwin's regiments hurriedly fell into column. With the Fourteenth Continental Regiment protecting the withdrawing column in guardian fashion because they were the brigade's crack fighting men—a true grenadier guard—and had suffered less than any other regiment of the brigade, Glover retired farther west toward the town just to the northwest. After fighting so long (most of the day) and with the number of cartridges in cartridge boxes now lower than ever before, discipline still remained firm in the veteran ranks of the Massachusetts Brigade, because pride in their recent accomplishments dominated the powder-stained men who had just seen their finest day. The embattled

New Englanders retired toward Eastchester with firm step and a resolution to turn and fight against the odds once again, if ordered to do so by Colonel Glover just in case Clinton again advanced in an attempt to gain the Eastchester Road to pose another serious threat to the life of Washington's army.

All the while, the relatively fresh soldiers of the Fourteenth Continental Regiment continued to protect the withdrawal of Massachusetts men, who held their heads high because of what they had accomplished against the odds. Then, after marching a short distance northwest along the Boston Post Road, the New Englanders, with muskets on shoulders, reached Eastchester, which was located on higher ground just to the northwest. As fate would have it, the men of Glover's brigade would never see their tents and baggage, which had been left behind in the encampment. No time had been allowed to retrieve these personal articles and everything would be burned when the British and Hessians finally arrived to take possession. But, of course, this loss was a small sacrifice for what had been achieved in overall strategic terms on October 18, after the Massachusetts men had fought most of the day against the odds and held Howe's force at bay. Most important in overall strategic terms, Glover's brigade had succeeded in denying the best and most direct route—the Eastchester Road—leading west to Washington's army, which could hardly have been more vulnerable at this time. After all, Glover and his boys were yet protecting the easternmost flank of Washington's command by blocking the Eastchester Road, and duty would again call if Howe unleashed any aggressive thrust to the west.

At long last and after it seemed like an eternity passed for the weary soldiers of Glover's brigade, the blazing October 18 sun dropped, after the most exhaustive and important day in their military careers. Most significant, Glover's tiny brigade had kept thousands of Hessians and British far away from Washington's vulnerable command in full retreat until the sun finally set over the Hudson River. In the darkness so as not to reveal that he was withdrawing farther west along the Eastchester Road after having departed the Boston Post

Road and after a job remarkably well done, Glover led his troops rearward toward Valentine's Hill and then eventually northwest toward Jeremiah Dobb's Ferry on the Hudson about seven miles distant. At no point had reinforcements been dispatched from Washington's army to ensure that October 18 had been strictly Glover's fight.[51]

Clearly, Glover and his Massachusetts troops had accomplished a great deal against impossible odds, succeeding in denying Howe possession of the Eastchester Road that led west to Washington's army—his primary mission on this day of destiny when the life of the Continental Army and the infant nation hung in the balance. One soldier summarized the crucial close-range October 18 fight in an October 23 letter with a great deal of pride for what Glover and his men had accomplished on their own:

> We continued fighting them and retreating the whole afternoon, until they came to a stand, where they now remain, stretching down along the south, toward Connecticut, we suppose for forage. Our men behaved like soldiers, conformed to the orders of the officers, and retreated in good order, which is the life of discipline.[52]

As indicated by this Bay State soldier's revealing letter, the most important strategic development that resulted from the defensive stand of Colonel Glover's brigade was strategically important: General Howe's ambition of thrusting deep into the interior of Westchester County and west along the Eastchester Road to trap and annihilate Washington's army had been stopped from surging toward the Hudson to strike a death blow to Washington's army. After the severe punishment inflicted by Glover's brigade, Howe had decided not to pursue any push to the Hudson, which saved Washington's army from a cruel fate.

With an obvious exaggeration in part to magnify his own accomplishments and those of his troops far beyond what they had actually achieved on this day when glory had been within his grasp but he had let it all slip away, General Clinton wrote how "the rebels being forced to quit the high [or the upper] road, the gross of our army lay this night [October 18] on their great communication [road, which was the Boston Post Road] with New England."[53] In much the same way, General Howe "grossly overestimated" the number of Americans he faced to justify the stunning setback and missed opportunity to end the war in one stroke.[54]

To his delight, Colonel Baldwin had seen far more damage inflicted upon the enemy on October 18 than on April 19, 1775, when the Massachusetts militiamen and minutemen had so severely punished the redcoats when they had withdrawn along the dusty road toward Boston's safety under a hail of gunfire from a throng of defenders, who blasted away from behind trees and stone fences. Far more than the East River evacuation of Washington's men off Long Island at the end of August, Colonel Glover was proud of his men for having thwarted the overpowering advance of General Howe's invasion into Westchester County's interior, when the lives of the disorganized rebel army and revolution were at stake. Because of what Colonel Glover had achieved by the narrowest of margins and against the laws of percentages, Washington's army would never be struck while retreating north to White Plains, which would have resulted in an absolute disaster.

Even Glover was astounded by what his troops had accomplished against the odds in "fighting all day without victuals or drink," wrote the ecstatic colonel from Marblehead. Saving Washington's army from a tragic fate indicated the wisdom of Glover's tactical vision in having created his masterful defense in depth and in having kept Captain Courtis and his Fourteenth Continental Regiment on high ground as a strategic reserve for the rest of the three undersized regiments of his brigade positioned on lower ground.[55]

And of course, Colonel Glover was equally pleased that so few of his men had been killed and wounded in a long and bloody fight, thanks to relying on the stone fence defenses and the element of surprise. Glover's innovative tactical plan had been conceived in large part to minimize casualties of a small command which could ill-afford to lose men from the ranks, because buying as much time as possible for Washington was paramount and this meant that command cohesion and combat capabilities had to be maintained by minimizing losses as much as possible. But naturally, the Marblehead colonel lamented the wounding of one of his top lieutenants, "Colonel Shepherd, a brave officer," in Glover's typically understated words.[56]

Colonel Glover was fully prepared to fight to the finish on the night of October 18, if necessary. Glover's initial northwest withdrawal had been only a relatively short distance to Eastchester and then west up the Eastchester Road after having departed the Boston Post Road, because he still guarded this strategic road to protect Washington's army, if General Howe's forces continued to push inland and farther west. In Glover's words about the successful withdrawal under the protective view of nighttime: "At dark we came off and marched about three miles [along the Eastchester Road], leading to Dobb's Ferry" on the Hudson River.[57]

The night of October 18, meanwhile, the redcoats and Hessians remained vigilant at their heavily guarded encampment, sleeping on their arms, as if expecting that Glover and his men might yet attack and unleash still another surprise, because these hard-fighting New England Yankees had already demonstrated their combative spirit, tactical wiles, and cunning with their tactically innovative defense in depth, which had thoroughly wrecked Howe's ambitious plans for a speedy thrust inland. As Thomas Sullivan scribbled in his journal how the British troops "laid that night upon their arms, with the left upon the Creek [the Hutchinson River] opposite to Eastchester, and the right near to Rochelle" to the northeast and located on the banks of the Long Island Sound.[58]

During the cool night, Colonel Glover positioned his troops in guardian fashion across the Eastchester Road, which was also called the Dobb's Ferry Road, that led west to General Washington's army, which was still in the midst of the most disorganized of retreats. Operated by Jeremiah Dobb and located in Westchester County southwest of White

Plains and about half a dozen miles from Eastchester, the ferry had long taken passengers across the wide Hudson River. Glover prudently aligned his Massachusetts troops across the Eastchester Road with the knowledge that he was still in relatively close proximity to an overwhelming number of British and Hessian troops, whose aggressiveness might return at any moment. For the most part, Colonel Glover was now following a strategic plan that had been decided upon at General Washington's October 16 commanders' meeting, especially in regard to safeguarding the strategic Eastchester Road. Out of necessity to achieve a greater good when the stakes were still high for America, the pugnacious colonel was prepared to use his diminutive force as bait, if necessary, to buy additional time, which Washington's army still desperately needed to complete the long withdrawal north to White Plains. If hard pressed, rather than risk destruction, Glover planned to fall back in order "by over movements, to lead them into the country" and farther away from Washington's army if they followed, which meant moving either north or south, but still relatively close to the coast, in the hope that the enemy would follow in pursuit in the English fox-hunt tradition beloved by aristocratic British leaders. If drawn deeper in the interior of Westchester County if Glover's force was followed away from Washington's army, then Howe's forces could not receive timely supplies, ammunition, or reinforcements from the armada of British warships in the Long Island Sound: basically, an effective way of wage a logistical war to ensure the continued safety of Washington's army.[59]

Across the narrow, dirt road leading northwest to Dobb's Ferry, situated on the Hudson's east bank and around twenty-two miles north of New York City, the Massachusetts soldiers held firm in another good defensive position carefully chosen by Glover to effectively block the Eastchester Road. The Bay State men remained vigilant in a defensive stance during a tense situation because of the belief that Howe would certainly attempt to push his way through Glover's brigade, while "laying as a picket all night, the heavens over us and the earth under us, which was all we had, having left our baggage at the old encampment we left in the morning."[60]

Like his tactical movements on the battlefield in having leap-frogged his troops rearward from one good defensive position to another and from one stone fence to the next one farther north, Glover's withdrawal had been orderly and disciplined while keeping up a bold front, which played its part in deterring Howe from pursuing the Continentals. During the thankful respite without Howe desiring to push to the Hudson, the Marblehead colonel had even directed his men to return to Eastchester on the following two nights, after the Friday battle, to retrieve the precious supplies stored in the town and in St. Paul's Episcopal Church, located on a commanding knoll as if to advertise God's love to the world. However, at one point, the stately church fell under British cannon fire that scored direct hits on the house of worship, knocking holes into its walls to infuriate its parishioners. A soldier penned in a letter how the bloodied British and Hessian troops respectfully kept their distance "so that our people on Saturday and Sunday nights [easily] brought off more than one hundred barrels of pork left in the store at East-Chester without any molestation."[61]

Finally, for the first time all day, Colonel Glover received orders from General Charles Lee. As recorded by Major William Raymond Lee in his orderly book: "All the wounded to be immediately carried to Valentine's Hill, at the second Liberty Pole where Surgeons should repair to dress them [and then] They are afterwards to be forwarded to Fort Washington."[62]

Confident because of the masterful tactical success recently reaped and believing that General Howe's invasion could yet be thwarted if necessary, one of Glover's men penned in a letter the next day, which revealed how a single Continental brigade continued to pose an obstacle to General Howe who continued to rely on stealth: "They are trying to surround us [but] It won't be easy; and I am mistaken if they don't meet some severe" reversals.[63]

But thanks to the brilliant tactical performance of Colonel Glover and his tiny Massachusetts Brigade throughout October 18, General Washington would not now either be either surrounded or defeated during the autumn of 1776, which was the vital key to keeping the revolution alive so that America's primary army would live to fight another day. It would not be until three days later, on October 21, when General Howe finally secured a solid foothold in Westchester County by occupying the town of New Rochelle, located just northeast of Pell's Point on Long Island Sound: in overall strategic terms, this was the best way to bypass Colonel Glover and his tough little brigade and any possible reinforcements from Washington's army. Thanks to what Glover and his men had accomplished just northwest of the Pell's Point Peninsula when the life of Washington's army had been at stake like the very existence of the revolution itself, General Howe had been unable to push inland deeper in this part of Westchester County to strike the flank and rear of Washington's army as planned, because he feared the countryside, covered in those hated stone fences, was filled with many more hard-fighting defenders like the seasoned Continentals of Glover's Brigade and under talented leaders like Glover.[64]

A Thankful General Washington

As could be expected, Washington, therefore, had nothing but glowing words of praise for Glover and his Massachusetts troops in his general orders on October 20. However, he did not completely know the exact tactical details (Glover's tactical masterpiece that was not unlike the more famous Cowpens strategy of General Daniel Morgan nearly a half decade later that resulted in the vanquishing of Lieutenant Colonel Banastre Tarleton's famed British Legion of Loyalists) of what exactly happened in tactical terms at Pell's Point and why, because he had been deeply involved in the demanding job of attempting to withdraw his disorganized army to White Plains in the army's most risky retreat to date, when the stakes were exceptionally high for America: ironically, an unfortunate situation that has ensured the general obscurity of the Battle of Pell's Point to this day. Unfortunately for the historical record, the "hurried situation of the Gen. that last two days have prevented him from paying him attention to Colonel

Glover and the officers and soldiers [during] a skirmish on Friday last that their merit and good behavior deserved."[65] Of course, for General Washington to have described the all-important Battle of Pell's Point as nothing more than a mere "skirmish" was not only a great injustice to what Glover had accomplished, but also one of the most enduring myths of the American Revolution, which was America's most mythical and romanticized conflict.

Indeed, in overall historical terms, this enduring myth about the insignificance of what has been deemed not even a battle on Friday October 18 in Westchester County by General Washington and others has been a key factor that has led to the battle's obscurity in the historical record for nearly two and a half centuries. Because of his lack of knowledge about this key engagement more than half a dozen miles from where he was located when he was preoccupied with his army's withdrawal, Washington lacked even the most basic details about this crucial battle: the situation that resulted in a great disservice to Glover and his men by reducing one of the hardest fought and most important battles of the American Revolution to nothing more than a mere "skirmish"—perhaps the greatest misnomer of the American Revolution. This unfortunate development was one fundamental reason that explained why generations of American historians, including even leading scholars of the American Revolution, have ignored the all-important Battle of Pell's Point to this day, including not even mentioning the critical engagement in many cases in full-length books about America's struggle for liberty. Clearly, this has been one of the great ironies of the American Revolution and the historiography of America's creation story because "a failure by Glover at Pell's Point could put Howe once again in a position to roll up Washington and the Revolution" to very likely bring an end to the war.[66]

However, having gained more knowledge about this forgotten battle in a remote section of Westchester County, Washington later correctly emphasized that "Glover's rear guard action was vital to the successful withdrawal of the entire Continental Army to safety in Westchester County" at White Plains.[67]

England-born and second-in-command of the Continental Army, General Charles Lee, who commanded the division (formerly Major General William Heath's Division) of which Glover's Bay State brigade (formerly Major General James Clinton's brigade before Glover took command on September 4, 1776) was a part, knew more intimately the tactical details of Glover's brilliant defense in depth at Pell's Point. In consequence, he wrote with sincerity how:

> General Lee returns his warmest thanks to Colonel Glover and on the brigade under his command, not only for their gallant behavior yesterday but for their prudent, cool, orderly and soldier-like conduct in all respects. He assures these brave men that he shall omit no opportunity of showing his gratitude.[68]

The Forgotten Showdown That Saved Washington's Army
Colonel John Glover's remarkable tactical success on Friday October 18 has to be placed within the proper strategic and tactical context to be fully understood and appreciated to dispel the myth that this forgotten battle was nothing more than a minor skirmish of no significance. In regard to the Battle of Pell's Point, the stage already had been set in the New York Campaign for the war to be won or lost and General Washington came perilously close to losing the war more than once. The summer of 1776 had seen both the high point and the low point of the American Revolution, which seemed to reveal some of its inherent contradictions, including the fact that this was America's first civil war.

On July 4, the issuing of the Declaration of Independence had seen the zenith point of the struggle for liberty, bringing forth a new nation conceived in lofty Enlightenment ideology during the high-stakes gamble to throw off the shackles of the mother country by force of arms. But less than two months after the heady signing of the idealistic document in Philadelphia that ushered forth a new day of freedom for the common man of a kind unknown in Europe, a large percentage of General Washington's fledgling army—an untrained, undisciplined, and inexperienced fighting force of amateurs in rebellion—was easily routed by the superior might and tactics of General William Howe, who commanded the largest expeditionary force sent forth in British history, at the Battle of Long Island near the end of August 1776. Defeat on Long Island was the war's greatest disaster to date for the young republic and its young citizen-soldier army, mocking the seemingly over-optimistic bid to win independence against the world's most powerful nation.

Worst of all and as demonstrated throughout the campaign of 1776 and almost to December's end, the army's novice commander in chief, General Washington, proved hopelessly inept in overall tactical terms—his Achilles' heel that was glaringly and repeatedly exposed for all to see. From the campaign's beginning, Howe had transformed the business of defeating the rustic amateurs of mostly farmers into little more than a game that proved almost as easy as child's play for such skilled professional opponents of a regular army. By the narrowest of margins, consequently, Washington had barely escaped a trap when he evacuated his seemingly doomed soldiers from Long Island and across the wide East River to Manhattan Island's safety under cover of darkness, thanks largely to Colonel Glover's efforts and that of his mostly Marblehead mariners who manned the transports and boats.

Even worse and because he was following the out-of-touch dictates of the political amateurs in the Continental Congress like in the case of defending Long Island, Washington also made the mistake of attempting to defend not only New York City but also Manhattan Island, which simply could not be held with too few inexperienced troops against superior troops and experienced British leaders primarily because the British Navy controlled the intricate system of waterways around New York City and Manhattan Island. Therefore, General Howe's formidable army was able to conduct an amphibious landing on Manhattan Island at any point north of New York City and north of Washington's army as long as it continued to commit the folly of remaining too long in defensive positions on Manhattan Island, as if just waiting to be trapped and destroyed at will.

Therefore, General Howe's overall strategic objective was to early encircle, cut off, and entrap Washington's army on Manhattan, where it could be easily crushed in detail. Still another golden opportunity was presented to Howe when Washington decided to hold a doomed position, although perched on fortified high ground, at Harlem Heights, which was located about halfway between New York City and the northern end of Manhattan Island. When Washington finally decided to escape Manhattan Island—a fatal trap—before it was too late and retire north into the New York mainland of Westchester County in a desperate attempt to reach safety of the high ground at White Plains, General Howe then resorted to moving north by water from Kip's Bay to conduct a secret amphibious landing in a bid to gain the eastern flank of Washington's withdrawing army to inflict a fatal blow. The morning of October 18 landing of Howe's more than six-thousand-man army, under Sir Henry Clinton's immediate command, on the western edge of Pelham Bay just above the southern tip of Pell's Point presented by far the most serious threat of the New York Campaign that possessed the potential for the British and Hessians to destroy Washington's withdrawing army just to the west to end the revolution by inflicting a fatal blow from which the rebellious colonies could never recover. In this most disadvantageous of situations, the fate of Washington's army and America was entirely in the hands of Colonel John Glover and his diminutive brigade of only four regiments to do the best under impossible circumstances —a classic case of do or die.

What most of all has been overlooked by generations of historians, both American and British, was the fact that the Battle of Pell's Point was a tactical and strategic success of the first magnitude, even though Glover's Brigade had been forced to withdraw and abandon the field. In technical terms, the British and Hessians won the battle— still another reason why so many American historians have chosen to ignore or minimize this all-important engagement to this day since it has been long viewed as a losing effort—because Howe possessed the field after the day's end and secured a toehold on Westchester County soil. Most important, however, Glover's last stand achieved far-reaching strategic gains of saving Washington's army and the revolution, because it "permitted them to advance only a short distance from the water's edge" in relative terms, which was the key development that allowed Washington to retreat safely to White Plains.[69]

Historian John R. Alden summarized the strategic importance of the defiant last stand of Colonel Glover's Brigade and thankfully for Washington's army laboring north in dismal retreat along the Albany Post Road just to the west: "the restraint imposed upon the British army by Glover convinced Howe that his flanking movement was too late to be successful [and] Howe made no strenuous attempt to execute it."[70]

This respected historian's opinion that revealed the battle's supreme importance can be fully verified from an ample number of primary sources. In a letter, one American soldier described the real strategic victory won by the hard fighting and tactical skill of Glover and his outnumbered men at Pell's Point, because of the severe punishment that the invaders had received on October 18, General Howe only "sent some light parties along the shore, as far as New Rochel [sic] and Maroneck, but their main body moved very little" to ensure the safety of Washington's army and unmolested retreat all the way to White Plains.[71]

And later in regard to General Howe's tactical movements for the next week after the Battle of Pell's Point and as revealed in a soldier's letter, "the enemy advanced [on October 25 or a week after the battle] a little into the country, but with great precaution," thanks to the sterling performance of the Massachusetts men on October 18.[72]

And two modern historians have agreed with a new appreciation of the battle's supreme importance, concluding how, "All day the engagement kept up [by Colonel Glover] with heavy casualties inflicted on the British and this delay was sufficient to permit Washington's army to escape encirclement."[73]

However, historian George Athan Billias perhaps said it best, writing without exaggeration how the Battle of Pell's Point "deserves to be ranked among the more decisive battles of the Revolutionary War [because Glover and his undersized Massachusetts brigade] saved [Washington's] army from encirclement and complete destruction."[74]

For General Howe, the Battle of Pell's Point was another Bunker Hill on a smaller scale but much more important in overall strategic terms, because the life of Washington's army was at stake like that of the revolution itself. In the attack on the fortified summit of Breed's Hill during the Battle of Bunker Hill, after a successful amphibious landing, General William Howe, the senior major general under General Thomas Gage, had orchestrated three headlong assaults of around 1,500 British soldiers up a narrow peninsula—the Charlestown Peninsula or Neck—against Massachusetts militiamen, who were posted behind strong defensive positions. In many ways, the Battle of Pell's Point seemed to have been little more than a tactical repeat, because of Howe's high losses (by far predominately Hessians) from repeated offensive efforts in vain on October 18.[75] In the words from a letter of one of Glover's men, who saw the battle firsthand and lived to tell one of the forgotten truths about the October 18 fight: "The Enemy were tho't at the lowest Computation to have lost 500 Men, some think not less than a thousd [thousand]. We had but very few killed, & as fat as I can learn not more than 50 or 60 Wounded."[76] This same writer never forgot how the enemy, especially the Hessians, "were seen to fall in great Numbers."[77]

"General Gage reported the entire loss in killed and wounded at Bunker Hill as one thousand and fifty-four; so that this battle [on October 18], which many historians ignore, was almost equally disastrous to the British arms," and even more so than in the world famous Battle of Bunker Hill.[78] However, Colonel Glover's repeated last stands in multiple ambush positions had succeeded in thwarting Howe's invasion from achieving far greater gains, especially in regard to gaining the strategic Eastchester Road and then striking Washington's weak, disorganized army while in retreat.

General Howe, who was yet traumatized from the "horror" of the decimation of so many of his disciplined redcoats at Bunker Hill on

June 17, 1775, had now just witnessed a bloody repeat on October 18 less than a year and a half later. Most of all in overall strategic terms because this was a costly victory comparable to the fate of Lord Cornwallis's Army at the Battle of Guilford Courthouse, North Carolina, in a war of attrition in the Southern theater on March 15, 1781, and although it was also technically a British victory, "Britain could not afford to win many peninsulas at similar cost."[79]

Indeed, this analysis has been the forgotten significance of the Battle of Pell's Point because it was basically another bloody Bunker Hill–like fiasco, but far more strategically important, in terms of total losses that General Howe's army could not afford to lose for a successful conclusion of the 1776 campaign with winter, when active campaigning would conclude in the European military tradition, on the horizon. Therefore, the brutal punishment administered by the four small regiments of Glover's Brigade upon Howe's finest troops, especially the Hessians, had saved the day, ensuring that a vigorous British drive west to smash into Washington's army and a decisive defeat were not forthcoming during this autumn, when America's life hung in the balance.[80]

Indeed, despite having gained "the rear of the left [if facing south] of our army" of the naive amateurs in rebellion, General Howe failed to deliver a fatal blow and only moved forward "with great caution," to Major General William Heath's utter astonishment, because he knew what was at stake.[81] With an innovative and creative tactical flair all his own that was uniquely American, Colonel Glover had succeeded in his crucial mission in an all-day battle of extreme importance, because, in the words of one of Glover's men from a letter, "their main body [of Howe's invasion force] did not move but very little," after having been so severely punished by the stubborn Bay State men, who had blazed away from behind successive stone fences in what were multiple ambushes of a defense in depth.[82]

Indeed, General Howe knew that he could not afford to suffer additional high losses of his best troops, both British, such as those regulars of the "King's Own" Regiment, and Hessians, including light infantrymen of the Third Grenadier Battalion, who could not be replaced in what was gradually turning into a lengthy war of attrition—the key to decisive American victory in this war—with each missed new opportunity to destroy Washington's army during the New York Campaign. After what he and his men had learned the hard way on October 18 and as mentioned, Howe also realized that this entire Westchester County countryside inland was laced with the high stone fences that reminded Howe what kind of serious damage could be inflicted by only a single Continental brigade—or even militia—if they rose up again from these fences of stone and stood firm like Glover's men: a realization that ended his dream of striking Washington's army to deliver a fatal blow.

In the end, what Howe had learned the hard way was that the patriots did not need a commanding hilltop like Breed's Hill and strong earthworks and fortified positions to inflict Bunker Hill–like losses on England's finest troops—a new tactical equation in the art of American warfighting that was steadily changing and evolving as demonstrated by Colonel Glover. Because of the many high stone fences that covered this fertile farming land with relatively little woodlands, even the general terrain could be easily transformed by the Americans into strong fortified positions and become the deadliest of ground—a true killing field—for General Howe's advancing troops. And, thanks to what had happened just northwest of the Pell's Point Peninsula on October 18, 1776, this was a bloody lesson that Howe would never forget not only for the campaign's remainder but also for the rest of his life, because he had missed a great opportunity to deliver Washington's army a fatal blow. In consequence, he thereafter would be haunted by the sight of stone fences that had once blazed such a deadly fire from its determined defenders from Massachusetts.

Quite simply, Colonel Glover's sparkling success in thwarting the British invasion from streaming inland and farther west like a juggernaut, the Battle of Pell's Point

saved the American army; for Howe had received such a check as to convince him that he could not advance into the country with impunity [and therefore] delayed his movements until the twentieth, when he advanced to the heights above New Rochelle, he was joined by the second division of the Germans [some eight thousand troops].[83]

Clearly, to achieve future success, Howe now knew that he needed additional strength—in part to replace the around one thousand German and British troops lost on October 18—before he attempted to march across a Westchester County laced with seemingly countless stone fences on ground favorable like those from which so many Glover-like defensive stands could be made and prove most costly to his ambitions. By this time, Howe was experiencing a degree of trauma when it came to launching offensive efforts directed against stone walls and for ample good reason.

As noted, because of Glover's repeated defensive stands and the heavy losses inflicted by the Massachusetts Continentals that had resulted in Howe's great "restraint," General Washington's army had been saved by some of the most spirited fighting of the war by only a relative handful of determined men, who had defied the odds, thanks largely to the superior leadership abilities and tactical skills of Colonel Glover. So successful was Glover's tactical masterpiece on October 18 that even an opportunity to have repelled the invasion had been missed by way of an American counterstroke in the estimation of some American fighting men on the scene. But in the end, Generals Washington and Lee forfeited the opportunity of supporting Glover with more troops or a greater success could have been achieved in pushing Howe's troops back down Pell's Point Peninsula or trapping him on the peninsula. One of those soldiers who witnessed Glover's tactical masterpiece on this unforgettable Friday wrote with complete confidence in a letter on October 23, only five days after this forgotten battle raged in full fury in Westchester County, "had we been reenforced with half their number, we might have totally defeated them."[84]

And as appearing in the October 31, 1776, issue of the *Maryland Gazette,* the Continental Congress received the dramatic news and timely intelligence of Glover's impressive success that raised spirits across Philadelphia and the infant American nation, although the details about this battle in New York were then not known:

> On Friday the 18th instant, one of the enemy's advanced parties near East-Chester fell in with part of col. Glover's brigade, when a smart and close engagement ensured; in which our men behaved with great coolness and intrepidity, and, [drove] the enemy back to their main body.[85]

Indeed, the joy stemming from Glover's remarkable tactical success in keeping a formidable invasion force at bay was well-founded. In overall strategic terms, Colonel Glover's tactically innovative defensive stand caused General Howe to significantly slow his push inland, allowing Washington's army sufficient time to withdraw safely to White Plains and concentrate in time to successfully meet General Howe's next tactical movement, but much belated to the point of an offensive strike having been unleashed far too late to additionally ensure Washington's survival. Thanks to the success of Glover's defensive efforts, Washington had gained sufficient time and preparations to defend the fortified high ground of White Plains in preparation for meeting General Howe's army, which finally arrived on October 28. Most important, Colonel Glover's men had bought Washington and his reeling army, which was in bad shape after successive defeats and withdrawals, a precious ten days of time that proved invaluable.[86]

The precarious situation of Washington's army, more than half a week after the Battle of Pell's Point, and the army's extreme vulnerability during the long withdrawal from Harlem Heights to White Plains can perhaps best be understood by the words of Tench Tilghman, Washington's faithful aide-de-camp, from a letter written on October 22 (four days after the Battle of Pell's Point) from "Valentine's Hill, 4 Miles from Kingsbridge": "We are just setting off from for the White Plains where the General [Washington] intends to fix Head Quarters for the present."[87]

Most important, thanks to the time bought by the series of clever defensive stands of a well-conceived defense in depth that allowed Glover to succeed in his critical mission that he had imposed upon himself and his badly outnumbered men by aggressively advancing on the enemy invasion force without orders instead of retreating, General Washington's army "was no longer seriously threatened with encirclement."[88]

Indeed, the Battle of Pell's Point had effectively "served to check the British and thus give time for the withdrawal of the men and army stores from N.Y. Island [and] By it Glover had the honor of being the first to resist the landing of a British Army on the main land of America."[89]

In the words of Thomas Fleming, Glover's Massachusetts troops had accomplished the impossible against the odds, because there

> was not the slightest attempt [of Howe's invasion force] to advance toward White Plains and seize the high ground [even though] the eighteen miles between [the British and Hessian invaders] and that strategic village and discover that it was defended by nothing but a handful of militia.[90]

Thus, Colonel Glover's personal battle on a Friday in early autumn against an invading army had led to strategically important consequences, after having orchestrated multiple defensive stands on ever-higher ground in a leapfrog tactic that served as a highly effective deterrent to a vigorous British advance inland. The sheer audacity and spirited defensive stands of the relatively handful of men of Glover's Brigade had been decisive in convincing Howe that these hard-fighting Massachusetts soldiers must have been motivated to stand so firm against the odds and with such defiance by the knowledge that sizeable reinforcements from Washington's army were nearby and ready to descend upon him: the tactical deception created by Colonel Glover's tactical masterpiece of an innovative and intricate defense in depth.

> Indeed, while Washington's army was extremely vulnerable during its gloomy withdrawal to White Plains only around

half a dozen miles away by way of a straight road, at East-chester [or the Eastchester Road], were William Howe's elite light infantry and grenadiers. Unquestionably, they could have smashed Washington's army to pieces in a single day's march. Or Howe could have led these light troops to unassailable positions in the hills above White Plains. Instead, he did nothing while Washington's army crawled painfully to these same hills and took possession of them.[91]

Little more than an old but time-honored cliché, the stereotypical explanation for Howe's failure to destroy Washington's army has been the general's incompetence, pro-American sentiment, and lack of a killer instinct. In this regard thanks to the convenience of hindsight, history has been most unkind to General Howe and unfair when it came to his invasion of the Pell's Point Peninsula. What has been most forgotten was the fact that Howe might have won it all, if he had not been thwarted by Glover and his men on October 18 in one of the remarkable defensive stands of the American Revolution. The unfortunate Howe has long served as the convenient scapegoat for British missed opportunities and military folly as to obscure the vision of historians to ascertain the real cause for British failure to reap decisive success. In truth, it was Glover who was most responsible for not only slowing but also thwarting Howe to ensure that the British and Hessian invasion force would not attack Washington's army during its lengthy retreat, while ensuring the Continental Army's survival.

In striking contrast to the simplistic stereotype of Howe's excessive incompetence and ineptitude of a typical aristocratic British general too inflexible and unimaginative to inflict a lethal blow and thereby robbing Great Britain of decisive victory, General Howe was actually a highly capable commander and one of England's best and brightest. His distinguished 1759 role at Quebec in leading the British Army of the brilliant General James Wolfe, Howe's mentor, up the rocky way up the cliffs to catch the French, under the Marquis de Montcalm, and paving the way for the reaping of decisive victory on the Plains of Abraham won Canada and the French and Indian War (known as the Seven Years' War in Europe) for Great Britain. In fact, Howe had learned the ways of waging modern warfare in a professional manner under Wolfe, who "was one of the great improvisers in military history," before the gifted young commander was killed at the Battle of Quebec along with Montcalm.[92]

Also, General Howe's tactical brilliance had been early evident in having been "partly responsible for the development of light infantry tactics" that were then "adapted and modified by Napoleon, which [then] enabled him to sweep Europe."[93] This gifted British aristocrat was also a master in the concept of amphibious warfare and the art of outflanking his opponent with textbook efficiency and consummate skill, as repeatedly proven during the New York Campaign. Howe's most successful flanking movement had been demonstrated at Long Island near the end of August 1776. Here, a complete victory had been easily won by smashing into the exposed American left and then rolling up the lines like an old carpet after catching the hapless Americans by surprise, while also gaining their rear because Washington had long expected an attempt from the opposite direction, west. By his successful amphibious landing on the Pell's Point Peninsula that caught the Americans by surprise like at Long Island, Howe once again skillfully placed himself into a most advantageous position by which to trap and strike Washington's retreating army, if he pushed west with vigor. But Colonel Glover's time-consuming and highly effective multiple stands of a brilliant defense in depth throughout October 18 ended the possibility of Howe reaping decisive victory as fondly envisioned.

All in all, it is almost incredible that such as important battle as Pell's Point has been forgotten and overlooked by even leading historians for more than two centuries. After all, Glover and his small band of Massachusetts soldiers had not only thwarted large numbers of some of the best trained and disciplined troops, both British and Hessians, in the world, but also thwarted Howe's brilliant strategy to destroy Washington's army and end the war in one masterstroke—in consequence, one of the war's most decisive battles. In truth, the real answer to the enduring mystery that best explained General Howe's missed golden opportunity on October 18 was the heavy losses that had been inflicted by Glover's men and their tenacious defensive stands that made Howe believe that he was facing many more troops than simply a single brigade and that other units of Washington's army were either nearby or on their way to reinforce the defenders.

And in overall strategic terms, the remarkable success of Glover in blunting General Howe's advance and buying precious time paid high dividends in allowing Washington to bypass the mighty invasion force just to the east and then to strengthen the fortifications at White Plains to successfully resist the next offensive effort unleashed by Howe, which came too late in consequence. Indeed, the high-stakes game of strategic maneuver between Howe and Washington culminated in the indecisive Battle of White Plains on October 28, ten days after Glover had bought the Continental Army precious time by delaying the advancing tide of thousands of British and Hessian troops and keeping them from delivering a death stroke to Washington's army: the guarantee that America's struggle for liberty would continue unabated in the years ahead in a war of attrition that ultimately proved fatal to Great Britain.

The first phase of a key turning point of the revolution, Glover's spirited defensive stand also set the tempo for the remainder of the New York–New Jersey campaign and for the rest of the year of decision, 1776, including even in having played a role in allowing Washington the opportunity to strike back at Trenton and Princeton to keep the flame of revolution alive. From now on and as if having been frustrated by a relative handful of Continentals of a small Massachusetts brigade of four regiments on October 18, General Howe would commit the ultimate folly of focusing more on capturing and occupying strategic points rather than smashing General Washington's army: the exact formula for eventually losing the war in a conflict never fully understood by London's strategists and King George III, who remained clueless and without answers from beginning to end.

Thanks to what had happened around the Pell's Point Peninsula on October 18 that resulted in a dramatic change in Howe's strategic thinking and overall level of aggressiveness, Glover's key role in saving the day assisted in setting the stage for Washington's unexpected crossing of the Delaware, in which Glover and his mariners played still another vital role, and the surprising victory over the Hessian brigade of three regiments at Trenton on December 26, 1776, and a dramatic reversal in patriot fortunes to turn the tide of the revolution. Quite simply, without Glover's success at Pell's Point, there would have been no surprising victories at Trenton and Princeton in less than three months to reverse the course of the American Revolution.[94]

Colonel Glover's Grim Harvest on an Autumnal Day

Ironically, the strategic importance of the Battle of Pell's Point also has been overlooked for so long partly because the American and British losses, unlike those of the Hessians, were insignificant, which has made this all-important showdown in Westchester County long seem like nothing more than a mere skirmish of little significance. After all, Colonel Glover's outsized gains that had been reaped at Pell's Point came at an incredibly small cost that almost defied logic and rational thought, but it has been indicative of the sheer brilliance of the Marbleheader's clever battle plan, which had been fashioned by him in short order on the fly in large part to minimize losses because of the smallness of the force, when battling in a key showdown a good distance from the army: the tactical situation that forced Glover to create his own ad hoc tactical plan out of urgent necessity because he was on his own. In an October 19 letter, one of Glover's soldiers wrote of the relatively small price paid for saving the day and the very life of Washington's army and the people's revolution itself: "We lost a few, thirty or forty killed and wounded."[95] In fact, no sacrifice so small has achieved so much for America during the war than at the Battle of Pell's Point.

Equally amazed by the diminutive loss of life in the four Massachusetts regiments, one of Glover's soldiers described in an October 23 letter how: "Our loss is about nine or ten killed, and about thirty wounded."[96] This figure was close to the colonel's eight killed and thirteen wounded in a letter to his mother, Tabitha. Privates Ezekiel Fuller, Daniel Deland, and Samuel Cole were killed in the ranks of Colonel Read's Thirteenth Massachusetts, while Sergeants Charles Adams, and James Scott of Shepard's Third Massachusetts were killed, along with Private Thaddeus Kemp.[97]

Ireland-born Thomas Sullivan, a member of the Forty-ninth Regiment of Foot at only age twenty-one, described a heavier American loss that was as inaccurate as it was exaggerated. Writing in his journal, he described how: "The Enemy's Loss upon this occasion was a Lieut. Colonel killed, a Major wounded, and about 90 men killed and Wounded." In a more accurate analysis, the close-range nature of the bitter contest on October 18 and the amount of punishment inflicted upon Howe's troops, especially the Hessians, had convinced Sullivan, though with some understatement, that this was indeed "a smart engagement."[98]

In part, the supreme importance of the Battle of Pell's Point in regard to slowing Howe's push inland and convincing him to proceed with much greater caution and care perhaps can be best seen in the high number of casualties inflicted upon General Howe's forces. However, these significant losses have been minimized largely for political reasons by Howe, which also has played a large part in obscuring the reality that the Battle of Pell's Point was an all-important clash of arms and not a mere meaningless skirmish—the most enduring myth about the dramatic showdown in Westchester County, when so much was at stake for America. General Howe had a habit of minimizing losses for personal and political reasons and the Battle of Pell's Point was no exception to the rule. In regard to the attack on Fort Washington, for instance, even one Briton at the time admitted how Howe's loss on November 18, 1776, "was much greater than G. Howes returns."[99]

Of course under the circumstances of a forced withdrawal before being overpowered by thousands of British and Hessian troops, Glover and his men had no time to count the number of dead or wounded

British and Hessians lying before the multiple fences of stone, because they left the field in a hurry during a fight that had spanned for hundreds of yards north up Split Rock Road and on both sides of the main artery leading deeper inland.

But General William Heath was not wrong when he generalized by writing more accurately than British sources how: "Shepard's, Read's, Baldwin's and Glover's regiments, had the principal share in this action. The Americans had between 30 and 40 men killed and wounded [but] The loss of the British was not known, but must have been considerable."[100]

In this context, even the use of the word "considerable" used by General Heath was in fact quite an understatement. However, gained from the firsthand oral accounts of officers and men in Glover's brigade, Heath's intimate knowledge of the massive destruction inflicted upon Howe's attackers had provided him with the basis for his on-target estimation of how the British and Hessian losses were "considerable." Meanwhile, General Howe reported to London that among his British troops, he lost eight killed and thirteen wounded, which was certainly an understatement in the extreme. Indeed, he had only continued his own and the usual British military procedure of minimizing British losses and entirely excluding losses among the Hessians, who composed not only three-quarters of the invasion force but also engaged almost all of the fighting on bloody October 18.[101]

General Howe's non-reporting of Hessian losses also played a role in the enduring myth, which has continued to this day nearly 250 years later, that the Battle of Pell's Point was nothing more than a meaningless skirmish of no significance. In his journal, Thomas Sullivan, who spoke with a distinctive Irish brogue like so many soldiers in red uniforms, wrote about only British losses: "Lieut. Colonel [Thomas] Musgrove commanded the 1st Battalion of Light Infantry, and Capt. [William Glanville] Evelyn of the 4th Regiment were both wounded; the latter soon died: 3 men were killed and 20 wounded."[102]

Besides the unfortunate Captain Evelyn, only one other British fatality of the "King's Own" Regiment has been identified from long-obscure British muster rolls, Private John Hudson or Hodgson of Captain Holmes's Company. The redcoat private died from his wounds on October 19. And other soldiers of the Fourth Regiment of Foot died in upcoming weeks, indicating that some of these British fatalities had gone down mortally wounded during the raging battle and later died of their injuries. One of these unlucky redcoats was John Burley or Burleigh, who died on November 5, less than three weeks after the battle, and Robert Cooper, who died on November 14. But General Howe most of all lamented the loss of the promising young Irish captain of light troops, writing on November 30 how Captain William Glanville Evelyn was "since dead, and much to be regretted" by the army.[103]

With a philosophical flair on reflecting upon his life's end but never losing his contempt for American rebels, the mortally wounded Captain Evelyn, who was a "dutiful and affectionate son," had written out his final will and testament in which he stoically described how: "As all Men who have taken upon them the profession of Arms, hold their Lives by a more precarious tenure than any other Body of People; and as the fatal experience of this Day shews us how particularly it is the case of those who are engaged in war, even with the most despicable Enemy."[104]

And it appeared that Lieutenant Colonel Musgrave, who commanded the British light brigade, had been mortally wounded at the time, but such was not the case. On November 30, General Howe reported back to London with joy how Musgrave was "in a fair way of recovery" from his wound.[105]

Longtime Lingering Mystery Solved about Hessian Losses
In his fine 2002 book *The Battle for New York*, historian Barnet Schecter described the greatest mystery surrounding the bloody battle fought on October 18 with such intensity on both sides for most of the day in regard to Hessian losses: "The number of Hessian dead [and wounded] in the Battle of Pelham Bay remains conjectural and controversial" to

this day.[106] But in truth, the close-range nature of the combat—the unleashing of more than twenty-five point-blank volleys by Glover's men, especially when muskets were steadied for a more accurate fire when they rested their flintlocks atop the stone fences during multiple ambushes from ever-higher ground positions, into the enemy's dense ranks—tell the tragic story of extremely high Hessian losses: undeniable facts and not mere conjectures based on idle speculation.

The leading American expert and prolific author of the Hessian experience during the American Revolution, Bruce E. Burgoyne, who has translated many Hessian-related primary documents, letters, and memoirs from German to English, responded many years ago in a nice letter to this current author's inquiry about information concerning Hessian losses during the Battle of Pell's Point: "Sorry I can not help you. I can not remember any Hessian document that I have translated that has any information on Pell's Point."[107] Clearly, the great mystery about Hessian losses had long remained solidly intact even among a foremost American expert of the German fighting man during the American Revolution.

The general obscurity of Hessian losses was neither accidental or surprising under the circumstances. First, Hessian losses were not reported by the British Army or by English officers back to London by General Howe or any other British commander, because Hessian officers reported losses directly to the princes of their German principalities and not British leaders. Casualty lists of Hessian soldiers went straight to the princes of the German states and were not published in patriot, Loyalist, or British newspapers, obscuring the total number of losses among the German troops from the eyes of almost everyone at the time and then historians of later generations on both sides of the Atlantic and well into the twenty-first century. In fact, Hessian casualty reports that were brought back to Germany have either been lost, destroyed during the chaos of the Second World War, or lay yet undiscovered by historians to this day.

In addition, yet another factor explained why the total number of fallen troops among Howe's invasion force have been obscured and lost to the historical record for so long. The high Hessian losses were deliberately minimized or even silenced in order to deflect criticism for this unpopular foreign war among the British people and the members of Parliament, or the Tories, who opposed the faraway overseas conflict with considerable zeal in the halls of government of their constitutional monarchy. Likewise, the manipulation of British losses for political reasons to much lower levels also occurred in regard to previous battles in the struggle for New York. For instance, young Massachusetts-born Private Joseph Plumb Martin, who was one of Washington's young soldiers of a Connecticut regiment, emphasized how in regard to the Battle of Harlem Heights in September 1776: "How many of the enemy [both British and Hessians] were killed and wounded could not be known, as the British were always as careful as Indians to conceal their losses."[108]

In his memoirs and like so many others, General Heath could only speculate. However, he was fundamentally correct about the ultimate cost paid by Howe at the Battle of Pell's Point, writing how, "The loss to the British was not known" to anyone on the American side, but they were "considerable." What General Heath meant to say was that the Hessian—not British—loss on October 18 was "considerable."[109]

The Unvarnished Truth About Enemy Losses
Therefore, for the first time, this present work has been partly focused on presenting as much new primary evidence and documentation as possible to validate the battle's supreme importance and also to provide substantial proof of Howe's higher casualty rates—especially among the Hessians—than previously believed or even imagined by generations of American historians to finally end the most major controversy about this long-overlooked engagement, while proving that the October 18 showdown was the antithesis of a mere skirmish. Therefore, British and Hessian losses should no longer be open to either conjecture or debate, given the new evidence revealed from

primary documentation and evidence found in this current book to end the enduring central mystery about the battle that has existed for nearly two and a half centuries.

Most important, contemporary estimates of total Hessian losses of Lieutenant General Leopold Philip de Heister's First Division at Pell's Point were as high as one thousand, as revealed from primary accounts and sources from both sides. In a letter written on October 19, or the day after the battle, one of Glover's men wrote: "Two deserters from the enemy say they lost one thousand" men, both killed and wounded.[110] This lofty figure of one thousand was no exaggeration, because it is entirely in agreement with the effectiveness of Glover's tactical masterpiece and the accuracy of the fire of the Massachusetts soldiers. As emphasized in a letter from one of the Marblehead colonel's men who wrote how, "some think not less than a thousd." of the attackers were cut down during the Battle of Pell's Point.[111]

Like the overall course of the lengthy battle, especially in regard to multiple close-range ambushes that resulted in the unleashing of more than twenty-five volleys on ever-high ground and the overall brilliance of Glover's tactical masterpiece (a true Battle of Cowpens-like defense in depth) in which frontline defenders fell back, as ordered at the right time, to successive stronger defensive positions on ever-higher ground, other primary accurate and valid evidence have supported these high estimates of Hessian losses and far more than assumed by generations of modern historians, coinciding with the tally of the total casualties emphasized from the firsthand reports of deserters, both English and Hessian, from the British Army. Only five days after the battle on October 23, 1776, one American soldier, who had witnessed the battle, wrote in a letter how: "The enemy, a deserter says lost two hundred killed on the spot, and a great number wounded."[112]

And an October 22 letter from another American soldier at Fort Lee [the former Fort Constitution], New Jersey, situated on the Hudson's west bank, revealed some of the latest intelligence about losses in the battle to provide another estimation based on first-hand information: "A deserter at headquarters informs that the loss of the enemy, on Friday instant [October 18], would have been seven or eight hundred."[113]

Indeed, the most important details of what really happened during the course of the bloody battle, especially in regard to enemy losses, can be glimpsed from the words and views of participants of the swirling, close-range combat on Friday October 18. For instance, the ever-reliable Colonel William Baldwin wrote how, "The enemy must have lost at least two hundred men dead [which] I jud[g]e from what I saw myself [lying before his Massachusetts Regiment] and good information."[114]

Another one of Glover's men described in an October 19 letter that, "I have the best opinions to believe they lost one hundred and fifty or upwards [in killed], as our men fired with great coolness" for an extended period from three separate and well-established defensive lines or ambushes, extending from south to north.[115]

And one of Washington's men, evidently a member of Glover's Brigade, described in a November 6, 1776, letter that revealed intimate, long-overlooked details of the battle: "The enemy were thought at the lowest computation to have lost five hundred men, some think not less than a thousand."[116] All in all, the fall of a thousand British and Hessian attackers on October 18 was not only well within the realm of possibility, but also certainly the case based on existing evidence and collaborating accounts from multiples sources, including from both sides. Indeed, in the conclusion of one insightful American historian,

> It is difficult to believe that [Glover's men,] familiar with the use of firearms, sheltered by ample defenses from which they could fire deliberately and with their guns rested on the tops [of stone fences], could have fired volley after volley [more than twenty-five in total] into a large body of men, massed in a compacted column in a narrow roadway, without inflicting as [much] extended damage as this

one thousand attackers, both British and Hessian.[117]

These most revealing estimations of enemy losses from Washington's soldiers, both officers and enlisted men who knew intimately about the details of the nature of the intense combat on October 18 because they witnessed the battle, are most significant for two reasons, because they have corresponded closely with the British-Hessian deserter estimates, and because these were made not long after this crucial engagement to ensure greater accuracy rather than if written long after the war.

Even if the total casualty figure of the German troops seems too lofty at first glance, then the number of Hessian fatalities only correlated to the high number of German wounded. If such estimates are indeed correct as they certainly seem to be because of overwhelming primary evidence and multiple sources, especially when hundreds of Massachusetts men used lethal "buck & ball" rounds and laid muskets atop the stone fences to ensure greater accuracy during the unleashing of more than twenty-five volleys, then around two hundred estimated fatalities have revealed the traditional three-to-one ratio of wounded men to killed men, which then brings the total Hessian losses close to the one thousand total loss estimate. By way of comparison at the Battle of Bunker Hill on June 17, 1775, a total of 226 British soldiers were killed to reveal how the Battle of Pell's Point was actually much more like another Bunker Hill in scale and scope, especially in regard to enemy losses than generally has been believed by generations of historians, but during a battle that was a far more important overall strategic situation because the lives of Washington's army and the infant nation were at stake.[118]

If this two hundred fatality number of enemy losses is correct which was almost certainly the case, then relying on the standard formula of one killed to at least three wounded, then a total casualty figure approaching one thousand can be easily reached in a basic combat equation that was standard in the eighteenth century and well into the nineteenth century. Historian George Athan Billias wrote how on October 19, two deserters from General Howe's force "testified that the total German and British casualties reached 1,000 men, and several days later two more deserters verified a severe toll by setting the losses at 800 men."[119] As mentioned, the vast majority of these losses never reported by General Howe to his superiors and government were among the Hessian troops, because they made up three-fourths of Howe's forces and they were the overwhelming majority of front-line troops who launched repeated attacks on October 18.[120]

Although not mentioning specifics or details like most writers and historians, Thomas Fleming was correct in his evaluation that Glover's disciplined troops "inflict[ed] heavy losses, particularly on the German regiments as they advanced inland."[121] During the sweeping attack on Fort Washington, New York, located on the east bank of the Hudson across from Fort Lee, on November 16, 1776, which was defended by nearly three thousand Continentals and contained tons of invaluable supplies and munitions, and a good many cannon badly needed by Washington's army, the Hessians also took the brunt of the losses like during the Battle of Pelham Heights less than a month before and largely for the same political reasons. In total, some fifty-eight Hessians were killed in the assault upon a strong fortified position defended by Washington's crack Continental troops and another 272 wounded, for a total of 330 casualties in one of the major clashes of the American Revolution, which ironically became very well known, unlike the Battle of Pell's Point.[122]

If the one thousand estimated Hessian casualties inflicted at Pell's Point was correct, then the Hessians suffered a loss three times higher on October 18 than their frontal assaults on Fort Washington, which contained multiple defensive lines that protected the strong earthen fort proper, which dominated a powerful defensive position far more elevated and formidable than Glover had used at Pell's Point. In contrast, Colonel Glover's men made their multiple defensive stands against greater odds in more open country and less-elevated terrain without a fort or earthen defenses and where only stone fences, which their savvy Marblehead commander exploited to the fullest, offered the only effective means by which to create a defensive arrangement to thwart Howe's mighty invasion.

But General Howe's repeated assaults on Breed's Hill at the Battle of Bunker Hill was more revealing by way of comparison to what happened on the Pell's Point Peninsula on October 18. On that scorching hot June 17, 1775 day and nearly a year before the signing of the Declaration of Independence, General Howe ordered British troops to advance up the hill of death with fixed bayonets in three sweeping assaults against earthen and fence-rail defenses held by hardy New England militiamen, guaranteeing the loss of 1,054 men on the war's bloodiest day to date. Howe lost almost half of his British attackers before the arrival of the German Hessians of the First Division in time for the New York Campaign, with 226 men killed and another 828 wounded in the bloody holocaust known as the Battle of Bunker Hill.

In striking contrast, on October 18, 1776, General Howe led thousands of troops against only around 750 Massachusetts soldiers—or around four times fewer New England defenders than at the Battle of Bunker Hill—and lost nearly as many troops at Pell's Point as at Breed's Hill, if the estimates of one thousand total casualties at the Battle of Pell's Point were accurate, which almost certainly was the case. Most significant and like no other battle of the American Revolution, a far lesser number of Bay State Continentals of Glover's brigade inflicted higher losses that were far more out of proportion to their own numbers: a seemingly impossible situation on a traditional battlefield that caused Howe and Clinton to believe that they faced thousands of American soldiers at Pell's Point. In truth, the answer to the mystery was Glover's tactical masterpiece and the high-quality of his men.

Therefore, in many ways, the forgotten Battle of Pell's Point, which was another "Bunker Hill all over again" in which the same British commander led the offensive effort, was more impressive than even the Battle of Bunker Hill, because far fewer Americans inflicted a higher percentage of casualties than at Breed's Hill and Glover's multiple defensive stands had been made entirely on the fly, without prepared defensive positions, and on less-advantageous terrain. As during the war's beginning, General Howe could no longer boast that one British regular in a scarlet uniform was more than equal to multiple Americans on the field of strife, after the dramatic show-down at Pell's Point.[123]

If he had only lived to fight another day beyond bloody October 18, Captain William Evelyn, the diehard Irishman of the "King's Own" regiment, would have entirely agreed. He had survived the bloody frontal assaults straight up Breed's Hill by some miracle, when so many other British soldiers had fallen in sickening bunches around him. The young captain from the Emerald Isle had been horrified when his company that he led was decimated to the point of having been "torn to shreds" by the scorching fire pouring down from the New England farmers, who stood firm atop Breed's Hill until their ammunition began to run out. But for the numbers engaged and the damage inflicted upon the attackers, the repeated British and Hessian assaults on the multiple stone fences held by Glover's men proved even more deadly to Howe's attackers than at Breed's Hill. Described by General Howe as "a gallant officer," the young Irish captain named Evelyn had been mortally wounded when struck by three bullets. He was fated to never again see his beloved Green Isle across the sea.[124]

Captain Evelyn was only one of hundreds of casualties who were cut down on bloody October 18, especially among the Hessians who suffered the lion's share of the losses by far. Historian William Abbott correctly concluded how Howe's overall losses at the Battle of Pell's Point "was greater than at Monmouth," which was one of the major and most famous battles of the American Revolution. Here, in north-eastern New Jersey on a sweltering June 28, 1778, an estimated 361 British soldiers became casualties in one of the hardest-fought contests of the war. In fact, Howe's casualties, especially among the Hessians, at Pell's Point were nearly three times as high as those suffered by the British at Monmouth Courthouse.[125]

Such a high estimation of German fatalities at Pell's Point corresponded with the long-accepted report—based on local oral tradition—that ninety Hessians wounded in the battle later died in the ad hoc hospital that had been set up by the British in St. Paul's Episcopal Church at Eastchester. Here, they were treated by German surgeons and medical attendants (unlike the British and Continental Armies in which a surgeon was assigned to each regiment, the Hessians assigned a junior surgeon to each individual company of the regiment). But in the end, ninety German soldiers died after the battle and then were buried nearby in the church cemetery. Local legend also has it that the Hessian dead on the battlefield were piled "in a mass grave" somewhere on the field of strike—most likely before the stone fences near Split Rock Road—whose exact location today is known only to God.[126]

This accurate estimate, which was almost certainly the case, of one thousand Hessian losses at the Battle of Pell's Point made it one of the most costly and bloodiest armed clashes of major significance during the entire colonial period. Like the Battle of Bunker's Hill, the greatest British disaster of the French and Indian War saw a loss comparable to what had been inflicted upon Howe's invasion force on October 18. General Edward Braddock lost nearly one thousand men, both British and colonials, when the French, Canadians, and Native Americans sprung their ambush in the wilderness near the present-day Pittsburgh, Pennsylvania. This perfectly timed ambush virtually destroyed Braddock's large task force, including the commander himself, who had to be hastily buried to keep his body out of vengeful Native American hands, as feared by his men, including a young George Washington. Colonel Glover's brilliant battle plan, based upon an innovative and unique series of clever ambushes and a staggered defense in depth with his regiments well-placed in echelon, inflicted as many casualties as had been lost by General Braddock's army in July 1755 during the greatest disaster of the French and Indian War.

Therefore, because of the defense's tenacity and the battle's intensity that lasted for most of the day, Glover's masterful orchestration of his defense in depth, the high number of inflicted casualties, and because it had taken a flank movement of a "corps" under Lord Cornwallis to finally dislodge a small brigade of only 750 men, General Henry Clinton believed that he had faced an astounding total of "at least 14,000" Americans on the Pell's Point Peninsula on October 18.[127]

This incredibly high estimation given of American strength by General Clinton was more than fifteen times larger than the actual number of soldiers in Glover's brigade, which has revealed the sheer tenacity and brilliance of the Marblehead colonel's tactical masterpiece. In many ways and beyond all doubt, this gross overestimation of American strength by Clinton was certainly the most fitting tribute to the combat prowess and overall tactical performance of Colonel Glover and his men. In overall percentage terms, Glover and his seasoned Continentals inflicted one of the highest casualty rates on British-Hessian forces during the war, making the Battle of Pell's Point not only one of the bloodiest engagements of the American Revolution, but also one of the war's most important battles: forgotten aspects of this long-overlooked engagement and its extreme importance within the overall context of not only the American Revolutionary history, but also of American history.

Ironically, Glover's amazing tactical success that he achieved against the odds on a picturesque October day just northeast of New York City when everything was at stake highlighted a brutal reality for the British war—yet not realized by leading officials in London, including Lord Germain, and especially King George III—in America, as emphasized in a Briton's letter that appeared in the *Pennsylvania Evening Post* on June 29, 1775: "the military coercion of America will be impracticable . . . America [is] like Hercules in the cradle [for] Neither shall we be able to sustain the unhallowed war at so remote a distance—unexplored deserts, wood-land ambuscades," which will make the conquest of America an impossibility in the end.[128]

And as written in another letter from London that appeared in the pages of the *Maryland Gazette*, of Annapolis, Maryland, and predicted that the American revolutionaries would rise to the challenge, like at Pell's Point, by embracing the right winning tactical formula for decisive success, thwarting England's best designs and well-laid plans, especially "if the provincials act with their usual spirit and prudence; that is, if they occupy good posts, intrench well, avoid a general action [and] Add this their superior knowledge of the country [which] will enable them to do, to as to distress if not destroy the invading army."[129]

Clearly, this most revealing letter was prophetic in regard to what Colonel Glover's innovative tactics, which were hastily created on the fly in a true emergency situation when time was of the essence, and the fighting prowess of the Massachusetts brigade had accomplished against the odds at Pell's Point. Ironically, while the much-celebrated defensive stand of the Anglo-Celtic revolutionaries of Texas during the late winter of 1836 at the Alamo during the Texas Revolution has become world famous, the even more remarkable story of a much more impressive defensive stands by a relatively small band of Americans on October 18, 1776, when far more was at stake—the life of Washington's army and that of the nation—has been long overlooked and forgotten to this day. Indeed, in overall percentage terms, the Massachusetts soldiers of an undersized Continental brigade inflicted a stunning amount of punishment upon the invaders of the American mainland to a degree not seen in any other battle of the American Revolution in overall percentage terms. By comparison, the world famous defense of nearly two hundred men at the old Spanish mission known as the Alamo inflicted a loss of barely three hundred upon the Mexican attackers, because they had been caught completely by surprise by a nighttime assault just before the chilly dawn of March 6, 1836.[130]

Not surprisingly, Colonel Glover and his band of Massachusetts warriors received a good deal of thanks, including from a grateful General Washington, for what they had accomplished against the odds on October 18. For ample good reason, General Charles Lee was so proud of what his tiny brigade of Massachusetts soldiers of his division had accomplished against such formidable odds in such a key situation that he advised one of Glover's men that "we shall none of us leave the army, but all stay and be promoted."[131]

Quite likely, there simply would have been no existing primary army of the infant republic from which to receive these coveted thanks and promotions had Colonel Glover and his men failed to thwart Howe's ambitious plans to destroy the Continental Army. Had General Howe gained the vulnerable right flank of Washington's army in a chaotic withdrawal north to White Plains, then in all probability the revolution might have ended in the autumn of 1776. Having been bestowed precious time by Glover's ingenious defensive stands, Washington's army miraculously and narrowly survived the New York Campaign to shortly escape south to New Jersey and eventually to strike back before the year's end. Washington was then able to reverse the tide of the revolution at Trenton and Princeton in less than three months partly because Glover and his Massachusetts Brigade ensured that the Continental Army yet remained a viable fighting force to cross the Delaware River, that Glover orchestrated with his usual skill like the withdrawal off Long Island, strike back with spirit, and win the December 26, 1776, battle that changed the course of the American Revolution. But in truth, the beginning of the reversing of the revolution's course began by Colonel Glover at Pell's Point.

With more than six thousand men who were unable to crush Glover's 750-man brigade and push it aside to continue west to strike Washington's army during its retreat not far from the Hudson River, Howe missed one of the war's best opportunities to destroy the Continental Army and end the revolution in one masterful strike. General Howe proved wholly unable to quickly and easily push aside the Massachusetts men on a hot October day in Westchester County as he had fully anticipated and expected without reservation, which would have been the key to winning a decisive victory over Washington's reeling army.[132]

The Forgotten Saving of Washington's Army

In his fine book *The Battle for New York*, Barnet Schecter has been one of the few modern historians to have placed this crucial battle in a proper historical perspective: "the tremendous strategic significance of the battle is beyond dispute. By obstructing the British advance for a day, Glover and his men helped Washington win the race to White Plains [and] it seems in retrospect that no general could have done better than [Colonel] Glover" on this day of destiny in Westchester

County.[133] However, perhaps Washington's chief engineer, Colonel Rufus Putnam, said it best in regard to the supreme importance of the army having safely reached White Plains, after a long and miserable retreat north that took far longer than anyone had anticipated: "we arrived at White Plains . . . and thus was the American army saved (by an interposing providence from a probable total destruction)."[134]

Indeed, despite having been forced to forsake the field of strife, Glover and his Massachusetts soldiers had actually won (although not technically but in regard to strategic results) one of the war's most one-sided, especially in terms of the ratio in regard to the odds and casualties inflicted on an overpowering opponent, successes during one of the bloodiest battles of the American Revolution: a long-forgotten reality revealed to have been true by an ample amount of primary evidence and documentation utilized in full in this book about this decisive battle that helped to decide America's destiny and future. Consequently, the Battle of Pell's Point should be rightly considered by Americans and historians as a rare American success story in the difficult and tragic year of 1776 before the Battle of Trenton, because it resulted in nothing less than the timely saving of Washington's army from destruction: hence, one of the most decisive battles of the American Revolution and in world history. A letter from a member of General Charles Lee's Division emphasized the extent of what was actually a sparkling success on October 18: "had we been reinforced with half their Number might have totally defeated them."[135]

This revealing letter, which was most likely written by a Continental officer, well summarized the ebb and flow of this forgotten battle of such critical importance, when so much was at stake for Washington, the army, and America: on the morning of October 18

> we were alarmed [by the news that] the Enemy landed at Rodman's Pt (a place about four miles from our Encampment) with their whole Force. The Brigade under the command of Col. Glover, consisting of about Seven hundred Men [and] We marched down towds the place where the Enemy were

advancing with a body of Sixteen Thousd with a very large Artillery. The first attack was made by a small party of their advanced guard, which were effectually routed & forced to retreat to the main body; who when they came up were fired upon by two [of Glover's] Reg[iments] advantageously posted by Col. Glover & Major Lee [who returned from Lee's headquarters at some point after having warned of the landing and "who behaved gallantly"] . . . which bro't many of them to the Ground. Thus we continued fighting them & retreating the whole Afternoon until they came to a Stand, where they now remain . . . Our men behaved like Soldiers, conformed to the Orders of their Officers & retreated in grand Order [and] As to [the enemy's] Courage, the whole Body of 16 Thousd were forced to retreat by the first of a single [Massachusetts] Regiment, & many of them old Troops. The fourth Regt [the "King's Own"] was one that run.[136]

This proud member of Charles Lee's Division then penned in his letter how: "The next day G[eneral] Lee (under whose commd we are] came & publicly returned his Thanks to Col. Glover & the Officers and Sold[iers] under his Commd for their noble, spirited, & soldier-like conduct during the Battle" on bloody October 18, 1776.[137] All in all, the dramatic showdown at the Battle of Pell's Point was not only the finest day for Colonel John Glover and his men, but also for America and its amateur army.

Unfortunately, the only known surviving Hessian account of the battle has come from the diary of Captain Andreas Wiederhold, of the Knyphausen Regiment, which was part of Major General Werner von Mirbach's Brigade of three regiments, Heister's First Division:

The enemy, in possession of the opposite shore, which they were entrenching, fled their posts as soon as our cannons, on land as well as on the frigate, opened fire. As soon as we had been carried across, which occurred in the presence of [Admiral Richard, who was the brother of William Howe], Lord Howe, we were formed and marched toward the hills. Then a battalion of [Massachusetts] riflemen, who lay hidden behind a stonework and close to our direction of march, let loose a heavy and unexpected discharge of weapons on the front of an English Light Infantry battalion, which had not taken the precaution to sending out patrols to the side. The riflemen then fled at a gallop. However, the result was only the death of one [British] sergeant and the wounding of two privates. Next the enemy had fortified the hills opposite us and greeted us with some cannon fire, which however, did no harm as it was fired above us. I skirmished with the enemy, for which I sent one of them into the next world with my rifle. We lay here for still another night, without tents. The region was called East Chester.[138]

But most important of all, because of an ingenious battle plan based on innovative tactics that had resulted in the desperately-needed "obstructing the British advance for a day, Glover and his men helped Washington win the race to White Plains."[139] By the narrowest of margins while retreating north thanks to Colonel Glover's masterful battle plan, Washington's army was able to slip past Howe's mighty invasion force and reach the safety of White Plains. Indeed, in the understated words of one historian, "by delaying the British advance Glover's brigade had bought Washington precious time to withdraw the patriot army . . . Glover's plucky initiative and his men's gallantry may well have averted catastrophe for Washington's army."[140]

For this reason, General Washington only belatedly bestowed recognition to Glover and his men for saving the day. In his orderly book, Major William Raymond Lee recorded Washington's forgotten words about the battle's importance:

The hurried Situation of the Gen. the two last days having prevented him from paying that attention Col. Glover and the Officers and Soldiers who were with him in the Skirmish on Friday last, their merit and good behavior deserved. He flatters himself that his thanks, though delayed be acceptable to them, as they are offered with great Sincerity & Cordiality—at the same time he hopes that every other part of the Army will do their duty with equal Bravery & Zeal whenever calld upon, & neither danger nor difficulties nor Hardships will discourage Soldiers engaged in the cause of Liberty, & while we are contending for all that free men hold dear and Valuable.[141]

In an army—like all armies throughout history and to this day—in which the usual Machiavellian games of backdoor politics, including backstabbing, slander, and endless fawning upon superiors to ease into their good graces, Colonel John Glover proudly stood apart in his typical independent fashion like during his brilliant orchestration of the Battle of Pell's Point. Like in civilian life back in the fishing port of Marblehead that overlooked a magnificent harbor of blue, he had always allowed his own skills and achievements to rise to the fore and speak for themselves. Glover was the antithesis of the typical Continental colonel and brigade commander, because he was the most unorthodox and versatile commander in Washington's army and, appropriately, he commanded the unconventional and can-do regiments in Washington's army of mostly rustic revolutionaries: the exact qualities necessary for both a colonel and his undersized brigade to do the impossible against the odds at Pell's Point on a pleasant autumn day in New York, when so much was at stake for the young American nation and a people's republic conceived in liberty.

Clearly, Colonel Glover and his mostly Marblehead regiment were a perfect fit and match for not only each other but also for the daunting challenge of meeting Howe's invasion head-on during the most crucial of situations on Friday October 18, 1776, when they were on their own in a do or die in a dramatic showdown of extreme importance. Indeed, only unorthodox, free-thinking, and unconventional men, like Glover, were capable of rising to the fore under the most disadvantageous of situations on the battlefield, while outfoxing and outfighting some of the world's best military thinkers of conventional military schools across Europe and who commanded a seemingly invincible army that had yet to lose a battle in the New York Campaign. It was precisely such rare qualities and abilities seldom seen in any traditional army that had allowed Colonel Glover and his outgunned men to repeatedly save the life of a conventional army, which had little, if any, chance of succeeding at anything other than hastily retreating before a superior opponent like throughout the course of the New York Campaign. And significantly, if Glover and his men had failed to rise to three stern challenges of supreme importance, especially at the Battle of Pell's Point, from late August to late December 1776, America would have certainly lost the war and its desperate bid for independence to forever change the course of world history.

Epilogue

After his fragile health, fortune, and most cherished hopes for a brighter personal future had been destroyed by the long years of arduous service in the cause of America's independence, John Glover, who had won a coveted general's rank in early 1777 that was certainly well-deserved, discovered to his shock that he faced a most painful readjustment to civilian life in the seafaring port of Marblehead, the once prosperous commercial center which had been reduced to poverty by the war. Like so many hardened veterans of this lengthy war of attrition, Glover attempted to readjust to the relative boredom and mundane realities of civilian life in a transition that was neither easy or painless for him, after years of battling for the great dream of liberty.

In fact, Glover's return to civilian life was a most difficult transition for the dynamic and gifted man who had played such stirring roles in having repeatedly saved Washington's army during the long struggle against Britain, especially in the crucial turning point year of 1776: rising magnificently to the fore in orchestrating the risky evacuation across the East River from Long Island to Manhattan and the Battle of Pell's Point when everything had been at stake, and then in serving as the driving force behind Washington's dramatic crossing of the Delaware River to surprise the Hessian brigade at Trenton, where the commander in chief finally won his first victory in this war. Because his first wife, Hannah Gale, had died in mid-November 1778 to leave a giant hole in his heart and soul, Glover became the sole provider and emotional foundation for his large family, which he adored so exceedingly that he considered it a distinct personal "weakness" (which was one of the very few that he possessed) after the war's conclusion.[1]

Writing in a late January 1781 letter, Glover described the sad plight of his family, barely two years after Hannah's tragic death:

> My helpless orphan children [and] being all very young, and by no means capable of taking care of themselves, except a daughter of eighteen, who has the charge of eight others, a burden much too great for so young a person; and what makes it exceedingly more so, they live in a seaport town [of Marblehead], where the necessaries of life are very dear and hard to come at, even were they possessed of the means, which I present . . . they are not.[2]

After the war and like in having repeatedly saved Washington's army on three different turning point occasions from late August to late December 1776, Glover devoted all his tireless energies and efforts to faithfully sustaining "my little flock," as he called his nine beloved children, in Marblehead during the difficult years after having reaped so many outstanding successes that played key roles in saving the day and the winning of American independence. Clearly and perhaps out of a sense of guilt for his long absence from home in fighting his country's battles, Glover was determined to make it all up to his children while serving as one of Washington's top and best lieutenants, because of so many missed birthdays and children growing up from infants to young adults, when their father had been absent risking his own life at obscure places like Pell's Point.[3]

But unfortunately, and unlike during the revolutionary struggle, Glover's best efforts in a postwar Marblehead were largely thwarted because of what the war's heavy burdens and horrors had done to his heart and soul and his declining finances to darken his future. His sailing ships, like the schooner *Hannah*—named in honor of his beloved wife when she had been alive and the first ship of Washington's infant navy—had been destroyed, and his fortune, acquired through so much hard work and determination for decades, had been ruined by this lengthy war.

Ironically, a self-made man who had long worked as hard in peacetime as he fought British and Hessian soldiers at Pell's Point and other fields of strife, Glover's tragic road to ruin actually began with the revolution's beginning. He had early abandoned his thriving business ventures and future prospects as a member of Marblehead's social and political elite merely for the honor of leading the Marblehead regiment to join General Washington's army in a holy war against the British and King George III. Out of his own deep pockets and taken from the mouths of his many children because of urgent necessity of answering the patriotic call and pressing wartime requirements, Glover's hard-earned money had early paid for the enlistment of his Marblehead soldiers and the equipping of these elite fighting men, who became Washington's most versatile and dependable troops, especially in 1776. As a cruel fate would have it, Glover was not reimbursed for his considerable financial commitment and sacrifice, and his large family suffered accordingly, while ensuring a bleak future in Marblehead.

Even more, Glover's once-robust health had been destroyed by the war's excessive demands and some of the most arduous campaigns of Washington's army, including the key winter campaign of 1776–1777 that saw sparking victories won at Trenton and Princeton. As a disillusioned Glover lamented in a sad mid-May 1778 letter to General Washington of a tragic reality and one that he had never believed possible at the war's beginning, "When I entered the service in 1775 I had as good a constitution as any man of my age [early forties], but it's now broken and shattered to pieces."[4]

Therefore, even before the war's end in 1783, he had been forced to virtually start life anew in Marblehead but with more pressing responsibilities than ever before and with a large family of nine children to support and with no wife to provide assistance to him, after he had played such a key role in ensuring the independence of a new nation that now lived on as the world's newest republic in part because of his timely contributions in the remarkable year of 1776, especially at Pell's Point and both before and after October 18. Without his characteristic vigor or energy that had once taken him far out to sea year after year and then across the Delaware River on a stormy December night and saddled with the formidable task of rebuilding his lost fortune without a military pension or land bounty in payment for his many years of faithful service, Glover could only survive on a meager subsistence as a lowly cobbler, which had been his first vocation as a young man, during the difficult decades after the American Revolution.[5]

What made Glover's personal predicament such a stiff challenge was because the war had ravished Marblehead and its people in the most insidious fashion. Few towns in America suffered or lost more as a result of its considerable efforts to support the revolution than the once-thriving port of Marblehead. In the dimming light of harsh New England winters when the icy winds sweeping off the Atlantic howled through Marblehead's snow-covered crooked streets and cut like a knife, Glover worked late at night by candlelight in repairing leather shoes of the townsfolk year after year in a paradoxical life that had strangely come full circle. At this time, the glory won by Glover and his men at Pell's Point seemed like a distant dream that was more unreal than real.

Despite the stiff odds and like during the crucial showdown at Pell's Point, he attempted to do the best that he could in a now-impoverished port town which once had been the prosperous cod fishing capital of America, while working as hard as possible to earn a meager living year after year in a struggle for simple survival, which far outlasted the long difficult years of the American Revolution. Unlike in that epic struggle for liberty in which a new nation had been born and then won its independence on the battlefield during a conflict in which he had repeatedly reaped glory, this was one personal fight that John Glover could not win in the end, because the obstacles were too steep and the odds too great, despite his best efforts to succeed.

But year after year after having been just barely able to scratch out a subsistence living as a cobbler of lower-middle-class status after having descended from his once lofty position as a member of the

"Codfish aristocracy" in prosperous prerevolutionary days, Glover at least gained a measure of supreme personal satisfaction in the end. He was able to find a rare and lasting measure of inner peace—which everyone hopes to find in life but seldom ever obtains despite many years of fruitless searching—and personal contentment, when he found the time to contemplate upon what all that he and his seafarers and fishermen had so often accomplished against the odds in the eventful year of 1776 to truly astound both friend and foe. As he penned in a letter with a sense of an intimate understanding of the endless cycles and twisting contours of history, including how the amazing success of the American Revolution, in which he had repeatedly played as a lead character in multiple stirring roles in 1776, had changed the world forever: "After a complete conquest over our enemies, to look back and reflect upon the toil & danger we surmounted to obtain victory, must afford us the greatest satisfaction & compel the world to admire the patience & firmness of the Conquerors, as well as applaud their bravery."[6]

With his once-robust health ruined by the war's stern demands when in a deplorable situation that only grew worse in his declining years because of the natural aging process, Glover would not live to see the turn of the century. But before he died at age sixty-four on January 30, 1797, and was laid to eternal rest beside his beloved first wife, Hannah Gale, in the Old Burial Hill—perhaps the most picturesque cemetery in New England—which overlooked the sparkling blue waters of Marblehead Harbor and while performing the mind-numbing drudgery of repairing seemingly endless shoes of the men, women, and children of Marblehead year after dreary year, he thought back on his glory days, when he had been a younger man and before so many of his life's once vivid personal dreams and bright ambitions had been shattered forever by life's cruelties and unfairness. And none of Glover's military feats that he recalled with so much fondness after the war had been more impressive and important— even more than the evacuation of Washington's forces off Long Island or the icy Delaware River crossing before Washington's great victory at Trenton—than his defiant defensive stand in Westchester County against impossible odds, while facing a massive British-Hessian invasion on his own, which saved General Washington's army and the American Revolution. And thanks in part to what he and his band of Massachusetts Continental soldiers had repeatedly accomplished against the odds during the struggle for independence in only a few months during 1776, the picturesque home port of Marblehead was never attacked by either British warships or armies and remained free from bitter retribution.

Ensuring a warming fondness and inner glow that cheered his sagging spirits during the steady physical decline of his twilight years, Glover thought about what had exactly happened that October 18, 1776 day and its long-term repercussions when he had boldly led his 750-man Massachusetts brigade on his own without any hope for much-needed reinforcements against a mighty invasion force of the finest British and Hessian soldiers in America pouring north up the Pell's Point Peninsula and then reaped a most improbable success to guarantee the continued survival and existence of the infant Continental Army and the United States of America.

When no one had believed that such a battlefield success of keeping thousands of well-trained invaders at bay and far away from Washington's withdrawing army could possibly be reaped in such a seemingly impossible situation—any kind of positive outcome seemed utterly inconceivable and unimaginable to one and all except for Glover—on fateful October 18, he had achieved the improbable by creating a masterful tactical plan of a defense in depth to slow down the advance of more than six thousand Hessian and British soldiers in Westchester County. Quite simply, he and his small New England brigade "saved the American army from encirclement and complete destruction." Therefore, even in old age when his fortunes had declined so dramatically, Glover felt great comfort with what he had achieved during his eventful life and what he had accomplished against the odds at an obscure place called Pell's Point, which overshadowed—at least for a moment in his troubled and overly-burdened mind when he was saddled with seemingly endless responsibilities and heavy burdens—the exceedingly high personal price that he and his family had paid for the survival of a new nation conceived in liberty during the exceedingly difficult years after the war.[7]

In a heartfelt letter and using words seldom, if ever, put to paper by him during the course of the American Revolution, General Washington had only belatedly given Colonel Glover his just due more than six months after the October 18 battle was fought, after gaining more knowledge about what had really happened at Pell's Point. He, consequently, wrote with great sincerity to the dynamic Marblehead leader, who had been one of his finest top lieutenants during the American Revolution's darkest days, especially during the turning point year of 1776: "But I think I may tell you without flattery, that I know of no man better qualified than you to conduct a brigade."[8]

On that unforgettable day in Westchester County, New York, when the life or death of Washington's army hung in the balance and as he revealed in an October 22, 1776, letter written only four days after the battle without a hint of hyperbole, Glover described how he and his Massachusetts men had saved the day at a critical time when "my country, my honour, my own life, and every thing that was dear, appeared at that critical moment [on October 18] to be at stake." And the ever-modest Glover was one who was never guilty of exaggeration, especially in regard to what he and his Massachusetts soldiers had accomplished at the Battle of Pell's Point, when General Howe had landed a mighty invasion force in Washington's rear, which today certainly "deserves to be ranked among the more decisive battles of the Revolutionary War."[9]

This undeniable, but long-forgotten, reality was only belatedly recently recognized by a Bronx Borough historian, who perhaps best placed Colonel Glover's contribution on October 18 in a proper historical perspective: "I feel an indebtedness of John Glover and I think all Americans should because, very simply, without him we wouldn't be Americans" today. And historian Lloyd Ultan additionally emphasized without any exaggeration how, "It was an extremely significant battle [because] If that battle did not take place, the American Revolution would have been over."[10]

Indeed, during the fall of 2001 and not long after the devastating terrorist attacks on New York City, historian Roberta Hershenson asked an on-target question that summarized the importance of Colonel Glover's tactical masterpiece, when no other American troops were available to oppose the landing of thousands of General Howe's troops, and its far-reaching strategic consequences that stemmed from the hard-fought Battle at Pell's Point, which helped to change the course of history in a decisive way on October 18, 1776: "Would there be a United States without the battle of Pell's Point . . . maybe not" at all.[11] In the end, the Battle of Pell's Point was one of the most decisive showdowns in the annals of the American Revolution and America's creation story and one that ensured the long life of the United States of America.

Endnotes

1. George Athan Billias, *General John Glover and His Marblehead Mariners* (New York: Henry Holt and Company, 1960), pp. 110–111.
2. Barnet Schecter, *The Battle For New York* (New York: Walker and Company, 2002), pp. 229–230.
3. Edward G. Lengel, *General George Washington, A Military Life* (New York: Random House, 2005), p. 161.
4. Troyer Steele Anderson, *The Command of the Howe Brothers During the American Revolution* (Cranbury, N.J.: The Scholar's Bookshelf, 2005), p. 187.
5. Ibid., pp. 1–7, 187.
6. Sharon Seitz, "George Washington May Have Made Par Here," *New York Times*, May 2, 2004.
7. *Maryland Gazette*, Annapolis, Maryland, December 5, 1776.
8. David McCulloch, *1776* (New York: Simon and Schuster, 2005), p. 212; Russell W. Knight, editor, *General John Glover's Letterbook, 1776–1777* (Salem, Massachusetts: Essex Institute, 1967), p. xiii; Russell F. Weigley, *The American Way of War: A History of United States Military Strategy and Policy* (Bloomington: Indiana University Press, 1977), pp. 9–10.
9. Richard F. Snow, Review of *The Winter Soldiers, American Heritage* Magazine, December 1973.
10. Lawrence E. Babits, *A Devil of a Whipping: The Battle of Cowpens* (Chapel Hill: University of North Carolina Press), pp. xiii–160; *New York Times*, August 10, 1901; *Maryland Gazette*, December 5, 1776; Thomas J. Fleming, *1776 Year of Illusions* (New York: W. W. Norton & Company, Inc., 1975), pp. 159–160, 328–329, 341–342, 367, 370–371; Barnet Schecter, *The Battle for New York* (New York: Walker and Company, 2002), pp. 4–5, 225–230.
11. *Maryland Gazette*, December 5, 1776; *New York Times*, August 10, 1901 and January 4, 1902; Babits, *A Devil of a Whipping*, pp. xiii–160.

Chapter 1

1. Schecter, *The Battle for New York*, pp. 4–5; Daniel Vickers, editor, *The Autobiography of Ashley Bowen, 1728–1813* (Peterborough: Broadview Press, 2016), pp. 9, 12–14.

2. Schecter, *The Battle for New York*, pp. 85, 92; Marcus Cunliffe, *George Washington, Man and Monument* (New York: Mentor Books, 1958), p. 74; Phillip Thomas Tucker, *How the Irish Won the American Revolution* (New York: Skyhorse Publishing, 2015), pp. 229–232.

3. Henry P. Johnston, *The Campaign of 1776 around New York and Brooklyn* (Cranbury: Scholar's Bookshelf, 2005), p. 241

4. John J. Gallagher, *The Battle of Brooklyn 1776* (New York: Castle Books, 2002), pp. 12–14.

5. Charles Bracelen Flood, *Rise, and Fight Again: Perilous Times Along the Road to Independence* (New York: Dodd, Mead and Company, 1976), p. 86; Johnston, *The Campaign of 1776 around New York and Brooklyn*, pp. 132–133.

6. Johnston, *The Campaign of 1776 around New York and Brooklyn*, p. 132.

7. L. G. Shreve, *Tench Tilghman, The Life and Times of Washington's Aide-de-Camp* (Centreville: Tidewater Publishers, 1982), p. 64.

8. *Pennsylvania Journal*, Philadelphia, Pennsylvania, August 28, 1776.

9. Johnston, *The Campaign of 1776 around New York and Brooklyn*, p. 67.

10. Ibid., p. 131.

11. Ibid., p. 76.

12. F. A. Gardner, *Glover's Marblehead Regiment in the War of the Revolution* (Salem: The Salem Press Company, 1908), p. 1; Christopher L. Ward, *The Delaware Continentals, 1776–1783* (Cranbury, N.J.: Scholar's Bookshelf, 2005), p. 63; Flood, *Rise, and Fight Again*, p. 86; Willard M. Wallace, *Appeal to Arms, Military History of the American Revolution* (New York: The New York Times Book Company, 1951), p. 114; O'Donnell, *The Indispensables*, p. 7.

13. O'Donnell, *The Indispensables*, p. 247; Gardner, *Glover's Marblehead Regiment in the War of the Revolution*, p. 6.

14. Don Cook, *The Long Fuse, How England Lost the American Colonies 1760–1785* (New York: The Atlantic Monthly Press, 1995), Douglas Southall Freeman, *Washington* (New York: Simon and Schuster, 1995), p. 292; O'Donnell, *The Indispensables*, p. 251.

15. Joseph Plum Martin, *A Narrative of a Revolutionary Soldier* (New York: Penguin Books, 2001) pp. v, 31.

16. Joseph Lee Boyle, *From Redcoat to Rebel: The Thomas Sullivan Journal* (Westminister, Md: Heritage Books, Inc., 2004), pp. 54–55.

17. Upham, *A Memoir of General John Glover*, p. 17.

18. Fleming, *Now We Are Enemies*, p. 41.

19. Ibid.

20. Upham, *A Memoir of General John Glover*, p. 4; Ronald N. Tagney, *The World Turned Upside Down: Essex County During America's Turbulent Years, 1763–1790* (West Newbury: Essex County History, 1989), p. 273.

21. Cunliffe, *George Washington*, p. 80.

22. Heath, *Memoirs*, p. 52; O'Donnell, *The Indispensables*, p. 251.

23. Phillip Thomas Tucker, *George Washington's Surprise Attack: A New Look at the Battle That Decided the Fate of America* (New York: Skyhorse Publishing, 2014), pp. 8–12; Graydon, *Memoirs*, p. 147; Gardner, *Glover's Marblehead Regiment in the War of the Revolution*, pp. 2–3; Vickers, ed., *The Autobiography of Ashley Bowen*, pp. 12–14; O'Donnell, *The Indispensables*, pp. 4–6; Virginia C. Gamage and Priscilla S. Lord, *The Lure of Marblehead* (Marblehead: Marblehead Publications, 1973), pp. 2–3, 5, 7, 13–14, 23, 28–29, 31, 44; Nick Bryant, *When America Stopped Being Great: A History of the Present* (New York: Bloomsbury Continuum, 2021), p. 187.

24. Graydon, *Memoirs*, pp. 148–149.

25. Ibid., p. 164.

26. Upham, *A Memoir of General John Glover*, p. 14.

27. O'Donnell, *The Indispensables*, pp. 253–254.

28. Freeman, *Washington*, p. 293.

29. Schecter, *The Battle for New York*, pp. 1–9; Russell Shorto, *The Island at the Center of the World* (New York: Vintage Books, 2005), pp. 1–2, 8.

30. Shreve, *Tench Tilghman*, pp. 67–68.

31. Schecter, *The Battle for New York*, pp. 1–2.

32. Upham, *A Memoir of General John Glover*, p. 17.

33. O'Donnell, *The Indispensables*, p. 250.

34. Ibid., pp. 250–251; Mark Mayo Boatner, *Encyclopedia of the American Revolution* (New York: David McKay Publishing Company, 1966), p. 799.

35. O'Donnell, *The Indispensables*, p. 254.

36. Ibid., pp. 247–271; Freeman, *Washington*, p. 296.

37. Moncrieff J. Spear, *To End the War at White Plains* (Baltimore, Maryland: Literary Press, Inc., 2002), pp. 2–3; Schecter, *The Battle for New York*, p. 5.

38. Washington Irving, *George Washington: A Biography* (New York: Da Capo, 1994), p. 276.
39. Ward, *The Delaware Continentals, 1776–1783*, p. 73; Schecter, *The Battle for New York*, p. 75; Knight, ed., *General John Glover's Letterbook*, p. ix; William Heath Biography, William Heath Papers, Massachusetts Historical Society, Boston, Massachusetts.
40. O'Donnell, *The Indispensables*, p. 257.
41. Alden, *A History of the American Revolution*, p. 272.
42. Ibid.
43. Fleming, *1776*, p. 366.
44. Ibid., pp. 348, 366.
45. Ward, *The Delaware Continentals, 1776–1783*, p. 76; Schecter, *The Battle for New York*, p. 4.
46. Spear, *To End the War at White Plains*, p. 6.
47. Michael Williams Craig, *General Edward Hand: Winter's Doctor* (Lancaster, Pennsylvania: private printing,1984), pp. 1–34.
48. Fleming, *1776*, p. 366; Spears, *To End the War at White Plains*, p. 9.
49. Boatner, *Encyclopedia of the American Revolution*, pp. 1099–1100; Schecter, *The Battle for New York*, pp. 221–222; Fleming, *1776*, p. 367.
50. Freeman, *Washington*, pp. 293, 297–298.
51. Ward, *The Delaware Continentals, 1776–1783*, p. 76; Shreve, *Tench Tilghman*, p. 73.
52. Johnston, *The Campaign of 1776 around New York and Brooklyn*, p. 267.
53. Schecter, *The Battle for New York*, pp. 221–222; Alden, *A History of the American Revolution*, p. 271; Fleming, *1776*, p. 367.
54. Alden, *A History of the American Revolution*, p. 272; Fleming, *1776*, p. 367; Spear, *To End the War at White Plains*, p. 6.
55. *Maryland Gazette*, April 24, 1777.
56. Ibid., November 6, 1776.
57. Freeman, *Washington*, pp. 298–299; Fleming, *1776*, p. 367.
58. Freeman, *Washington*, p. 299.
59. Heath, *Memoirs*, pp. 59–60; Craig, *General Edward Hand*, p. 35.
60. Ward, *The Delaware Continentals, 1776–1783*, p. 76.
61. Spear, *To End the War at White Plains*, p. 6; Craig, *General Edward Hand*, p. 53.
62. Boyle, *From Redcoat to Rebel*, p. 61; O'Donnell, *The Indispensables*, p. 262.

63. Ward, *The Delaware Continentals, 1776–1783*, p. 76; Craig, *General Edward Hand*, p. 53.
64. *Maryland Gazette*, October 31, 1776.
65. Boyle, *From Redcoat to Rebel*, p. 61.
66. Heath, *Memoirs*, pp. 62, 64; Craig, *General Edward Hand*, p. 53.
67. Edward G. Lengel, *General George Washington: A Military Life* (New York: Random House, 2005), pp. 160–161; O'Donnell, *The Indispensables*, p. 263.

Chapter 2

1. *Maryland Gazette*, December 5, 1776.
2. Ibid.; Gardner, *Glover's Marblehead Regiment in the War of the Revolution*, p. 6.
3. Martin, *A Narrative of a Revolutionary Soldier*, p. 44.
4. Irving, *George Washington*, p. 275.
5. *Maryland Gazette*, October 31, 1776.
6. Schecter, *The Battle for New York*, pp. 224–225; Ward, *The Delaware Continentals, 1776–1783*, pp. 25, 77; Lengel, *General George Washington*, p. 161; Tagney, *The World Turned Upside Down*, p. 276; O'Donnell, *The Indispensables*, p. 264.
7. Schecter, *The Battle for New York*, p. 225.
8. Ibid.
9. Ward, *The Delaware Continentals, 1776–1783*, p. 25.
10. Schecter, *The Battle for New York*, p. 225; Ward, *The Delaware Continentals, 1776–1783*, p. 77; Lengel, *General George Washington*, p. 161.
11. Ezra Stiles, *The Literary Diary of Ezra Stiles*, volume 2 (2 volumes, New York: Charles Scribner's Sons, 1901), p. 86.
12. Wallace, *Appeal to Arms*, p. 115.
13. Fleming, *1776*, p. 368; Ward, *The Delaware Continentals, 1776–1783*, p. 78; Spear, *To End the War at White Plains*, p. 29; Martin, *A Narrative of a Revolutionary Soldier*, pp. 44–46.
14. Schecter, *The Battle for New York*, pp. 222, 225–226.
15. Ibid., pp. 225–226; O'Donnell, *The Indispensables*, p. 264.
16. Freeman, *Washington*, p. 299; Ward, *The Delaware Continentals, 1776–1783*, p. 78; Schecter, *The Battle for New York*, p. 79; Gardner, *Glover's Marblehead Regiment in the War of the Revolution*, p. 7.

17. William Heath, *Memoirs of Major-General William Heath* (New York: Arno Press, 1968), p. 63.

18. Ibid.; Schecter, *The Battle for New York*, p. 226; Ketchum, *Winter Soldiers*, p. 106; *New York Times*, August 14, 1921.

19. Freeman, *Washington*, p. 298; *New York Times*, August 14, 1921; Stiles, *The Literary Diary of Ezra Stiles*, vol. 2, p. 87.

20. Bolton, *The Private Soldier Under Washington*, p. 233.

21. Thomas Fleming, *Now We Are Enemies* (New York: St. Martin's Press, 1960), pp. 17–18; Boatner, *Encyclopedia of the American Revolution*, pp. 902–903; Cunliffe, *George Washington*, p. 75.

22. *Maryland Gazette*, December 5, 1776; Stiles, *The Literary Diary of Ezra Stiles*, vol. 2, p. 86.

23. Schecter, *The Battle for New York*, p. 226; Graydon, *Memoirs*, pp. 148–149, 164; Freeman, *Washington*, p. 299; Stiles, *The Literary Diary of Ezra Stiles*, vol. 2, p. 86; Roads, *History and Traditions of Marblehead*, p. 169; Heath, *Memoirs*, p. 76; Stiles, *The Literary Diary of Ezra Stiles*, vol. 2, p. 87; Tagney, *The World Turned Upside Down*, pp. 276–277.

24. Freeman, *Washington*, p. 266.

25. Stiles, *The Literary Diary of Ezra Stiles*, vol. 2, p. 85; Rick Atkinson, *The British Are Coming: The War for America, Lexington to Princeton, 1775–1777* (New York: Henry Holt and Company, 2019), p. 330.

26. Stiles, *The Literary Diary of Ezra Stiles*, vol. 2, p. 297; Flexner, *Washington*, pp. 62–63.

27. Flexner, *Washington*, pp. 62–63.

28. Wallace, *An Appeal to Arms*, p. 115.

29. O'Donnell, *The Indispensables*, p. 255.

30. Cunliffe, *George Washington*, p. 74.

31. Cunliffe, *George Washington*, p. 54.

32. Johnston, *The Campaign of 1776 around New York and Brooklyn*, p. 267.

33. Schecter, *The Battle for New York*, p. 226; Heath, *Memoirs*, p. 63.

34. Upham, *A Memoir of Gen. John Glover*, p. 21; Richard A. Brayall, *Washington's Savior: General John Glover and the American Revolution* (Bowie: Heritage Books, 2013), pp. xiii, 84; Heath, *Memoirs*, p. 63; Gamage and Lord, *The Lure of Marblehead*, pp. 33–34; Gardner, *Glover's Marblehead Regiment in the War of the Revolution*, pp. 3, 8.

35. Schecter, *The Battle for New York*, p. 187; Atkinson, *The British Are Coming*, p. 440.

36. Upham, *A Memoir of Gen. John Glover*, pp. 2–6; Knight, ed., *General John Glover Letterbook*, p. xv; Gamage and Lord, *The Lure of Marblehead*, p. 33.

37. Sanborn, *Gen. John Glover and His Marblehead Regiment*, p. 35; Knight, ed., *General John Glover Letterbook*, p. xv; Gamage and Lord, *The Lure of Marblehead*, p. 9.

38. Upham, *A Memoir of Gen. John Glover*, p. 24; Knight, ed., *General John Glover Letterbook*, pp. xii, xiv.

39. Fleming, *Now We Are Enemies*, p. 7.

40. Knight, ed., *General John Glover Letterbook*, p. xviii; O'Donnell, *The Indispensables*, pp. 8–9.

41. Upham, *A Memoir of Gen. John Glover*, p. 38; Knight, ed., *General John Letterbook*, p. x; Brayall, *Washington's Savior*, pp. xi–xiii, 27–31, 33–60; Vickers, ed., *The Autobiography of Ashley Brown*, p. 9; O'Donnell, *The Indispensables*, p. 9.

42. Knight, *General John Glover Letterbook*, p. x.

43. Ward, *The Delaware Continentals, 1776–1783*, p. 71.

44. Ibid., pp. 490–491.

45. Ibid., pp. 71, 490–491; O'Donnell, *The Indispensables*, p. 263.

46. O'Donnell, *The Indispensables*, pp. 6–7, 352; Graydon, *Memoirs*, p. 149.

47. Gamage and Lord, *Marblehead*, pp. 26–27; Sylviana A. Diouf, *Servants of Allah: African Muslims Enslaved in the Americas* (New York: New York University Press, 1998), pp. 4–48; Hammond Innes, *The Conquistadors* (New York: Alfred A. Knopf, 1969), pp. 12–21.

48. Graydon, *Memoirs*, pp. 25–26, 77–78; W. Jeffrey Bolster, *Black Jacks: African American Seamen in the Age of Sail* (Cambridge, Mass.: Harvard University Press, 1997), p. 28.

49. Gamage and Lord, *Marblehead*, pp. 26–27; Bolster, *Black Jacks*, pp. 3–9, 11–12, 15, 27–28, 68–70, 75; Billias, *General John Glover and His Marblehead Mariners*, p. 69; O'Donnell, *The Indispensables*, pp. xii, 6–7.

50. Billias, *General John Glover and His Marblehead Mariners*, pp. 68–69.

51. John U. Rees, *"They Were Good Soldiers": African-Americans Serving in the Continental Army, 1775–1783* (Warwick: Helion and Company Limited, 2019), p. 51; O'Donnell, *The Indispensables*, p. 352.

52. O'Donnell, *The Indispensables*, p. 352.

Chapter 3

1. Alden, *A History of the American Revolution*, p. 271.
2. Benton Rain Patterson, *Washington and Cornwallis: The Battle for America, 1775–1783* (New York: Taylor Trade Publishing, 2004), p. 62.
3. Boyle, *From Redcoat to Rebel*, pp. 60–61.
4. Alden, *A History of the American Revolution*, p. 272; Fleming, *1776*, p. 367; Fleming, *Now We Are Enemies*, pp. 182–183.
5. *Maryland Gazette*, April 24, 1777.
6. Fleming, *1776*, p. 367; Gardner, *Glover's Marblehead Regiment in the War of the Revolution*, pp. 6–7.
7. David L. Jacobson, *Essays on the American Revolution* (New York: Holt, Rinehart and Winston, Inc., 1970), p. 189.
8. Upham, *A Memoir of General John Glover*, p. 24.
9. Alden, *A History of the American Revolution*, p. 272; Weigley, *The American Way of War*, p. 9; Fleming, *1776*, p. 367.
10. Fleming, *1776*, p. 367.
11. Schecter, *The Battle for New York*, pp. 225–226.
12. Ward, *The Delaware Continentals*, p. 77.
13. Ibid.
14. Weigley, *The American War of War*, p. 10.
15. Boatner, *Encyclopedia of the American Revolution*, pp. 335, 904–905; Freeman, *Washington*, p. 290.
16. William Baldwin October 20–23, 1776, letter to wife, William Baldwin Papers Collection, Harvard University Library, Cambridge, Massachusetts; Gardner, *Glover's Marblehead Regiment in the War of the Revolution*, p. 7; Spear, *To End the War at White Plains*, p. 17; Heath, *Memoirs*, p. 65.
17. William Baldwin October 20–23, 1776, letter to wife, William Baldwin Papers Collection, Harvard University Library, Cambridge, Massachusetts; Hufeland, *Westchester County During the American Revolution*, p. 115; Ketchum, *The Winter Soldiers*, p. 97; Upham, *A Memoir of General John Glover*, pp. 13,15; Lord and Gamage, *Marblehead*, p. 119; Brayall, *Washington's Savior*, p. 121; Ward, *The Delaware Continentals, 1776–1783*, 64; Gardner, *Glover's Marblehead Regiment in the War of the Revolution*, p. 7; *New York Times*, April 28, 1878; Heath, *Memoirs*, p. 63; Knight, ed., *General John Glover Letterbook*, p. 2.

18. Alden, *A History of the American Revolution*, pp. 256–257; Shorto, *The Island at the Center of the World*, p. 160; *New York Times*, April 28, 1878; Heath, *Memoirs*, p. 63; Eve LaPlante, *American Jezebel, The Uncommon Life of Anne Hutchinson: The Woman Who Defied the Puritans* (San Francisco: HarperCollins Publishers, 2004), pp. 208–237; Gardner, *Glover's Marblehead Regiment in the War of the Revolution*, p. 7.

19. Gardner, *Glover's Marblehead Regiment in the War of the Revolution*, p. 7; Fleming, *1776*, pp. 258; Spear, *To End the War at White Plains*, pp. 4, 30; Shorto, *The Island at the Center of the World*, pp. 163–164, 290; Edgar J. McManus, *A History of Negro Slavery in New York* (Syracuse: Syracuse University Press, 1966), pp. 46–47; Ferling, *Almost a Miracle*, pp. 121–122; Joshua Pell (1710–1781), Family Search, internet; Joshua Pell (1710–1781), Ancestry.com, internet; Phillip Thomas Tucker, *Ranger Raid: The Legendary Robert Rogers and His Most Famous Frontier Battle* (Guilford: Stackpole Books, 2021), pp. 1–21.

20. Knight, ed., *General John Glover Letterbook*, p. x; Billas, *General John Glover and his Marblehead Marines*, p. 27; Tucker, *George Washington's Surprise Attack*, p. 13.

21. *Maryland Gazette*, April 24, 1777.

22. Ibid., October 31, 1776; Patterson, *Washington and Cornwallis*, p. 62

23. *Maryland Gazette*, September 19, 1776.

24. Ibid., October 3, 1776.

25. O'Donnell, *The Indispensables*, p. 263; Gardner, *Glover's Marblehead Regiment in the War of the Revolution*, p. 7; Fleming, *Now We Are Enemies*, pp. 81–82; Ferling, *Almost A Miracle*, pp. 121–122; William Baldwin October 20–23, 1776, letter to wife, William Baldwin Papers Collection, HUL.

26. Vickers, ed., *The Autobiography of Ashley Bowen*, p. 116.

27. Ferling, *Almost A Miracle*, p. 120.

28. Fleming, *Now We Are Enemies*, pp. 83, 85.

29. William Baldwin October 20–23, 1776, letter to wife, William Baldwin Papers Collection, HUL; Upham, *A Memoir of General John Glover*, pp. 14–15; Gardner, *Glover's Marblehead Regiment in the War of the Revolution*, p. 7.

30. Alden, *A History of the American Revolution*, p. 265; Ferling, *Almost a Miracle*, p. 122.

31. Ferling, *Almost A Miracle*, p. 123.

32. Bolton, *The Private Soldier Under Washington*, pp. 77–82; Gardner, *Glover's Marblehead Regiment in the War of the Revolution*, p. 7.

33. *FJ and NHG*, November 26, 1776; William Baldwin October 20–23, 1776, letter to wife, William Baldwin Papers Collection, HUL; Brayall, *Washington's Savior*, p. 231; Upham, *A Memoir of General John Glover*, p. 2; Heath, *Memoirs*, p. 64; O'Donnell, *The Indispensables*, p. 264; Gardner, *Glover's Marblehead Regiment in the War of the Revolution*, p. 7.

34. Bolton, *The Private Soldier Under Washington*, p. 143; Gardner, *Glover's Marblehead Regiment in the War of the Revolution*, p. 3; Atkinson, *The British Are Coming*, p. 440.

35. William Baldwin October 20–23, 1776, letter to wife, William Baldwin Papers Collection, HUL; Files of St. Paul's Church National Historic Site, Eastchester, New York; Brayall, *Washington's Savior*, p. 119.

36. Hufeland, *Westchester County During the American Revolution*, p. 122; Brayall, *Washington's Savior*, p. 119; Gardner, *Glover's Marblehead Regiment in the War of the Revolution*, p. 25.

37. Hufeland, *Westchester County During the American Revolution*, p. 122; Pelham Bay Park, Official Website of the New York City Department of Parks and Recreation, internet.

38. *New York Times*, August 14, 1921; Boatner, *Encyclopedia of the American Revolution*, p. 850; Heath, *Memoirs*, p. 64; Spear, *To End the War at White Plains*, p. 17; Boyle, *From Redcoat to Rebel*, p. 62.

39. *Maryland Gazette*, April 24, 1777.

40. Boyle, *From Redcoat to Rebel*, p. 62.

41. O'Donnell, *The Indispensables*, p. 264; Fleming, *1776*, p. 366.

42. *FJ and NHG*, November 26, 1776.

43. William Baldwin October 20–23, 1776, letter to wife, William Baldwin Papers Collection, HUL; Brayall, *Washington's Savior*, pp. 119, 121.

44. Heath, *Memoirs*, p. 64.

45. Ibid.

46. Spear, *To End the War at White Plains*, p. 19.

47. Ibid., p. 29.

48. Heath, *Memoirs*, p. 64; Jenkins, *The Story of the Bronx*, p. 144; Brayall, *Washington's Savior*, p. 120.

49. *Maryland Gazette*, December 5, 1776.

50. William Baldwin October 20–23, 1776, letter to wife, William Baldwin Papers Collection, HUL; Stephen Jenkins, *The Story of the Bronx: From the Purchase Made by the Dutch from the Indians in 1639 to the Present*

Day (New York: G. P. Putnam's Sons, 1912), p. 144; O'Donnell, *The Indispensables*, p. 264; Christopher Matthew and Matthew Trundle, editors, *Beyond the Gates of Fire: New Perspectives on the Battle of Thermopylae* (South Yorkshire: Pen & Sword Books, 2013), pp. 20–26.

51. Boyle, *From Redcoat to Rebel*, p. 62; O'Donnell, *The Indispensables*, p. 264.

52. Hufeland, *Westchester County During the American Revolution*, p. 115; Roads, *The History and Traditions of Marblehead*, p. 169.

53. Ketchum, *The Winter Soldiers*, p. 140.

54. O'Donnell, *The Indispensables*, p. 263; Ketchum, *The Winter Soldiers*, pp. 118–119; Brayall, *Washington's Savior*, p. 121.

55. *Maryland Gazette*, April 24, 1777; *New York Times*, August 14, 1921.

56. *FJ and NHG*, November 26, 1776; Billias, *General John Glover and His Marblehead Mariners*, p. 114; Matthew and Trundle, eds., *Beyond the Gates of Fire*, pp. 20–26.

57. *FJ and NHG*, November 26, 1776; Fleming, *Now We Are Enemies*, p. 182.

58. Boyle, *From Redcoat to Rebel*, p. 48.

59. Fleming, *Now We Are Enemies*, p. 146.

60. Ibid., pp. 146–147.

61. Ibid., pp. 320–321.

62. Billias, *General John Glover and His Marblehead Mariners*, p. 114; O'Donnell, *The Indispensables*, p. 264.

63. Bolton, *The Private Soldier Under Washington*, pp. 169, 219, 237–238; Brayall, *Washington's Savior*, p. 119.

64. Don N. Hagist, *A British Soldier's Story, Roger Lamb's Narrative of the American Revolution* (Baraboo, Wisconsin: Ballindalloch Press, n.d.), p. 56.

65. Johnston, *The Campaign of 1776 around New York and Brooklyn*, p. 268.

66. Bolton, *The Private Soldier Under Washington*, p. 115; Fleming, *Liberty*, pp. 176, 344.

67. Bolton, *The Private Soldier Under Washington*, p. 144.

68. Upham, *A Memoir of General John Glover*, p. 17.

69. Ibid.; Alden, *A History of the American Revolution*, p. 253.

70. Cunliffe, *George Washington*, p. 75.

71. Lincoln Diamant, *Chaining the Hudson, The Fight for the River in the American Revolution* (New York: Carol Publishing Company, 1994), p. 64.

72. *FJ and NHG,* November 26, 1776; McCulloch, *1776,* p. 351; William Baldwin October 20–23, 1776, letter to wife, William Baldwin Papers Collection, HUL.

73. William Baldwin October 20–23, 1776, letter to wife, William Baldwin Papers Collection, HUL; Upham, *A Memoir of General John Glover,* p. 19; *New York Times,* August 14, 1921; Stiles, *The Literary Diary of Eliza Stiles,* vol. 2, p. 91.

74. Alden, *A History of the American Revolution,* p. 255.

75. Miscellaneous Notes from New York Historical Society, New York, New York.

76. Roads, *The History and Traditions of Marblehead,* p. 131.

77. *Maryland Gazette,* December 5, 1776.

78. Spear, *To End the War at White Plains,* p. 17; Ferling, *Almost a Miracle,* p. 126; O'Donnell, *The Indispensables,* pp. 249–250.

79. Ferling, *Almost a Miracle,* p. 127.

80. Patterson, *Washington and Cornwallis,* pp. 27–29.

81. Alden, *A History of the American Revolution,* pp. 219–220, 229–230; Victor Wolfgang von Hagen, *The Germanic People in America* (Norman: University of Oklahoma Press, 1976), pp. 2–3, 151–153, 156, 158, 160; Joseph Lee Boyle, *From Redcoat to Rebel: The Thomas Sullivan Journal* (Westminister, Md: Heritage Books, 2004), p. 47; O'Donnell, *The Indispensables,* pp. 219–220; Johnston, *The Campaign of 1776 Around New York and Brooklyn,* p. 133; Donald M. Londahl-Smidt, *The German Troops in the American Revolution: Hessen, Cassel* (Oxford: Osprey Publishing, 2021), pp. 3–7, 12; O'Donnell, *The Indispensables,* pp. 8, 266.

82. Hagen, *The Germanic People in America,* pp. 156, 160.

83. Alden, *A History of the American Revolution,* pp. 219–220, 229–230; Fleming, *1776,* p. 263.

84. Hagan, *The Germanic People in America,* pp. 151–153.

85. Fleming, *1776,* pp. 316–317.

86. Hagan, *The Germanic People in America,* p. 162.

87. Alden, *A History of the American Revolution,* p. 248.

88. Ibid., pp. 223–224; Fleming, *Now We Are Enemies,* pp. 5–7; Fleming, *1776,* pp. 244–245.

89. Bell, Norman A., "Thursday February 06, 2014, A Description of the Revolutionary Battle of Pelham Published in 1926 for the

Sesquicentennial," A Description of the Celebration Revolutionary Battle of Pelham, internet, hereafter cited as Bell, Battle of Pelham.

90. *FJ and NHG*, November 26, 1776; Fleming, *1776*, pp. 319–320; *Maryland Gazette*, September 12, 1776; Schecter, *The Battle for New York*, pp. 145–150, 194–200.

91. *FJ and NHG*, November 26, 1776; Billias, *General John Glover and His Marblehead Mariners*, p. 66; Craig, *General Edward Hand*, p. 36; Gamage and Lord, *The Lure of Marblehead*, p. 12; Gardner, *Glover's Marblehead Regiment in the War of the Revolution*, pp. 16–17.

92. *FJ and NHG*, November 26, 1776.

93. Roads, *The History and Traditions of Marblehead*, p. 119.

94. Knight, ed., *General John Glover's Letterbook*, pp. xiv, xv.

95. Roads, *The History and Traditions of Marblehead*, p. 170; Archives of Old North Church, Marblehead, Massachusetts; Billias, *General John Glover and his Marblehead Mariners*, pp. 19–21.

96. Boyle, *From Redcoat to Rebel*, p. 62.

97. Knight, ed., *General John Glover's Letterbook*, p. 4.

98. O'Donnell, *The Indispensables*, p. 7; Braydon, *Washington's Saviors*, p. 121; O'Donnell, *The Indispensables*, pp. 115, 263; Graydon, *Memoirs*, pp. 148–149, 164; LaPlante, *American Jezebel*, p. 231; Pelham Bay Park, Official Website of the New York City Department of Parks and Recreation, internet.

99. *FJ and NHG*, November 26, 1776; Michael Cecere, *They Behaved Like Soldiers: Captain John Chilton and the Third Virginia Regiment, 1775–1778* (Bowie: Heritage Books, 2004), p. 15; O'Donnell, *The Indispensables*, p. 265.

100. Alden, *A History of the American Revolution*, p. 272.

101. Upham, *A Memoir of General John Glover*, p. 17.

102. Fleming, *1776*, p. 369; *Maryland Gazette*, November 6, 1776.

103. Johnston, *The Campaign of 1776 around New York and Brooklyn*, p. 134.

104. *Maryland Gazette*, November 6, 1776.

105. Upham, *A Memoir of General John Glover*, 19; Brayall, *Washington's Savior*, p. 121; O'Donnell, *The Indispensables*, p. 8; Atkinson, *The British Are Coming*, p. 440.

106. Spear, *To End the War at White Plains*, p. 26.

107. Hufeland, *Westchester County During the American Revolution*, p. 107; O'Donnell, *The Indispensables*, p. 265.

108. William Baldwin October 20–23, 1776, letter to wife, William Baldwin Papers Collection, HUL; *FJ and NHG,* November 26, 1776; O'Donnell, *The Indispensables,* p. 266; Jenkins, *The Story of the Bronx,* p. 145; *Maryland Gazette,* December 5, 1776.

109. O'Donnell, *The Indispensables,* p. 266.

110. Histories of the 16th and 17th Regiments of Light Dragoons, regimental websites; Fleming, *1776,* pp. 346, 368; James Kochan, *Don Troiani's Soldiers of the American Revolution* (Mechanicsburg, Pa.: Stackpole Books, 2007), pp. 34–35; Brendan Morrissey, *Monmouth Courthouse 1778* (Oxford, England: Osprey Publishing, 2004), p. 20; Boyle, *From Redcoat to Rebel: The Thomas Sullivan Journal,* pp. 8–9, 11; Boyle, *From Redcoat to Rebel,* p. 62.

111. Boyle, *From Redcoat to Rebel,* p. 61.

Chapter 4

1. O'Donnell, *The Indispensables,* p. 266; Roads, *The History and Traditions of Marblehead,* p. 170; Boyle, *From Redcoat to Rebel,* p. 62; Tagney, *The World Turned Upside Down,* p. 277.

2. O'Donnell, *The Indispensables,* p. 266.

3. *Maryland Gazette,* April 24, 1777; Boyle, *From Redcoat to Rebel,* p. 62.

4. Roads, *The History and Traditions of Marblehead,* p. 171; Schecter, *The Battle for New York,* pp. 199–201; O'Donnell, *The Indispensables,* pp. 104–105.

5. Hufeland, *Westchester County During the American Revolution,* p. 107.

6. *FJ and NHG,* November 26, 1776; Roads, *The History and Traditions of Marblehead,* pp. 171–177; *Maryland Gazette,* April 24, 1777; O'Donnell, *The Indispensables,* pp. 104–105, 351–352.

7. William Baldwin October 20–23, letter to wife, William Baldwin Papers Collection, HUL.

8. Ibid.; Priscilla Sawyer Lord and Virginia Clegg Gamage, *Marblehead, The Spirit of '76 Lives Here* (New York: Chilton Book Company, 1972), pp. 1–47.

9. *FJ and NHG,* November 26, 1776; Jenkins, *The Story of the Bronx,* p. 144; *New York Weekly Journal,* New York, New York; December 24, 1733; O'Donnell, *The Indispensables,* pp. 352, 266, 270; Gardner, *Glover's Marblehead Regiment in the War of the Revolution,* p. 17.

10. *FJ and NHG,* November 26, 1776; Upham, *A Memoir of General John Glover,* p. 12.

11. Marblehead Cemetery Records, Old Burial Hill, Marblehead, Massachusetts; Glover Letter Book, John Glover Papers, 1775–1781, Columbia University, Columbia University Library, Rare Book and Manuscript Collection, New York, New York; Billas, *General John Glover and His Marblehead Mariners,* p. 66; Roads, *The History and Traditions of Marblehead,* p. 556; O'Donnell, *The Indispensables,* p. 352.

12. Billias, *General John Glover and His Marblehead Mariners,* pp. 66, 75; O'Donnell, *The Indispensables,* p. 351; Gardner, *Glover's Marblehead Regiment in the War of the Revolution,* p. 19; Glover Letter Book, CUL.

13. Billias, *General John Glover and His Marblehead Mariners,* pp. 20–21, 66–67, 72–84; Upham, *A Memoir of General John Glover,* p. 7; Roads, *The History and Traditions of Marblehead,* pp. 555, 558; O'Donnell, *The Indispensables,* pp. 151–154, 351.

14. Glover Letter Book, CUL; American Silversmiths Genealogy, Thomas Grant, on internet; Roads, *The History and Traditions of Marblehead,* p. 559; Billias, *General John Glover and his Marblehead Mariners,* pp. 78–79; O'Donnell, *The Indispensables,* p. 352.

15. Billias, *General John Glover and his Marblehead Mariners,* pp. 9, 66; Roads, *The History and Traditions of Marblehead,* pp. 550–551.

16. *FJ and NHG,* November 26, 1776.

17. O'Donnell, *The Indispensables,* p. 266.

18. *FJ and NHG,* November 26, 1776; Heath, *Memoirs,* p. 11.

19. William Baldwin October 20–23, 1776, letter to wife, William Baldwin Papers Collection, HUL; Billias, *General John Glover and His Marblehead Mariners,* p. 117; *New York Times,* August 14, 1921; Spear, *To End the War at White Plains,* pp. 19–20; *FJ and NHG,* November 26, 1776.

20. Spear, *To End the War at White Plains,* pp. 19–20; *FJ and NHG,* November 26, 1776.

21. Wright, *The Continental Army,* pp. 217–218.

22. Billias, *General John Glover and His Marblehead Mariners,* p. 117; Spear, *To End the War at White Plains,* pp. 19–20.

23. William Baldwin October 20–23, 1776, letter to wife, William Baldwin Papers Collection, HUL.

24. Upham, *A Memoir of General John Glover,* p. 19.

25. Wright, *The Continental Army,* pp. 217–218.

26. Heath, *Memoirs*, p. 41, note 2.
27. Virtual American Biographies, William Shepard; Boatner, *Encyclopedia of the American Revolution*, p. 1003; Alfred Minot Copeland, *"Our County and Its People," A History of Hampden County, Massachusetts*, vol. 2 (3 vols: Boston: Century Memorial Publishing Company, 1902), pp. 414–417.
28. Wright, *The Continental Army*, pp. 206–207; Billias, *General John Glover and His Marblehead Mariners*, p. 117.
29. William Baldwin October 20–23, 1776, letter to wife, William Baldwin Papers Collection, HUL; Billias, *General John Glover and His Marblehead Mariners*, p. 117; Stuart Reid and Marko Zlatich, *Soldiers of the Revolutionary War* (Oxford, England: Osprey Publishing, 2002), p. 18; O'Donnell, *The Indispensables*, p. 268.
30. Reid and Zlatich, *Soldiers of the Revolutionary War*, pp. 11, 18, 32, 48; Fleming, *Now We Are Enemies*, p. 185; Ward, *The Delaware Continentals, 1776–1783*, pp. 51–52.
31. Ward, *The Delaware Continentals, 1776–1783*, pp. 51–52.
32. William Baldwin October 20–23, 1776, letter to wife, William Baldwin Papers Collection, HUL; Loammi Baldwin, Jr., Papers, William L. Clements Library, The University of Michigan, Ann Arbor, Michigan; Virtual American Biographies, Loammi Baldwin; William Richard Cutter, *Historic Homes and Places and Genealogical and Personal Memoirs Relating to the Families of Middlesex County, Massachusetts* (New York: A. M. Lewis Publishing Company, 1908), pp. 1–254; Fleming, *Liberty*, pp. 119–120; Reid and Zlatich, *Soldiers of the Revolutionary War*, p. 48; Boatner, *Encyclopedia of the American Revolution*, pp. 55–56; O'Donnell, *The Indispensables*, p. 105.
33. William Baldwin October 20–23, 1776, letter to wife, William Baldwin Papers Collection, HUL; Billias, *General John Glover and His Marblehead Mariners*, p. 117.
34. *FJ and NHG*, November 26, 1776; Jenkins, *The Story of the Bronx*, pp. 144–145.
35. *Maryland Gazette*, December 5, 1776.
36. Johnston, *The Campaign of 1776 around New York and Brooklyn*, p. 269.
37. Upham, *A Memoir of General John Glover*, p. 25; Boyle, *From Redcoat to Rebel*, p. 62; Brayall, *Washington's Savior*, p. 123; Paul Cartledge,

Thermopylae, The Battle that Changed the World, (New York: Overlook Press, 2006), p. 145.

38. Upham, *A Memoir of General John Glover*, p. 26.
39. Ibid., p. 27.
40. Lord and Gamage, *Marblehead*, p. 125; Fred Anderson, *A People's Army, Massachusetts Soldiers and Society in the Seven Years' War* (Chapel Hill, North Carolina: University of North Carolina, 1984), pp. vii–x, 3–25, 222–223.
41. William E. Connelley, *A Standard History of Kansas and Kansans* (Chicago: Lewis Publishing Company, 1918), pp. 1819–1820; Lord and Gamage, *Marblehead*, pp. 83, 125..
42. Lord and Gamage, *Marblehead*, pp. 101, 104, 106, 125; Roads, *The History and Traditions of Marblehead*, p. 170; Connelley, *A Standard History of Kansas and Kansans*, pp. 1819–1820.
43. Billias, *General John Glover and His Marblehead Mariners*, p. 66; *FJ and NHG*, November 26, 1776.
44. Spear, *To End the War at White Plains*, p. 19.
45. *FJ and NHG*, November 26, 1776; Bell, Battle of Pelham, internet.
46. *FJ and NHG*, November 26, 1776; O'Donnell, *The Indispensables*, p. 266; Fleming, 1776, p. 368; *Maryland Gazette*, December 5, 1776; Boyle, *From Redcoat to Rebel*, p. 62.
47. *Maryland Gazette*, December 5, 1776.
48. Boyle, *From Redcoat to Rebel*, p. 62.
49. *FJ and NHG*, November 26, 1776; Spear, *To End the War at White Plains*, pp. 19–20; Bell, Battle of Pelham, internet; British Army Muster Rolls, King's Own Regiment, Chris Woolf Collection, London, England; Chris Woolf e-mail to author, March 15, 2006.
50. *FJ and NHG, November 26, 1776.*
51. Stuart Reid, *Culloden Moor 1746* (Oxford: Osprey Books, 2002), pp. 42–72; Fleming, *Now We Are Enemies*, p. 186; Bell, Battle of Pelham, internet; British Army Muster Rolls, King's Own Regiment, Chris Woolf Collection; Chris Woolf e-mail to author, March 15, 2006; *Maryland Gazette*, April 24, 1777; Reid and Zlatich, *Soldiers of the Revolutionary War*, p. 158; Londahl-Smidt, *German Troops in the American Revolution*, p. 15.
52. Fleming, *Now We Are Enemies*, pp. 48–49.
53. Ibid., p. 107.
54. Bolton, *The Private Soldier Under Washington*, p. 122.

55. Alden, *A History of the American Revolution*, p. 256.

56. *FJ and NHG*, November 26, 1776; Bell, Battle of Pelham, internet; Fleming, *Now We Are Enemies*, p. 186; *Maryland Gazette*, April 24, 1777; O'Donnell, *The Indispensables*, p. 266; William Seymour *The Price of Folly, British Blunders in the War of American Independence*, (Washington, D.C.: Brassey's Ltd., 1995), pp. ix-x, 30–32.

57. *FJ and NHG*, November 26, 1776; Fleming, *Now We Are Enemies*, p. 203; Brayall, *Washington's Savior*, p. 123; *Maryland Gazette*, April 24, 1777.

58. *FJ and NHG*, November 26, 1776; O'Donnell, *The Indispensables*, p. 266; Fleming, *1776*, p. 368; Spear, *To End the War at White Plains*, pp. 19–20; *Maryland Gazette*, April 24, 1777; Bell, Battle of Pelham, internet; Boyle, *From Redcoat to Rebel*, p. 62; Fred Anderson, *The War That Made America, A Short History of the French and Indian War*, pp. 57, 69–71; Stiles, *The Literary Diary of Ezra Stiles*, vol. 2, p. 87.

59. Fleming, *1776*, p. 368; Fleming, *Now We Are Enemies*, pp. 146, 194, 321; *Maryland Gazette*, April 24, 1777; Bell, Battle of Pelham, internet; Boyle, *From Redcoat to Rebel*, p. 62; O'Donnell, *The Indispensables*, pp. 102, 266.

60. *Maryland Gazette*, April 24, 1777; Boyle, *From Redcoat to Rebel*, p. 62.

61. *Maryland Gazette*, April 24, 1777; Fleming, *Now We Are Enemies*, p. 194.

62. Boyle, *From Redcoat to Rebel*, p. 62.

63. Johnston, *The Campaign of 1776 around New York and Brooklyn*, p. 124.

64. *FJ and NHG*, November 26, 1776; Upham, *A Memoir of General John Glover*, p. 19; *Maryland Gazette*, December 5, 1776.

65. *Maryland Gazette*, December 5, 1776.

66. *Maryland Gazette*, October 3, 1776.

67. Upham, *A Memoir of General John Glover*, p. 19.

68. *FJ and NHG*, November 26, 1776; *Maryland Gazette*, April 24, 1777 and December 5, 1776; Bell, Battle of Pelham, internet; O'Donnell, *The Indispensables*, p. 266.

69. *New York Times*, August 14, 1921; O'Donnell, *The Indispensables*, p. 266.

70. *FJ and NHG*, November 26, 1776: Reid, *Culloden Moor*, pp. 68–87; Arthur Herman, *How the Scots Invented the Modern World* (New York: Three Rivers Press, 2001), pp. 150–153; Fleming, *Now We Are*

Enemies, p. 186; Brayall, *Washington's Savior*, p. xiii; Thomas Bartlett and Keith Jeffery, editors, *A Military History of Ireland* (Cambridge: Cambridge University Press, 1996), pp. 200–202; Roads, *The History and Traditions of Marblehead*, p. 171; *Maryland Gazette*, December 5, 1776; Atkinson, *The Redcoats Are Coming*, p. 440.

71. Roads, *The History and Traditions of Marblehead*, p. 171; Brayall, *Washington's Savior*, pp. xiii, 84.

72. Spear, *To End the War at White Plains*, pp. 19–20; Bell, Battle of Pelham, internet; *Maryland Gazette*, April 24, 1777; Johnston, *The Campaign of 1776 and New York and Brookyln*, p. 136.

73. William Baldwin October 20–23, 1776, letter to wife, William Baldwin Papers Collection, HUL; Spear, *To End the War at White Plains*, pp. 18, 21; *Maryland Gazette*, December 5, 1776 and April 24, 1777; *New York Times*, August 14, 1921.

74. William Baldwin October 20–23, 1776, letter to wife, William Baldwin Papers Collection, HUL; Benton Rain Patterson, *Washington and Cornwallis, The Battle for America, 1775–1783* (New York: Taylor Trade Publishing, 2004), pp. 27–29.

75. William Baldwin October 20–23, 1776, letter to wife, William Baldwin Papers Collection, HUL; Billias, *General John Glover and His Marblehead Mariners*, p. 121; *New York Times*, August 14, 1921.

Chapter 5

1. Upham, *A Memoir of General John Glover*, p. 19; *FJ and NHG*, November 26, 1776; *Maryland Gazette*, December 5, 1776; Londahl-Smidt, *German Troops in the American Revolution*, p. 7.

2. Upham, *A Memoir of General John Glover*, p. 19; *New York Times*, August 14, 1921; *Maryland Gazette*, December 5, 1776.

3. *FJ and NHG*, November 26, 1776; *Maryland Gazette*, December 5, 1776; Londahl-Smidt, *German Troops in the American Revolution*, pp. 12–15.

4. *FJ and NHG*, November 26. 1776; Roads, *The History and Traditions of Marblehead*, p. 170; Brayall, *Washington's Savior*, p. 121; *New York Times*, August 14, 1921.

5. *Maryland Gazette*, December 5, 1776.

6. Ibid.; *FJ and NHG*, November 26, 1776.

7. *Maryland Gazette*, December 5, 1776.

398 • SAVING WASHINGTON'S ARMY

8. *FJ and NHG*, November 26, 1776; Roads, *The History and Traditions of Marblehead*, pp. 170–171; Bolton, *The Private Soldier Under Washington*, p. 108; Schecter, *The Battle for New York*, p. 229; Brayall, *Washington's Savior*, p. 121; British Army Muster Rolls, King's Own Regiment, Chris Woolf Collection; *Maryland Gazette*, December 5, 1776.

9. Roads, *The History and Traditions of Marblehead*, p. 170.

10. *Maryland Gazette*, December 5, 1776.

11. *FJ and NHG*, November 26, 1776; Upham, *A Memoir of General John Glover*, p. 19; Spear, *To End the War at White Plains*, p 18; *New York Times*, August 14, 1921; *Maryland Gazette*, December 5, 1776.

12. *FJ and NHG*, November 26, 1776; Jenkins, *The Story of the Bronx*, p. 146; *Maryland Gazette*, December 5, 1776.

13. *FJ and NHG*, November 26, 1776; Upham, *A Memoir of General John Glover*, p. 19; *Maryland Gazette*, December 5, 1776; Brayall, *Washington's Savior*, p. 121; O'Donnell, *The Indispensables*, p. 267.

14. *Maryland Gazette*, December 5, 1776.

15. *FJ and NHG*, November 26, 1776; Upham, *A Memoir of General John Glover*, p. 19; Jenkins, *The Story of the Bronx*, p. 146; *New York Times*, August 14, 1921; Spear, *To End the War at White Plains*, p. 18.

16. Roads, *The History and Traditions of Marblehead*, p. 170; FJ and NHG, November 26, 1776.

17. Upham, *A Memoir of General John Glover*, p. 19.

18. Roads, *The History and Traditions of Marblehead*, p. 170; FJ and NHG, November 26, 1776; Upham, *A Memoir of General John Glover*, p. 19; *New York Times*, August 14, 1921; Spear, *To End the War at White Plains*, p. 18.

19. *FJ and NHG*, November 26, 1776.

20. Jenkins, *The Story of the Bronx*, p. 146.

21. Bolton, *The Private Soldier Under Washington*, pp. 122–123.

22. *FJ and NHG*, November 26, 1776; O'Donnell, *The Indispensables*, p. 267.

23. *FJ and NHG*, November 26, 1776.

24. Ibid.

25. Roads, *The History and Traditions of Marblehead*, p. 171.

26. Upham, *A Memoir of General John Glover*, p. 19.

27. *Maryland Gazette*, December 5, 1776.

28. *FJ and NHG*, November 26, 1776.

29. Roads, *The History and Traditions of Marblehead*, p. 171.
30. *FJ and NHG*, November 26, 1776; Brayall, *Washington's Savior*, p. 121.
31. *FJ and NHG*, November 26, 1776.
32. Roads, *The History and Traditions of Marblehead*, p. 171; *Maryland Gazette*, December 5, 1776.
33. Spear, *To End the War at White Plains*, p. 18; Brayall, *Washington's Savior*, p. 121; Atkinson, *The British Are Coming*, p. 442.
34. *FJ and NHG*, November 26, 1776; Spear, *To End the War at White Plains*, p. 18; *Maryland Gazette*, December 5, 1776; *New York Times*, August 14, 1921; Boyle, *From Redcoat to Rebel*, p. 62.
35. Roads, *The History and Traditions of Marblehead*, p. 170; FJ and NHG, November 26, 1776.
36. *FJ and NHG*, November 26, 1776; "William Shepard," Encyclopedia.com, internet; Alfred Minot Copeland, *A History of Hampden County, Massachusetts*, vol. 2, pp. 414–417; Brayall, *Washington's Savior*, p. 121; Christopher Dawson, *Dynamics of World History* (Wilmington: ISI Books, 2002), p. xvii.
37. Copeland, *"Our County and Its People," A History of Hampden County, Massachusetts*, vol. 2, pp. 414–417; Heath, *Memoirs*, p. 65.
38. Copeland, *"Our County and Its People," A History of Hampden County, Massachusetts*, vol. 2, pp. 414–417; Heath, *Memoirs*, p. 65; O'Donnell, *The Indispensables*, p. 189.
39. William Baldwin October 20–23, 1776, letter to wife, Baldwin Papers Collection, HUL; *New York Times*, August 14, 1921.
40. *FJ and NHG*, November 26, 1776; Upham, *A Memoir of General John Glover*, p. 19.
41. *FJ and NHG*, November 26, 1776; Spear, *To End the War at White Plains*, p. 18; *New York Times*, August 14, 1921; Boyle, *From Redcoat to Rebel*, p. 62; William Baldwin October 20–23, 1776, letter to wife, Baldwin Papers Collection, HUL.
42. Spear, *To End the War at White Plains*, p. 21; *Maryland Gazette*, December 5, 1776; *Boyle, From Redcoat to Rebel*, p. 62; *New York Times*, August 14, 1921; O'Donnell, *The Indispensables*, p. 268.
43. *FJ and NHG*, November 26, 1776; *Maryland Gazette*, December 5, 1776; *New York Times*, August 14, 1921; O'Donnell, *The Indispensables*, pp. 257, 351.
44. *FJ and NHG*, November 26, 1776; Spear, *To End the War at White Plains*, p. 18; Boyle, *From Redcoat to Rebel*, p. 62; *New York Times*,

August 14, 1921; William Baldwin October 20–23, 1776, letter to wife, Baldwin Papers Collection, HUL.

45. *FJ and NHG*, November 26, 1776; *New York Times*, August 14, 1921; Gardner, *Glover's Marblehead Regiment in the War of the Revolution*, p. 7.

46. *Maryland Gazette*, December 5, 1776.

47. Gardner, *Glover's Marblehead Regiment in the War of the Revolution*, p. 7.

48. *FJ and NHG*, November 26, 1776; *Maryland Gazette*, November 7, 1776 and December 5, 1776; "William Shepard," Encyclopedia. com, internet; Gardner, *Glover's Marblehead Regiment in the War of the Revolution*, p. 7.

49. *Maryland Gazette*, December 5, 1776.

50. Brayall, *Washington's Savior*, p. 125; Gardner, *Glover's Marblehead Regiment in the War of the Revolution*, p. 7.

51. *FJ and NHG*, November 26, 1776; Roads, *History and Traditions of Marblehead*, pp. 169–170; Tagney, *The World Turned Upside Down*, p. 278; Gardner, *Glover's Marblehead Regiment in the War of the Revolution*, p. 7.

52. Roads, *History and Traditions of Marblehead*, pp. 170–171; Gardner, *Glover's Marblehead Regiment in the War of the Revolution*, p. 7.

53. Spear, *To End the War at White Plains*, pp. 22, 33; Gardner, *Glover's Marblehead Regiment in the War of the Revolution*, p. 7; O'Donnell, *The Indispensables*, p. 269.

54. O'Donnell, *The Indispensables*, p. 269.

55. *FJ and NHG*, November 26, 1776; Gardner, *Glover's Marblehead Regiment in the War of the Revolution*, p. 7.

56. *FJ and NHG*, November 26, 1776.

57. Ibid.

58. Boyle, *From Redcoat to Rebel*, p. 62.

59. *Maryland Gazette*, November 6, 1776; Gardner, *Glover's Marblehead Regiment in the War of the Revolution*, p. 7.

60. *FJ and NHG*, November 26, 1776; Gardner, *Glover's Marblehead Regiment in the War of the Revolution*, p. 7.

61. *New York Times*, December 30, 1888; *Maryland Gazette*, December 5, 1776; *New York Times*, April 28, 1878.

62. William Raymond Lee's Orderly Book, Massachusetts Historical Society, Boston, Massachusetts.

63. Upham, *A Memoir of General John Glover*, p. 19.

64. Patterson, *Washington and Cornwallis*, p. 63; Gardner, *Glover's Marblehead Regiment in the War of the Revolution*, p. 7.
65. Brayall, *Washington's Savior*, pp. 126–127.
66. Ibid.
67. Ibid., p. 127.
68. Ibid., p. 126; Gardner, *Glover's Marblehead Regiment in the War of the Revolution*, p. 6.
69. Alden, *A History of the American Revolution*, p. 272; Bell, Battle of Pelham, internet.
70. Alden, *A History of the American Revolution*, p. 272.
71. *Maryland Gazette*, December 5, 1776.
72. Ibid.
73. Lord and Gamage, *Marblehead*, p. 119.
74. Billias, *General John Glover and His Marblehead Mariners*, pp. 110–111.
75. Alden, *A History of the American Revolution*, pp. 181–182.
76. Stiles, *The Literary Diary of Ezra Stiles*, vol. 2, p. 87.
77. Ibid.
78. Jenkins, *The Story of the Bronx*, p. 147.
79. Alden, *A History of the American Revolution*, p. 182.
80. Ibid., pp. 181–182, 272.
81. Heath, *Memoirs*, pp. 65, 68.
82. Stiles, The *Literary Diary of Ezra Stiles*, vol. 2, p. 88.
83. Jenkins, *The Story of the Bronx*, p. 148; Bell, Battle of Pelham, internet.
84. Alden, *A History of the American Revolution*, p. 272; Roads, *The History and Traditions of Marblehead*, p. 171.
85. *Maryland Gazette*, October 31, 1776.
86. Alden, *History of the American Revolution*, p. 272.
87. Shreve, *Tench Tilghman*, p. 73.
88. Ibid., pp. 272–273.
89. Upham, *A Memoir of General John Glover*, p. 15.
90. Fleming, *1776*, p. 368.
91. Ibid., p. 369.
92. Fleming, *Now We Are Enemies*, pp. 180–181.
93. Ibid.
94. Seymour, *The Price of Folly*, pp. 30–32; Weigly, *The American Way of War*, p. 22; Tucker, *George Washington's Surprise Attack*, pp. 8–16, 549–558.
95. Upham, *A Memoir of General John Glover*, p. 19.

96. Roads, *History and Traditions of Marblehead*, p. 171.
97. Brayall, *Washington's Saviors*, p. 125; William Baldwin Papers Collection, Harvard University Library, Cambridge, Massachusetts; Miscellaneous Papers, Massachusetts Historical Society, Boston, Massachusetts.
98. Boyle, *From Redcoat to Rebel*, p. 62.
99. Stiles, *The Literary Diary of Ezra Stiles*, vol. 2, p.84.
100. Heath, *Memoirs*, p. 65.
101. Schecter, *The Battle for New York*, p. 229; *Maryland Gazette*, April 24, 1777; Atkinson, *The British Are Coming*, p. 442.
102. Boyle, *From Redcoat to Rebel*, p. 62; Atkinson, *The British Are Coming*, p. 442.
103. British Army Muster Rolls, King's Own Regiment, Chris Woolf private collection; Maryland Gazette, April 24, 1777.
104. O'Donnell, *The Indispensables*, p. 267; Atkinson, *The British Are Coming*, p. 441.
105. *Maryland Gazette*, April 24, 1777.
106. Schecter, *The Battle for New York*, p. 229.
107. Bruce E. Burgoyne email to author, July 1, 2006.
108. Martin, *A Narrative of a Revolutionary Soldier*, p. 37; Atkinson, *The British Are Coming*, p. 442.
109. Heath, *Memoirs*, p. 65.
110. Roads, *History and Traditions of Marblehead*, p. 171.
111. Stiles, *The Literary Diary of Ezra Stiles*, vol. 2, p. 87.
112. Alden, *History of the American Revolution*, pp. 272–273; Roads, *The History and Traditions of Marblehead*, p. 171; Billas, *General John Glover and His Marblehead Mariners*, p. 121.
113. *Maryland Gazette*, November 7, 1776.
114. Billias, *General John Glover and His Marblehead Mariners*, p. 121.
115. Upham, *A Memoir of General John Glover*, p. 19.
116. *Maryland Gazette*, December 5, 1776.
117. O'Donnell, *The Indispensables*, p. 269.
118. Alden, *A History of the American Revolution*, p. 182.
119. Billias, *General John Glover and His Marblehead Mariners*, p. 121.
120. Ibid., pp. 120–121; Atkinson, *The British Are Coming*, p. 442.
121. Fleming, *1776*, p. 368.
122. Ketchum, *The Winter Soldiers*, pp. 115–130.
123. Alden, *History of the American Revolution*, p. 251; *New York Times*, January 4, 1902; Fleming, *Now We Are Enemies*, p. 329; Stiles, *The*

Literary Diary of Ezra Stiles, vol., 2, p. 87; O'Donnell, *The Indispensables*, p. 269.

124. Fleming, *1776*, p. 368; Fleming, *Now We Are Enemies*, p. 266; Spear, *To End the War at White Plains*, p. 20.

125. *New York Times*, August 10, 1901; Morrissey, *Monmouth Courthouse 1778*, p. 76.

126. *New York Times*, July 8, 1943 and October 25, 1998; Londahl-Smidt, *German Troops in the American Revolution*, pp. 5, 47.

127. Spear, *To End the War at White Plains*, p. 21; *New York Times*, August 14, 1921.

128. *Pennsylvania Evening Post*, Philadelphia, Pennsylvania, June 20, 1775.

129. *Maryland Gazette*, October 3, 1776.

130. Roger Borroel, *The Texan Revolution of 1836: A Concise Historical Perspective Based On Original Sources* (East Chicago, Indiana: La Villita Publication, 2002), pp. 57, 92

131. Roads, *The History and Traditions of Marblehead*, p. 171.

132. Schecter, *The Battle for New York*, p.4; *Maryland Gazette*, December 5, 1776; Bell, Battle of Pelham, internet; *New York Times*, August 10, 1901, January 4, 1902, and October 25, 1998.

133. Schecter, *The Battle for New York*, pp. 229–230.

134. Johnston, *The Campaign of 1776 around New York and Brooklyn*, p. 139.

135. Stiles, *The Literary Diary of Ezra Stiles*, vol. 2, p. 91.

136. Ibid., pp. 90–91.

137. Ibid., p. 91.

138. Burgoyne, *Defeat, Disaster, and Dedication*, p. 65.

139. Schecter, *The Battle for New York*, p. 229.

140. Tagney, *The World Turned Upside Down*, p. 278.

141. William Raymond Orderly Books, Massachusetts Historical Society, Boston, Massachusetts.

Epilogue

1. Sanborn, *Gen. John Glover and His Marblehead Regiment*, p. 46; Billias, *General John Glover and his Marblehead Mariners*, pp. 21–22.

2. Sanborn, *Gen. John Glover and His Marblehead Regiment*, p. 38.

3. Ibid., p. 35.

4. Ibid., p. 34; Upham, *A Memoir of General John Glover*, p. 4.

5. Sanborn, *Gen. John Glover and His Marblehead Regiment*, p. 46; Bolton, *The Private Soldier Under Washington*, pp. 245–246.

6. Sanborn, *General John Glover and His Marblehead Regiment*, p. 46; Upham, *A Memoir of General John Glover*, p. 48.

7. Sanborn, *Gen. John Glover and His Marblehead Regiment*, p. 46; Billias, *General John Glover and His Marblehead Mariners*, p. 111; *Maryland Gazette*, December 5, 1776; *New York Times*, October 25, 1998; Knight, ed., *General John Glover's Letterbook*, pp. xv–xvi.

8. Brayall, *Washington's Savior*, p. 158.

9. *FJ and NHG*, November 26, 1776; Billias, *General John Glover and His Marblehead Mariners*, pp. 110–111.

10. *New York Times*, October 25, 1998.

11. Ibid., October 14, 2001.

Index

About the Author

Phillip Thomas Tucker, PhD, is the award-winning author of more than eighty books in many fields of history and, in total, more than 180 works in history, including scholarly articles. He received his PhD in History from St. Louis University, St. Louis, Missouri, in 1990. Tucker has long specialized in producing groundbreaking history in multiple fields of study, including Women's history and African American history. He has been recognized as "the Stephen King of History," after more than three decades of authoring important books of unique distinction.